ISSUES IN SOCIAL JUSTICE

FRANK TRIDICO
Western Michigan University

JOSEPH M. PELLERITO, JR.
Wayne State University

JACOB ARMSTRONG
Western Michigan University

ISBN 978-0-9734159-7-1

1. Issues in Social Justice. Tridico, Frank (Ed.)
                          Pellerito, Jr., Joseph M. (Ed.)
                          Armstrong, Jacob (Ed.)

Sociology/Criminal Justice
Library & Archives Canada/Bibliothèque & Archives Canada

Printed and bound in Canada

 Landon Elsemere Press
    Canada – United States – Great Britain
32-B Queen Street East, Sault Ste. Marie, ON CANADA P6A 1Y3

CONTENTS

PREFACE

The study of social justice is a study of conflict. Within the context of power, dissenters vie for varying forms of change against adversaries who are more likely to resist change. Those who ascend to power, regardless of ideological perspectives, synthesize into a culture of static elitism. In an effort to maintain and sustain its power, such a culture resists change, limits dissent and adheres to varying principles of unequal relations. Power is fostered and preserved through unequal relations.

However, to dissenting factions who perceive varying forms of marginalization, change is considered a required medium to attain egalitarianism. Of crucial concern is whether egalitarianism has ever been reached in societies around the world. Has inequality been a consistent historical process? If it has, the question then becomes *'Can egalitarianism be possible?'*

The concept of justice is complicated insofar as it can be defined differently by different persons. For example, the criminal justice system has been designed by the State to enforce its own laws, expand its power and enhance its legitimacy. Dissenters who break the covenant of law are scrutinized through the State's own institutional structure. Hence, laws place limits on acceptable and unacceptable behavior and in doing so, force dissenting parties to work from the outside by the State's rules, or from the inside within the State's organizational structure.

The U.S. Constitution is regarded as a higher authority, but it is Supreme Court Justices, who are appointed by legislators, are afforded the power to interpret the document and apply it to case law. Hence, the Constitution itself is not a guarantor of fundamental rights; it rests on the Justices to decide if they are fundamental rights and if they can be extended to the individual.

Justice is defined as a concept of moral righteousness based on ethics, rationality and egalitarianism. Yet many cases within the courts indicate varied interpretations of applied justice. Justice then, from a criminal justice perspective, is subject to varying processes. Through this it can be argued that we can arrive at three premises in understanding justice through this context:

(1) Justice is subjectively defined.
(2) Ideology plays an influential role in the interpretation of the Constitution.
(3) Justice, then, is subject to the ideological shift of Supreme Court Justices.

Most grievances do not make it to the U.S. Supreme Court. Indeed, many forms of conflict do not enter the legal realm. However, if justice cannot be guaranteed within the courts, how can it be guaranteed elsewhere? History has shown us that collective identity is achieved through shared disenfranchisement. It is through the process of perceived and/or realized marginalization that social movements form. The collective, inspired by in-group hegemony also strengthens itself through out-group hostility. Forms of dissent, or conflict, should not be defined as chaotic or disruptive to the system. Rather, it is through challenges to institutional power that abuses of power can be minimized.

Every social movement is unique in its organizational structure, strategies and tactics it employs its goals and the nature of collective action it undertakes. There are however, themes that can be discerned that make some social movements similar to one another. This helps bring some understanding to the phenomena but it does not serve as a comprehensive analysis. For example, some collective movements have similar themes yet the nature of their struggles is bound by different criteria. Internal and external constraints play significant roles in how the social movement organization fares against its adversary.

In faring against more powerful adversaries, social movements often must enter the realm in which the adversary is situated. In some models, the dissenter is able to engage its adversary within its own jurisdiction. Regardless of its location, conflict will either result in the dissenter's goals being realized (to different extents) or being rebuked through resistance. Legitimacy plays an important factor in the struggles, with the more legitimate faction having an advantage prior to, and during conflict. Legitimacy, whether it is real or perceived, is a crucial element in a faction's ascent to power.

Social justice then is not only a concept; it must be understood as a process of conflict. Further, the conflict that ensues is likely to instill two *separate* and *unique* definitions of justice. The faction that has power may perceive dissent as disruptive and negative; the dissenting faction may perceive its real or perceived marginalization as abuses of power and denial of fundamental rights. How can social justice then be attained if two very different definitions of the concept emerge *within* conflict?

To critically analyze and understand power, it must be examined in its *entirety*, including through the lens of disenfranchised sectors. We examine their struggles. We watch how collective identity is formed through the process of leadership styles, strategies and tactics, attainment and distribution of resources, goals, and the manner by which it mobilizes itself against a more powerful adversary.

Whether it is the marginalization of homosexuals within a broader religious structure, or the institution of the State, or the disenfranchisement of the homeless within society, or the economically disadvantaged within a broader system, or the overrepresentation of racial minorities in prisons, each dissenting faction has a story to tell. It is here where their voices are heard.

Issues in Social Justice is the first in an ongoing volume by Landon Elsemere Press. It brings together 13 writers in the field to dissect the myriad of issues that concern contemporary society. These issues should not be examined independently. Although different in terms of context, the themes that emerge are similar. Each sees dissent as an instrumental medium to confront their disenfranchisement, and sees dissent as a necessary process to achieve social justice.

Examining such issues through what makes them *similar*, as opposed to what makes them *different* helps us understand common themes in the pursuit of egalitarianism. This book will examine the complexity of each struggle and the implications of its process. These issues form a timeline in the evolution of social justice. History has shown us justice cannot be guaranteed. The struggles within each issue of this book tell us that there are still those who wish to find it.

CHAPTER 1
RELIGION AND HOMOSEXUALITY

Frank Tridico, Jacob Armstrong and David Barry

Abstract: Although political and legal reform regarding homosexuality in the United States has taken place in recent years, resistance and opposition to the normalization of homosexuality in American society remains visible, and religion remains a powerful force in the ongoing debates over the place of homosexuality in American culture. The authors contend that the relationship between Church and State has been one of consensus, rather than conflict, and that organized religion mimics the State in terms of its organizational structure, conservative ideology, resistance to change and quelling of internal and external dissent. Recent literature and research has examined the ways that groups connected to the gay-affirming and ex-gay Christian movements revise longstanding doctrinal interpretations that marginalize homosexuality, create alternative Christian identities, and challenge heterosexist ideology from within Christianity itself. It is argued that these movements will face considerable challenges in attaining legitimacy and overcome heterosexism while operating within the larger religious system that subordinates them.

Opposition to homosexuality has been a central tenet of many orthodox wings of established religions. This historical facet has been a force for preserving in-group hegemony within organized religion. Through the identification and condemnation of a minority sexual identity sector, organized religion has set the parameters for acceptable and unacceptable principles and actions. Thus, homosexuality could be regarded as a direct assault on the traditions of most faiths and attempts to gain tolerance or acceptance of homosexuality have been met with resistance to forceful opposition.

It is clear then, that a discourse on gay movements and their relationship with organized religion must involve the concept of power. Religion gains its legitimacy through several processes. These include but are not limited to:

(1) **Its relationship to a predecessor**. History has shown that many new religions help temper the transition by amalgamating some of the established tenets of a previous religion with revised principles. This process has benefitted them in two ways. First, they borrow from the predecessor's legitimacy. In doing so they make it easier to attract adherents who may still identify themselves with the older religion. Second, they minimize the degree of dissent by focusing on ways of building on tenets or principles, rather than completely rejecting them. Where there is an overt and complete rejection of the predecessor, the new religion not only works from a disadvantage but runs the risk of being stigmatized as a radical movement or cult. This compromises their legitimacy and limits their effectiveness in building a new identity.

(2) **Numbers of adherents to the movement**. Many new religions have utilized aggressive pushes for attaining membership, much of this through conversion. Judaism, as one of the world's oldest and more established religions has been an exception. Christianity, as having branched off of Judaism, has been successful at rapidly gaining adherents by spreading its influence across broader regions. Whether it is from forced conversion, to proselytizing, new religions have attained added legitimacy with large numbers of adherents.

(3) **The strength of its organizational structure**. Most organizations attain and maintain continuity through highly sophisticated and hierarchically structured dynamics. Members are ascribed status through the positions they hold within the organizational structure. However, an adherence to the larger entity (religion, and/or a god through the religion) also entails subscription to subordination of individual identity. Forms of dissent that can lead to changes must be resisted to preserve the existing order and structure of the organization. Hence, the acceptance and promotion of conservative ideology, along with the rejection and resistance to liberalized ideals, help solidify the organization's power.

(4) **Tenure of movement**. Historically, new religions have been regarded as illegitimate forms of dissent and challenged by the State and/or more established religions. Early Christians faced

persecution for several centuries prior to the religion being accepted as legitimate. While new religions face varying degrees of stigmatization, much of this can be quelled over time if they can sustain themselves and incorporate many of the afore-mentioned processes. Tenure then becomes paramount to how outsiders and potential adherents may perceive new religions. Legitimacy is attained and enhanced through tenure.

(5) *Strength of ideology and opposition to dissent.* Many new religions carry from predecessors entrenched tenets that ideologically unify adherents. Conservative ideals that have enjoyed tenure and legitimacy serve to strengthen in-group hegemony while at the same time reinforcing out-group hostility. By clearly identifying and denouncing ideology or behavior that runs contrary to internal group tenets, the religion strengthens its own identity. Adherents are rewarded for accepting the established ideals through inclusion, and bear witness to the realized and perceived rejection of dissenters through exclusion. By resisting, limiting, and/or aggressively challenging forms of dissent, religion enhances its own identity.

(6) *Its relationship to the State.* Religions are born within existing political structures of nation-states. Hence, to dismiss or underscore the relationship religions have with the State would ignore the extent to which legitimacy is challenged or attained. Alliances of Church and State have been effective measures in the preservation of social order. Examples of such include Islamic law in the Middle East, Judaism as a central component of Israel and identification of Christianity imposed on natives during colonialism of the Americas and the Philippines. In all afore-mentioned regions, religion has been used as an ideological force to attain and maintain State power.

There have been historical accounts of separation of Church and State as effective measures in the preservation of social order in other regimes. Examples of these include fascist movements in Italy and Japan, National Socialism in Nazi Germany, the advent of communism in the former Soviet Union and the Peoples Republic of China. In these regimes, subordination to a religion was perceived to weaken the subordination to the State. In subordinating solely to the State, dissent could be minimized and order and structure could be preserved.

History tells us that the relationship between Church and State has been one born of *consensus* and not *conflict*. Conflict served to test the nature of the relationship. Nonetheless, where conflict has ensued, it has been limited, decisive and has led to new development. Such development has always been in the interests of the State. If the Church could be useful for the continuance of the State, then it was afforded tenure. If the Church was deemed to be a corrosive force in the order and structure of things, it was altered, minimized or completely eliminated.

The advent of gay movements that have sought to create a new religious identity has been met with particular resistance within already established religions, particularly Christianity. Within this context, gay movements must be examined as challenging the entrenched tenets of a more powerful adversary. To understand the degree of power and legitimacy established religions have, they must be understood from an historical process. Hence, the discourse must include the understanding of Christianity in its relationship to Judaism, Protestant sects in their relationships to Roman Catholicism, and ultimately, Christianity itself in its relationship to the State. New religions, or sects within Christianity, have attained and preserved legitimacy through relationships with more established entities, including to some degree those which they have branched off of.

If the State resists change and limits dissent, why does it allow and forge alliances with religion? Examining the conservative structure of both the State and religion allows the reader to ascertain greater similarities rather than differences between these structures, and studying one helps us to gain a greater understanding of the other. The organizational structures of more established religions mimic that of the State itself. Power and legitimacy is attained through similar contexts. Hence, to understand the evolution of religion, it is integral to first assess the internal dynamics of the State.

State Power and Organized Religion

Every nation has adopted some form of law. The purpose of such law is to maintain order within a society. The State therefore enacts and legitimizes rules of acceptable and unacceptable behavior. The legitimacy of law suggests that the law is just, beyond reproach and representative of both the wants and needs of the majority of its citizens. Social order is defined by obedience of, and adherence to laws enacted by persons who ascend to power and influence. The political and legal realms then, serve to create and enforce laws. Here, the State has greater power than religion because it can force obedience to, and impose sanctions on parties who violate law.

Religion must promote and enforce conservative tenets to maintain order within its organization much like the State, and much of that control must be achieved through the voluntary adherence of its membership. Religion ensures both its own continuance and its authority by defining the terms of acceptable and unacceptable behavior and doing this on its own playing field. Tenets become legitimate because they are subject to enforcement by the religion. The Church can impose sanctions for violations of its tenets; these can include forms of censure to overt excommunication. In this process, the individual must work *within* the system and adhere to its established norms. By doing so, the individual accepts a subordinate position within the broader structure, therefore granting it power and legitimacy.

There are two central premises that are necessary to maintain law and order within civil society. The State and organized religion need to (1) be perceived as legitimate and (2) be able to use its power and influence to enforce its own laws/tenets. The latter is a more aggressive approach in that it moves beyond the ideological stage to the concrete form. Those that deviate from the legitimized law are met with resistance. In endorsing behavior that is not legal, and thus, not formally legitimized, deviants are confronted with immediate disdain from those who find such behavior challenging.

If the State or organized religion do not enforce its own laws/tenets then credibility and legitimacy is compromised. If they lose their perception of legitimacy, they cannot enact laws/tenets that will be respected and adhered to by the wider society. Legitimacy, then, serves as the foundation for power and influence. Any behavior that challenges this legitimacy will more likely be met with resistance by the State or organized religion. In doing so, they afford themselves continuity.

It would be incorrect to posit that the State or organized religion do not allow dissent. It would be correct to assert that the State and organized religion allow for dissent only in areas where it can (1) compartmentalize dissent (2) minimize dissent, and (3) ensure it affords itself means by which dissent can be quelled.

Compartmentalizing Dissent

Organization is an important facet of both the State and organized religion. The organizational structures entail highly sophisticated and hierarchically structured roles. Each unit of the bureaucratic organization (1) accounts for its own jurisdictional responsibility, (2) is accountable to a superior unit and ultimately the whole or body, and (3) works to preserve it and other units by maintaining its current operating system. Change is rarely perceived as progressive. Rather, it is perceived as a disruptive force that threatens the organizational structure of, and the legitimacy of, the bureaucracy itself.

Just as organization is integral to the sustenance of its continuity, it is also used as a medium to contain dissent. Dissent needs to be (1) identified (2) measured with regard to the level of threat is poses, if at all, and (3) categorized. This categorization entails that the potential disruptive force must be contained, and perhaps controlled. Both State and religion preserve their sustenance through organization and deals effectively with dissent through organization itself. The identification, measured threat and categorization of dissent afford the organization to control the variables, and ultimately the playing field.

External and Internal Forms of Dissent

When the forces of dissent originate from outside of the organization, the State or established religion maintains the advantage. This is what can be referred to as the *External Force Model*. Here, there arises dissatisfaction with a particular phenomenon from within the wider society. These can include organized or unorganized protests or collective behavior. Dissenters may initiate tactics and strategies to confront that which they oppose. Here, it moves beyond the general ideological stage and emerges as tangible strategies (Tridico, 2003; Oberschall, 1992; Offe, 1985).

There is concentration on accentuating the dissenters' strengths while targeting their opponent's weaknesses. Dissenters may engage in necessary battle that will determine their own fate. The end result can include (i) having their goals being met, (ii) having a significant portion of their goals fulfilled, (iii) having some of their goals being satisfied, (iv) having none of their goals realized but having been successful at having their concerns being formally raised and addressed or (v) having all of their concerns being rejected in their entirety. Both the State and religion hold the advantages of power and legitimacy (Tridico, 2003; Oberschall, 1992; Nedelmann, 1984).

External dissent has led to some changes. Christianity began as a Jewish sect (Esler, 2000; Robinson, 2001) and thus, like Judaism and Islam, is classified as an Abrahamic religion (*see also Judeo-Christian*). (Anidjar, 2003; Fowler, 1997) Originating in the eastern Mediterranean, it quickly grew in size and influence over a few decades, and by the 4th century had become the dominant religion within the Roman Empire. During the Middle Ages, most of the remainder of Europe was Christianized, with Christians also being a religious minority in the Middle East, North Africa and India. Following the Age of Discovery, Christianity spread to the Americas and the rest of the world through colonization (McManners, 2001).

Early Christianity then, can be seen as a form of dissent against Judaism because it wanted to change and/or expand the tenets of an established religion. Early Christianity can be seen as a form of dissent within the lens of the Roman Empire; this new pagan religion was perceived to be a potential threat to an existing political power. The persecutions of early Christians continued until the 4th Century, when Roman Emperor Constantine I issued an edict of toleration in 313. On 27 February 380, Emperor Theodosius I enacted a law establishing Christianity as the official religion of the Roman Empire (Bettenson, 1999). Constantine was also instrumental in the convocation of the First Council of Nicaea in 325, which sought to address the Arian heresy and formulated the Nicene Creed. This is still used by the Roman Catholic Church, Eastern Orthodoxy, Anglican Communion, and many Protestant churches. From at least the 4th Century, Christianity has played a prominent role in the shaping of Western civilization (Orlandis, 1993).

Internal dissent has led to significant change within Christianity, but that has largely come from the relationship between Church and State. The Church of England broke from Roman Catholicism to establish a new sect of Christianity. Much of this influence came from, and gained legitimacy from the State itself. Hence, one can argue that an alliance between England and the new sect of Christianity was forged to break from the grasp of Roman Catholicism (which was once heavily influenced by the Roman Empire).

The reform or change to establish a new Christian sect arose from internal dissent. However, this was not completely radical. It retained a significant identity from its predecessor. The Church of England can be understood to be both Catholic and Reformed. At the time of its establishment, Henry VIII caused the independent Church of England to cut ties with the Roman hierarchy, but the organization, liturgy, and doctrine of the church remained Roman Catholic (Melton, 2003). This is also expressed in its strong emphasis on the teachings of the early Church Fathers, in particular as formalized in the Apostolic, Nicene, and Athanasian creeds. However, it also views itself as being shaped by some of the doctrinal and institutional principles of the 16th century Protestant Reformation. Under Edward VII, doctrinal statements and religious articles that exemplified the reformed position were prevalent in the church (Melton, 2003), and the influence of Reformation liturgical and doctrinal principles continued under Queen Elizabeth I.

The oldest Protestant groups separated from the Roman Catholic Church in the 16th Century. The Protestant Reformation was followed in many cases by further divisions (McManners, 2001). The Methodist Church branched out of Anglican minister John Wesley's evangelical and revival movement in the Anglican Church. Several Pentecostal and non-denominational Churches evolved from the Methodist Church (Melton, 2003).

It has been internal dissent that has led to the expansion of Protestant denominations, with each schism adopting much of the former's identity while instilling marginal changes. Many of these changes, however, have not liberalized the ideology or structure of the denominations. Indeed, many remain largely conservative in both religious tenets and organizational dynamics. In this vein, we see a continued preservation of the broader religious doctrine of Christianity through the maintenance of tradition, conservative ideology and limiting of dissent.

While it can be argued that with each schism (from Roman Catholicism to multiple Protestant denominations), dissent has led to changes in the names of Churches, one can also argue that dissent has not necessarily led to changes in the ideological framework of most. This is particularly pronounced in areas of abortion and homosexuality, two central and historical premises of concern for established orthodox wings of Christian religions. While there is entrenched doctrine for opposition to abortion and homosexuality in Roman Catholicism, such opposition has been pronounced to varying degrees in Protestant denominations. Indeed, one can argue that the Evangelical movement has adopted concerted emphasis on such opposition (Smith, 2005).

Advent of Christianity in the United States

In general, Christianity has been an ever-present religious force throughout the development of the United States as a nation, and Protestant Christianity has been the predominant religious influence in America from before the United States officially existed as a nation. Some of the earliest settlements in Colonial America were established by religious groups whose beliefs and doctrines emerged in the 17th century Protestant Reformation, and from America's colonial beginnings to today Protestantism has remained one of the most prevalent and influential religious orientations in American society.

In *The Churching of America 1776-2005,* Finke and Stark (2007) provide an interesting analysis of the growth of Christianity in the United States. They begin their study by describing the religious establishment within the British colonies, and they found that both the dominant colonial religions (e.g., Congregationalist and Episcopalian) and a majority of the smaller religious bodies (Quaker, Presbyterian, Baptist, Methodist, Lutheran, etc.), were Protestant Christian denominations. Despite Finke and Stark's claim that the majority of the colonial population was far less religious than previously believed, and that 20% or less of the colonial population were religiously affiliated, it is nevertheless evident that Protestant Christianity was an essential aspect of religious and social life in America even before the United States emerged as a nation.

After the American Revolution, the dominant Protestant (Congregationalist and Episcopal) churches were gradually replaced as the leading religious bodies in America by other denominations (e.g., Baptist and Methodist) that spread throughout the American frontier and eventually dominated the American religious landscape. While the other Protestant groups (Presbyterian, Lutheran, etc.) did not grow at the same rate as the Baptists and Methodists, they were nevertheless significant religious congregations in the formative years of the United States and up to the present day.

As Protestantism expanded, Catholicism also began to grow in the U.S. in the 1800s. By the early 20th century Catholics had also become a considerable American religious body, although still small in comparison to the combined proportion of Protestant congregations. Throughout the 19th and 20th centuries the American religious landscape was constantly in flux, and included the growth of mainstream Protestant denominations and Catholicism, the emergence of many nondenominational and evangelical Protestant churches, and the appearance of various new religious movements (Mormons, Jehovah's Witnesses, etc.). Despite these changes, the whole of America's religious history has been primarily dominated by Christian belief systems, and the religious roots of the U.S. are still reflected in the predominant Christian religious composition of America today (Balmer & Winner, 2002).

Christianity as a Cultural Force

Christianity has been a powerful religious and cultural force throughout all of American history thus far. Not only can vestiges of these belief systems be readily seen on American monetary currency (e.g., '*In God We Trust*') and heard in many of the nation's patriotic anthems (e.g., America the Beautiful, My Country 'Tis of Thee, etc.), but also some of the most foundational and famous governmental documents, like the Declaration of Independence, are imbued with themes of Christian ideology. Additionally, despite the long standing separation of Church and State in the United States, Christianity also continues to play a role in the contemporary political arena. For instance, when Barak Obama, an admitted Christian, was sworn in as the 44th President of the United States he finished the inaugural oath with the pronouncement, '*So help me God.*' When Mitt Romney recently campaigned for the Republican presidential nomination, his Mormon faith received considerable attention in the mass media and some commentators even questioned his ability to govern in the office of the President of the United States because of his allegiance to his religion.

The preeminent role of Christianity in American history is also reflected in the contemporary religious landscape of the United States. According to the 2008 U.S. Religious Landscape Survey conducted by the PEW Forum on Religion and Public Life, 78% of all American adults are affiliated with a Christian religious tradition. Over half are affiliated with a Protestant Christian denomination and nearly 25% of American adults claim a catholic affiliation. Contrary to the predictions of secularization (Bruce, 2002; Berger, 1967) made by many social scientists over the past 40 years (e.g., that the role of religion in public life would decline and eventually disappear as societies become more modern, rational, and scientifically advanced) the United States continues to show high levels of religious belief and participation (Berger et al., 2008; Berger, 1999).

Religious beliefs also continue to influence modern perceptions and opinions regarding important social and political issues, including many of the issues surrounding homosexuality in American society. For example, in November 2008 a hotly contested California ballot proposition (Proposition 8) resulted in an amendment to the state Constitution that banned same-sex marriage. The role played by various religious organizations in supporting and campaigning for Proposition 8 became more apparent in the post-ballot media coverage. After the proposition passed, gay-rights advocates staged rallies and protests outside of church buildings and temples belonging to The Church of Jesus Christ of Latter Day Saints (Mormons), believing that Mormon support for Proposition 8 was a major factor in the amendment's passage. While Mormons were among a larger coalition of religious organizations that supported the amendment including Catholic, Evangelical, and Orthodox Christian groups and organizations, it is nevertheless clear that Christian religious beliefs concerning morality and homosexuality played an influential role in the recent re-definition of the institution of marriage in California.

Not long thereafter, the well known Evangelical Christian pastor, Ted Haggard, appeared in the national media to discuss the extra-marital homosexual relationships that contributed to his public 'disgrace'. He admitted to engaging in homosexual behaviors with a male volunteer, and he also admitted to paying for the services of a male prostitute. This was all the more controversial given the position he had voiced that the Bible clearly states that homosexuality is sinful and that God intended intimate relationships to be monogamous relationships between men and women.

Even the 2009 Miss America Pageant became a nationally televised stage for the debate over the political correctness of gay marriage. Carrie Prejean (Miss California), a student at an evangelical Christian college, was asked by an openly gay pageant judge whether she thought all U.S. states should legalize gay marriage. Upon her response that she believed marriage should be between a man and a woman she received both heckling and cheers from the audience. However, much of the post-pageant commentary and media coverage attributed her loss of the pageant to her publicly pronouncing the belief that marriage should be a heterosexual institution.

These examples demonstrate that Christian belief systems continue to perpetuate marginalized views of homosexuality that reinforce sexual inequality in America's cultural and religious institutions. However, it is also evident that heteronormative views of sexuality are also being challenged in American society, to the extent that five U.S. states (e.g., Massachusetts, Connecticut, Maine, Iowa, and Vermont) have now legalized same-sex marriage. While a great deal of mass media attention and social-scientific research has been paid to the political and social issues surrounding homosexuality in the United States, far less consideration has been given to the ways that the stigmatization of homosexuality in Christian beliefs and doctrine is being challenged from within Christianity itself.

Christian Ideology and Heterosexism

Christianity in general and Protestantism in particular, have been an ever-present religious force throughout the development of the United States as a nation. Through this, the continual influence of Christian religious beliefs affected American cultural institutions and practices with regard to homosexuality. It can be argued that within religious beliefs and doctrines of varying Christian denominations throughout American history have endorsed and legitimized heterosexuality while homosexuality has typically been viewed as sinful, immoral and worthy of condemnation.

According to Wolkomir (2006) the justification for stigmatizing homosexuality within Christian doctrine can be found in the traditional interpretations of several passages in the bible that label homosexuality as sinful and condemn those who engage in homosexual practices (e.g., Genesis 19:4-11; Leviticus 18:22-23; 20: 13-14; Deuteronomy 23: 17-18; 1 Corinthians 6:9, and the Sodom and Gomorrah story). Given that Christianity has been such a powerful and enduring force in American society for over 200 years, it is not difficult to conceive of these beliefs shaping the moral order in American society and affecting America's national culture and institutions as it developed and evolved.

The national culture of a society is often shaped over time by its religious traditions, and religious traditions and values become a part of, and are transmitted by, institutions that impact not only religious individuals in a given society but also those who have no connection to institutional religion (Inglehart & Baker, 2000). Religious institutions can become established moral communities (Stark & Glock, 1970) that impact cultural values and norms, and according to Smith (2003), it is inevitable for the institutions of a society to be infused with rules and values that are based on conceptions of morality and moral order, and these institutions, in turn, transmit and reinforce standards by which people judge themselves and others.

This becomes important when discussing the marginalization of homosexuality in American society because Christian doctrines and beliefs have been one of the most powerful and pervasive forces in defining, transmitting, and reinforcing heteronormative conceptions of gender, morality, and sexuality. Homosexuality has been stigmatized within Christian ideology for centuries, and some scholars argue that Christian doctrine continues to function as one of the primary means through which heterosexism is maintained in contemporary society (Wolkomir, 2006).

Thus, the term heterosexism refers to the cultural intuitions, ideologies, and belief systems that promote normative heterosexuality and perpetuate the marginalization of other sexual orientations (Herek, 2004; Niesen, 1990). Many social scientists have argued that heterosexism is an ongoing social problem and that heterosexist belief systems continue to oppress homosexuals in modern American society. However, recent research has shown that the gay-affirming and ex-gay Christian movements represent a challenge to heterosexism from within Christianity itself, and researchers have recently studied these groups to analyze how heterosexist ideologies are challenged and revised. The next sections introduce readers to the gay affirming and ex-gay Christian movements and demonstrate how the symbolic interactionist approach to social research can be used for understanding how gay-affirming and ex-gay Christian groups attempt to challenge heterosexism by reinterpreting and revising Christian ideology.

The Gay-affirming and Ex-gay Christian Movements

Members of gay-affirming or ex-gay Christian groups have experienced varying degrees of conflict between their religious identity and homosexual desires, and their Christian religious identity is so central to their self-concept that they seek out ways to hold on to that important part of their self and somehow come to terms with their sexuality. Previous research has consistently found that individuals who perceive their sexual desires and practices as being contradictory to their religious beliefs often experience a great deal of psychological and emotional conflict (Wolkomir, 2006; Wilcox, 2003; Rodriguez & Oulette, 2000; Yip, 1997; Mahaffy, 1996; Thumma, 1991). Given the fact that there exist segments of Christianity where homosexuality is viewed as being completely contrary to Christian doctrine and beliefs (Roof &McKinney, 1987), many whose identity is strongly tied to their Christian religious beliefs experience considerable internal turmoil.

Prior to the late 1960s there were not many options for Christians who experienced same-sex desires. Typically, gay Christians would either hide their sexuality from their families and friends, often fearing the consequences of exposure. Revealing their sexuality to others often meant the loss of important relationships and exclusion from their religious communities. However, as the gay-rights movement began to take hold the gay-affirming and ex-gay Christian movements emerged and offered different ways for dealing with and situating homosexuality within Christianity beliefs and doctrine.

Generally speaking, gay-affirming Christian ministries and groups are characterized by the view that homosexuality is not contrary to Christian doctrine; that God makes and loves homosexuals just as he makes and loves heterosexuals, and therefore homosexuality is not an abomination but acceptable in the sight of God. The Metropolitan Community Church, one of the first and largest gay-affirming organizations in the U.S. also asserts the view that homosexuality adheres to biblical tenets and standards as long as homosexual practices take place within committed monogamous/marriage relationships (Wolkomir, 2006).

By contrast, ex-gay Christian ministries can generally be characterized as reinforcing the belief that homosexuality is sinful and contrary to God's will, but diverges from mainline Protestant ideology is the sense that the sin of homosexuality is not viewed as being any worse than other types of sin. Ex-gay groups are often oriented towards healing homosexuality and helping Christians overcome same-sex desires (Erzen, 2006; Wolkomir, 2006) so they can develop a heterosexual identity that is in line with God's will.

Despite the stark contrast in the ways gay-affirming and ex-gay groups situate homosexuality within Christian doctrine and beliefs, researchers have found that many of the strategies used by these groups to challenge traditional interpretations of biblical doctrine and theology are quite similar (Wolkomir, 2006), which may provide additional insight into how subordinate groups (homosexuals) come to challenge heterosexism as they learn how to reconcile the perceived tension between being gay and Christian.

Revising Beliefs and Identities: A Symbolic Interactionist Approach

So the question remains, how is it that Christians who have internalized strong religious beliefs that completely reject homosexuality come to terms with their same-sex desires? It may be difficult to challenge long standing doctrines and theological beliefs that have been internalized as truthful and divine. Berger (1967) claimed that other-worldly (religious) beliefs are even harder to change than secular beliefs because they are grounded in God's authority as opposed to humankind's. Dominant belief systems are also difficult to alter because they are fundamental to the way people come to view themselves and others in the worlds they inhabit (Wolkomir, 2006, 2001; Schwalbe, 1998).

One way of understanding how individuals come to challenge dominant Christian ideologies though interaction and participation in gay-affirming and ex-gay groups is by analyzing the ideological work done by these groups through a symbolic interactionist perspective (Wolkomir, 2006, 2001; Thumma, 1991). The symbolic interactions approach (Berger & Luckmann, 1966; Goffman, 1959; Mead, 1934) in social research is often used to describe how individual and social identities are created, transmitted, maintained, and changed through processes of socialization and human social interaction, and recent studies have shown that the use of this approach can be valuable for exploring the processes involved in revising dominant ideologies and integrating seemingly incompatible sexual and religious identities (Wolkomir, 2006, 2001; Yip, 1997; Thumma, 1991).

One of the most important functions of gay-affirming and ex-gay groups that social scientists have discovered is that they offer individuals a safe social space in which they learn through social interaction with others that it is possible for their religious beliefs to be altered in such a way that either allows them to integrate their Christian religious identity with their sexuality (gay-affirming), or maintain their Christian identity while reshaping beliefs about homosexuality that reinforce and justify the struggle against homosexual desires (ex-gay). To understand how gay-affirming and ex-gay groups help Christian men come to terms with their beliefs and sexuality by challenging dominant Christian ideology, Michelle Wolkomir (2006; 2001) studied a support group affiliated with Exodus International, a leading ministry in the ex-gay movement, and a gay-affirming bible-study group connected with Metropolitan Community Church. She found that through a process she refers to as ideological maneuvering (2001), members within both of these groups were able to confront the nature of certain dominant Christian beliefs and ideology by exposing traditional interpretations of biblical doctrine regarding homosexuality as biased and incorrect.

Wolkomir (2006) explains that in the gay-affirming group, heterosexist ideology was challenged by placing an emphasis on teaching members that interpretations of Christian doctrine that condemn homosexuality are flawed because such interpretations were made by individuals, not God. As such, they may be subject to bias. This was done by having members attend group bible-study classes where they were guided through the reading of certain biblical passages in different versions of the bible (e.g., King James and NIV) to see how certain interpretations condemn homosexuality whereas others do not. By identifying the condemning interpretations, members were able to question the divine authority of heterosexist doctrine, which allowed them to bring it into the secular realm and reconstruct a Christian ideology that is accepting of homosexuality. The ex-gay group used a similar strategy of ideological maneuvering. However, in lieu of constructing a completely different ideology, they challenged the divine authority of biblical interpretations of homosexuality for being more damning than other types of sin. This allowed them to reinterpret those passages and place homosexuality on the same parallel as other types of sin.

Once the work of invalidating certain elements of Christian doctrine was accomplished members were able to re-conceptualize what it meant to be a good Christian, but the groups still had to provide members with social and religious resources that helped them to internalize and affirm their revised identities as gay or ex-gay Christians. The validation of the new identity was achieved by providing members with positive social interactions that made group participation emotionally rewarding (Wolkomir, 2006), and offering members the change to legitimize the new identity by being engaged in meaningful group activities and experience acceptance (Thumma, 1991) within their respective groups.

It is important to remember, however, that neither the gay-affirming or ex-gay groups attempted to discredit the overall belief system of Christianity. Their overall goal was to challenge and revise certain aspects of dominant Christian doctrine so they were able to *maintain* their Christian identity while allowing for certain doctrinal accommodations (e.g., acceptance of homosexuality or redefining the severity of homosexual sin so that it can be viewed as conquerable).

While it is apparent that both gay-affirming and ex-gay groups challenge long-standing Christian conceptions of morality and sexuality, it is integral to measure the extent such groups are able to overcome heterosexism and influence social change in the larger society. Wolkomir (2006) argues that the gay and ex-gay Christian movements have had an impact within American culture by creating alternative Christian identities and expanding cultural perceptions of religion and sexuality, but she also contends that the overall impact of these groups upon larger issues of sexual equality are constrained and minimized because these groups remain connected to the larger ideological framework (Christianity) that oppressed them from the first.

This raises important questions about the extent to which marginalized groups are able to affect real social change when they are acting within larger cultural and ideological systems that continue to reaffirm their subjugation. To gain a better understanding of the potential for gay and ex-gay Christian groups to affect change towards sexual equality, the next section discusses sociological perspectives of power and authority in society and the larger social consequences of marginalized groups acting within dominant structures of ideology and power.

Reaffirming Heterosexism or Genuine Social change: Critical Perspectives

As discussed in earlier sections, the religious tradition and associated moral order of a society has a considerable impact on the cultural institutions and practices that develop within that society. Thus, Christian belief systems have played a role in the normalization of heterosexuality and the marginalization of alternative sexualities in American cultural institutions and practices. Given that gay and ex-gay Christian movements are functioning within an overall religious belief system (Christianity) that subordinates homosexuals and a larger cultural system where homosexuality is also marginalized, it is questionable whether such groups can overcome inequality under such conditions. Indeed, one may question whether they actually may be reaffirming the heterosexist ideologies that oppress them.

Doctrinal Reinterpretation as Social Change

What is social change? What is a social movement? Can the gay-affirming and ex-gay Christian movements be seen as influencing social change? For the purposes of this study, social change is understood as the transformation of elements of society, and these elements can include culture, institutions, and ideological systems such as beliefs, norms, and values (Macionis, 2008). Social movements can be thought of as collective acts that influence social change, or the acts that transform elements of society (Macionis, 2008).

David F. Aberle (1966) constructed four types of social movements based on who is affected and the strength of change that may provide insight into the type of social change that results from the gay-affirming and ex-gay Christian groups. These include:

(1) *alterative social movements* that affect specific individuals while being limited in its strength of change,
(2) *redemptive social movements* that also affect specific individuals but are far more radical in change,
(3) *reformative social movements* that affect large populations while having limited strength, and
(4) *revolutionary social movements* that affect large populations and have radical strength of change.

While differing interpretations of Christian doctrine are abundant throughout the world, it is nevertheless a very difficult task to challenge and revise long-standing and widely shared aspects of theological ideology, which is precisely what takes place within gay-affirming and ex-gay Christian groups. As previously discussed, in comparison to secular beliefs, modifying components of religious ideology is far more difficult because these beliefs are perceived as transcendent, divine, sacred, and beyond the power of man (Berger, 1967). Secular ideologies on the other hand are grounded in the everyday human realm, making changes to secular beliefs easier to undertake.

The social change that comes from the ideological work that takes place within the gay-affirming and ex-gay movements includes the alternative beliefs and norms that allow individuals to construct alternative Christian identities as gay and ex-gay Christians. These movements also expand cultural perceptions of religion and sexuality (Wolkomir, 2006), and have a real impact in the lives of their members, allowing them to feel empowered as they work to resolve the issues they have been struggling with.

However, based on Aberle's (1966) types of social movements, the gay and ex-gay Christian movements would likely be classified as alterative social movements. While they affect specific individuals involved in these movements, the strength and scope of social change made possible by these movements is limited and constrained. The next section addresses how relations of power and authority constrain the extent to which these movements are able to overcome sexual inequality both within Christianity and in the larger society.

Relations of Power and Authority

Over the centuries, many philosophers and scholars have attempted to describe the different ways that power and authority function within societies and constrain the ability of subordinate groups to overcome oppression and inequality. One such perspective provided by Lukes (2005) appears to be applicable to the current discussion. According to Lukes' third dimension of power, individuals in a society behave according to unwritten rules and expectations that can have great power in maintaining a dominant agenda. For example, a popular cultural value in the United States is the belief that one can achieve anything through hard work and determination. With all things being equal, if an individual wants something (e.g., better vehicle, home, occupation, etc.), the opportunities for obtaining these thing are available, if only individuals work hard enough to achieve their goals. Not only is this cultural value not shared among all other cultures throughout the world, some would argue that this is not even a reality in the United States.

In applying Lukes' third dimension of power to this example, one may suppose that the belief that anything can be achieved by working hard enough may in fact reinforce a variety of other cultural agendas. For example, if everyone is working hard to achieve and attain more and better things, this would mean they are continually consuming and pumping money into the economy, reinforcing the practice of American consumerism. Thus, the influence of a shared cultural ideology in a given society has a deep power relation that reinforces and maintains other dominant agendas.

Given that Christianity has played a role in the institutionalization of heterosexuality in American culture, and because heterosexist cultural ideologies and institutions continue to be reinforced by Christian belief systems, it is possible that maintaining the dominance of traditional Christian ideology reinforces dominant cultural agendas that have developed around heteronormative culture in the United States. Moreover, by functioning within the larger Christian ideology as opposed to discarding the larger ideology that subjugates them, gay and ex-gay Christians may be seen as behaving according to unwritten heterosexist rules and expectations that actually reaffirm the belief systems that marginalize homosexuals, limiting the potential of these groups to affect any social change towards sexual equality in Christianity and the larger society.

In conjunction with Lukes' contribution, Schwalbe, Godwin, Holden, Schrock, Thompson and Wolkomir's (2000) analysis of the direct and indirect processes that dominants (those in positions of power) use to establish and maintain control over subordinates is also useful for exploring the social consequences of the gay and ex-gay Christian movements. Schwalbe and his colleagues contend that those in power use the ideas and norms of society to indirectly influence people's behavior according to the dominant agendas. This is accomplished not by controlling all aspects of people's behavior, but only those parts that affect the dominant agendas. This allows for the mirage of change to take place without actually threatening dominant agendas. This indirect and subtle form of establishing and maintaining control is far more successful than direct force, where subordinates would likely rise against the dominant agenda (Scott, 1990). Therefore authority is established and sustained by creating a situation that allows subordinates the illusion that change can happen while at the same time reinforcing the dominant agendas (Schwalbe et al., 2000). Michel Foucault (1980a; 1980b) also understood power as being more successful if its mechanisms are hidden, thereby allowing control to be endured by those being dominated.

By applying these conceptualizations of power to the process of ideological maneuvering described by Wolkomir, the notion that gay and ex-gay Christian groups may be reaffirming systems of sexual inequality becomes clearer. Typically, those who join gay and ex-gay groups do so because they have already internalized and legitimated a Christian belief system that shapes and defines their self-concept. Insofar as religious identity comes into conflict with their same-sex desires, they seek out ways to maintain their religious identity and somehow reconcile their sexuality within the Christian belief system they have already legitimated.

Although members of these groups achieve a sense of empowerment by revising elements of the dominant heteronormative Christian ideology (Wolkomir, 2006) they are also validating the overall legitimacy of the Christian belief system that subjugates them. Despite the mirage of change (Schwalbe et al., 2000), the dominant ideology that marginalizes homosexuality isn't truly challenged, but it is actually reaffirmed. Additionally, by reaffirming the larger Christian belief system, it is possible that these groups are reaffirming an ideological framework that reinforces heterosexist cultural ideologies and institutions in the larger society, thereby constraining the overall potential for overcoming sexual oppression.

Conclusion and Discussion

Political reform regarding homosexuality has occurred in recent years. The gay rights movement has achieved varying success at such reform by *removal from*, rather than *inclusion of*, religious identity. What can be discerned is that the same stigmatized compartmentalization as a sexual minority ascribed by organized religion, has been used by this sector to lobby for legal and constitutional rights. Legal reform of homosexuality in the United States has occurred through constitutional challenges but it has been met with significant opposition.

Constitutional challenges to laws against homosexuality have come after challenges to issues regarding contraception and abortion. What is consistent in all three challenges is that they have been argued under privacy rights of the Fourteenth Amendment of the U.S. Constitution. The first successful challenge, *Griswold v. Connecticut*, 381 U.S. 479 (1965), was a U.S. Supreme Court landmark case that accorded Constitution protection for privacy rights. The case examined a

Connecticut law that prohibited the use of contraceptives. By a majority vote of 7-2, the Supreme Court invalidated the law on the grounds that it violated the right to marital privacy.

It would be *Griswold* however, that would be the precedent case that would set the course for the broader expansion of privacy rights. The three privacy victories that grew from Griswold's methodology were:

(1) *Eisenstadt v. Baird (1972)*. Here, Harlan's interpretation of the Equal Protection Clause of the Fourteenth Amendment extended privacy rights for usage of contraceptives from married couples to unmarried couples.

(2) *Roe v. Wade (1973)*. The Court ruled that this law was a violation of the Due Process Clause of the Fourteenth Amendment. The law was struck down, legalizing abortion for women up through the first trimester, and some restrictions for the second and third trimesters.

(3) *Lawrence v. Texas (2003)*. The Court ruled that state law prohibiting sodomy between homosexuals was unconstitutional. This essentially overruled a decision 17 years earlier in *Bowers v. Hardwick* (1986) which upheld a Georgia statute prohibiting sodomy. The Fourteenth Amendment was used again in this case to grant privacy rights over intimate relations.

Eisenstadt v. Baird (1972) extended privacy rights of contraception for all couples. *Roe v. Wade* (1973) extended privacy rights for abortion for women. *Lawrence v. Texas* (2003) extended privacy rights to gay Americans over intimate relations. It can be argued then, that the Equal Protection Clause of the Fourteenth Amendment was essential in interpreting privacy rights where the Constitution fails to textually address it.

The 17 year lapse between *Bowers v. Hardwick* (1986) and *Lawrence v. Texas (*2003) suggests two things. First, there was significant political and legal rebuff of homosexual advances, even within the context of constitutional protection. Without constitutional legitimacy, homosexuality was limited in legal and moral advancement. Second, constitutional legitimacy, albeit gained through political and legal opposition, has not extended to advancement of homosexual acceptance within the moral auspices of organized religion. Indeed, the shift of moral opposition to homosexuality has met or exceeded that of abortion in many Christian religious denominations *after* constitutional and legal recognition (Tridico, 2009).

This polarizing process has benefitted the gay rights movement, rather than hindered it. Insofar as the movement has gained constitutional and legal legitimacy vis-à-vis sexual privacy and broader human rights, and limited advancement of legal rights vis-à-vis same sex unions and same sex marriage at the state level, opposition to it from the religious community has been able to be effectively curtailed. In advancing the *separation* of Church and State, and by concentrating on political and legal reform, the movement has helped define legitimacy through the *State* rather than the *Church*.

While it can be argued that overt moral rebuke of homosexuality has been contained within organized religion, the covert resistance toward full acceptance of its identity is pronounced in political, legal, economic and social contexts. Recognition on all afore-mentioned levels has been consistently resisted throughout history, and gains have only been achieved to varying degrees in recent decades. Religion and traditional moral context have slowed and limited the advancement of the gay movement within the State. It continues to provide resistance. In identifying homosexuality as an emerging moral threat vis-à-vis potentially changing the traditional definition of marriage, organized religion's opposition to homosexuality is enhanced.

The consistent overt moral rebuke of homosexuality within organized religion has shifted the gay movement away from the Church and directly to the State. Political and/or legal legitimacy gained therein does not necessary transcend toward moral legitimacy within organized religion. The move from the State to the Church, either by attempting to gain entry to established religions, or attempts to initiate reform through new sects within existing religions, will face significant resistance.

While new sects afford themselves legitimacy and recognition of Christian identity through its name, the movement cannot separate the historical and consistent opposition to homosexuality within religion itself. To varying degrees, most established sects within Christianity have instilled opposition to homosexuality as one of its central tenets. The establishment of divergent ideals from new sect(s) within Christianity will more likely be identified as a threat to an established structure, rather than progressive reform.

References

Aberle, D. R. (1966). *The Peyote Religion among the Natives*. Chicago, IL: University of Chicago Press.

Anidjar, G. (2003). *The Jew, the Arab: A History of the Enemy (Cultural Memory in the Present)*. Stanford, CA: Stanford University Press.

Balmer, R. & Winner, L. F. (2002). *Protestantism in America*. New York, NY: Columbia University Press.

Berger, P. (1967). *The Sacred Canopy: Elements of a Sociological Theory of Religion*. New York, NY: Anchor Books.

Berger, P. (Ed.). (1999). *The Desecularization of the World: Resurgent Religion and World Politics*. Grand Rapids, MI: William B. Eerdmans Publishing Company.

Berger, P., Davie, G. & Fokas, E. (2008). *Religious America, Secular Europe? A Theme and Variations*. Hampshire, UK: Ashgate Publishing Limited.

Berger, P. & Luckmann, T. (1966). *The Social Construction of Reality*. Garden City, NY: Doubleday.

Bettenson, H. (1999). *Documents of the Christian Church*. New York, NY: Oxford University Press.

Bruce, S. (2002). *God is Dead*. Malden, M.A.: Blackwell Publishing.

Esler, P. F. (2000). *The Early Christian World*. New York, NY: Routledge.

Ezren, T. (2006). *Straight to Jesus: Sexual and Christian Conversions in the Ex-Gay Movement*. University of California Press.

Finke, R. & Stark, R. (2007). *The Churching of America 1776-2005: Winners and Losers in Our Religious Economy*. New Brunswick, NJ: Rutgers University Press.

Foucault, M. (1980a). *Power/Knowledge: Selected Interviews and Other Writings, 1972-1977*. Brighton: Harvester.

Foucault, M. (1980b). *The History of Sexuality, Vol. 1*, trans. Robert Hurley. New York, NY: Random House.

Fowler, J. D. (1997). *World Religions: An Introduction for Students*. Portland, OR: Sussex Academic Press.

Goffman, E. (1959). *The Presentation of Self in Everyday Life*. Garden City, NY: Doubleday.

Herek, G. M. (2004). Beyond "Homophobia": Thinking About Sexual Prejudice and Stigma in the Twenty-First Century. *Sexuality Research & Social Policy*, 1(2), p. 6-24.

Inglehart, R. & Baker, W.E. (2000). Modernization, Cultural Change, and the Persistence of Traditional Values. *American Sociological Review*, 65(1), p. 19-51.

Lukes, S. (2005). *Power: A Radical View*. New York, NY: Palgrave Macmillan.

Macionis, J. (2008). *Sociology, 12th ed*. Upper Saddle River, NJ: Pearson Education Inc.

Mahaffy, K. (1996). Cognitive Dissonance and its Resolution: A Study of Lesbian Christians. *Journal for the Scientific Study of Religion*. 35, p. 392–402.

McManners, J. (2001). *Oxford Illustrated History of Christianity*. New York, NY: Oxford University Press.

Mead, G. H. (1934). *Mind, Self, and Society*. Chicago, IL: University of Chicago Press.

Melton, G. (2003). *Encyclopedia of American Religions. 7th ed*. Detroit, MI: Gale.

Nedelmann, B. (1984). New Political Movements and Changes in Processes of Intermediation. *Social Science Information*. 23(6): 1,029-1,048).

Neisen, J. H. (1990). Heterosexism: Redefining Homophobia for the 1990s. *Journal of Gay & Lesbian Psychotherapy*,1(3), p. 21-35.

Oberscshall. (1992). *Social Movements: Ideologies, Interests and Identities*. Engewood Cliffs, NJ: Transaction Publishers.

Offe, C. (1985). New Social Movements: Challenging the Boundaries of Institutional Politics. *Social Research*, 53(4).

Orlandis, J. (1993). *A Short History of the Catholic Church*. New York, NY: Scepter Publishers.

Pew Research Center (2008). U.S. Religious Landscape Survey. Retrieved June, 2009: http://religions.pewforum.org/pdf/report-religious-landscape-study-full.pdf

Rodriguez, E. & Ouellette, S. (2000). Gay and Lesbian Christians: Homosexual and Religious Identity Integration in the Members and Participants of a Gay-Positive Church. *Journal for the Scientific Study of Religion*, 39(3), p. 333-347.

Roof, W., & McKinney, W. (1987). *American Mainline Religion: Its Changing Shape and Future*. New Brunswick, NJ: Rutgers University Press.

Schwalbe, M. (1998). *The Sociologically Examined Life. 2nd ed*. Repr. Mountain View, CA: Mayfield Publishers, 2001.

Schwalbe, M., Godwin, S., Holden, D., Schrock, D., Thompson, S. & Wolkomir, M. (2000). Generic Processes in the Reproduction of Inequality: An Integrationist Analysis. *Social Forces*, 79(2), p. 419-452.

Scott, J. (1990). *Domination and the Arts of Resistance: Hidden Transcripts*. New Haven, CT: Yale University Press.

Smith, C. (2003). *Moral, Believing Animals*. Oxford, UK: Oxford University Press.

Smith, M. (2005). The Politics of Same-Sex Marriage in Canada and the United States. *PS, Political Science and Politics*, 38(2), p. 225-228.

Stark, R. & Glock, C. (1970). Churches as Moral Communities. In Phillip E. Hammond and Benton Johnson (Eds.), *American Mosaic: Social Patterns of Religion in the United States*. (p. 290-298). New York, NY: Random House.

Thumma, S. (1991). Negotiating a Religious Identity: The Case of the Gay Evangelical. *Sociological Analysis*, 52(4), p. 333-347.

Tridico, F. (2003). *The Social Construction of Reality*. Sault Ste. Marie, ON: Landon Elsemere Press.

Tridico, F. (2009). *Law and Social Order*. Sault Ste. Marie, ON: Landon Elsemere Press.

Wilcox, M. (2003). *Coming Out in Christianity: Religion, Identity, and Community*. Bloomington, IN: Indiana University Press.

Wolkomir, M. (2001). Wrestling with the Angels of Meaning: The Revisionist Ideological Work of Gay and Ex-Gay Christian Men. *Symbolic Interaction*, 24, p. 407-424.

Wolkomir, M. (2006). *"Be Not Deceived": The Sacred and Sexual Struggles of Gay and Ex-gay Christian Men*. New Brunswick, NY: Rutgers University Press.

Yip, A. (1997). Attacking the Attacker: Gay Christians Talk Back. *British Journal of Sociology*, 48, p. 113–127.

CHAPTER 2
DISCRIMINATION FACED BY MEMBERS OF THE LESBIAN, GAY, BISEXUAL, AND TRANSGENDER (LGBT) COMMUNITY

Carrie Buist and Andrew Verheek

Abstract: In the forthcoming article, the authors will highlight some of the problematics associated with the discrimination that the LGBT community faces in several facets of their everyday lives, with special attention being placed on gays and lesbians. In order to explore this topic, an overview of sexuality and identity will be highlighted along with the social construction of gender and sexuality and the prevalence of heterosexism in the United States. The importance of sexual identity and the connectivity between identity and sexuality will be used as an example of why discrimination towards gays and lesbians is just as detrimental to American society as racism and sexism. The areas of discrimination that will be examined include the impact and rate of hate crimes in the United States, marriage equality, and housing and employment discrimination.

The genesis of the gay rights movement began on the evening of June 28, 1969 when the Stonewall Inn, a bar that was frequented by homosexuals, was raided by police officers. This raid was not an unusual occurrence as during this time in history; establishments that welcomed homosexuals were often investigated or raided. What was unusual on this night was that the patrons of the Stonewall resisted with spontaneous and violent demonstrations, forcing the police officers to essentially surrender their raid. This served as a catalyst for the gay liberation movement, forging collective identity through the creation of new lobbyist groups (Stein, 2004; Seidman, 2003).

Political, Legal and Economic Contexts

In the 40 years since the Stonewall Riots, there have been tangible gains for the Lesbian, Gay, Bisexual and Transgender community, albeit *concerted*, *diminutive* and with *significant resistance* from the political, legal and economic realms. Political resistance to the advancement of the gay rights has been the most historic and consistent. At the federal level and to a lesser extent, there have been two issues that have served as political obstacles for the LGBT community. First, same sex marriage has been perceived as a threat to the definition of traditional marriage. This issue has helped forged an alliance between conservative religious factions and conservative ideology within both major political parties (Tridico, 2009). Hence, the preservation of traditional definitions of marriage and the family have served to resist and limit what have been perceived to be forms of organized dissent. Second, the lobby to have sexual orientation be added for protection in federal hate crimes legislation in 1999 was rebuffed. While it did prompt more aggressive lobbying and subsequent some successes at the state level, the rejection of the Hate Crimes Prevention Act at the federal level demonstrates political resistance to change (Tridico, 2004).

Legal challenges have also been met with profound resistance. While many state laws banning sexual acts between consenting same sex adults have been purged, sodomy laws continued to be in place until 2003. In *Bowers v. Hardwick* (1986), the United States Supreme Court decided by a narrow 5-4 majority, at least with regard to *homosexual sodomy*, a Georgia statute making *all* sodomy criminal. This decision was an ideological shift toward conservatism, and a direct rebuff of the arguments in *Roe v. Wade* (1973). The Supreme Court essentially added constitutional legitimacy to state discrimination against gays, since homosexual sodomy could now be legally prosecuted without address (Tridico, 2009).

Despite its 17 year tenure (from the 1986 ruling to the Supreme Court essentially striking down *Bowers v. Hardwick* in another decision in *Lawrence v. Texas* in 2003) many states rejected the Court's constitutional recognition of prohibition of sodomy. Many state statutes were repealed as a symbolic denunciation of what could be considered a denial of application of the Fourteenth Amendment (Tridico, 2009). Even despite constitutional legitimacy, the repeal of statutes at the state level served as a powerful symbolic victory for the gay community.

Tridico (2009) argues that while it was expected that the Bowers decision in 1986 would have long reaching effects on state laws, it did the opposite. In affirming the Georgia statute, many states repealed their laws. In doing so, it negated any power of prosecuting sodomy. Many states essentially did what the Supreme Court failed to do: grant the right of privacy to adults (regardless of their sexual orientation) to engage in sodomy, even though the Supreme Court stated that this was *not* a *fundamental right*. This would explain why the decision remained unchallenged for 17 years. Many states repealed sodomy laws and those that retained them rarely pursued charges against individuals who violated such laws.

There are laws in some states that have never been repealed (e.g., prohibition against interracial marriage, or marital aids) but continue to go unchallenged because the enforcement of them have been nonexistent. Unless legislatures repeal the laws, or someone charged challenges their constitutionality, they remain intact. So too did the Supreme Court's decision in Bowers remain as constitutional precedent, until it was challenged in 2003. This suggests that at the legal level, despite consistent and historical resistance toward change vis-à-vis the gay community, there have been gains, albeit recent and it is within this realm where challenges to laws enacted by the political sector can be challenged.

The political and legal resistance to full recognition of the LGBT community has helped foster additional economic challenges. Legislation continues to exist that fails to protect this sector from overt and covert discrimination. For example, the resistance toward full inclusion of marriage recognition at the federal level, and on most state levels denies same sex partners the rights afforded to opposite sex partners vis-à-vis insurance spousal benefits and issues regarding estates in wills. Further, housing and employment discrimination continue to exist at federal, state and local levels, with the local sector serving as the most difficult to have grievances addressed at.

Sexuality and Identity

Sexuality as it is related to identity is an important topic to review before one can delve into the specific types of discrimination that people in the LGBT community face. Coupled with the importance of sexuality, gender is also paramount for the discourse of sexuality in society. It can be argued that gender and sexuality are dichotomous variables that should not be interconnected. However, both sexuality and gender are topics that have traditionally been viewed through a binary lens; an individual is either heterosexual or homosexual, and individual men are to be masculine, while individual women are to be feminine. Additionally, these binaries have been researched and presented as being linear in their approaches, however, the argument that shall be presented here is that neither sexuality or gender are linear concepts (Rust, 1993), but moreover would be better served if observed on a *continuum*.

The social construction of gender is a concept that is not unfamiliar to many sociological scholars, the concept of gender as a social construct and sex a biological fact (Oakley as cited in Messerschmidt, 2004) have been explored for generations; we are born either male or female (in most cases) and from the time of our births, the way in which we act and react in society is fashioned by a set of societal standards based on gender roles, such as the previously mentioned masculinity of men and femininity of women. Furthermore, women are expected to be more emotional while men expected to be more rational beings (Adler, Proctor II, and Towne, 2005). These gender role expectations are in essence, gender role *ideals* that society both creates and perpetuates both as a whole and on the individual level. This reciprocal nature is reminiscent of Giddens' (1984) structuration theory that posits that we both feed into the structures in society while those structures in turn, feed into how we act and react in society.

Messerschmidt (2004) has indicated that gender in and of itself is a learned behavior that we can unlearn, however this is a difficult task for many of us, as we have been conditioned from the time of our births until the time of our deaths to act in a manner that is acceptable to society as a whole. These actions that we have learned are performances, or have also been referred to as '*doing gender*.' Some of us are more successful in performing our gender roles while others find it more difficult to fit into the roles that have been assigned to us and both the ability to pass or fail societal expectations of our gender roles are interpreted by our interactions with others in society (Barak et al., 2007; Butler, 1990).

Gender roles are an important component to our identities in society. An example of this could be the wider society's expectations and perceptions of men through reinforced cultural stereotypes. A male may be expected to be strong both physically and emotionally. Given these expectations of such characteristics, the individual may attempt to represent himself in the way that reinforces the broadly accepted norms. Failure to do so may potentially lead to negative censure from the wider society. For example, demonstrating signs of physical and emotional frailty may be perceived as signs of weakness, and therefore undermine the socially accepted and defined standards of masculinity (Kimmel 2007). Conversely, a female may be expected to be physically weaker and passive in her demeanor and may feel social pressure to conform to these standards. Failing to adhere to social norms may lead to societal rebuke, where her femininity is brought into disrepute. Expectations of men and women have been one of the defining factors in sexuality research of the past, during a time when many people assumed that gay men were men who should have been born women and lesbians are women who should have been born men (Seidman, 2003).

These ideals are often not fulfilled by men and women. In reality, in what is described to operate on a gender continuum, individuals incorporate gendered traits that can be considered both masculine and feminine. The ideal perceptions of what gender is supposed to mean to each individual or society is a stagnant ideal that when examined more thoroughly and closely can be dismantled, if through nothing else, than the basic life experiences that each individual has had. Those experiences are what make gender roles static and dynamic.

The binary system of defining gender roles, or sex for that matter, is also used regarding sexuality; simply put, one is either heterosexual or homosexual. Certainly, it could be argued that sexuality is not that simple, and when we look at sexuality on a continuum just as we should approach gender roles, we see that sexuality is clearly not that simple. While some individuals would indicate that they are completely heterosexual and others completely homosexual, others could fall somewhere in between these two factions.

Historically, sexuality has not been addressed as *fluid* or *changing*. This approach can be used for people who identify themselves as heterosexual, homosexual, or bisexual. An individual can at one point in their life identify her/himself as a heterosexual, yet at another time, could become involved in a relationship with someone of the same sex. Outsiders looking into this relationship may be quick to categorize the once heterosexual person as now homosexual or bisexual, yet the person involved in the relationship might still personally identify has a heterosexual, who at present is partnered with someone of the same sex.

Rust (1993) found this to be true regarding lesbians and bisexual women in her study as some women, both lesbian and bisexual began to question their exclusively heterosexual identities in their mid to late teen years and some still did not begin the coming out process until their early to mid twenties. Sexuality may also be part of an identity continuum that could change or at the very least delineate from the simplistic idea that one is heterosexual or homosexual by choice or by birth. When looking at the process of sexuality and identity, it is important to note the possibility that sexuality can in fact be fluid and can therefore *change* or *evolve* based on an individual's social interactions and personal experiences. Furthermore, an individual may have had same-sex attractions from their earliest memories on into their adult life, yet never self-identify as gay or lesbian.

The authors of this chapter do not endorse the theory that sexuality is a choice; in fact, the authors *do* support that sexuality is more of a biological component of one's physiological make-up. However, when looking at the process of sexuality and identity, it is important to note the possibility that sexuality can in fact be *fluid* and can therefore *change* or evolve based on an individual's social interactions and personal experiences.

The standpoint of ignoring the homosexual experience in society is often referred to as heterosexism. Heterosexism looks at all aspects of life and society through a heterosexual lens; heterosexism leaves those who do not fit into the heterosexual category at the margins of society. The focus on heterosexuality as the norm and therefore the only acceptable sexual orientation privileges heterosexuals over homosexuals not only on an individual basis but also in many aspects of everyday life, such as legislation (Walls, 2008; Seidman, 2003). Heterosexism supports the subordination of the LGBT community and therefore helps to silence the LGBT population and in many aspects act, whether it be intentionally or passive-aggressively, as oppressors of the minority group, similar to the way in which whites once (and in some respects, still do) oppress African-Americans or are privileged over any other race or ethnicity, as well as the way patriarchy in society has had an oppressive affect on women.

Additionally, one could equate heterosexism as one of the contributing factors as to why gays and lesbians may be fearful of 'coming out,' the process of not only accepting but for many announcing one's sexuality. With the majority of society identifying as heterosexual, straight men and women do not have to proclaim their sexual preference to anyone; it is merely assumed. While some gays and lesbians are more forthcoming in revealing their sexuality, others resist doing so perhaps in part to discrimination that gays and lesbians may face. Indeed, the possibility of gays and lesbians living seemingly heterosexual lives in order to avoid being disowned by their family and friends and in an effort to avoid discrimination does exist. The gay liberation movement has lobbied for overt identification of sexual orientation to help offset negative stereotypes and to help foster and strengthen in-group hegemony.

The process of '*coming out*,' while extremely personal can also be very political as well. The impact that the ramifications of coming out can have on individuals can be equally satisfying and terrifying as well, one is not only having to negotiate what their family and friends reactions my be, they also must negotiate how they will be perceived in the workplace, in their churches, at school, and every other facet of their lives. Again, this echoes the importance of the meaning behind the process, as well as the meanings behind sexuality and if nothing else the process of realizing one's sexual orientation and in turn deciding on how one will negotiate society as a member of the LGBT community. This negotiation, or even the entertainment of the notion of negotiation, is part of how one performs their roles or interacts with others in society.

The idea that sexuality can be fluid should not be mistaken for the notion that for each individual this is applicable. For some, one's sexuality is not in fact fluid. In the LGBT community, the negotiation of one's sexuality is both similar to the negotiation of gender roles in society and the importance of identity formation. While the importance of coming out cannot be denied when concentrating on equal rights and anti-discrimination legislation actually being passed in the United States, when looked at on an individual basis the fear of coming out can be seen as a personal paralysis, that can prevent individual members of the LGBT community from doing so. This fear may be substantiated by the rising numbers of hate crimes that LGBT people face every year in the United States (Tridico, 2004; Craig, 2002).

Hate Crimes

It is important to note that official statistics for hate crimes against members of the LGBT community are difficult to ascertain, mainly because of the lack of self-reporting to law enforcement officials. One of the main sources for acquiring official statistics regarding hate crimes in the U.S. is the FBI's, Uniform Crime Reports and while these statistics for hate crimes and a myriad other crimes are often used in research it should also be mentioned that reporting of crimes to the UCR is done voluntarily by departments across the country and therefore there is no real uniformity in the Uniform Crime Reports with regards to what is being reported and what agencies are reporting crimes to the FBI.

According to the National Gay and Lesbian Task Force, gays and lesbians face a disproportionate amount of crime based on their sexual orientation. According to the Uniform Crime Reports for 2007, 15.9 percent of hate crimes were attributed to the sexual orientation of the victim, since the estimated average percentage of gay and lesbians in society today is between 4 to 10 percent according to the Gay and Lesbian Alliance Against Defamation (GLAAD), this highlights just how disproportionate hate crimes against gays and lesbians are. Additionally, from that 15.9 percent of victimization towards gays and lesbians 58.9 percent of those victims were male. This indicates that those in the LGBT community have been a targeted group for both physical and emotional violence based solely on their sexual orientation. Furthermore, victims of hate crimes based on sexuality could have been targeted based on the *assumption* of their sexual orientation. This assumption further highlights the social construction of what society deems as acceptable gender roles.

Hate crimes encompass bias motivated crimes against gays and lesbians, but also, persons of color, religious orientation, and disability. These crimes are not considered unique crimes based on the actual crime taking place. For example, if someone commits an assault against a member of the LGBT community, the crime is not necessarily reported as a hate crime or bias crime, unless that assault was *motivated* by the sexual orientation of the victim. An assault would not have been made on the person, if that person did not identity or was not assumed to be gay or lesbian, bisexual, or transgender. This demonstrates the complexity of hate crimes and underscores the implications it has on disenfranchised sectors.

According to the National Gay and Lesbian Task Force, 12 states and the District of Columbia have hate crime legislation that includes both sexual orientation and gender identity, while 19 states have hate crimes legislation regarding sexual orientation, but do not mention gender identity. However, 18 states do not offer any hate crime legislation or protection against hate crimes based on either sexual orientation or gender identity, five of which have no hate crime protection for any group (Arkansas, Georgia, Indiana (no hate crime penalty laws), South Carolina, and Wyoming).

These findings raise specific issues of concern. First, there are caveats to the hate crime legislation in specific states, such as Utah having laws on the books that note a violation of the law if one commits acts of '*intimidation or terrorism*' however, it does not indicate the categories of people or groups that are protected under the law. Secondly, it is interesting to note that Wyoming is without hate crime laws, even after having been the location of one of the most vicious hate crime acts against a gay man, Matthew Shepard, in this country's history. In fact, the 2009 legislation entitled the Federal Law Enforcement Hate Crimes Prevention Act that passed in the House of Representatives on April 29, 2009 has also been referred to as the Matthew Shepard Act.

Official statistics on the violence inflicted on transgender individuals is limited; yet according to the Human Rights Campaign (HRC) through the use of a report conducted by Kay Brown (1999), transgender people have a 1 in 12 chance of being murdered. Self-reporting of hate crimes is limited due in part to the fear of the LGBT community that authorities will not take their complaints seriously. This is most certainly the case when hate crimes against transgender individuals is examined. HRC further notes that the fear of transgender people to report crimes to the police is based on the lack of knowledge that police officers and other authorities have regarding transgender individuals, this can also be considered the case with other members of the LGBT community as well.

Foreman (2003) has indicated that research in nearly the last 20 years has demonstrated that sexual orientation is biologically predetermined. Despite the findings, other research has suggested otherwise, and the debate within society continues to house varying opinions. Regardless of the opposing positions, consensus should be reached on eradicating discrimination against this disenfranchised sector within the context of human rights (Mohr, 2007). A similar argument and comparison can be made when one discusses Constitutional concerns, specific to the Fourth, Fifth and Sixth Amendments. Tridico (2009) shows that the Due Process Revolution of the 1960s afforded Constitutional protection to individuals, while limiting the powers of the State vis-à-vis prosecutors, law enforcement and the courts. This shift allowed for rights entrenched within the Constitution to be protected.

Marriage Rights

Currently five states in the US allow for same sex marriage: Massachusetts, Vermont (until September 2009), Connecticut, Maine and Iowa. In both New Hampshire and New Jersey, couples can enter into civil unions however they are not recognized outside of those locations. In May of 2008, California also passed legislation that allowed same sex marriage, yet the legislation was overturned quickly after it was passed. It appears that the choice of whether or not gay men and lesbians will have marriage equality will be on the state rather than the federal level and regardless of the strides that have been made in the handful of states mentioned, there are several issues surrounding same sex marriage that cause debate.

One of the arguments forwarded by some religious groups and individuals is that the Bible defines homosexuality as wrong and therefore attempts at legalizing gay marriage threaten traditional beliefs. Corvino (1996) contends that if the Bible is to be interpreted literally, then there are a myriad of issues that should raise dissent, among them the use of loaning money with interest within the Church, or the prevalence of slavery represented in the Bible. Corvino posits that when some who attach themselves to this way of Biblical thinking are confronted with these issues their response is usually focused on how times have changed. Ironically, the concept of change is not extended to the religious tenet of opposition to homosexuality.

One of the reasons why same sex marriage is not widely accepted in society today is based on the standards of a heterosexist society and heteronormativity, a concept illustrated in queer theory and highlighted through the work Cameron (2005) in relation to gender and sexuality. It can be argued that legislative efforts to legitimize same sex marriage have been shifted from the federal to state levels, and in doing so two processes emerge. First, the federal government relieves itself of addressing the issue, and second, in doing so, it promotes a form of laissez-faire discrimination through denial of this address. Legal legitimization of same sex marriage is therefore constricted within the boundaries of the state, and not through other state and federal recognition.

Couched within the heterosexist framework is the idea that the sanctity of the family will be diminished if homosexuals are allowed marriage equality. This notion falsely presupposes unfounded positions that homosexuals, especially gay men are promiscuous and/or child predators. These antiquated stereotypes that go back decades to the time when the vast majority of society thought that being gay was a mental abnormality (Mohr, 2007; Seidman, 2003). The concept of marriage equality has and continues to be largely influenced by heteronormative perspectives.

Employment and Housing Discrimination

Employment and housing discrimination has an inglorious and harmful past and continues to affect a wide range of individuals within the United States to this very day. A number of authors (Roscigno, 2007; Gregory, 2003; Cohn, 2000; Dovidio & Gaertner, 1986) have detailed the harmful effects of employment discrimination as this practice applies to racial minorities and women. Roscigno (2007) details how exclusion through the hiring process was the fourth most common form of employment discrimination (6 percent) detailed in the approximately 60,700 discrimination cases filed in Ohio from 1988 through 2003. From a qualitative interview conducted for this same study, a younger African American man details how his application for employment was continuously turned down by a perspective employer for close to a year with an explanation given that there were no open positions at that time. However, this man indicated that inside information provided by a friend employed by the company indicated that there were a variety of openings during this same time period.

Beginning at the front-end of the employment process, then, African American men and women face the harmful effects of employment discrimination. Tomaskovic-Devey (1993) found that employment discrimination faced by black men and women at this step in the process reduces the labor force experiences and on-the-job training that is of the utmost importance in developing human capital within individual workers.

Moving beyond the hiring stage, minorities face discrimination in additional areas within the employment realm. Roscigno (2007) found that the most often reported form of employment discrimination in his study was through the firing process with fully 60 percent of all discrimination cases filed in Ohio during the study's time frame related to termination decisions. Isolation, retaliation, and overt racism are examples of the discriminatory employment issues faced by visible minorities within their work environments (Roscigno, 2007). Due to practices related to employment discrimination, racial minorities often find themselves working in a number of different occupations with these particular occupations often occupying the lower slots on a given prestige scale (Cohn, 2000). As Cohn (2000) points out, the reason this occurs is that racial minorities are often restricted in terms of their access to higher paying and higher access employment.

Housing discrimination is an additional harm faced by racial minorities and women. In a historical sense, as evidenced by such authors as Massey and Denton (1993) in their work *American Apartheid* to the research accomplished by Charles (2003), racial segregation through housing discrimination has produced a wide swath of problems in terms of the health, education, and economic well-being of racial minorities. Ross and Turner (2005) have contributed to this debate over the harmful effects of housing discrimination with their research that replicated a 1989 paired testing study that examined housing discrimination and racial minorities and found that the magnitude of housing discrimination faced by racial minorities has declined from the first study in 1989 to 2000.

The authors note with caution that this decline is mitigated for African Americans as this population is still experiencing what Massey (2005) refers to a less observable form of housing discrimination in the form of steering racial minorities to neighborhoods or rental properties where there is a more concentrated number of other racial minorities (Ross & Turner, 2005). Housing segregation has also manifested itself without rental/real estate agents having to come to face-to-face with racial minorities hoping to either rent an apartment or buy a house (Massey and Lundy, 2001). Discrimination as it applies to housing occurs even over the phone with Massey and Lundy (2001) finding that real estate agents practiced discriminatory practices related to housing based upon the vocal patterns they discerned from individuals during telephone conversations. In particular, lower socio-economic status African America women were found to experience the greatest level of housing discrimination in this particular study (Massey & Lundy, 2001).

Gender issues also play into housing discrimination faced by women within the United States (Roscigno, 2007). Women who are single parents face additional discriminatory housing practices due to the increased likelihood that they will have custody and need to care for their children. Roscigno (2007) reported the additional housing issues that single women with children face as renters may refuse to rent to single mothers with children due to concerns ranging from increased noise in the apartment to the possibility of property damage to the rented apartment with landlords undertaking such tactics as listing an apartment with fewer available bedrooms as there really are in the apartment or simply stating that there are too many children in the apartment building and not renewing contracts. Adding in issues related to race and the problems faced by women with regards to housing are increased.

Roscigno's (2007) study of discrimination cases in Ohio found that African American women represented over 60 percent of the serious cases of sex and family discrimination cases, compared to the 21 percent level of Caucasian women, filed during the time period of the study. African American women may also face additional issues related to filing housing discrimination cases as there is a concern as to whether to file a lawsuit under the auspices of a race discrimination or gender/sex discrimination case. This conflict may produce a situation where the housing discrimination claim may not lead to its adjudication within the legal system (Roscigno, 2007). As Roscigno (2007) points out, housing discrimination in the form of the sexual harassment experienced by women has a number of further considerations of potential harm and defenselessness for women involved in these situations.

Although long viewed through these lenses of racial and gender studies, discrimination within the employment and housing realms has also impacted a number of other groups within the United States through the years. Stefan (2002) provides an overview of discriminatory employment practices in terms of individuals who suffer from psychiatric disabilities. Some of the discriminatory practices illustrate how some individuals have experienced discrimination in terms of their employment through being fired after employers have learned of their psychiatric disabilities; being denied promotions due to their psychiatric disabilities; or being fired by having their employer learn of their psychiatric disability through other means (e.g., the employee keeping the psychiatric disability a secret and not telling the employer when initially hired into the organization).

Despite legislative efforts vis-à-vis the Americans with Disabilities Act (ADA), (Stefan, 2002) argues that employment discrimination continues to be practiced. Individuals with psychiatric impairments may actually exacerbate psychiatric disabilities as employees with this form of disability have detailed how discriminatory practices within the workplace have contributed to breakdowns and subsequent hospitalizations and loss of self-worth. Missing from many studies involving housing and employment discrimination is a glaring lack of attention to the effect of these discriminatory practices on gay men and lesbians. Many of the authors quoted earlier, including Roscigno (2007), and Tomaskovic-Devey (1993) fail to bring out in their discussions how gay men and lesbians suffer from discrimination within the employment and housing realms.

Cohn (2000) lays out 26 arguments regarding sex and racial discrimination within the employment realm that cover such details as how prejudice and attitudes fail as an explanation of discrimination as employees and employers are not always able to act upon their personal preferences in addition to employment discrimination being the primary roadblock to increasing the level of black employment. In terms of gender discrimination at work, Cohn indicates that employment discrimination is of principal importance in confining women to subordinate job positions with lower status and prestige. Cohn distinctly fails to mention or simply include in any of the discussions throughout his text or in the delineated arguments the importance of sexual orientation and how this may play into the discrimination faced by gay men and lesbians within private and public employment opportunities.

Housing discrimination studies appear to be consistent in this regard. Through the three chapters devoted to housing discrimination faced by women and African Americans in Roscigno's (2007) study, there is no mention of the harms of this type of discrimination as it applies to the issue of sexual orientation. With Herek (2009) reporting that one in 10 gay men, lesbians, and bisexual experiencing some form of housing and/or employment discrimination, the importance of addressing these discriminatory practices in light of sexual orientation becomes more apparent.

Most literature with regards to employment discrimination and sexual orientation is found with regards to the difficulties and discrimination faced by gay men and lesbians in the public sector (Colvin, 2000; Lewis, 1997; Portwood, 1995). Although homosexual men and lesbians faced employment discrimination for years with the dismissal of Walt

Whitman by the Interior Department in 1865 (Lewis, 1997), more recent literature addressing employment discrimination and sexual orientation fashions the post World War II era as a starting point of recent employment discrimination history (Lewis, 1997; Portwood, 1995).

Lewis (1997) details how Presidents Truman and Eisenhower began to see gay men and lesbians as potential security threats as the specter of communism fell over the United States. As Lewis (1997) relates, the chairman of the Republican National Committee launched a full-fledged attack against homosexuals within public employment as this group of citizens represented as grave of a threat against the United States as the communists presented during the same time frame. Based upon the belief that homosexual behavior as being immoral and a behavior that is intentionally closeted, both Lewis (1997) and Portwood (1995) illustrate that the Hoey Committee sought to root out homosexual employees based upon the erroneous assumption that gay men and lesbians are more susceptible to blackmail that may out an individual as being homosexual. Thus, gay men and lesbians may be more likely to be drawn into treasonous behavior. The moral stance taken by this committee, that one homosexual employee within a public government agency can besmirch the entire office, still finds adherents in public employment to this day (Portwood, 1995).

These discriminatory employment experiences continue to be experienced by gay men and lesbians up to and through the current age. Colvin (2000) reports that between 16 percent and 46 percent of the gay men, lesbians, and bisexuals that responded to a survey noted that they had experienced some form of discrimination during their terms of employment. Portwood (1995) details how gay men and lesbians who are employed within education settings (more specifically grade and secondary schools) have faced continued employment discrimination through the years.

Economic Marginalization

Two specific court cases, *Rowland v. Mad River Local School District* (1985) and *Acanfora v. Board of Education* (1974), illustrate free speech considerations and what Portwood (1995) regards a '*Catch-22*' situation that the decisions in both of these legal cases created in through the decisions handed down by the courts. Gay men and lesbians face discriminatory employment practices in terms of hiring and termination practices through the mere admittance of a homosexual or lesbian sexual orientation. Freely providing information related to sexual orientation may prevent the hiring of gay men and lesbians due to the current moral climate within the United States while potentially making valid points regarding employment discrimination and sexual orientation becomes difficult by simply entering the debate due to this current moral climate (Portwood, 1995). In short, the 'Catch-22' situation comes in where if an individual admits to being a homosexual male or lesbian as the admittance is seen as a possible disruption to the classroom environment while remaining closeted creates a situation where that form of speech is left unprotected (Portwood, 1995).

Badgett (1995), Klawitter and Flatt (1998), Levine (1979), Levine and Leonard (1984), and Schnieder (1986) have all reported on the effects of employment discrimination on gay men and lesbians within the United States. Levine and Leonard (1984) reported that while nearly one third of the lesbians that responded to their survey expected to experience some form of employment discrimination because of their sexual orientation, approximately 13% of the respondents had experienced discriminatory practices with 8 percent of the lesbians responding to the survey actually losing their employment due to their sexual orientation or almost losing their employment due to their sexual orientation.

Badgett (1995) applies a more direct economic effect to the employment discrimination faced by gay and bisexual men as his study found that this population earn, in terms of wages, 11 percent to 27 percent less than heterosexual males with the same levels of experience, education, type of occupation, region of residence, and (admittedly surprising) marital status. Lesbian and bisexual females were also found to earn less than heterosexual women but these were of a lower strength (in terms of statistical significance) and were considered somewhat non-significant by Badgett (1995). Levine (1979) found that systematic employment discrimination was experienced by gay men in terms of hiring, firing, and promotion situations. Using stereotypes to justify these discriminatory practices, employers often tracked gay men into fields that were inconsistent with the educational attainment of the applicant (Levine, 1979). Higher educated gay men were tracked into fields that required lower levels of education.

What may be of even greater interest, however, is the tactics that gay men and lesbians employ to deal with these discriminatory environments.

Ford (1997), Klawitter and Flatt (1998), and Schnieder (1986) report that gay men and lesbians present a number of different strategies to deal with discrimination in the employment field. Klawitter and Flatt (1998) found that gay men and lesbians may take to limiting their financial income through the choosing of employment situations where the chances are greatest in terms of being able to avoid discriminatory behavior on the part of employers and fellow employees.

Ford (1997) found similar results through a survey that was administered to 120 lesbians from 26 different states. A majority of respondents reported that they chose employment opportunities where they could safely disclose their sexual orientation to employers and employees alike. Other respondents to this survey reported that they had eliminated specific occupations based upon the anticipated discrimination they expected to experience (Ford, 1997). Levine and Leonard (1984) showed that in order to avoid discriminatory employment practices, 72 percent of the lesbians in their study remained partially hidden in terms of providing information on their sexual orientation while 28 percent remained completely closeted in order to avoid expected discrimination within the workplace.

These avoidance tactics employed by gay men and lesbians to avoid employment discrimination may come with a legal price. Portwood (1995) suggested that gay men and lesbians may be in a no-win situation through the closeting of their sexual orientation or fully detailing their sexual orientation at the onset of an employment opportunity. However, Levine and Leonard (1984) have suggested what could amount to a major legal hurdle by gay men and lesbians keeping their sexual orientation hidden and to themselves. Recall that Stefan's (2002) description of several concerns with the ADA and other legislation enacted to combat discrimination against individuals with psychiatric disorders that centered on the generalizability of what may amount to individualized acts of discrimination.

Opponents of ratifying anti-discrimination legislation with regards to sexual orientation often employ this same viewpoint and suggest that a majority of discrimination cases (in this case employment discrimination) are in fact not widespread and are primarily individualized to the single person filing the discrimination complaint (Levine & Leonard, 1984). As Levine and Leonard (1984) point out, without the proof of widespread employment discrimination aimed at gay men and lesbians, there is no need for additional legal protections that seek to shield gay men and lesbians from employment discrimination.

Although literature that examines discrimination in light of the sexual orientation of individuals tends to touch upon issues related to housing discrimination there exits very little literature that focuses specifically upon answering the question of whether gay men and lesbians experience housing discrimination when attempting to rent an apartment or buy a house. This makes it difficult to draw out any firm indication of the width and breadth of this type of discriminatory behavior.

Two recent studies do attempt to draw out these practices. Herek (2009), while not focusing exclusively upon housing discrimination found that a number of gay men and lesbians had experienced some form of employment or housing discrimination within the time frame of the study. Gay men and lesbians, when compared to bisexual men and women, were statistically more likely to have experienced either housing or employment information. Page (1998) conducted a telephone interview, as in the same manner as Massey and Lundy (2001) had done in their research study, in two Canadian cities and one city in Michigan with the intent of determining if rental/housing agents discriminated against gay men and lesbians with regards to housing matters. Participants in this study who referenced to themselves as being homosexual during the telephone conversation significantly reduced the likelihood that individual would have a room or flat described as being available (Page, 1998).

Although there is little research geared specifically to the experiences of gay men and lesbians in terms of housing discrimination, Larson (2006) suggests that the experiences of gay men and lesbians in terms of housing discrimination may be similar to those experienced by women as detailed by Roscigno (2007). Single women and single mothers caring for their minor children often faced housing discrimination at the hands of landlords and real estate agents that were based upon faulty evidence and explanations that single mothers and their children will create more property damage on the property or may create a louder living situation with more than two or three occupying an apartment at the same time (Roscigno, 2007).

Gay men and lesbians also face similar discriminatory situations when trying to rent an apartment or purchase a house. Larson (2006) reported that gay men and lesbian couples attempting to rent an apartment, as an example, run into the same discriminatory housing ordinances which dictate a specific moral orientation through the limitation of unmarried persons to reside in the same apartment/household. This mandating of morality becomes easier for landlords and other rental/real estate agents to undertake by ensuring that the rules and procedures for renting/purchasing apply to everyone and that these administrative policies work to prevent overcrowding in the apartment complex or neighborhood in question (Larson, 2006). Rental/real estate agents are thus able to hide their overt opinions regarding same sex couples in a blanket prohibition that applies to all possible renters/buyers.

Disenfranchisement of Different Sectors of Society

Care should be taken, however, when trying to equate the experiences of gay men and lesbians in terms of employment and housing discrimination with the unique experiences of African Americans within these discrimination areas. Lewis (2003) details the concerns that have been voiced that gay men and lesbians, along with their supporters, have co-opted the civil rights movement and experiences of African Americans as analogous to the current struggle against discrimination in the housing, employment, and other fields.

Wadsworth (1997) details how reaching out to African American evangelicals in an attempt to win support of Amendment 2 during 1992 in Colorado, white evangelicals took the position that gay men, lesbians, and their supporters who equate gay rights and freedom from discrimination in the same light at the Civil Rights Movement diminishes the real suffering experienced by African Americans. White evangelicals relied upon social science findings that many African Americans are conservative in their views with regards to sexual orientation (Wadsworth, 1997). Even though this was the case in Colorado back in 1992, Lewis (2003) points out that his research suggests that once issues related to religion and education are controlled for, African Americans become less likely to oppose anti-homosexual employment discrimination. Further, African Americans within the same religious circles and have the same levels of education as whites become more likely to support efforts to assist gay men and lesbians overcoming employment discrimination tactics.

Over the years there have been a number of arguments forwarded by any number of individuals and groups to justify the discrimination (in this case housing and employment discrimination) faced by gay men and lesbians within the United States. Samar (1994) delineates six different moral arguments used to justify discrimination based upon sexual orientation with these arguments encompassing a need to maintain the stability of society through the exclusion of deviant groups; morality is undermined through the protections afforded to gay men and lesbians; and that the right to the free exercise of religion may conflict with the rights of gay men and lesbians to face a life of non-discrimination.

These arguments are caste aside by Samar (1994) as he illustrates how these moral arguments, when framed in the contexts of utilitarianism, rights theory, and communitarian points of view, simply fail to justify the discrimination faced by gay men and lesbians. In order to protect homosexual individuals from housing and employment (among other discriminatory practices) discrimination, Samar (1994) argues that anti-discrimination laws assist in the forging of social attitudes that rest on opportunity free from discrimination for all individuals regardless of sexual orientation. Further, law can also assist in the elimination of the most egregious, overt forms of discrimination.

Caution should be taken when relying on the law, as advocated by Samar (1994), to deal with housing and employment discrimination within the context of sexual orientation. Portwood (1995) provides a detailed explanation of how the courts in the United States have generally not been friendly to the employment discrimination faced by gay men and lesbians within the public sphere. More specifically, when looking at issues related to the equal protection guarantees found within the Fifth and Fourteenth Amendments to the United States Constitution, federal courts have generally not been inclined to add homosexuality/sexual orientation to the list of suspect statuses such as race, national origin, and alienage due to the finding that homosexuality and homosexual behavior is primarily behavioral in nature (Portwood, 1995). This is in opposition to the position taken, as detailed by Portwood (1995) that racial minorities, as an example, exhibit more immutable characteristics and have been experienced an extended history of discrimination based upon stereotypes and have been unable to obtain relief and protection through the non-judicial branches of government.

Colvin (2000) also contributes to these concerns by adding that legal protections for gay men and lesbians in regards to employment discrimination within the public sector may not be effective. Policies may provide a legal course of action for those that are discriminated against in terms of employment but these legal protections may not progress far enough in terms of adding additional protections against possible retaliatory actions taken by employers. These legal solutions may promote non-discrimination policies in an environment which is not interested in fully implementing these employment protections for gay men and lesbians. Without an environment that is supportive of such policies, there is good reason to believe that these legal protections will fail to adequately address employment discrimination faced by this sector.

Overcoming employment discrimination in terms of sexual orientation is a most difficult undertaking. Portwood (1995) cited social science evidence to show how public bias contributes to the fear of and discrimination experienced by gay men and lesbians regardless of the professional abilities that they bring to their employment within public school settings. When speaking towards housing discrimination as it applies to racial minorities, Massey (2005) quotes Lieberson (1985) and his observations with regards to social research that as previous avenues through which discrimination is observed and employed are overcome or closed down, newer discriminatory paths and practices that are less obvious and more subtle are forged and put into practice by the majority population within a society to maintain privilege and power over minority populations. As gay men and lesbians continue to gain greater and wider acceptance into everyday life within American society, the means through which discrimination in the housing and employment realms may become more subtle.

Although same-sex marriage is gaining in terms of acceptance and legal status in a growing number of individual states within the United States, same-sex couples still face discriminatory practices in a majority of states with regards to employment benefits in terms of gaining health insurance for same-sex partners. Sexual orientation continues to play an important part in the broader discussions of housing and employment discrimination and may provide new opportunities to explore these issues in a more inclusive context rather than simply focusing upon racial and gender categories and considerations.

Conclusion

The impact that societal expectations have had on sexuality as well as gender, along with the connectivity between both gender and identity and sexuality and identity are crucial in addressing discrimination faced by the LGBT community. The social construction of gender and the problematics that may be experienced by members of this sector can be better understood during the process of identifying and expressing their sexual identity. Both gender and sexuality contain components of performance and social interaction. Societal standards of acceptance and successful gender and sexuality performance are based on heterosexist standards that may help perpetuate or inadequately respond to the discrimination of gays and lesbians.

While much more attention has been paid in recent years to the discrimination that individuals in the LGBT community are faced with, this is an area that deserves further attention and far more breadth and depth than can be provided here. The emergence of gender studies, feminist theory, queer theory, and the importance of advocacy groups and organizations such as the National Gay and Lesbian Task Force, GLAAD, and Human Rights Campaign are integral resources in researching any topics regarding the LGBT community and the authors suggest that these sources be used for further information.

References

Adler. R. B., Proctor II, R. & Towne, N. (2005). *Looking Out, Looking In.* Belmont, CA: Wadsworth Thomson.

Badgett, M.V.L. (1995). The wage effects of sexual orientation discrimination. *Industrial and Labor Relations Review, 48*(4), 726-739.

Barak. G, Leighton, P. & Flavin, J. (2007). *Class, Race, Gender, & Crime: The Social Realities of Justice in America.* Lanham, MD: Rowan and Littlefield Publishing.

Brown, K. (1999) 20th Century Transgender History and Experience. *Human Rights Campaign.* Retrieved May 2009. http://www.hrc.org/issues/1508.htm#referece1

Bulter, J. (1990). *Gender Trouble: Feminism and the Subversion of Identity.* New York, NY: Routledge.

Cameron, D. (2005). Language, Gender, and Sexuality: Current Issues and New Directions. *Applied Linguistics 26(4) 482-502.*

Charles, C.Z. (2003). The Dynamics of Racial Residential Segregation. *Annual Review of Sociology, 29,* 167-207.

Cohn, S. (2000). *Race and Gender Discrimination at Work.* Boulder, CO: Westview Press.

Colvin, R.A. (2000). Improving State Policies Prohibiting Public Employment Discrimination Based on Sexual Orientation. *Review of Public Personnel Administration, 20*(5), 5-19.

Corvino, J. (1996). The Bible Condemned Usurers, Too. *The Gay Moralist.* Retrieved October 2007. http://www.johncorvino.com/article_archive/26725.html

Craig, K. (2002). Examining Hate-motivated Aggression: A Review of the Social Psychological Literature on Hate Crimes as a Distinct Form of Aggression. Aggression and Violent Behavior, 7: 85-101.

Dovidio, J.F. & Gaertner, S.L. (1986). Prejudice, Discrimination, and Racism: Historical Trends and Contemporary Approaches. In Dovidio, J.F. & Gaertner, S.L. (Eds.), *Prejudice, Discrimination, and Racism* (p. 1-34). Orlando, FL: Academic Press, Inc.

Federal Bureau of Investigation (2007). Hate Crime Statistics. *Uniform Crime Report.* Retrieved May 2009. http://www.fbi.gov/ucr/hc2007/victims.htm

Ford, H.W. (1997). The Influence of Sexual Orientation on the Early Occupational Choices of Young Lesbians using Astin's Model of Career Choice and Work Behavior. *Dissertation Abstracts International Section A: Humanities and Social Sciences, 57*(12-A), 5061.

Foreman, J. (2003). The Biological Basis of Homosexuality. *The Boston Globe.* Retrieved May 2009. http://www.boston.com/news/science/articles/2003/12/02/the_biol ogical_basis_of_homosexuality

Freedman, E. B. (2002). *No Turning Back: The History of Feminism and the Future of Women.* New York, NY: Random House Publishing.

Gay and Lesbian Alliance Against Defamation (2009). Where Do Gays Live? How Many Households Are There? *GLAAD Advertising Media Program.* Retrieved May 2009. http://www.commercialcloset.org/common/news/reports/detail.cf m?classification=report&qid=5425&clientid=11064&topicid=38 4&subsection=resources&subnav=resources

Giddens, A. (1984). *The Constitution of Society*. Berkeley, CA: University of California Press.

Gregory, R.F. (2003). *Women and Workplace Discrimination: Overcoming Barriers to Gender Equality*. New Brunswick, NJ: Rutgers University Press.

Herek, G.M. (2009). Hate Crimes and Stigma-Related Experiences Among Sexual Minority Adults in the United States: Prevalence Estimates from a National Probability Sample. *Journal of Interpersonal Violence, 24*(1), 54-74.

Human Rights Campaign (2009). How Do Transgender People Suffer from Discrimination? Retreived May 2009. http://www.hrc.org/issues/1508.htm#referece1

Kimmel, M. (2007). Masculinity as Homophobia. In Rothenburg , P.S. (ed). *Race, Class, and Gender in the United States*. New York, NY: Worth.

Klawitter, M. & Flatt, V. (1998). The effects of state and local antidiscrimination policies for sexual orientation. *Journal of Policy Analysis and Management, 17*(4), 658-686.

Larson, N. Gay Families, Keep Out! *The Advocate*. July 18, 2006. Issue 967, p. 34.

Levine, M.P. (1979). Employment Discrimination against Gay Men. *International Review of Modern Sociology, 9*(2), 151-163.

Levine, M.P. & Leonard, R. (1984). Discrimination against Lesbians in the Work Force. *Signs, 9*(4), 700-710.

Lewis, G.B. (1997). Lifting the Ban on Gays in the Civil Service: Federal Policy toward Gays and Lesbian Employees since the Cold War. *Public Administration Review, 57*(5), 387-395.

Lewis, G.B. (2003). Black-White Differences in Attitudes toward Homosexuality and Gay Rights. *The Public Opinion Quarterly, 67*(1), 59-78.

Lieberson, S. (1985). *Making It Count: The Improvement of Social Research and Theory*. Berkeley, CA: University of California Press.

Massey, D.S. (2005). Racial Discrimination in Housing: A Moving Target. *Social Problems, 52*(8), 148-151.

Massey, D.S. & Denton, N.R. (1993). *American Apartheid: Segregation and the Making of the Underclass*. Cambridge, MA: Harvard University Press.

Massey, D.S. & Lundy, G. (2001). Use of Black English and Racial Discrimination in Urban Housing Markets: New Methods and Findings. *Urban Affairs Review, 36*(4), 452-469.

Messerschmidt, J.W. (2004). *Flesh and Blood: Adolescent Gender Diversity and Violence.* Lanham, MD: Rowman & Littlefield.

Mohr, R.D. (2007) Anti-Gay Stereotypes. In Rothenburg , P.S. (Ed). *Race, Class, and Gender in the United States.* New York, NY: Worth.

National Gay and Lesbian Task Force (2009). *Hate Crime Laws in the U.S.* Retrieved May 2009. http://www.thetaskforce.org/downloads/reports/issue_maps/hate_crimes_4_09.pdf

Page, S. (1998). Accepting the Gay Person: Rental Accommodation in the Community. *Journal of Homosexuality, 36*(2), 31-39.

Portwood, S.G. (1995). Employment Discrimination in the Public Sector Based on Sexual Orientation: Conflicts between Research Evidence and the Law. *Law and Psychology Review, 19*, 113-152.

Roscigno, V.J. (2007). *The Face of Discrimination: How Race and Gender Impact Work and Home Lives.* NY: Rowman & Littlefield Publishers, Inc.

Ross, S.L. & Turner, M.A. (2005). Housing Discrimination in Metropolitan America: Explaining Changes between 1989 and 2000. *Social Problems, 52*(2), 152-180.

Rust, P. (1993). "Coming Out" in the Age of Social Constructionism: Sexual Identity Formation among Lesbian and Bisexual Women. *Gender & Society 7(1), 50-77.*

Samar, V.J. (1994). A Moral Justification for Gay and Lesbian Civil Rights Legislation. *Journal of Homosexuality, 27*(3-4), 147-178.

Schnieder, B. (1986). Coming out at work: Bridging the private/public gap. *Work and Occupations, 13*(4), 463-487.

Seidman, S. (2003). *The Social Construction of Sexuality.* New York, NY: W.W. Norton & Company.

Stefan, S. (2002). *Hollow Promises: Employment Discrimination Against People with Mental Disabilities.* Washington, DC: American Psychological Association.

Stein, M. (2004). Pride Marches and Parades. In *Encyclopedia of Lesbian, Gay, Bisexual, and Transgender History in America.* New York, NY: Charles Scribner's Sons.

Tomaskovic-Devey, D. (1993). *Gender & Racial Inequality at Work.* Ithaca, NY: ILR Press.

Tridico, F. (2009) *Law and Social Order.* Sault Ste. Marie, ON: Landon Elsemere Press.

Tridico, F. (2004) *Contemporary Issues in Law and Society*. Sault Ste. Marie, ON: Landon Elsemere Press.

Wadsworth, N.D. (1997). Reconciliation Politics: Conservative Evangelicals and the New Race Discourse. *Politics & Society, 25*(3), 341-376.

United States Census Bureau (2005). *Number, Timing, and Duration of Marriages and Divorces: 2001*. Retrieved May 2009. http://www.census.gov/prod/2005pubs/p.70-97.pdf

Walls, N. E. (2008). Toward a Multidimensional Understanding of Heterosexism: The Changing Nature of Prejudicial Attitudes. *Journal of homosexuality 55 20-70.*

CHAPTER 3
HUMAN TRAFFICKING

Darrick Brake

Abstract: Imagine living in a social environment where the everyday, accepted norm, entailed the buying and selling of people of all ages, sexes, and nationalities. Further, imagine a world in which your neighbors, friends, and family could sell you into a life of permanent and perpetual bondage for profit. Never to be seen again, a person once sold, could be forced to work in industry, mines, prostitution, or outright sex slavery. For many people in developing countries across the globe this is a harsh and ever present reality. Millions of people are bought and sold worldwide in a global trade that has a transnational network operating on profits in the billions of dollars. This profitable trade, referred to as human trafficking, shows that even in a modernized, global, 21st century social world we are still dealing with the brutal realities of an ancient problem, that of modern slavery.

Introduction

The purpose of this chapter is to investigate and explore the social problem of human trafficking in its modern context. In doing so, we will be considering four major aspects that help assess the problem as it currently exists. These include:

(1) *Defining the problem*: that is, discussing and defining the terms, context, and factors that lead to an increase in human trafficking.
(2) *How these crimes are committed and who commits them*: that is, how is the crime performed or perpetrated in the first place, and what are the motivating factors that foster and sustain human trafficking.
(3) *Focus on victims*: that is, what are the consequences of being trafficked, and what are the outcomes associated with human trafficking for the victims of these types of crimes?
(4) *Actions to address the problem*: that is, how has the global community responded to the situation of a growing human trafficking problem? What specific political and legal initiatives have been taken to prevent this problem?

These four aspects along with the answers to the questions contained within them will provide a holistic approach to studying the problem of human trafficking. In addition, it will provide an overarching perspective that will allow the proper depth, width, and scope of the problem at hand to be expressed. This will be beneficial as we unravel the complexities associated with this modern problem.

Defining the Problem

Human trafficking can be defined as the purposeful movement of any person(s) to places in which they are sold, or purchased into forced labor or bondage such as prostitution, industrial work, domestic work, or sex slavery (Aronowitz, 2009; Lee, 2007; King, 2004). Not only are people purchased but the traffickers (sellers) use deceptive techniques such as violence, verbal or physical threats, or other types of coercion in order to force their victims into a life of bondage (UNODC, 2006; King, 2004). This differs from outright slavery because human trafficking, while not marked by formal, legal ownership of humans (which is the case with slavery proper), still entails temporary ownership, debt bondage, forced labor and hyper-exploitative contractual agreements (Bales, 2005; 2000). While the terminology associated with this type of exploitative practice has changed, the actual term human trafficking can still be conceptualized as a form of slavery (Bales, 2005; Lee, 2007; Ould, 2004). It can be conceptualized in this manner because trafficking represents the entire process associated with slavery as opposed to the condition or result of slavery.

Human trafficking has come to represent an umbrella term with several different types of forced labor and bondage that fall along a wide array and range of illegal, selling and purchasing of humans. There are eight forms of bondage that fall under the category of human trafficking. These include:

(1) ***Industrial forced labor.*** This refers to persons who are trafficked and sold to businesses for the purpose of performing industrial services such as manufacturing and production for no restitution (UNODC, 2006; King, 2004). Victims sold into this type of bondage work in unregulated and unsafe work environments that other employees in a country would not work in because of hazard or risk of injury, or in some cases death. Many of these companies operate just under the radar in places where weak

industrial laws allow for them to flourish and profit off the very lives of the people forced work there. The majority of the people sold into this type of bondage tend to be males (Aronowitz, 2009, 45); this is especially the case in countries where working in industry is considered a male occupation.

(2) *Mining forced labor*. This is labor in which people are purchased by mining companies in order to perform work related to mining such as: digging new mines, retrieving mineral resources, or working with light to heavy mining equipment (Aronowitz, 2009; UNODC, 2006). Similar to industrial forced labor, victims are mandated to work in mines owned by companies that are largely unregulated and pose significant health hazards. Workers face over exposure to deadly toxic chemicals such as sulfur, carbon monoxide, arsenic, and several different types of lethal acids. In addition, many of the mines that these trafficked people are forced to work in are just unsafe and collapse or explode due to lack of regulation. The majority of the persons sold into this type of bondage are male but children are also used to crawl and navigate narrow mines as well.

(3) *Forced domestic labor*. This refers to a type of labor in which humans are purchased to perform a myriad of household duties which include, but are not limited to: cleaning, cooking, taking care of the outside of a house or home, raising kids, or being forced to do anything consider domestic or house related work (UNODC, 2006; King, 2004). This type of work is generally done by older women or younger women who are forced into other individuals private homes through purchase. Unlike industrial or mining forced labor, domestic forced labor involves an individual representing a household to purchase individual humans. There are two main risks associated with this type of bondage: (1) when a person (usually a woman) is too old or unable physically to continue in her duties she is often either resold or put to death and; (2) Any person sold into this type of bondage is at the mercy of the household owner.

(4) *Forced prostitution*. This entails forced and unwilling selling of one's body for the purpose of sexual acts, or any physical activity (Aronowitz, 2009; Gerdes, 2006; UNODC, 2006). This

type of bondage involves the selling of men and women (mostly women) to brothels, pimps, gangs, mail order bride companies, and match maker services. The hazards associated with this specific type of include being beaten, tortured and raped, being expected to engage in sexual acts with numerous customers each day and night and increased risks of contracting sexual diseases. Many people forced to work in these conditions often die either from starvation, beatings, physical abuse, or due to transmitted diseases such as HIV/AIDS, tuberculosis, syphilis, etc.

(5) *Forced child prostitution* or *forced child sex slavery*. Child prostitution can be defined as the forced and unwilling selling of the body of a minor under the age of 18 for the purpose and use of sexual activities, or physical activities. This type of forced labor is perhaps the most disconcerting insofar as it involves the usage of children for sexual gratification. Similar to forced prostitution, these children face the same risks associated with their type of bondage. However, they also face the increased risk of permanent damage to their reproductive organs due to the body's lack of physical development in this area, and an increase in death due to inability to endure the physical beatings, torture, and sexual under-development (Willis & Leavy, 2006).

(6) *Bonded or indentured labor*. This involves a deal with an individual purchaser (or trafficker) whom a person voluntarily offers to work or provide services under the pretense that they will receive some type of service or debt relief in exchange (Picarelli, 2007; UNODC, 2006). For example, an unemployed factory worker may offer her or his services to a trafficker or forced labor purchaser. In exchange for doing so, that person may receive a passport, proper documentation, and travel to a country that is in better economic shape than the one they are currently living within. This promise of a better, more financial secure life sounds enticing for the individual choosing to become an indentured servant who believes she/he will gain their freedom once the debt has been paid.

This arrangement is subject to reevaluation and subjectively altered to benefit the traffickers, who intend to profit off of the victim's misfortune. The traffickers raise the debt to considerable amounts, using excuses that range from cost of

expenses, to increases in challenges for fake documentation and fake passports, to charges for complications in sending or providing transportation to other countries. With the debt incurred in transit to another country mounting, the indentured laborers are now forced to repay an amount of money that could take years to clear. This is the underlying intent of the human traffickers; they want to maximize profits from indentured laborers for as long possible.

(7) *Military bondage*. This entails the unwilling recruitment of persons to be used in military service, or military actions at home, or abroad (Aronowitz, 2009; UNODC, 2006). This type of forced labor is highly prevalent in countries that are war torn, or are currently engaged in perpetual battles. In times of war, voluntary enlistment in the military may decrease. As the need for soldiers may increase, new recruits may be taken by force. Civilians, including children may be forced into military service through the threat or administration of violence. Attempts to defect can be met with other severe consequences such as physical violence, torture, rape or rape of family members, death, or death of one's family. The civilians and children forced into this type of labor (or service) also face death on the battlefield as they have little to no military training before being sent into combat (Aronowitz, 2009).

These several subtypes or categories of human trafficking represent the kinds of forced activities that many people around the world are forced to accept and endure on a regular daily basis even though international and many national laws forbid its practice. Along these same lines, official state sanctioned slavery has ceased to exist worldwide, and yet human trafficking functions as a major worldwide industry that provides forced human labor.

Context of the Trade

With global recognition that the afore-mentioned exists, it is imperative that it is put into context to help the reader understand how this is made possible to thrive. There is an expanding black market for the sell and purchase of human beings. It has been estimated that there are currently anywhere from 12.3 to 27 million people (U.S. State Department, 2008) either living in slavery (bondage) or who were trafficked, living around the world at any given time. The business of selling humans, as the U.S. Department of State points out, is highly profitable as every year it pulls in an estimated 32 billion dollars, if both the sale of the individual and the value of their exploited labor or services are taken into account (U.S. Department of State, 2008). Hence, the motivating factor for the trade is financial, making it one of the largest multi-billion dollar global enterprises.

Given the industry's economic premise of supply and demand (Aronowitz, 2009) argues that trafficking markets flourish and expand as the demand for cheap labor and keeping the costs of production low increases. No matter what subtype or category of forced labor one chooses, this economic principle is a universal. Moreover, supply and demand for trafficked individuals increases in both developing and industrialized nations because both types of countries operate under this underlying economic principle. This suggests that expanding markets for human trafficking presents the issue as a global problem.

A second factor that increases human trafficking has been *globalization.* The transformation of individual nation states into a more complex singularly integrated global system has been highly economically advantageous. It has produced integrated economic, technological, scientific, and communication systems that now allow countries to freely interact and learn from one another (Aronowitz, 2009; King, 2004). However, it has also produced ambitious conditions from which human traffickers can thrive within because it allows traffickers to easily transport people around the world (King, 2004, 2). There are global networks that extend beyond national or regional borders. The advent of globalization has improved efficiency, including that of illegal enterprises.

A third contributor to the increase for human trafficking is a weak economic system (Aronowitz, 2009; U.S Department of State, 2008; Lee, 2007; UNODC, 2006; King, 2004). In countries that are either developing or have stalled economic development, trafficking flourishes because the traffickers themselves have a large population of people from which they can exploit. Acknowledging that persons are vulnerable to any promise of poverty relief, debt relief, or a better life that can exist away from their current situation, the risks of victimization are enhanced. In countries that have corrupt and/or fragile governments, conditions are rife for perpetrators to carry on their industry without legal address.

Some political and/or military rogue parties assist and/or actively take part in the enterprise, adding a perverted legitimacy, as well as strength to the trade.

Within widespread poverty, the need for survival creates and shapes a system in which traffickers can make profit on the misery and misfortune of others. It creates conditions by which persons consider the selling of friends, neighbors, and family members to traffickers. Parents can be reduced to selling children or other relatives on the promise of money or that their loved one will receive perceived opportunities for better quality of life.

A weakened economic system also encourages the use of trafficked persons in labor throughout developing countries. A cycle is created in which a developing country is struggling to meet labor demands because of an increase in wages or willingness to perform in hazardous conditions, or due to the fact that there is no industry. In order to combat labor shortages, for any reason, people are bought and sold into a life of forced labor to sustain businesses, and in an attempt to stabilize the need for cheap workers (Rodriguez, 2006). This is another situation in which traffickers thrive because the need for employees and cheap laborers will only increase in countries that are developing, and they can pull humans from countries in which economic development has stalled. Thus, they have a cycle set up that allows them to profit even if a country is developing or not. In both situations, a human trafficker can profit and it is the weak economic system that fosters and sustains this system.

A fourth factor that causes trafficking entails war. This increases the need for trafficked humans for two specific reasons. The first reason involves forced military labor or service because as the duration of a war increases so does its need for military personnel. The second reason in increased trafficking during war is due to the growing numbers of refugees that develop throughout the duration of the conflict. It is estimated that there are around 50 million refugees displaced worldwide every year (King, 2004: 22). Refugees are easy targets to coerce or take by force given the conditions of crisis (UNODC, 2006; King, 2004). Rogue regimes often force large amounts of unregulated and untracked people into foreign countries they are not familiar with; traffickers are able to prey upon these groups of vulnerable individuals. Refugees are often placed into temporary camps or sets of living areas that are near to or next to a nation's border, making them accessible for human transfer.

A fifth factor that causes trafficking is the legal and illegal prostitution being tolerated in some countries. These countries enhance the spread of human trafficking because there is *legal* and *illegal* money to be made. Sex trafficking alone accounts from an estimated 7 to 19 billion dollars per year. Perhaps even more frightening is that the International Labor Organization (ILO) estimates that the profits from individuals sold into the sex trade are at a staggering 217.8 billion dollars a year or 23,000 dollars per person (U.S. Department of State, 2008).

In countries where prostitution is legal, human trafficking for the purpose of sex can be a very profitable business. Since the only crime traffickers commit is the actual selling of humans, selling to countries with legal prostitution encourages the enterprise. When perpetrators are charged with prostitution in a foreign country they are often deported or transferred back to their country of origin. Traffickers selling to countries where prostitution is legal can resell humans, maximizing their profits and strengthening the cyclical model of human trafficking for the sex trade.

This situation changes in countries where prostitution is illegal because the trafficker is involved in both trafficking humans and perpetuating the crime of prostitution. In order to combat this problem, traffickers mainly sell to countries that have weak laws or have more acceptable attitudes towards prostitution. By doing this, perpetrators know that legal reprisals will be limited or less likely. This is one of the reasons why human trafficking of forced sex laborers takes place in countries where they have weak central governments (e.g., war torn, politically torn, religious torn, etc.) or the governments and/or officials within the governments are corrupt and condone or take part in the enterprise.

How These Crimes are Committed

The crime of human trafficking is often committed and perpetrated through the use of various creative but sinister propositions. For instance, some traffickers use what is known as a '*bait and switch*' scheme (King, 2004: 2) to lure people into forced labor. In this context, a person is promised better quality of life in another region. The motivation of ambition offers voluntarism on the part of the victim; this facilitates easier transfer of the victim. The victim may not fully appreciate her or his circumstances until the individual is placed in a vulnerable circumstance. The cycle of victimization is then accentuated because the victim often times becomes dependent on the trafficker or subsequent perpetrators for survival.

Traffickers may advertisement in newspapers, local magazines, the internet, or use local people that spread information of ideal circumstances to entice others (Aronowitz, 2009). Persons who find themselves in desperate or vulnerable situations will respond to these advertisements and set up meetings with people who they think are legitimately trying to help them. Instead, they are setting up meetings with people who wish to sell them into a life time of forced labor. Traffickers are able to successfully use this technique because they make up or create elaborate stories of new possibilities that they can provide. They offer these potential victims opportunities such as the promise of a foreign job, the opportunity of an education, the possibility of new job skills, or the chance to leave the country they are living in for a chance to make it in another foreign country (Aronowitz, 2009, King, 2004).

Perhaps even more troubling is the problem of human traffickers posing as Non-Government Organizations or NGO's and employing the use of *'bait and switch'* schemes. In this case, individuals are promised the possibility of being helped in a myriad of ways such as (i) being made into a refugee and receiving *'official'* refugee status, (ii) being offered documentation to leave the country, or (iii) the chance to leave the country under the context that they will work abroad. Similar to the afore-mentioned scheme, this one has the same result. Once an individual agrees to the terms set by the trafficker they are transported and sold to another trafficker to be used at the discretion of the purchaser.

Another version of the *'bait and switch'* scheme involves the luring in of potential victims by making them become *indentured* or *bonded* to the trafficker. Here, a potential victim is promised a better life or opportunity just like before. However, the potential victim agrees to the terms of the promised benefit or better life under the condition that they will work off any and all debt incurred for doing so. Next, the trafficker will give them an estimate of how much money it will take to make this opportunity happen. Based on this estimate, a person will be forced to work off their debt in a job that the trafficker chooses.

This job is often not the one promised, but rather one of the numerous types of forced labor. Conditions of the arrangement change to the benefit of the trafficker and the detriment of the indebted victim. This strategy is employed so that perpetrators maximize their profit per victim. Victims find it difficult to reimburse their traffickers for reasons that may include (i) earning an abysmal wage working in any type of forced labor, (ii) accruing interest for not having the debt paid in full, (iii) the debt may have interest pre-applied to it, and the debt is exasperated, and/or (iv) the cost of maintaining or feeding the victim is also applied to the debt (Aronowitz, 2009). In either one of these situations, the individual's victimization is prolonged.

Another technique used to capture victims for the purpose of being trafficked is abduction. While not as complex as afore-mentioned strategies, it is similarly effective. Some traffickers scour the streets and public areas to find their next victims in cities across the world. In these cases, traffickers seek the most vulnerable and the most profitable, depending on the form of trafficking they are concentrating on. The most vulnerable of targets include street children, teenagers, and homeless adults. In war torn countries, traffickers are able to choose their victims because law enforcement is at a minimum and war tends to disorganize large groups of people. It also creates vast amounts of refugees to abduct and kidnap that can easily be sold.

A final way in which trafficking is committed is particularly disconcerting insofar as it involves the selling of relatives, friends, and neighbors by people that the victims know. Gaon and Forbord (2005) posit that many cases involve parents who sell their children and babies to human traffickers under for several reasons: (1) under the pretense that their daughter or son may receive a better quality of life outcome; (2) some children are sold under the pretense that the parents need money to survive and their children are a natural and renewable resource that can be replenished; and (3) the assumption that they can only afford to raise and take care of the child that is the most beneficial (in some cases this means smartest or most talented child).

Along these same lines, there are instances in which people have been sold to traffickers and into forced labor by their friends, neighbors, and relatives. In a situation such as this, individuals are often deceived by the persons they have relationships with. These betrayals are particularly distressing because it creates a social reality in which no one can be truly trusted, anyone could be a potential trafficker and hence a threat to one's own well being. These types of transfers are effective because it involves deception, voluntarism on the part of the victim who is being deceived, no clear resistance and financial incentive for the parties who are assisting the traffickers in their enterprise.

Who Commits These Crimes

In terms of the crimes committed, human traffickers represent a group of people that prey upon the weak, vulnerable, and unprotected individuals that often live in under-developed or developing countries around the globe. The criminals themselves have no real universal identifiers or commonalities because they represent individuals and groups of people that are from diverse ethnic backgrounds and operate globally. Traffickers are primarily focused on the selling for profit, but Shelley (2007) suggests some use trafficking to fund other enterprises such as terrorism, insurgencies, and regional guerilla warfare.

Many of the individuals who turn to this type of criminal activity do so because it is viewed as, and thought of as being the most lucrative form of criminal activity (King, 2004). Given the disparity between risk (of being held liable legally) and reward (profits attained through trafficking), perpetrators have accepted the enterprise as the perfect crime. Traffickers operate from within countries in which the crime is considered a small or negligible problem in comparison to other, more pressing issues such as drugs, gun smuggling, or war. Corruption within rogue regimes affords the enterprise continuity. It is easier because the context with which the traffickers are operating is one that feeds upon desperation, necessity or need to survive, and disorganization (Phongpaichit et al., 1998; Ruggiero 1997).

Traffickers also have a unique perspective when it comes to human beings. They categorize humans as a type of renewable natural resource that can be recycled or reused over and over again (Shelley, 2007). The dehumanization of victims transforms them into commodities that can be traded, bartered, and sold for a price to the highest bidder. People are no longer humans from their perspective because they lack any differentiation, individuality, and perhaps most importantly they lack a story to tell. Instead, human traffickers reduce people to nothing more than an abstract object, a tangible material good that can be exchanged for profit at their discretion.

Adding to this calculating perspective is the notion that the trafficker does not see humans as a long term investment. Individuals can only perform the task they are sold into for limited tenure. While humans are renewable, and reusable (they can perform different tasks if needed), they do have a finite life span. Due to this, victims' lives are directly correlated to what they can provide in terms of financial return. Without financial value, they are at risk of possible injury or disposal.

Categorizing the Victims

Although women and children are at particular and accentuated risk, this is largely correlated with the form of labor (or service) they are likely to provide. For example, women are at greater risk of being targeted for prostitution because of the profits involved in the sex trade, where most clientele are males in search of females (Aronowitz, 2009; Lee, 2007; King, 2004). Children are at greater risk of being targeted for military service since they are less likely to resist and can less appreciate the risks of what they will face in armed combat (Aronowitz, 2009). Moreover, they have longer tenure and can provide greater return for the purchaser's investment. Men are more likely to be targeted for hard labor, where efficiency can be attained (Aronowitz, 2009; King, 2004). Put simply, they are more likely to offer maximum production in labor than women and children, who may be physically weaker than them.

Victims are also targeted based on the threat posed to abductors. This may be gauged by the risks associated with being held legally accountable if caught. Persons who are displaced and may lack documentation are particularly vulnerable since they may be more difficult to trace if they are missing. Those living in poverty or the less educated and naive may be particularly vulnerable to traffickers because they may be less likely to resist. Those physically weaker may pose less of a threat to abductors through resistance, and thus may be perceived as attractive targets.

These situations put potential victims into a position in which traffickers can thrive and take advantage of their undesirable circumstances. By having a steady stream of possible victims that are desperate, weak, and vulnerable the traffickers know that they have a constant supply of potential victims to sell for profit. It fosters and enhances a system in which persons are readily available to be sold into a life of forced labor.

What Are the Outcomes?

The victims of human trafficking are the ones who pay the ultimate price when this crime is committed. Persons sold into forced labor and bondage suffer on a daily basis from a myriad of negative consequences placed upon them because of their captors. For example, many individuals endure sessions of brutal physical harm throughout the duration of their labor. Some are beaten on a daily basis to remind them of who is in charge, others are beaten for not performing as expected, and some are beaten and tortured just for the sake of making an example out of potential deserters or trouble makers. In some instances, people are sold and trafficked to people who purchase individuals only for the purpose of beating of them.

People also suffer physically (Aronowitz, 2009; King, 2004) from performing long, grueling work in substandard conditions such as in the case of those people forced to work in industry and in mines. The same can be said for people sold into prostitution and sex slavery in that many of these victims are expected/ or forced to perform sexual acts with an untold amount of partners per day. The duration of performing these activities on a daily basis takes a terrible toll on many of the victims. Since many of the victims receive no health care their immediate (short term) and long term health is put into jeopardy.

This is also the case for children whom are especially vulnerable to physical harm because of lack of physical development. Many children are exposed to physical beatings and torture for the same reasons as adults: to exercise power and control, to force people to perform at a certain preset standard, or to discourage dissenters and deserters. Adding to the problem is the fact that many are forced to work in situations and conditions in which adults cannot perform the work. This is the case for children working in small, dark, and tight tunnels found in mines. Children working in these mines often find themselves exposed to hazards such as: unreliable mines that collapse, mines that are too narrow, unsafe exposure to toxic chemicals, etc. Each of these factors increases the chances of harm or injury (such as losing a limb), stunted growth (from over exposure to chemicals) and in some cases death.

Not only is physical harm a major problem for the victims of human trafficking but biological harm is also an issue. For instance, victims of forced prostitution have felt an explosion in HIV, AIDS, and STD's (sexually transmitted diseases) worldwide (Aronowitz, 2009; Lee, 2007; UNODC, 2006; King, 2004). Along these same lines, victims of forced prostitution have also experienced increased exposure to diseases such as hepatitis, tuberculosis, and other communicable diseases. These victims (regardless of being adult or child) often find themselves in a double bind caused by the fact that they may contract anyone of the above diseases from any partner, at any given time. The problem develops when a victim contracts a disease and they cannot take care of it. Since there is no health care made available from their captors victims are left to suffer and live with their disease. Even if a person escapes captivity, majority of the people, once they get home or break free (if they do), usually reside in countries with relatively little to no healthcare in the first place. Thus, for many treatment is not a realistic option because many of the trafficked victims reside in developing or underdeveloped countries.

Trafficked victims also find themselves exposed to various types and kinds of psychological harm. The stress caused by being captured and sold into forced labor can cause any kind of anxiety based problems, depression, post-traumatic stress disorder, flashbacks, nightmares and night terrors, and thoughts of suicide (Aronowitz, 2009; UNDP, 2009), just to name a few. Often victims of human trafficking crimes who survive or escape bondage need counseling and therapy in order to begin to cope with, and understand what has happened to them. However, many of the victims saved from a life of perpetual forced labor never receive this type of help because it is not made available. For the victims that do not escape, many are left to cope with the fallout of their psychological trauma on their own.

Children that are trafficked into forced labor suffer other indignities that adults do not. For example, children are often stripped away from their parents at young ages and never see their birth parents ever again. This even happens in cases where children are rescued or freed from force labor and bondage because no effort is made to find the child's parents. Instead, a child may find themselves under state control, in an orphanage, or wandering the streets as a homeless trafficked victim. These situations are particularly dangerous for children because it increases their chances of being resold into forced labor again.

Children can suffer from lack of sexual development. Since children have not fully developed their reproductive organs using them in forced labor such as prostitution and sex slavery has dire consequences.

Children's underdeveloped bodies suffer as each customer or sexual partner uses their genitals or other areas of the body for sexual gratification (King, 2004). Minors are exposed to sexual labor it can increase the chances that: they will have irreparable damage done to their reproductive system, that they will catch a disease (either a sexually transmitted or non-sexually transmitted one), that their genitals may be harmed, mutilated, or experimented upon. In addition, many female children can develop diseases that are associated with complications due to pregnancy at an early age.

King (2004) contends that trafficked children are also missing out and lose valuable opportunities to develop socially, to gain educational opportunities, to grow up within a family, and to develop as a child into an adult. By subtracting a child's ability to grow up in such an environment they are more vulnerable to, and susceptible to: psychological trouble, they are more likely to not fully develop both physically and mentally, they are more likely to be resold and re-trafficked, they have a reduced potential to succeed, and they can be exposed to the realities of a harsh and brutal adult world at too early of an age. All of these consequences can negatively impact the child's dignity and minimizes the potential for self-actualization.

Overall, the outcome for individuals that undergo the horrifying experience of being trafficked into forced labor is bleak at best. The hardships that victims are expected to endure are painful, and tragic. Adults and children alike are exposed to every type of underserved human behavior possible ranging from: lack of personal freedom, to physical and psychological harm, to even a cap off of human potential. None of the individuals captured and used for the purpose of forced labor or bondage deserve it, and certainly no one wants to be resigned to a life of servitude; and yet this is the situation that millions of people across the globe find themselves within on a daily basis.

Actions to Address the Problem

The crime of human trafficking is not only on the rise but it has become an epidemic affecting nearly every country, on every continent, on the globe. It has grown from a small time criminal pursuit to a transnational, multibillion dollar industry that preys upon the weak, vulnerable, and defenseless. It has ravaged and destroyed millions. The volume of people who become human trafficking victims has reached a critical point in which the international community has declared it to be a global problem rather than a regional one (UNODC, 2006).

Tangible responses have included the development of large international organizations. For example, in the year 1997 the United Nations formed an international organization known as UNODC or the United Nations Office of Drugs and Crime. This organization was created by merging the United Nations Drug Control Program and the Centre for International Crime Prevention. The combined resources of both programs allowed the newly formed UNODC to operate in regions throughout the world by utilizing an extensive network of field offices. These field offices report information back to UNODC in order to gain access to resources that will allow them to assist in the fight against drugs, crime, and terrorism.

The UNODC organization has three specific functions:

(1) It provides "field-based technical cooperation projects to enhance the capacity of member States to counteract illicit drugs, crime and terrorism."

(2) It assists with "research and analytical work to increase knowledge and understanding of drugs and crime issues and expand the evidence base for policy and operational decisions."

(3) It facilitates "normative work to assist States in the ratification and implementation of the relevant international treaties, the development of domestic legislation on drugs, crime and terrorism, and the provision of secretariat and substantive services to the treaty-based and governing bodies" (UNODC, 2009).

These key areas provide United Nations members educational and legal reform with regard to human trafficking (a social issue that falls under the general category of crime for UNODC). UNODC has the ability to create and provide resources to Non-Government Agencies or NGOs that function to eliminate and educate citizens about the issue of trafficking (UNODC, 2009). It provides specific training and assistance to law enforcement agencies both internationally and member state based in order to combat human trafficking.

UNODC also provides a myriad of educational tools and resources that teachers, researchers, persons who work in government agencies and

NGOs can use to fight against human trafficking. They prepare annual reports such as trafficking reports, global pattern reports, and an overall yearly report that emphasizes increases and decreases in trafficking behavior. The valuable knowledge gained from these types of reports allows numerous professionals who work with trafficking prevention to use data and research to their advantage. Some of these reports have been used to change and shape both international and national policies regarding laws on human trafficking. They have also been used to hold other countries, whether they are United Nations members or not, accountable for trafficking crimes (UNODC, 2009).

The United States has also responded to the global problem of human trafficking by enacting and adopting the Victims of Trafficking and Violence Protection Act of 2000. This legislation has facilitated sweeping changes in American policy and attitudes in human trafficking. The VTVPA has created the Interagency Task Force to Monitor and Combat Trafficking which serves several functions which include the evaluation and tracking of progress of other nations, along with the United States, in areas related to or pertaining to trafficking activities. It also actively participates in collecting data and creating research reports to illustrate the enterprise's changing nature. The Act has increased the need for interstate and global cooperation in terms of understanding and preventing trafficking (USDOJ, 2009).

The Act has helped foster liaisons between the United States government and NGOs or non-government organizations. Relationships between both types of organizations allow for greater potential resources to draw from. In addition, it has made the United States government and law enforcement officials accountable for increases in human trafficking due to the fact that a yearly report on the nature of trafficking crimes is presented to numerous house and international committees (USDOJ, 2009).

The Act has also changed U.S. law in relation to penalties for being caught trafficking. Not only have the penalties increased for the crime of trafficking but the definition of trafficking and criminals associated with this crime has also expanded. It now includes the traffickers, the transporters, and any and all accomplices, along with any persons known to purchase or use individuals in any form of forced labor (USDOJ, 2009). There is also a focus on charging more criminals in cases in which a person has been caught using purchased individuals for the purpose of sex slavery. Along these same lines, the VTVPA Act has also increased the need for law enforcement cooperation between states and nations around the world.

Another significant contribution that the VTVPA Act has made is its insistence on providing resources to the victims of human trafficking. Support has been increased as federal funds are now used to create protective shelters for victims, to open and operate hotlines, and to support non-government agencies, to create new agencies, and provide resources for public and private organizations that combat human trafficking (USDOJ, 2009). It has encouraged support for both legal and social services to be provided to trafficking victims. There has also been a focus on providing services to reintegrate trafficked victims back into their homes with their families. If this is not possible the Act also provides resources for integrating victims into the United States.

The international community has also responded by creating and developing numerous non-government agencies (NGOs) that operate with the sole purpose of ending human trafficking (Aronowitz, 2009). These agencies represent a mixture of public, private, and grass roots organizations that function to assist and help local, state, national, and international community initiatives to end trafficking. Examples of these types of organizations include Free the Slaves, Terre Des Hommes, Save the Children, La Strada and the International Labor Union (ILO) (Aronowitz, 2009: 146). Such organizations serve multiple functions in the fight against trafficking. They provide a range of services and assistance such as: counseling, trafficking prevention, assisting law enforcement, fighting corruption in local courts, educating others, providing research and reports, and in some instances shaping and reforming laws.

NGOs have been successful in the fight against human trafficking because they work on multiple levels (local, state, national, and international). They provide valuable assistance to many people, groups, and nations that might normally be overlooked on the large scale international level. The range of services and assistance they provide is invaluable and cannot be overlooked. Non-government agencies will continue to make an impact on the global fight against human trafficking.

Conclusion

While major initiatives such as the creation of UNODC and the passing of the VTPVA Act of 2000 provide resources to take action against human trafficking, it can be argued that it may still not be enough to curtail its spread. The formation of international organizations such as UNODC can and often do provide help in many cases to the victims of human trafficking, while also attempting to change international and state member laws. One limitation is that other countries may choose not to abide by the standards set by the United Nations. Violators are often relieved of international censures or sanctions from international standards, laws, or initiatives created by the United Nations or UNODC.

The VTVPA Act of 2000 falls short in its purpose a couple of reasons. First, the resources and availability of resources provided by this legislation is purely contingent upon the money that the federal government allocates for this purpose. The services and resources that this Act claims it can provide is dependent upon money budgeted in advance. As the economic system of the United States fluctuates, so too will the resources and services that this legislation provides. While there are laws and statues that provide minimum services to victims and resources to law enforcement the availability of these funds may prevent the VTVPA Acts full potential from ever being realized.

A second problem can be found in the expansion of duties expected of from law enforcement at all levels (local, state, and federal). While resources and money exists to fight against human trafficking from the act itself, many agencies are already over worked. Creating a large federal law that requires adherence to it may seem applicable, but law enforcement agencies may not have specialized divisions, or the resources along with it to fully address trafficking. This problem is accentuated as one moves from the federal level to state and local law enforcement factions.

Another law enforcement related problem has been with cooperating and coordinating efforts to prevent, prosecute, and protect victims with other countries. One limitation has been the resistance by governments, in what is perceived to be external interference in sovereign nations' affairs. Additional problems entail the difficulty in matching, or equivocating laws that will allow for extradition and removal of wanted traffickers. Some nations may not have specific and/or strict legislation pertaining to trafficking; this may create additional complications, particularly due to the fact that such nations may be less likely to release criminals into the hands of U.S authorities.

Non-government agencies have been successful at assisting with the various needs of trafficking related issues. However, their successes can have limited tenure. NGOs are negatively impacted from the problem of being funded through either federal money which is inconsistent, or private donations which is equally inconsistent. When the funding is low or resources are depleted, these organizations may be limited in the services they provide, or may have to cease operation.

Compounding both of these problems is the fact that interest in human trafficking related issues often wanes or is discontinued. There are periods in which trafficking is a prevalent topic because it is being mentioned in current politics, or NGOs are able to shore up support by advertising or educating people on trafficking through public means, or it is given exposure in media. As interest in the topic of trafficking fades, economic support and volunteer support may also decrease. Conversely, if interest is piqued, donations and volunteerism may be accentuated. This situation presents a major problem in that non-government agencies can suffer from inconsistency in terms of providing help and assistance for human trafficking.

NGOs can also fall into the trap of becoming more focused on their own political agendas rather than actually helping fight against trafficking. In this case, the organizations' lobby against human trafficking becomes a personal, or group statement about their own political beliefs on the issue of human trafficking. Instead of the focus being on the victims, the criminals, or trafficking prevention some NGOs lose sight of what they are trying to accomplish in the first place. In cases such as these the organizations are overly concerned with the politics of the situation and not the realities that develop out of it.

Problems endemic within UNODC and the legislative efforts still do not undermine or curtail the benefits that emerge from such processes. The impact of these types of programs is significant insofar as they offer sequential steps in combating injustice globally. While human trafficking may not be dissolved, it can be limited. This presents a much more palpable address to human suffering.

References

Aronowitz, A. (2009). *Human Trafficking, Human Misery: The Global Trade in Human Beings*. Westport, CT: Praeger Press.

Bales, K. (2005). *Understanding Global Slavery*. Berkely, CA: University of California Press.

Bales, K. (2000). Expendable People: Slavery in the Age of Globalization, *Journal of International Affairs*, 53: 461-485.

Gerdes, L. (2006). *Prostitution and Sex Trafficking: Opposing Viewpoints*. Farmington Hill, MI: Greenhaven Press.

Gaon, I., Davor, & Forbord, N. (2005). *For Sale: Women and Children*. Victoria, BC: Trafford Publishing.

King, G. (2004). *Woman, Child for Sale: The New Slave Trade in the 21st Century*. New York, NY: Chamberlain Bros.

Lee, M. (2007). *Human Trafficking*. Uffculme, UK: Willan Publishing.

Ould, D. (2004). Trafficking and International Law, in Christian van den Anker (ed.) *The Political Economy of New Slavery*. New York, NY: Palgrave Macmillan.

Picarelli, J. (2007). Historical approaches to the trade in human beings, in Maggy Lee *Human Trafficking*. Uffculme, UK: Willan Publishing.

Phongpaichit, P., et al. (1998). *Guns, Girls, Gambling, and Ganja: Thailand's Illegal Economy and Public Policy*. Chiang Mai, Thailand: Silkworm Books.

Rodriguez, O. (2006). Smuggling Deaths Likely to Rise with Fence. *Adelante*.
http://x.adelantesi.com/news/story/.php?ID=279

Ruggiero, V. (1997). Trafficking in Human Beings: Slaves in Contemporary Europe, *International Journal of the Sociology of Law*, 25:231- 244.

Shelley, L. (2007). Human Trafficking as a form of transnational crime, in Maggy Lee *Human Trafficking*. Uffculme, UK: Willan Publishing.

United Nations Development Program. UNDP. n.d. Trafficking and HIV/AIDS: The Link. Youandaids.
http://www.youandaids.org/Themes/Trafficking.asp

United Nations Office on Drugs and Crime. UNODC: Trafficking in Persons: Global Patterns, June 6, 2006.
http:www.unodc.org/unodc/en/human-trafficking/publications/html#Reports

United Nations Office on Drugs and Crime. (UNODC) 2009.
http://www.unodc.org/unodc/en/about-unodc/index.html
United States Department of Justice. (USDOJ) 2009.
http://www.ovw.usdoj.gov/laws/vawo2000/welcome.html
United States Department of State. Department of State Report:
Trafficking In Persons Report, June 2008.
http://www.state.gov/g/tip/rls/tiprpt/2008/index.htm
Willis, B. M., & Leavy, B. (2006). Child Prostitution Is a Global Health
Problem, in Louise Gerdes *Prostitution and Sex Trafficking*.
Farmington Hills, MI: Green Haven Press.

CHAPTER 4
DRIVING DISCONTINUANCE AND QUALITY OF LIFE AMONG THE ELDERLY

Joseph M. Pellerito Jr.

Abstract: Contemporary research indicates that the elderly view driving retirement as a negative experience with numerous disabling consequences resulting in decreased quality of life. Scholarship on successful aging, however, shows that seniors generally define aging neutrally or positively. Links between driving retirement and these aging identities have not been studied in full. Further, researchers have relied upon quantitative research methods that lack the kind of rich description gleaned from qualitative inquiries. Reducing driving retirement to a finite list of negative consequences does not fully convey meanings and lived experiences. In this study, qualitative research methods were employed to study driving retirement through historical, cultural, and social contexts. Variables such as social locations, gender, age, race/ethnicity, socio-economic status, marital status, and residential location are employed to remedy some of these gaps in the literature and to better understand the relationships between participants' social locations and their self-defined meanings of driving and driving retirement.

Introduction: Driving Retirement and its Consequences

Negative consequences have been associated with driving retirement in the literature. Examples include, but are not limited to, the following: (1) diminished spontaneity (Korner-Bitensky et al., 1994), (2) feelings of being a burden on family members (Cook & Semmler, 1991), and (3) a perceived loss of social status (Barnes & Hoyle, 1995; Cynkin & Robinson, 1990). Luborsky (1994b) used the cultural context as a backdrop against which he described popular cultural ideas of full adulthood and how they affect the social experiences, interpersonal interactions, and self-esteem of people with recently acquired disabilities. He also asserted that every culture's model of adulthood includes the notion that the realization of competence and mastery occurs when language and the ability to achieve and maintain willful movement is successfully acquired.

Duggan (2000) expanded this idea and described how the loss of independent motor control (e.g., mobility) threatens the experiences of full adulthood and a meaningful existence because social interaction and roles are negatively affected. People that comprise the geriatric population are all too familiar with being marginalized and disenfranchised as a result of aging and subsequent diminished personal and community mobility. Thus, for older individuals, driving or the resumption of driving, or at a minimum being able to identify viable alternative transportation options, is a major goal towards maintaining community integration and quality of life (Ranney & Hunt, 1997).

Statement of the Problem

In present-day societies, citizens young and old overwhelmingly depend on the automobile to meet their travel and community mobility needs (U.S. Department of Transportation, 2003, Molnar et al., 2003); however, not every adult is able to safely continue driving when contending with aging-related health conditions and other problems. Maintaining the skills necessary to drive provides a sense of *independence* and *competence* and enables access to essential goods and services, meaningful social interaction, and the ability to age in place in familiar surroundings (U.S. Department of Transportation, 2003). Independent community mobility also influences the construction of positive self-concepts and high self-esteem (Carr, 1993; Galski et al., 1992; Gillins, 1990; Kalz et al., 1990; Stubbins, 1977), roles people assume (Enterlante & Kern, 1995), formation and maintenance of primary and secondary group ties or networks (Pellerito, 2006), daily operation of households and businesses, and the pursuit of meaningful activities in a variety of social settings (Johnson, 1995; Victor, 1994; Carr, 1993).

Interaction is at the core of any relationship, and the maintenance of meaningful relationships with primary and secondary group members has been linked to an individual's physical and psychological well-being in both the general population and among groups comprised of people with disabilities. This is punctuated by the fact that the older Americans account for one-half of the 60 million people with disabilities in the United States (Duggan, 2000; U.S. Census Bureau, 2000; Anson, Stanwyck, & Krause, 1993; Ferrans & Powers, 1992; Flanagan, 1982; Andrews & Withey, 1976). Individuals with aging-related health conditions that are visible, as well as disabilities that are undetected by the general public, must strive to overcome attitudinal and physical barriers in their communities. The consequences of disability and aging (e.g., driving retirement) include (i) increased dependence, (ii) diminished productivity, (iii) social isolation, (iv) loneliness (Johnson, 1995; Korner-Bitensky et al., 1994; Gillins,1990; Kalz et al., 1990; Legh-Smith et al., 1986), and (v) marginalization and a threatened sense of life's meaning and purpose (Duggan, 2000; Gourgey, 1994).

Community participation after driving retirement also may be negatively affected. The combined effect of expanding geographic distances between group members and the lack of reliable, accessible, and affordable alternative transportation can dramatically weaken social ties. People in most contemporary urban centers and those living in suburban or rural areas often must travel great distances by automobile to engage in daily activities, routines and habits, paid or volunteer work, recreation and leisure, and self-care. The convenience that driving affords (e.g., shopping for goods and services, commuting to and from work, driving for pleasure) has been cited as a key factor that has fostered an increased reliance on the automobile (Lister, 1997).

Access to a motor vehicle facilitates speedy and efficient mobility. This helps to maintain one's mere existence while facilitating new and reinforcing existing social ties, which can result in expanded and strengthened social networks across vast geographic distances. Driving also provides timely access to essential goods and services and a robust social life within neighborhoods, work or retirement settings, and other contexts throughout the broader community.

There is a growing body of literature that has purported negative consequences associated with driving retirement and, conversely, positive outcomes when individuals possess the ability and means to continue driving. Conclusions have been extrapolated primarily from quantitative studies, however, that reflect perspectives that are void of the kinds of insights mined from rich descriptions of participants' points of view in well-designed qualitative studies. Previous studies have not considered driving retirement within the context of aging or against a socio-cultural backdrop that would enable analyses of driving retirement and its consequences within the broader contexts of history, culture, successful aging, and community participation.

Older Drivers as a Group

The proportion and number of older drivers in the United States has increased dramatically over the past two decades (Lundberg et al., 1998) and it is anticipated that this trend will continue (Freund & Szinovacz, 2002). There are 35 million Americans 65 years of age or older, which is approximately 13% of the total U.S. population; the number of older drivers is expected to double and reach 70 million by the year 2030 (U.S. Department of Transportation, 2003). Drivers age 55 and older comprised 28% of the driving population in 2000 and that number is expected to increase to 39% by the year 2050 (Cushman, 1996; Marottoli, 1993).

Older Americans resemble the broader population when it comes to their dependence on privately owned automobiles (U.S. Department of Transportation, 2003). More than four out of five trips undertaken by people over the age of 65 in the U.S. are in passenger vehicles that are usually their own (National Research Council, 1988). It is understandable that older Americans continue to drive even after experiencing the cumulative effects of aging and chronic disease, and the disabling effects of traumatic injuries, chronic disabilities, and the aging process (Molnar et al., 2003). There is significant variation in the functional abilities of older drivers as well. Although it has been estimated that about one-third of the population over age 65 have limitations that render them unable to perform a significant number of activities of daily living (ADL), more than two-thirds of these people continue to drive (Rosenbloom, 1993).

The effects of aging and the concomitant challenges associated with disabling health conditions can work in tandem to reduce the functioning, safety, independence, and well-being of older Americans. Lysack (2004) posited that when a person is hospitalized, current medical rehabilitation is considered complete after an individual (1) survives an initial or reoccurring disabling event; (2) reaches an optimal level of functioning that is primarily measured in physical terms; and (3) returns home or to an alternative destination to resume as many routines and meaningful activities as possible, which may or may not include driving. Community and public policy perspectives take into consideration the long-term consequences of aging and disabilities. They assert that social outcomes of rehabilitation should be measured by the extent to which a person can reconstruct a positive self-image, resume key life roles, re-engage with primary and secondary group members, return to meaningful work and leisure activities, and participate in the community.

There is growing concern among some health care professionals and the general public that there is mounting evidence that older driver sub-groups account for a disproportionate number of traffic accidents and morbidity and mortality. The oldest drivers (75 years of age or older) experience traffic accidents at a rate second only to the youngest drivers between 15 and 24 years of age (O'Neill, 1992; Williams & Carsten, 1989). More than 7,000 elderly drivers die in automobile accidents on U.S. highways and roads annually (Kulash, 2000); the number of older drivers 70 years of age and older killed in vehicular accidents nationwide has increased 39% over a 10-year period (Aging News Alert, 2000). Florida had the most elderly auto fatalities in 1999, followed by Texas, California, Pennsylvania, and Michigan (Aging News Alert, 2000). Motor vehicle accidents are the leading cause of accidental deaths for people age 65-74 and second leading cause (after falls) for older people in general (U.S. Department of Health and Human Services, 1991).

By age group, drivers 80 years of age or older have the highest fatality rate, drivers 65-79 the third highest, and drivers 16-24 the second highest (U.S. Department of Commerce, 1995). Physiologic changes, concomitant medical conditions, and medications associated with aging can impair driving ability (Molnar et al., 2003). Thus, as the number of older drivers increases, their competence to drive has become a growing concern for themselves and their families, professional caregivers, and physicians. Medical doctors possess an added responsibility because they have the legal authority and ethical responsibility to report individuals (e.g., their state's department of motor vehicles or DMV) they deem unsafe to drive (Underwood, 1992). Other health care team members and family caregivers also share the ethical responsibility and burden of helping to facilitate driving retirement when necessary. Safe driving is similarly the concern of the general public, the automobile manufacturing industry, researchers, and the insurance industry.

Alternative Transportation and Driving Retirement

Why some individuals continue to drive with cognitive, kinesthetic, visual perceptual or functional deficits may be partially explained by the fact that older adults overwhelmingly rely on the automobile for their primary means of transportation (Jette & Branch, 1992). However, the absence of alternative transportation options, however, including an available family member or friend in possession of a driver's license and a vehicle who is willing to assist, the lack of a comprehensive system of public transportation in some cities and throughout rural areas, and the absence of a 'co-pilot' who can assist with navigation and serve as a 'second pair of eyes' can exacerbate the problem. The availability of drivers who have access to reliable vehicles can facilitate a transition toward driving retirement only if they are willing and able to assist (Kington et al., 1994). Driving retirement can lead to a heavy dependence on informal support systems resulting in caregivers missing or reducing work, or giving up working altogether to care for their elderly loved ones (Freund & Szinovacz, 2002). Consequences such as these may partially account for the hesitancy to stop driving among some older drivers (Freund & Szinovacz, 2002).

In some instances, older men who do not have spouses that drive receive help from their wives who fill the role of co-pilot (Burkhardt et al., 1996). Fulfilling the role of a co-pilot may include assisting with topographical orientation and navigation through an unfamiliar area, or by watching the driving environment and offering verbal cues and guidance to their older driving partners. Foley and colleagues (2000) confirmed that 10% of older men with incident dementia reported to have continued driving with the help of a co-pilot. Co-piloting has recently received some scrutiny over the past several years (Foley et al., 2000; Bedard et al., 1998; Shua-Haim & Gross, 1996); however, its use as a potential driving compensation strategy versus a detriment (e.g., distraction) has not been studied in a systematic fashion (Freund & Szinovacz, 2002).

Reuben et al. (1988: 12) have succinctly presented the issue at the center of driving retirement: They argue that the concern over competency of driving has been raised, other ethical concerns will subsequently follow. The central debate focuses on competing interests, including the benefit of continued driving for the individual versus the risk to that person and society as a whole.

Successful Aging

There are two models of successful aging that are widely accepted in the research community. The first is the *selection-optimization-compensation model* developed by Baltes and Baltes (1990), which utilizes the concepts of variability and plasticity to outline the optimal psychological processes of successful aging. The other model is the *three-component model* developed by Rowe and Kahn (1997). This model defines successful aging by a set of objective measures to determine the absence or low risk of disease, high levels of psychological and physical functioning, and engagement in meaningful activities. The World Health Organization (WHO) defines active aging as *"the process of optimizing opportunities for health, participation, and security in order to enhance the quality of life as people age"* (WHO, 2002: 12). In this definition, *'active'* refers not only to one's ability to be physically active, but also to *'continue participating in social, economic, cultural, spiritual, and civic affairs'* (WHO, 2002).

When older people actively participate in meaningful activities and continue to engage in relationships with family members, colleagues, and members of their communities, as well as carry-out civic duties, they are actively aging, regardless of whether they are chronically ill or disabled or both (Hui-Chuan, 2007). This view of healthy or active aging considers the physical, mental, and social well-being of individuals, which presents an action-oriented conception of aging that emphasizes participation as a key to aging successfully. In most studies, however, researchers have identified physical functioning or a specific disease as the outcome measure, while mental and social health status have rarely been considered (Albert et al., 1995). There has been little scholarly inquiry into what older people consider to be the necessary prerequisites to successful aging.

Despite research findings that have reported negative consequences associated with driving retirement, successful aging literature reveals that older adults do have agency and a large degree of autonomy in influencing and ameliorating the impact of disease and disability. This can foster the maintenance of social ties, productivity and contributions to the broader community, and high levels of cognitive and physical functioning (Dillaway, 2005; Katz & Marshall, 2003). Older people rarely report feeling or being old (Kaufman & Elder, 2002; Cremin, 1992). This may be due to the following: older people view aging in a more positive light than researchers have assumed previously (Gannon, 1999); older people often continue to engage in meaningful occupations or activities, such as care giving, sexual intimacy, and paid work roles (Lysack & Seipke, 2002); and aging is a complex phenomena that is much more than the sum of a finite list of health conditions and disabilities (Laz, 2003). It is within the social contexts of one's past and present life experiences that a person assigns meaning to aging and the aging process, and whether or not they feel old (Lysack & Seipke, 2002).

Exploration of aging identities and meanings by employing qualitative research methods could help foster greater understanding of the positive or neutral experiences of driving retirement. These findings could advance our understanding by moving beyond the negative consequences of driving retirement reported in the literature previously. Aging studies have been predominantly quantitative, however, and have defined successful aging narrowly. This has resulted in the need for a broader conceptualization of what successful aging within the context of driving retirement really means.

Employing a sociological perspective that considered how social locations influence driving retirement promoted a deeper understanding of how people view and experience driving and driving retirement. Sociological perspectives in the study reported on in this chapter have complimented the current client- or person- based focus in contemporary driving retirement literature. This has been accomplished by examining the inter-relationship between individuals and groups, institutions, and other social structures, thus promoting micro- and macro-level analyses of successful aging within the context of driving retirement. Sociological perspectives also enabled me to focus on the relationships between social locations and health and aging disparities between groups (Weber, 2001). Finally, sociological theory and qualitative research methods can help to explain differences and similarities in how a phenomenon such as driving retirement is experienced and perceived by individuals and groups.

Symbolic Interactionism

Looking through the theoretical lens of symbolic interactionism, a researcher would contend that the ways in which older people see themselves is influenced by the broader societal view of seniors as a group. The mass media's typically critical depiction of older drivers has influenced both the public's collective perception of older Americans generally and older drivers specifically. This in turn has shaped how older people view themselves in general terms, such as their overall levels of competence, and as drivers specifically. This concept can be better understood when examined within the context of Mead's work on the 'self' (1934) and Cooley's conceptualization of the 'looking-glass self' (1902).

Socialization is a process of symbolic interaction that occurs when people use significant symbols and vocal gestures (e.g., language) to communicate. This ability uniquely enables human beings to interpret each other's attitudes and initiate action based on the meanings associated with these interpretations. Personal and meaningful experiences do not begin with the individual, which then influences society. Instead, it starts with society or the whole prior to the part or individual, with role-taking and the self as emerging and changing throughout an individual's life span.

Individuals learn to assume the role of others by interpreting gestures or symbols that are conveyed by others. Language or significant symbols play an important role in this process. Language enables individuals to develop the ability to envision themselves in the place of others and, in turn, imagine how others perceive them (Mead, 1934). The final stage of maturation for children occurs when one assumes or perceives and understands the role of the 'generalized other'. The 'generalized other' reflects the attitudes and beliefs of the broader community (Mead, 1934).

Mead's View of the Self

Mead's (1934) description of the self, by which he meant the person, is at the core of symbolic interactionism. Mead (1962, 1934) posited that, unlike functionalist perspectives that view the individual as a passive agent impacted by social and psychological influences, the self is a willful participant. The self is not a passive entity that simply receives and responds mechanistically to external stimuli.

Blumer (1975) reinforces the notion that the self can be *active* and *adaptive*, as contrasted with a functionalist view of the individual as a passive instrument controlled by social and psychological factors. Mead argued that people have the ability to formulate and control their behavior (e.g., actions and reactions) via self-interaction. Additionally, symbolic interactionism refutes a deterministic viewpoint by differentiating the self. Mead (1962) asserted that the self cannot exist without the '*other*'.

The self develops in two phases. First, socialization fosters a sense of self via an exchange of attitudes with others. During this phase the '*I*' or the unorganized response to the attitudes of others, is spontaneous, impulsive, creative, and reactionary. In the second phase, people organize attitudes of the generalized other or broader social group and are influenced and shaped by these experiences throughout their lives. The second phase features the '*me*' or a set of organized attitudes of others that a person internalizes before reacting to form perspectives on one's self (McCall & Simmons, 1966).

Mead's conceptualization provides an important theoretical foundation that is relevant and useful when examining the ways older people engage in meaningful activities associated with specific occupations, roles, habits, and interests. Conversely, a lack of engagement due to life changes such driving retirement can help to define the self as well. Upon retirement from work, driving, and other activities or occupations of interest, an older man or woman's sense of self is influenced by the broader social system or generalized other. The generalized other is often critical of their ability and in opposition to them continuing to participate in activities that might present a risk to themselves and others, such as driving a motor vehicle. A loss of one's sense of consciousness of the self eventually leads to fear and isolation (Mead, 1934).

Cooley's Looking-Glass Self

Cooley (1964, 1902) argued that a person's self grows from interaction with others and that an individual's self-awareness is a reflection of the ideas about himself that she or he attributes to the minds of others (Coser, 1971). To explain the reflected sense of the self, Cooley (1964) conceptualized the '*looking-glass self*' and posited three key elements of it. These include (i) the imagination of our appearance to the other person, (ii) the imagination of his judgment of that appearance, and (iii) some sort of self-feeling, such as pride or mortification. Thus, the '*self*' arises and matures via a process of interpersonal communication as it is reflected in one's consciousness within a socio-cultural context. Society is internalized in a person's psyche and becomes an integral part of the individual through interaction with others, which links them into an organic whole (Coser, 1971).

As people age and retire from driving, do these links weaken or break causing decreased connectedness between individuals and the community or generalized other? The study reported on in this chapter attempts to address this question and others within the theoretical framework of symbolic interactionism.

These elements of sociological theory provide a conceptual framework and foundation upon which discovery and analysis of patterns, themes, and topics emerged. Theory also stimulates other important questions such as the following: Do older people see the generalized other as critical of their ability to participate in meaningful activities such as driving a motor vehicle? Does this realization and internalization affect older people and, if so, how?

Since obtaining a driver's license is an important milestone event and a kind of rite of passage, it seems reasonable to deduce that driving retirement also is a milestone event that can have an important, even profound impact, on older Americans, especially if that person has limited or no access to the broader community. To address these and other important questions, sound research featuring qualitative methods that foster scientific and humanistic inquiry is warranted.

Purpose of the Study Reported on in this Chapter

The purpose of the study reported on in this chapter was to identify and describe the self-defined meanings of driving and consequences of driving retirement. Topical themes were identified in the literature that helped guide the construction of the interview guide used in this research project. The interview guide featured a series of open-ended questions with probes intended to stimulate participant verbalization to explore the lived experiences of driving and driving retirement. Topics and questions contained in the interview guide reflected key content that was identified in the literature as being important to older people as well as subjects interesting to the researcher, such as alternative transportation; redefined roles at home, work, and in the community; mental health and wellness; meanings of driving; circumstances causing driving retirement; and community participation and social networks. Gaps in the literature in terms of our understanding of this phenomenon were identified, which also influenced the construction of the interview guide. The interview guide was pre-tested by interviewing three initial volunteer participants who had retired from driving for a minimum of one month or longer.

The qualitative study drew from nearly equal numbers of women and men whose ages ranged from 51 to 90 with a mean age of 73 years. Initially a selection of 30 participants (e.g., until the data was saturated) (Hesse-Biber & Leavy, 2004) who had stopped driving due to ill health or traumatic injury or both and were living in the Metropolitan Detroit area were placed into 2 groups: older men (n=17) and older women (n=13). This was done to help ensure saturation of the data and that gendered perspectives were fully considered.

Characteristics of a Qualitative Research Tradition: Phenomenology

Qualitative methods employed in the study reported on in this chapter may not be fully familiar to all readers and is therefore briefly presented here. The methods are derived from phenomenology interviewing techniques (Strauss & Corbin, 1990a; Agar, 1984; Spradley, 1979). Methods incorporated semi-structured and structured, open-ended questions (Luborsky, 1994a) to explore the following topics: (i) the effects of driving retirement on quality of life and other factors; (ii) perceived barriers and resources that influenced responses to driving retirement; and (iii) strategies for maintaining or improving personal quality of life following driving retirement. Demographic data were collected as well; these questions were relatively brief and were used to establish the social locations that participants occupied, such as age, gender, race/ethnicity, and SES or class. Data explication included descriptive, content and theme, and narrative analysis (Luborsky, 1994a). Memo writing was undertaken to assist with the preparation of the final manuscript (Hesse-Biber & Leavy, 2004).

Data explication involved description and interpretation of the data collected resulting in narrative content. The content highlighted the socio-cultural behavior and perspectives of a participant and group (Creswell, 1998). These are preferred methods of inquiry when central concepts (e.g., cultural meanings of driving and community mobility, personal independence, subjective quality of life, driving retirement, and coping and adjustment) are underdeveloped in a given study population. They are also preferred when the researcher's goal is to develop a substantial description of the person, group, environment, and socio-cultural phenomenon under scrutiny. Finally, perceptions, meanings, and experiences are not amenable to standardized formats and quantitative approaches. Alternatively, qualitative research methods allow for understanding both personal meanings and experiences (Frank, 1996; Luborsky, 1994b; Kleinman, 1992, 1988; Scheer & Luborsky, 1991).

Phenomenology Reviewed

Notably the project reported on in this chapter combined sociological concepts and qualitative research methods to explore the meanings of driving and driving retirement and the self-described strategies used in response to the effects or consequences of driving retirement. Phenomenology was the qualitative tradition that was employed in the study reported on in this chapter.

The study reported on in this chapter met the criteria outlined by Creswell (1998) for using a phenomenological approach to research. For example, the study reported on in this chapter was undertaken to better understand the participants' lived experiences versus explaining 'why' using quantitative research methods. Also, a detailed description of participants' experiences was necessary to enhance understanding of their lives in the naturalistic environment or community. Further, this approach enabled results that were *interpretive*, rather than relying upon mechanistic and causative language that is used to describe statistical significance in a quantitative inquiry. Finally, the study reported on in this chapter gave voices to the respondents as they shared their unique perspectives on their lived experiences.

Qualitative analysis has at its foundation a more subjective approach to studying social phenomena. Irrespective of the fact that data was gathered from a number of respondents, qualitative analysis is not focused on the quantifying of qualitative data but rather to a process of interpretation. The researcher accounts for concepts and relationships that emerge, and then organizes them into a theoretical context (Strauss & Corbin, 1998).

Developing or building theory (e.g., building a conceptual or theoretical model) involves more than an exhaustive description of the phenomena being studied. Instead, detailed description allows for conceptual ordering by systematically organizing elements that emerge from the data into themes or categories, subcategories, and relationships. Strauss and Corbin (1980) described this as the interplay between *inductive* and *deductive* processes. A process is inductive when particular cases are examined in order to make empirical generalizations. It is deductive when subsequent cases are examined to see if the generalizations are supported. The research process followed in the study reported on in this chapter was intended to provide explanation and prediction of social phenomena (Strauss & Corbin, 1998).

While qualitative research findings can seldom be anticipated, ongoing research in related areas of aging, disabilities, and rehabilitation research has suggested that perceptions, views, and response patterns differ across groups and over time. Each participant's interests, needs, and insights reflect their unique life experiences and are influenced by a number of factors. These factors include, but are certainly not limited to, the existence and quality of social ties, socioeconomic status, and education. Life experiences, worldviews, and other social locations such as gender, age, and geographic location or place of residence influence participants' perspectives as well.

Natural History of Community Mobility

Personal narratives enable individuals to order and make sense of the disruptions in their lives by creating a subjective and temporal framework (Strauss & Corbin, 1990). Serious chronic illnesses and disabling conditions associated with ill health, traumatic injuries, or aging can cause a sharp disjunction in one's sense of self and impinge upon a biographical self-concept of what came before, what is going on, and how the future is anticipated (Luborsky, 1995). Listening to participants articulate how their lives had progressed through a series of stages or chapters was punctuated by meaningful transitions or milestone events.

Two such key events that were focused on in the study reported on in this chapter were driving and driving retirement. Life transitions also were illuminated by how participants viewed and adapted to ill health, traumatic injuries, and the aging process. Participant-centered voices revealed the meanings of driving and driving retirement and how the consequences of driving cessation were addressed. Perspectives on pitfalls and pathways to planning for, and coping with, driving retirement further expanded and illuminated our understanding of this phenomenon. While these data may be inferred during data explication, each participant's own description and statements about their unique and personal sense of how and why they have transitioned through these key life events was vital to interpreting the data in the final analysis. Notably narrative methods and qualitative questions were used to achieve this aim.

A brief life story of driving experiences, driving retirement, and responses to its consequences were appraised by employing a structured interview paradigm espoused by Luborsky (1993). This well-defined technique is a sensitive measure of subjective meanings, psychosocial functioning and distress, and processes of life reorganization (Luborsky & Rubinstein, 1995; Scheer & Luborsky, 1991). For example, participants were asked, *"Tell me the story of what it has been like to grow older and have stopped driving voluntarily or involuntarily?"* Content analysis was used to identify topics of concern and structures for portraying the experiences to others. Issues and changes in topical concerns and story structures were described in detail. Narrative elements predicting effective adaptation to driving retirement versus ineffective and unsuccessful adjustment were identified and summarized in both narrative and table form (Lysack, et al., 2003).

Each of the participants' stories was *personal* and *unique*. Stories were investigated and further examined to construct chapters and transitions around driving and driving retirement. For example, the interviewer asked: *"Thinking of your experience participating in your community since you have stopped driving, what different stages or chapters have you gone through? Tell me about the first one. What title or label would you give to the first chapter? What goes in there? What is the next one? How is that different from the previous chapter?"* The researcher completed a worksheet to structure the dialogue. Replies were then summarized under major topic headings and content was organized according to each particular stage or chapter. This structured method was used to identify potential stages in adjustment practices to driving retirement. Additionally, perceived barriers and helpful resources related to personally meaningful and productive response strategies prior to, and following, driving retirement were explored.

Successful adjustment to driving retirement over time emerged as a key factor in the achievement of satisfying levels of family, neighborhood, and community engagement, participation, and reintegration. Soon after driving retirement, some older people have difficulty imagining maintaining a satisfying family and community social life; persistent and repeated efforts that followed response strategies reported to be effective have to be undertaken before adaptation, personal networks, and meaningful community participation can be re-established (Lysack, et al., 2003).

Alternatively, some older persons sometimes reject longstanding relationships and community affiliations when they realize that they can no longer achieve the same level of community mobility as compared to when they were driving. To assess this topic, participants were asked, *"How long do you think it will take before you return to pre-driving retirement levels of community mobility and participation, if ever? How does your health impact your perspective on driving retirement? Do your health challenges put driving retirement 'in perspective' and make it easier or more difficult or both? Or is it neither and why?"*

Study Questions

This research project reported on in this chapter was dedicated to the collection, analysis, and presentation of interview data to provide a foundation upon which a better understanding of the meanings of driving and driving retirement could emerge. Hypothesis testing *is not* the focus of qualitative methodology. Nonetheless, several guiding research study questions were distinguished at the beginning of the study reported on in this chapter. The following questions framed recruitment of participants, data collection, and data explication at least in part.

  (1) How will older women versus older men define the meanings of driving and describe the effects or consequences of driving retirement on their quality of life?
  (2) How can the results from the study reported on in this chapter inform future studies designed to deepen our understanding of driving retirement?

Description of the Sample

Research participants comprised 13 women and 17 men. The ages of the women ranged from 62 to 93, and they had stopped driving between six weeks and six years prior to their interviews. Six women were black, five were white, one Native American, and one was biracial (West Indian and white). Eight women lived in an urban nursing facility, two lived in a suburban assisted living center, and two lived at home in an affluent suburban community adjacent to Detroit, Michigan.

The ages of the 17 men ranged from 51 to 90 years of age. They had stopped driving between four weeks and 22 years prior to their interviews. Eleven men lived in an urban nursing facility, four lived in a suburban assisted living center, and two lived at home in an affluent suburban community. Participants' education levels ranged from completion of elementary education (e.g., grade eight) to having completed a clinical doctorate (e.g., physician) and a doctorate in education (e.g., EdD). Most of the participants (all but six of the 30) were either unwilling or unable to provide information about their annual incomes; therefore, these data are not included here.

Meanings of Driving and Driving Retirement

Findings analyzed here are related to how participants described and assigned meanings to driving and driving retirement within historical and socio-cultural contexts. Included are the major themes and concepts to emerge from the data. Data presented will illustrate the importance of the rite of passage associated with earning a driver's license and the benefits driving afforded the participants. These results offer a foundation upon which a theoretical or conceptual model of driving and driving retirement emerged. The conceptual model attempts to succinctly explain both the meanings of driving and how older Americans experience and respond to driving retirement. Thus, the foundation of the conceptual model begins here, with the presentation of central and subordinate themes and concepts about the meanings of driving and driving retirement.

Major Themes and Concepts

The data revealed that earning a driver's license and driving a motor vehicle was a transformative event that had a profound influence on the participants' lives including their relationships, social networks, experiences, productivity, and social status, to name a few. The meanings of driving and driving retirement were explored and were informed by central themes culled from the data. Central themes are presented in an order which highlights the chronology of the lived experiences of the older Americans who participated in this study.

Two central themes born from the participants' views were identified during data explication: (1) driving as a rite of passage; and (2) the meanings of driving retirement. Driving as a rite of passage subsumed subordinate themes, such as obtaining a driver's license, mobility, freedom and pride, maturation; status, relationships and social life, driving to work, vehicle ownership, past driving records, and efficient transportation. Driving retirement subsumed subordinate themes including fun; family; status, image; and love. Finally, the phenomenon of driving retirement as a lived experience also was explored.

Driving As a Rite of Passage in American Culture

Obtaining a Driver's License: Symbol of Mobility, Freedom and Pride, and Maturation

The participants were asked questions that elicited descriptions of their lived driving experiences and what driving meant to them. Acquiring a driver's license marked a kind of rite of passage that afforded the participants the privileged status of becoming new drivers. Successfully obtaining a driver's license was a personal milestone for all but two of the participants (n=28). Driving status also presented a constellation of benefits (and some challenges) as the participants matured and progressed toward entering adulthood.

One of the participants that did not view the acquisition of a driver's license or driving as an important milestone was Ian. He was a 66-year-old black male who was married and living in a suburban assisted living center. He said, "*It [driving] didn't mean anything to me. I just got my driver's license and could drive, that's all. It was no big deal.*" Ian had no romantic illusions about his driving experiences. Jacob was the other participant who did not necessarily enjoy driving or think that acquiring a driver's license was a meaningful event or milestone in his life. He was an 86-year-old white male who was married and living in a suburban assisted living center. He stated, "*I didn't enjoy driving too much and it wasn't a big thing to get my license. I know that it was work. I didn't think of it as a job, but I used it as work.*" For Jacob, driving was associated with work and not necessarily with relationships, leisure, freedom, or other positive associations that some of the other participants identified.

The other 28 participants experienced a kind of rite of passage that was marked by the milestone event of earning a driver's license, which they regarded as a universal symbol of autonomy and independence or freedom. Gender appeared to influence the male participants' positive associations with obtaining a driver's license. Other social locations such as place of residence, age, education, and socioeconomic status (SES), however, did not appear to affect the participants' positive associations when they described when and how they successfully obtained a driver's license.

Once line-by-line coding and data explication had been conducted, focused coding helped me to sift through large amounts of data to identify the positive associations (or memories) of obtaining a driving license as an initial code, which helped me to understand and explain larger segments of data (Charmaz, 2006). Data that were identified during line by line coding featured participants' early driving stories accompanied by smiles and even robust laughter; this indicated that the participants' affects appeared to brighten as they described these distant memories.

All but one of the participants secured their licenses during their mid-teen years. All of the participants were able to recall in detail their lived experiences that centered on that milestone: acquiring a driver's license. David, a 65-year-old black male who was never married and living in a nursing home, associated maturation and a perceived elevation in his status with his rite of passage. He responded to the following question:

> [JP: *Can you remember, thinking back to when you got your driver's license, what that meant to you?*]
> [David: *Oh, yes! It was exhilarating! It was sort of like advancing in life to a new level. It was as if I had suddenly grown up and I was free. I would drive all over the east side of Detroit, to friends' houses; that type of thing, you know. To see people that I went to school with and we would really enjoy spending time together. Those were some of the best times of my life; anything was possible.*]

David and others (n=11) associated driving with freedom and autonomy, maturation and improved status, and the facilitation of movement over expanding geographic distances. David also valued the camaraderie with his primary group members that possessing a driver's license and driving afforded him. He was no longer dependent upon others or slower methods of community mobility, such as waiting for a bus, riding a bike, or walking. David characterized his rite of passage as being akin to '*advancing in life to a new level.*' Although none of the participants used the phrase '*rite of passage*,' 27 other participants used positive language similar to David's to describe their experiences. David also used positive terms such as *"exhilarating"* and feeling *"free"* when he described his lived experiences. Obtaining a driver's license and having access to a motor vehicle enabled him to connect with his primary group members (e.g., friends at school and people within his neighborhood and broader community) with greater ease and efficiency. He and four other participants framed their encounters and experiences in an historical context when asserting that they were *"the best times"* of their lives.

Perhaps David and the others used the word *"best"* to capture, in a word, a time in their lives when they were able to interact freely with the people that mattered most to them. David, for example, was a teenager in good health and without problems, such as the disabling health conditions that would confront him later in life when he suffered a stroke just before he was compelled to stop driving. Driving afforded him more than simply transportation to fulfill some functional need to move about in his community, such as commuting to and from work or visiting a sick relative in the hospital. Rather, it validated his feelings of well-being that were associated with feeling "free," as well as providing him with the means to reinforce existing, and foster new, meaningful relationships. Possessing a license meant having an active social life, at least in the way he described it.

Women in this sample also talked about driving in similar ways. Lisa, an 87-year-old white female, who had also stopped driving as the result of a stroke, was living in an urban assisted living center. Like David, she described experiencing a sense of freedom and pride when she stated, *"The thing I remember the most about getting a license to drive was the feeling I got when I used to go [drive] downtown and pick up my father in the afternoon. He'd go down [downtown] in the morning, be driven down, and then I would pick him up. That was a big deal for me. I was free and loved it!"* Betty, a 62-year-old black female who was never married, and living in an urban nursing home, echoed Candace's lived experience. She stated, *"I thought I was grown when I received my driver's license."* The emphasis that Candace and Betty placed on equating being 'grown' with possessing a driver's license, was a uniquely *gendered perspective*. Male participants, with the exception of David, focused more on the *independence* and *freedom* that securing a driver's license and driving afforded them.

Art was a highly articulate and open participant. His ability to describe his thoughts and feelings about driving and driving retirement made him an especially interesting subject to quote throughout this study. In fact, Art served as more of an informant than a participant alone, which informed my data explication and coding. He was a 63-year-old black male who was never married and living in an urban nursing home. In the following quote, he reinforced the importance of earning a driver's license and having access to a motor vehicle.

Art pointed out that he was a teenager when he earned his license and he underscored the freedom he experienced while traveling over vast geographic distances while travelling abroad. His love of travel and desire for extensive mobility was facilitated by the efficient means of transportation that driving afforded him. Physical boundaries were expanded and he seemed to take pride in his ownership of space; an ownership that extended over vast geographic distances. Amorphous boundaries were also expanded, such as existing or prospective personal and work relationships and networks, as well as the potential for connecting with people and things located in new and unfamiliar environments. Art described a '*love*' for driving and was almost poetic when he stated that driving was important to him because his "*world started at the point where the driveway ended and the street began.*" His time in the military enabled him to drive in other countries as well, and he appeared to take pride in this fact. More than two-thirds of the participants (n=22) talked about the freedom of mobility that driving enabled. For Art, driving was, in essence, nothing less than life affirming when he stated, "*it [driving] was my life.*"

Lisa was an older white female (87-years-old) living in a suburban assisted living facility, and Art and David were younger males (63- and 65-year-old black men, respectively) who were living in an urban nursing home. Robert, like Art and David, was also in his mid-sixties (a 65-year-old, divorced, white male living in a suburban assisted living center). He reminisced about his early driving days and interjected humor to describe the freedom and expanding social network that he enjoyed, which he associated with acquiring a driver's license and driving.

> [Robert: *I was sixteen going on thirty, and it was an event to be celebrated...because I could go anywhere and do anything I wanted; I was the top dog.*]

[JP: *And what was it like when you first started driving? Where would you go? What would you do?*]

[Robert: *Well, I grew up in a rural community and so, you drive through those types of lands; farm lands, you know, we would look at pretty sites, take girls places* (laughter).]

[JP: *How important was it to you that you were able to drive?*]

[Robert: *Oh, it was great. It meant the world to a young man living in the country; I finally got my wings and I could fly!*]

Robert described the independence and freedom that he felt, even power or control (n=3), once he earned a driver's license and began driving. It also revealed that he believed his status among his primary and secondary group members had been elevated in some tangible way. He noted that he grew up in a rural community and emphasized that driving *"meant the world to a young man living in the country"* Perhaps driving enabled him to escape a rural setting that he viewed as isolating and confining. Robert's rural upbringing was in contrast to Art's and David's and most of the other participants (n=27) who grew up in Detroit, or other urban and suburban areas. Not unlike most of the men who participated in this study (including Art and David), Robert associated earning a license and driving with the growth of intimate. Like David, Robert was articulate in describing how the rite of passage he experienced resulted in expanded social boundaries, increased freedom, and greater access to a shrinking world in terms of his expanding social network and elevated status.

Driving and Relationships

As hinted earlier, possessing a driver's license and driving also affected relationships, especially male-female dyads for the male participants. For example, 11 of the 17 male participants talked about how driving facilitated memorable social interactions with female companions. In contrast, only two of the 13 female participants recalled how motor vehicles facilitated, increased, or improved socialization with men. Instead of reminiscing about romantic relationships or driving to work, many female participants talked about driving memories that involved their immediate family members, such as their mothers, fathers, siblings, and grandparents. More than one-half of the female participants (*n*=7), for example, fondly recalled a time when their fathers or grandfathers taught them how to drive. Many grew up in an era when fathers acted as family patriarchs who prepared young women to assume the responsibilities that came with earning a driver's license and driving a motor vehicle (D'Emilio & Freedman, 1988).

Only one of the male participants reminisced about how an older male (his older brother) taught him how to drive. Perhaps it was prevalent for fathers or older brothers to teach their sons how to drive during this era; however, only one of the 17 male participants described having that experience. Ben, a 60-year-old black male who lived in an urban nursing home and reported to have had a stroke, reflected on the role his older brother played in his driver training. Ben's brother was apparently a father-figure to him. He described his brother as "*mean*," and then qualified (actually justified) it as "*what he knew was right*." Of all the memories that Ben could have identified, he chose to describe his brother's mentorship and role as his driving instructor as his "*most special*" driving memory.

As we have seen, both male and female participants discussed positive associations they had with obtaining a driver's license, as well as their early driving experiences. They often highlighted the fact that driving afforded them mobility across expanded geographical distances, which reinforced and enhanced interpersonal relationships that were meaningful to them. All but two of the participants (n=28) recalled at least one positive memory of their initial driving experiences. In fact, only five individuals recalled a stressful event in addition to the positive experiences they had when driving or riding in a motor vehicle or both. These five participants recalled experiences they deemed to be "*negative*" or "*stressful*," such as being involved in a car crash or being stranded by the side of the road after their vehicle had broken down. Associations with driving were predominantly positive, however, for most of the participants.

Vehicle Ownership

A key to understanding why most of the participants described their driving experiences in such a positive manner was that most of them (n=26) equated vehicle ownership with a personal sense of pride. Twenty-six participants reported that they were took pride in knowing that over the years they had previously owned (or later in their driving experiences leased) motor vehicles. Participants were asked if they could recall the first vehicle they had driven. Nearly two-thirds of the participants (n=19 or 11 men and eight women) were able to describe in detail the first car they had driven. They often described the person or people they were with when they first got behind the wheel, as well as the make and model of the first vehicle they had driven. Many participants also expressed a sense of pride and accomplishment when describing the first vehicle they owned.

Initial ownership was a greater milestone than driving for the first time for 11 of the participants (9 of 17 males and 2 of 13 females). These males appeared to enjoy describing in detail their first vehicles more than they enjoyed talking about obtaining a driver's license or their early driving memories. For example, Chris, a 72-year-old male who was widowed and living in an urban nursing home used the term "*beautiful*" and he did not simply describe the vehicle's color as '*blue*' but, instead, was specific in using the term "*metallic blue*." These descriptors indicated that Chris still cherished his memories of his first vehicle, which once played an important part in his life. Art equated the "good life" with owning and being able to afford multiple motor vehicles. For Art, multiple car ownership was tantamount to economic success. Ownership in general gave certain respondents some social status.

Social locations including race, location of residence, education level, and age did not influence whether or not the participants believed that the make and model of the vehicles they had driven inferred something about them to the wider society. Gender did make a difference, however. Almost one-third (n=9) of the participants did imagine that the types of vehicles they had driven influenced how others viewed them, but eight of these were men. Only one of the nine participants who felt this way believed that it affected his self-confidence or how he viewed himself as a "*man*" (e.g., whether he was fulfilling his roles and responsibilities successfully, such as commuting to and from work and chauffeuring his family while on vacation or to special events). The rest of the participants (n=21 or nine of the 17 men and 12 of the 13 women) expressed neutrality or no concern whatsoever with how others may or may not have viewed them as a result of the types of vehicles they had driven.

Past Driving Performance

In addition to vehicle ownership, more than two-thirds of the participants also talked about their past driving records (n=24), further illustrating the sense of pride they felt because they equated having a good driving record with being competent while behind the wheel of a motor vehicle. These participants believed they were '*very good*' or '*excellent*' drivers prior to their driving retirement. None of the participants felt that they were '*less than average*' or '*worse than other drivers.*' Driving records were another source of pride for many of the participants, similar to car ownership. They also took pride in knowing that they were once able to drive with a high degree of competence and had a driving record to prove it.

Driving and its Influence on Daily Life

For most Americans, consumption of automobiles satisfies a need for transportation, a need as basic as food, clothing, and shelter. The automobile has been and still is an indispensable method of transportation, as well as a personal and meaningful symbol of participation in mainstream American life (Berger, 2001). This symbol became solidified in both an American and Motor City culture within the 1940s and 50s (Berger, 2001) when these participants were either in early or mid-adulthood. Some participants (n=9) talked about the influence that cars had on people of their generations and how the automobile changed the daily lives of the average American, especially the average Detroiter and suburbanite, more than any other twentieth century innovation at the time (The Presidential Committee Report on the Impact of the Automobile, 1934).

Automobiles empowered people to move from place to place with speed, efficiency, reliability, and a personal style that was previously unavailable to the general public. Driving motor vehicles made popular pastimes that the participants' parents and grandparents enjoyed (e.g., walking and riding bicycles) essentially obsolete for both near and far community mobility. This was especially true for individuals and families that had the financial resources to purchase (and later lease) and maintain a motor vehicle. Detroit was the epicenter of motor vehicle development and manufacturing (Pellerito, 2006) and the automobile became an icon that symbolized more than efficient transportation. It projected personal taste, power, and status and helped to fuel rapid social change in Detroit and beyond (Berger, 2001). Xavier summed it up when he stated emphatically: "*In the Motor City, the car was king!*"

The fact that the participants once had access to a motor vehicle or vehicles influenced their daily habits, routines, and schedules. Just as bicycles and some forms of local mass transit (e.g., electric street cars) had empowered generations of Americans before the arrival of the automobile, cars offered the option to walk short community distances much less or even not at all. These and other cultural shifts were occurring in every urban area throughout most of the 20th century in the U.S., and Detroit's contributions were unique. Six of the participants specifically referred to Detroit as the "*Motor City*," a nick-name and term of endearment that became part of the American vernacular as a result of Detroit's role as the leading mass producer and distributor of motor vehicles in the world.

One respondent, Bill, took pride in both driving a Cadillac, but like many Detroiters, during the industrial boom, he was a part of the industrial complex that produced automobiles. His pride was evident and his perspective of the autos he was helping to build was that they were second to none. To drive a Cadillac meant, to Ben, that a man could be "*king of the hill*." Again this illustrated the power and control driving afforded many of the participants.

Victor, a 90-year-old male, who was remarried and living at home in an affluent suburban community remembered Detroit as a city that was once called the "*Golden City*." Victor was passionate about both his perceptions of the Motor City in a gone-by era and what he viewed as a city in decline today. Undoubtedly, his attitude about the current state of affairs in the city of Detroit was negatively affected after he was a victim of a violent car-jacking one year prior to this interview. I did not specifically ask any of the participants about driving and crime, but it was surprising that he was the only participant who initiated a story that associated driving with a violent crime that had been committed against him and his wife. Two armed assailants assaulted them in their suburban driveway and stole their vehicle. Fortunately they survived the attack and the perpetrators were later arrested; however, that event left an indelible mark on them and demarcated the point at which Victor stopped driving. The police recovered the stolen vehicle and it was eventually returned to Victor.

Only one other participant was overtly critical of the city of Detroit, and he had a great deal in common with Victor. Paul was a white male; he was 79-years-old, married, and living in an assisted living center in suburban Detroit. He was hoping to return to his suburban home to be with his wife, once he completed his rehabilitation program and his physical health and functional capacity improved. His residence was in the same affluent neighborhood where Victor and his wife lived. Theirs was a white, upper middle-class perspective that seemed to glorify a city they had experienced as younger men, but now saw as highly dysfunctional.

Another aspect of how motor vehicles influenced daily life and culture was described by three of the older participants who spoke about ways the automobile influenced the speed and efficiency by which city services were carried out. They recalled how cars and trucks led to an improvement in the quality of life, health, and well-being of the general population. Streets were cleaner and safer thanks to mechanized street cleaners and motorized police cars, fires were much less destructive because horse-drawn or steam-powered fire wagons were replaced with speedy and reliable gasoline-powered fire engines, and a person or animal with an injury or illness was better served thanks to ambulances and automobiles that transported sick and injured patients to hospitals and clinics post haste.

These participants lived through one of the country's rites of passage facilitated by a burgeoning transportation industry. While living in the Detroit Metropolitan area or the Motor City, they recognized the impact that motor vehicles had on everyone and everything around them. Irrespective of the situation, these participants acknowledged the fact that automobiles have played critical roles in helping people as they experienced life.

The Meanings of Driving Retirement

This section explores driving retirement in terms of when and how the participants stopped driving. Findings presented here also show how the participants responded to questions about what driving retirement meant to them. The central themes that were identified during data explication were gleaned from the following key questions: *"Was the participants' driving retirement voluntary or compulsory? Did the participants change their driving habits prior to their driving retirement, and were others involved in their decision to stop driving? Do they miss driving? Do the participants feel that they were viewed differently because they retired from driving?"* Each of these key questions or themes enabled me to continue building the conceptual model of driving and driving retirement.

Did the participants change their driving habits prior to driving retirement?

More than one-half of the participants (n=17) modified their driving behaviors prior to retiring from driving altogether. They limited or refrained from highway driving (n=6); drove fewer miles by selecting destinations that were considered more essential than others (n=7); drove only in familiar areas (n=6); and avoided driving at night (n=9) or during inclement weather (n=9).

One-half of the male participants (n=8) changed their driving habits prior to driving retirement, which was in contrast to nearly two-thirds of the female participants (n=9) who did so. Perhaps this is a slight indication that the females were less willing to take risks than their male counterparts. The nine women appeared to be more willing to trade the convenience and freedom that driving afforded them for a greater sense of safety as a result of altering their driving behaviors. This may mean that although both males and females talked about the freedom and independence that driving afforded them, they valued it differently.

Examples of ways in which participants modified their driving behaviors are as follows. Agnes was a 62-year-old, divorced black female, who was remarried and living in an urban nursing home. She described her declining health and the subsequent changes to her driving habits and routines prior to suffering a cerebrovascular accident (CVA). The CVA ultimately resulted in her retiring from driving. Agnes talked about modifying her driving behaviors as a result of her declining health and abilities. She was aware of the challenges posed not only by driving at night, but also any time of day when there was less than optimal light or too much light. Perhaps she was referring to the visual perceptual challenges that glare from the sun can pose for drivers of all ages.

Angie was a 70-year-old Native American female who was also married and living in an urban nursing home. She described the voluntary adjustments she made to her driving routines as the result of "leg problems" and other unspecified health-related challenges. Like Agnes, Angie described modifying her driving behaviors without reluctance. She was fully aware of her declining health and waning functional abilities and understood, albeit implicitly, the risks associated with driving continuance without modifying her behavior accordingly.

Contrary to the media's frequent portrayal of the elderly as being irresponsible and unwilling to modify their driving habits or retire from driving altogether (Detroit News and Free Press, 2005), these women believed that it was their responsibility to help ensure not only their own safety, but the safety and well-being of other road users as well. They accomplished this by self-regulating their driving behaviors. Art's decision to modify his driving behaviors (e.g., limiting his driving at night or in inclement weather) was, to a large extent, because he was aware of his declining functional capacity and subsequent performance limitations. Like Agnes, Angie, and the other participants who modified their driving behaviors, Art took responsibility for maintaining his safety and the safety of his passengers and other road users by modifying his driving behaviors and eventually retiring from driving altogether.

His perspective was in contrast to the female participants who seemed to be more accepting of their non-driver status. Some of the male participants were explicit in describing the negative outcomes they associated with modifying their driving behaviors initially and stopping driving eventually. Conversely just over one-half of the male participants (n=9), compared to only three female participants, did not modify their driving behaviors prior to driving retirement. For each of these participants, their retirement came abruptly because of either an emergent disabling condition due to illness (n=15) or a traumatic injury (n=2). Behaviors changed when the participants had concerns about their disabling medical conditions (e.g., diabetes mellitus, hip fracture, and stroke) and declining abilities. For these 21 participants, personal responsibility was a key factor in their decision-making.

Was the participant's driving retirement voluntary or compulsory and did they receive help in making their decisions?

Ten male participants voluntarily retired from driving versus seven men who experienced compulsory driving retirement. This was in sharp contrast to the female participants who overwhelmingly volunteered to give up their car keys (n=12) when they felt that they could no longer drive safely. Almost one-third of the sample, or four males and five females, talked about receiving others' assistance while transitioning from driving to driving retirement. The rest of the participants (n=21) described a decision-making process that was solitary and without the involvement of a professional (e.g., occupational therapist, physician, nurse), spouse, friend, or family member. This, of course, goes against public perception: most of the sample voluntarily and solitarily decided to retire.

Nearly all of the participants implicitly or explicitly contradicted the widespread reporting in the mainstream media that older Americans are unwilling to relinquish their keys, even at the expense of themselves and others because they would otherwise miss driving too intensely (Eby & Molnar, 2005). Data gathered from this project presents an alternative view of older Americans as a group, within the context of personal responsibility, successful aging, and driving retirement.

Participants revealed that they possessed key insights including the following: (1) they generally knew when it was time to stop driving, which was based on their understanding of their own diminished functional capacity and inability to drive a motor vehicle safely; (2) participants made the decision to stop driving without the help of others, such as their spouses, family members, or health care professionals (n=21); and (3) more than two-thirds of the participants voluntarily relinquished their driving privileges, irrespective of the potential or actual negative consequences (n=22).

Meanings of Driving

Driving and community mobility is a timeless topic. Modes of transportation may change, but transitions from being in control of one's mobility to becoming dependent on others for moving from location to location will not. Exploration of topics in this study followed phenomenological methodology to advance knowledge about the meanings of driving and how older women and men experience, interpret, and respond to driving retirement. This study also was conducted to understand and describe how social locations, such as gender, age, race, class, and place of residence impact these phenomena. By giving each of the participants a voice, both individually and collectively, via qualitative inquiry, the following study aim was addressed: Discover and describe the self-defined meanings of driving and driving retirement from gendered perspectives within the context of successful aging.

When given the opportunity, elders can effectively articulate self-defined meanings of driving and driving retirement. A theoretical or conceptual model of driving was constructed through phenomenological data explication. Explication included engaging the participants during the review process to ensure the conceptual model reflected their lived experiences. The conceptual model establishes a construct-focused framework for understanding the constellation of lived experiences the participants associated with driving and driving retirement.

Acquiring a driver's license marked a kind of rite of passage that afforded each of the participants the privileged status of becoming a driver. Driving marked a passage or transition between childhood and adulthood and impacted their lives in numerous ways. Driving improved community mobility, fostered a sense of freedom and pride, improved social status, bolstered new relationships for a more robust social life, and enabled an efficient mode of transportation that enabled them to engage in work, leisure, and self-care activities. Memories of vehicle ownership and past driving records also were described as meaningful by the participants in this sample because of the importance they attached to driving in general.

Males placed greater importance on licensure and vehicle ownership than women in this sample. They especially valued the first cars they drove, as well as the first vehicles they purchased. When compared to women, men also placed more weight on vehicle ownership than either acquiring a driver's license or reminiscing about early driving experiences. It was both the male and female participants, however, who associated driver licensure and driving with personal freedom, pride, maturation, and elevated or improved social status. Possessing a driver's license and driving also helped to reinforce existing relationships and foster new ones for both men and women in the sample.

The males in the sample asserted that driving facilitated relationships with female peers by giving them opportunities to develop romantic ties. Female interviewees, on the other hand, were more prone than men to talk about how driving helped to reinforce familial ties (e.g., they described happy memories of being taught to drive by their fathers or older brothers). Male and female participants believed that community mobility was made easier and more efficient because motor vehicles surpassed all other modes of transportation in terms of speed, privacy, and flexibility. The men remembered themselves as drivers, while the women recalled filling the roles of both drivers and passengers. Past driving records were a source of pride for men and women when they were void of traffic tickets, moving violations, and vehicular crashes.

Participants also associated driving with having fun with friends and family.

Aging was not identified as a factor and not associated with declining health by any of the participants. More males (n=13 of 17) than females (n=7 of 13) denied seeing themselves as old or aging, and most participants did not associate old age with driving retirement. Instead, participants overwhelmingly believed that disabling health conditions; that is, their physical health status led to driving retirement. One of the most interesting findings in this study, then, is the fact that participants in this study did not link driving retirement to aging. Participants saw the aging process as separate from the process of retiring from driving, and did not even make direct links between declining physical health and aging.

None of the participants in this sample received assistance from a professional caregiver in planning for or implementing their decision to retire from driving or both. Only four men and five women were helped by a friend or family member to stop driving as compared to 13 men and eight women who received no help whatsoever. This finding goes against our popular culture's image of physicians or driver rehabilitation specialists assisting clients with planning for and contending with driving retirement.

Although driving retirement planning should be a component of any comprehensive driver rehabilitation and community mobility program (Pellerito, 2006), it was apparent that none of the participants had access to facilities that offered these programs. Only one of the participants was reported as an unsafe driver to the State of Michigan's DMV. More than two-thirds of the participants, 11 men and nine women, stated that they missed driving. Finally, nine of the 17 men and three of the 13 women believed that they were viewed differently because they stopped driving. This was in contrast to eight men and 10 women who either did not believe or did not care that others' perceptions of them had changed for the worse.

Conclusion

Driving retirement in Michigan and nationally is very poorly understood due to an absence of systematically collected qualitative and quantitative population-based data. To my knowledge, no local, state, or national agency has ever collected such information in any comprehensive way. Future research initiatives could continue the process of gathering qualitative data but also begin gathering quantitative data systematically, to permit the development of the following:

(1) Greater understanding of the meanings and experiences of driving and driving retirement within the context of our larger social world

(2) Effective interactions with different groups of individuals as they retire (or contemplate retiring) from driving, within hospitals and health centers, among doctors, family members and friends

(3) Specific recommendations to guide professionals assisting individuals and caregivers affected by driving retirement after a disabling injury, illness, or because of the aging process

(4) A comprehensive database of older men and women affected by driving retirement in the Detroit Metropolitan area with the potential to become the state and national database template

(5) Recommendations for implementing standardized guidelines for re-licensing drivers as well as renewing insurance coverage and registration of motor vehicles for older drivers. Research could inform us about how standardized policies and procedures should be developed and implemented to maximize consumer engagement, which could lead to routine and standardized collection, analysis, and dissemination of traffic safety data with an emphasis on improving safety and enhancing health and well-being among people with disabilities, the elderly, and the general public.

For social psychologists and health care workers, the car culture's influence on social networks or the impact that driving retirement has on social and community relationships might be of interest. Further, influence of driving retirement in social and community relationships also may be relevant. For researchers studying successful aging, participant perceptions of aging and ill health within the context of driving retirement may be instructive.

This study attempts to advance knowledge and understanding of the meanings of driving, as a meaningful activity, and driving retirement, as a milestone event in the lives of older men and women. Everyone will continue to grow old and face challenges that spring from the tensions that arise between our awareness of who we were, who we are, and who we may eventually become. We begin our lives dependent for our mobility. We will come full circle through many wonderful transitions, where independence waxes before it wanes in time with old age or ill health or both. Very few will be fortunate to possess the right genetic make-up and experience the environmental influences that mitigate the eroding influence that time has on health, well-being, and productivity; most will not be so fortunate. As we grapple with these and other sobering realities, perhaps we will learn to listen to our elders, so that we can gain the insight that is necessary to discover new ways of defining what it truly means to age successfully and possess quality of life.

References

Aging News Alert (October 24, 2000). *Fatalities Rise among Older Drivers*. Silver Spring, MD: CD Publications. p. 11.

Albert, M. S., Jones, K., Savage, C. R., Berkman, L., Seeman, T., Blazer, D., et al. (1995). Predictors of Cognitive Change in Older Persons: The MacArthur Studies of Successful Aging. *Psychology and Aging*, 10, 578-589.

Andrews, F. M., & Withey, S. B. (1976). *Social Indicators of Well-being: America's Perception of Life Quality*. New York, NY: Plenum Press.

Anson, C. A., Stanwyck, D., & Krause, J. (1993). Social Support and Health Status in Spinal Cord Injury. *Paraplegia, 31,* 632-638.

Baltes, P. B. & Baltes, M. M. (Eds.) (1990). *Successful Ageing: Perspectives from the Behavioral Sciences*. New York, NY: Cambridge University Press.

Bedard, M., Molloy, D. W., & Lever, J. A. (1998). Factors Associated with Motor Vehicle Crashes in Cognitively Impaired Older Adults. *Alzheimer's Disease and Associated Disorders 12 (3),* 135-139.

Berger, M. L. (2001). *The Automobile in American History and Culture: A Reference Guide*. Westport, CT: Greenwood.

Burkhardt, J., Berger, A.M., & McGavock, A.T. (1996). The Mobility Consequences of the Reduction or Cessation of Driving by Older Women. In S. Rosenbloom (Ed.), *Proceedings from the Second NationalCconference on Women's Travel Issues*. Washington, DC: Federal Highway Administration, US Department of Transportation.

Carr, D. (1993). Assessing Older Drivers for Physical and Cognitive Impairment. *Geriatrics. 48*, 46-51.

Charmaz, K. (2006). *Constructing Grounded Theory: A Practical Guide through Qualitative Analysis.* London, ON: Sage.

Cooley, C.H. (1964). *Human Nature and the Social Order.* New York, NY: Schocken.

Cooley, C.H. (1902). *Human Nature and the Social Order.* New York, NY: Charles Scribner's Sons.

Coser, L. A. (1971). *Masters of Sociological Thought: Ideas in Historical and Social Contex*t. Orlando, FL: Harcourt Brace Jovanovich.

Cremin, M. (1992). Feeling Old versus being Old: Views of Troubled Aging. *Social Science & Medicine, 34(12),* 1305-1315.

Creswell, J. W. (1998). *Qualitative Inquiry and Research Design: Choosing among Five Traditions.* Thousand Oaks, CA: Sage.

Cynkin, S., & Robinson A. M. (1990). *Occupational Therapy and Activities Health: Towards Health through Activities.* Boston, MA: Little, Brown.

Davey, J. & Nimmo, K. (2003). *Older People and Transport.* Wellington, New Zealand: Institute of Research on Aging, Victoria University, for LTSA and MOT.

D'Emilio, J., & Freedman, E. B. (1988). *Intimate Matters: A History of Sexuality in America.* New York, NY: Harper & Row Publishers.

Eby, D. W., & Molnar, L. J., (2005). Self-screening by Older Drivers. *Public Policy & Aging Report, 15,* 18-20.

Ferrans, C., & Powers, M. (1992). Psychometric Assessment of the Quality of Life Index. *Research in Nursing and Health, 15,* 29-38.

Flanagan, J. C. (1982). Measurement of Quality of Life: Current State of the Art. *Arch Phys Med Rehabil, 63(2),* 56-59.

Foley, D. J., Masaki, K. H., Ross, G. W., & White, L. R. (2000). Driving Cessation in Older Men with Incident Dementia. *Journal of the American Geriatrics Society, 48,* 928-930.

Frank, G. (1996). Life Histories in Occupational Therapy Clinical Practice. *The American Journal of Occupational Therapy, 50,* 251-264.

Freund, B., & Szinovacz, M. (2002). Effects of Cognition on Driving Involvement among the Oldest Old: Variations by Gender and Alternative Transportation Opportunities. *The Gerontologist, 42*(5), 621-633.

Galski, T., Bruno, R. L., & Ehle, H. T. (1992). Driving after Cerebral Damage: A Model with Implications for Evaluation. *American Journal of Occupational Therapy, 46(4)*, 324-332.

Gannon, L. (1999). *Women and Aging: Transcending the Myths.* New York, NY: Routledge.

Gillins, L. (1990). Yielding to Age: When the Elderly can no Longer Drive. *Journal of Gerontological Nursing, 16*, 12-15.

Gourgey, C. (1994). From Weakness to Strength: A Spiritual Response to Disability. *Journal of Disability Rehabilitation, 1*, 69-80.

Hesse-Biber, S. N., & Leavy, P. (2004). *Approaches to Qualitative Research.* New York, NY: Oxford University Press.

Hui-Chuan, H. (2007). Exploring the Elderly People's Perspectives on Successful Aging in Taiwan. *Aging & Society, 27*, 87-102.

Jette, A. M. & Branch, L. (1992). A Ten Year Follow-up of Driving Patterns among the Community-dwelling Elderly. *Human Factors, 34(1)*, 25-31.

Johnson, J. E. (1995). Rural Elders and the Decision to Stop Driving. *Journal of Community Health Nursing, 12(3)*, 131-138.

Kalz, R. T., Golden, R. S., Butler, J., Tepper, D., Rothke, S., Holmes, J., et al. (1990). Driving Safely after Brain Damage: Follow up of 22 Patients with Matched Controls. *Archives of Physical Medicine and Rehabilitation, 71*, 133-137.

Katz, S., & Marshall, B. (2003). New Sex for Old: Lifestyle, Consumerism, and the Ethics of Aging Well. *Journal of Aging Studies, 17(1)*, 3-16.

Kaufman, G., & Elder Jr., G. (2002). Revisiting Age Identity: A Research Note. *Journal of Aging Studies, 16*, 169-176.

Kington, R., Reuben, D., Rogowski, J., & Lillard, L. (1994). Sociodemographic and Health Factors in Driving Patterns after 50 years of age. *American Journal of Public Health, 84*, 1324-1329.

Kleinman, A. (1988). *The Illness Narratives: Suffering, Healing, and the Human Condition.* New York: Basic Books.

Kleinman, A. (1992). Local Worlds of Suffering: An Interpersonal Focus for Ethnographies of Illness Experience. *Qualitative Health Research, 2*, 127-134.

Korner-Bitensky, N., Sofer, S., Kaizer, F., Gelinas, I. & Talbot, L. (1994). Assessing Ability to Drive Following an Acute Neurological Event: Are we on the Right Road? *Canadian Journal of Occupational Therapy, 61*, 141-148.

Kulash, D. (2000). *Safe Mobility for a Maturing Society: A strategic plan and national agenda.* Originally presented as proceedings from the International Conference, Transportation in an Aging Society: A Decade of Experience, November 1999.

Laz, C. (2003). Age Embodied. *Journal of Aging Studies, 17(4),* 503-519.

Legh-Smith, J., Wade, D. T., & Hewer, R. L. (1986). Driving after a Stroke. *Journal of the Royal Society of Medicine, 79,* 200-203.

Lister, R. (1999). Loss of Ability to Drive following a Stroke: The Early Experiences of Three Elderly People on Discharge from Hospital. *British Journal of Occupational Therapy, 62,* 514–520.

Luborsky, M. (1995). The Process of Self-report of Impairment in Clinical Research. *Social Science and Medicine, 40(11),* 1447-1459.

Luborsky, M. & Rubinstein, R. (1995). Sampling in Qualitative Research: Rationales, Issues, and Methods. *Research on Aging, 17(1)* 89-113.

Luborsky, M. (1994b). The Cultural Adversity of Physical Disability: Erosion of Full Adult Personhood. *Journal of Aging Studies, 8,* 239-253.

Luborsky, M. R. (1994a). Identification and Analysis of Themes and Patterns. In J. Gubrium & A. Sankar (Eds.), *Qualitative Methods in Aging Research* (p. 189-210). Thousand Oaks, CA: Sage.

Luborsky, M. (1993). The Identification and Analyses of Themes and Patterns. In J. Gubrium, & A. Sankar (Eds.), *Qualitative Methods in Aging Research.* New York, NY: Sage Publications.

Lysack, C., & Seipke, H. (2002). Communicating the Occupational Self: A Qualitative Analysis of Oldest Old American Women. *Scandinavian Journal of Occupational Therapy, 9,* 130-139.

McCall, G. J., & Simmons, J. L. (1966). *Identities and Interaction.* New York, NY: Free Press.

Mead, G. H. (1934). *Mind, Self, and Society.* Chicago, IL: The University of Chicago Press.

Molnar, L. J., Eby, D. W., & Miller, L. L. (2003). *Promising Approaches for Enhancing Elderly Mobility.* Ann Arbor, MI: University of Michigan Transportation Research Institute.

O'Neill, D. (1992). Physicians, Elderly Drivers, and Dementia. *Lancet.* 2, 99-104.

Pellerito, J. M. (Ed). (2006). *Driver Rehabilitation and Community Mobility: Principles and Practice.* St. Louis, MO: Elsevier Mosby.

Ranney, T. A., & Hunt, L. A. (1997). Researchers and Occupational Therapists can Help each Other to Better Understand What Makes a Good Driver: Two Perspectives. *Work: A Journal of Prevention, Assessment & Rehabilitation, 8,* 293-297.

Reuben, D. B. Silliman, R. A. & Traines, M. (1988). The Aging Driver: Medicine, Policy and Ethics. *J Am Geriat Soc, 36,* 1135-1142.

Rosenbloom, S. (1993). Transportation Needs of the Elderly Population. *Clinics in Geriatric Medicine, 9,* 297-310.

Rowe, J. W., & Kahn, R. L. (1997). Successful Aging. *The Gerontologist, 37,* 433-440.

Scheer, J., & Luborsky, M. (1991). Post-polio Sequelae: The Cultural Context of Polio Biographies. *Orthopedics, 14,* 1173-1181.

Spradley, J. (1979). *The Ethnographic Interview.* New York, NY: Holt.

Strauss, A, & Corbin, J. (1998) *Basics of Qualitative Research. Techniques and Procedures for Developing Grounded Theory, 2nd ed.* Newbury Park, CA: Sage Publications, Inc.

Strauss, A., & Corbin, J. (1990a). *Basics of Qualitative Research.* Newbury Park: Sage Publications, Inc.

Stubbins, J. (1977). *Social and Psychological Aspects of Disability: What about Leisure?* Baltimore, OR: University Park Press.

U.S. Department of Transportation. (2003). *Safe Mobility for a Maturing Society: Challenges and Opportunities.* Washington, DC: Government Printing Office.

U.S. Department of Commerce, Economics and Statistics Administration. (1995). *Statistical Abstract of the U.S.* 115th ed. Washington, DC, Bureau of the Census.

U.S. Department of Health and Human Services (1991). *Bound for Good Health: A Collection of Age Pages.* Bethesda, MD: National Institute on Aging.

Underwood, M. (1992). The Older Driver: Clinical Assessment and Injury Prevention. *Archives of Internal Medicine, 152(4),* 735-740.

Victor, C. (1994). *Old Age in Modern Society, 2nd ed.* London: Chapman and Hall.

Williams, A. F. & Carsten, O. (1989). Driver age and Crash Involvement. *American Journal Public Health, 79:* 326-327.

World Health Organization. (2002). *Active aging: A Policy Framework.* Geneva, Switzerland: WHO.

CHAPTER 5
THE ROLE OF THE AUTOMOBILE IN AMERICAN CULTURE

Joseph M. Pellerito, Jr., Frank Tridico and Catherine Lysack

Abstract: The value of the automobile to American culture has shifted from basic transportation to a myriad of symbolism which includes social status, freedom, and identity. The cultural transition of automobility from privilege to right is paramount in understanding its link to individual autonomy. This chapter focuses on the historical context and cultural synthesis of the role the automobile has had in American culture. Through social integration, entrenched values in society over generations helps define 'fundamental rights.' Limitations to mobility may serve to broaden marginalization of sectors of society that are already disenfranchised. If mobility is considered a fundamental right, its inaccessibility may be perceived as a denied fundamental right. Perceived marginalization becomes more powerful than actual disenfranchisement because of the cultural framework with which it operates within. As such, limitations to automobility serve as hindrances to individual autonomy, social integration and self-actualization.

The Meaning of 'Fundamental Rights'

The United States Constitution can be examined in three distinct areas: (1) Articles I-VII, (2) Amendments 1-10 (also known as the Bill of Rights), and (2) Amendments 11-27. Articles I-VII account for specific limitations to State power vis-à-vis executive, legislative and judicial branches. The Founding Fathers imposed limits to prevent potential abuses or collusion from those with access to power. The Bill of Rights went beyond limitations, and specified fundamental rights of the individual (e.g., First Amendment's freedom of religion, press and expression, Fourth Amendment's protection from search and seizure, etc.). Amendments 11-27 were passed after the adoption of the Constitution to account for new rights not clarified therein (e.g., 14th Amendment's citizenship rights) and Constitutional changes to strike down laws that violated definitions of inherent rights (e.g., 13th Amendment abolishing slavery and 15th Amendment forbidding race to be a factor in voting).

What becomes clear in Constitutional discourse is that the concept of *'rights'* is not necessarily entrenched in law. Laws are declarations of acceptable and unacceptable behavior, subject to enforcement by the State. Rights which may not be protected by law may still be inherent within the Constitution. Rights are also subject to the interpretation of Justices, who use the Constitution as a basis for deciding cases. Landmark cases then are used as precedent, where future similar cases are examined in accordance to past cases. Hence, the concept of *'rights'* is subject to external oversight, external interpretation and external power.

The Ninth Amendment of the U.S. Constitution states *"The enumeration in the Constitution, of certain rights, shall not be construed to deny or disparage others retained by the people."* While it has rarely been used in jurisprudence, it has been subject to usage to rationalize and legitimize ideological positions. This can be found in some Supreme Court Justices asserting that the Ninth Amendment is relevant to interpret the Fourteenth Amendment. Justice Goldberg (joined by Chief Justice Warren and Justice Brennan) juxtaposed this in *Griswold v. Connecticut* (1965) which invalidated Connecticut law that prohibited the use of contraceptives for married couples:

> *"The Framers did not intend that the first eight amendments be construed to exhaust the basic and fundamental rights... do not mean to imply that the...Ninth Amendment constitutes an independent source of rights protected from infringement by either the states or the federal government...While the Ninth Amendment - and indeed the entire Bill of Rights - originally concerned restrictions upon federal power, the subsequently enacted Fourteenth Amendment prohibits the states as well from abridging fundamental personal liberties. And, the Ninth Amendment, in indicating that not all such liberties are specifically mentioned in the first eight amendments, is surely relevant in showing the existence of other fundamental personal rights, now protected from state, as well as federal, infringement."*

In *Eisenstadt v. Baird* (1972), this *interpretation* of the Equal Protection Clause of the Fourteenth Amendment extended *privacy* rights for usage of contraceptives from married to unmarried couples.

Since Griswold, some Justices have tried to use the Ninth Amendment to legitimize enforcing rights that are not specifically enumerated. For example, in *Roe v. Wade* (1973), the District Court heard that the Ninth Amendment secured an individual's right to have an abortion. Not all agreed with this view. *Roe* itself was granted primarily on privacy rights found to be within the Fourteenth Amendment even though the Constitution itself doesn't specifically account for privacy other than in a limited role within the Fourth Amendment.

The Ninth Amendment was added to the Bill of Rights to ensure that fundamental rights were not denied because they were not specifically enumerated in the Constitution. The discourse moves full circle to the concept of *'fundamental rights'*. What are fundamental rights? If they are fundamental why aren't they found within the document itself? Why do they need to be interpreted? Further, do rights become *'fundamental'* over time through shared norms or culture?

The Presidential Committee Report on the Impact of the Automobile (1934) stated *"It is probable that no invention...so quickly exerted influences that ramified through the national culture, transforming even habits of thought and language."*

Our consumption of automobiles satisfies a real need for transportation, a need as basic as food, clothing, and shelter, but this need has changed as the social and spatial patterns of American culture have changed.

To fully assess the integrated symbolism, meaning and value of the automobile to culture, it must be analyzed through an historical lens. This chapter examines the automobile as a historically situated form of transportation, one appropriate to a particular stage in capitalist development. We also suggest that the automobile was and continues to be simultaneously a *cause* and *consequence* of the rise of consumerism. This chapter discusses how the automobile came to be this indispensable method of transportation and a personal and meaningful symbol of what it means to participate fully in mainstream American life.

It is however, important to discern that entrenched values in society over generations helps define *'fundamental rights.'* The value of the automobile to American culture has shifted from basic transportation to a myriad of symbolism which includes *social status*, *freedom*, and *identity*. Access to mobility, thus, enhances social integration. Conversely, restrictions to mobility may serve to broaden marginalization of sectors of society that are already disenfranchised. Where economic disparity limits mobility, individuals are not only denied access to the tangible component of the automobile, but the cultural symbol that underlies it. If mobility is considered a fundamental right, is inaccessibility to mobility a denied fundamental right?

The Distant Past and Themes of Mobility, Movement, and Progress

Throughout history civilizations have advanced in part by trading ideas, goods, and services. Transportation methods have thus been central to the continiuty of cultures. Rich oral traditions and detailed written histories have emphasized accounts of efficient and even supernatural mobility as central themes within traditional stories meant to be instructive and edifying for members of the community. Examples include, but are not limited to:

(1) the pioneers crossing the uncharted and sometimes hostile American frontier during the nineteenth century
(2) the Underground Railroad in North America that featured covert escape routes and support systems for enslaved African Americans and the abolitionists who opposed the cruelties associated with the slave trade during an era that saw a nation deeply divided and at war with itself
(3) the wave of immigrants who left Europe in masses during the late 19th century and throughout the first half of the 20th century, crossing the Atlantic Ocean with minimal personal and financial resources in hopes of finding a better life in North America; and finally the creation and refinement of the assembly line that not only revolutionized how motor vehicles are built, but countless other products as well

Moreover, the critical role efficient mobility has played throughout history and today is evident when examining how a person's life can depend on the speed and efficiency of public officials expeditiously arriving on the scene of an accident in order to intervene and ameliorate personal and public emergencies (e.g., an ambulance driver responding to motor vehicle crashes and firefighters to a forest or building fire). The critical role played by efficient mobility is also highlighted when one reflects on the many amazing structures and mobility systems that have been constructed throughout time, including the Great Pyramids,

Stonehenge, the International Space Station, and the Autobahn, to name a few. These timeless symbols of humankind's ingenuity are also a testament to the efficient and purposeful movement of people and materials in extraordinary ways.

The Emergence of an American Car Culture

Just as mobility has been instrumental in helping to ensure the survival of sentient and unconscious creatures throughout time, community mobility, in the form of driving a motor vehicle, has also been a critical aspect of contemporary society. Perhaps no invention in modern history has had a more profound influence on how people work and persue leisure activities than the automobiles and the infrastructure that supports it.

Despite the vast array of scholarship on the topic of the automobile and its many dimensions, there is disagreement on the origins of the automobile itself. For example, many people still debate whether the automobile was invented in Europe or the United States. It is generally accepted, however, that the drive, ingenuity, strength, and perseverance of the American inventors, designers, industrialists, and autoworkers ensured that the automobile would become a global phenomenon (Olson & Cabadas, 2002).

The automobile has changed the lifestyle of the average American more than any other 20th Century innovation with the possible exception of television and perhaps computers and information technology. It has brought a flexible and individual form of transportation that makes everything from employment to leisure time pursuits easier and more enjoyable than it has ever been.

Moving from place to place with greater speed and efficiency has affected how and where people live, work, and spend their leisure time activities. In a gone-by era trolleys powered by electricity enabled urban centers to expand into suburbia; however, it was the automobile that afforded people and commodities to move from place to place more efficiently and according to individual schedules (Sandler, 2003). Coal- and wood-burning steam locomotives moved large numbers of people vast distances across rivers, over flat prairie lands, and even directly through mountains that resulted in a network of railways crossing continents and connecting East and West and North and South, as well as rural with urban and suburban areas throughout North America and wherever there was land, people, and industrialization.

However, railroads eventually gave way to the automobile because automobiles powered by the internal combustion engines eventually outpaced walking, running, bicycles, horse-drawn carriages, and steam- and electric-powered vehicles. Under the right circumstances, automobiles could meet and exceed speeds attained by some locomotive trains, and automobiles were able to gain acceleration faster from a standstill. The burgeoning infrastructure, that supported the automobile, empowered persons to move from place to place with speed, efficiency, reliability, and a personal style that was previously unavailable to the general public. All of this was accomplished because the automobile enabled individuals to choose when and where to move based on their self-determined schedules versus depending on a predetermined and often unreliable train schedule or restricted by the limitations in speed and distance that were associated with the horse and carriage, or even the earlier steam - or electric-powered vehicles.

The reasons why the automobile has assumed such a central place in the lives of Americans is complex, but it can be argued that at least two broad cultural beliefs helped to propel the ascendancy of the automobile to the heights it has attained today. These cultural beliefs go well beyond the practical advantages of horse-drawn carriages of the past and the numerous types of trolleys, buses, and trains that have been transporting people and things for more than a century. These are (1) the belief in the power of science and technology to bring progress and improvement for all in society; and (2) the individually held belief that through personal freedom and independence all individuals can achieve the American Dream (or some semblance of it). Both are powerful metaphors in the story of the automobile in American life.

Science and Technology

Vast infrastructure projects undertaken by the government provided major labor opportunities to assist America out of the Great Depression. The ensuing network of superhighways transformed the economy nationally and locally. Industry and manufacturing jobs brought wealth to average Americans during this period, but the shape of work life and commerce, not to mention family life, were radically reorganized to be accessible by automobile. The cultural view of the time was that '*good old American know-how'* could be applied to most any economic or social enterprise, and the result would be successful. There was an optimism that abounded, and a myriad of scientific discoveries and technologic innovations were made in arenas as diverse as medical treatments to kitchen appliances. At the foundation of this thinking was the belief that progress was possible through science. This sense of scientific optimism has fueled the automotive industry since its inception.

Freedom and Independence

The second broad cultural belief was that through personal freedom and independence all individuals could achieve the American Dream. The substance of that dream is found in the Declaration of Independence: *"We hold these truths to be self-evident, that all men are created equal, that they are endowed by God, Creator, with certain inalienable Rights, that among these are Life, Liberty, and the pursuit of Happiness."* The American Dream meant hope: an unshakable belief that happiness and security were truly possible for anyone who pursued it. There was an internalized contention that whether native born or immigrant, individuals were afforded a unique opportunity to make a better life for themselves, their families, and broader communities (e.g., Little Italy in New York City, Chinatown in San Francisco, and other ethnic cleavages in the United States). The automobile assumed a critical place in the American Dream because it helped foster personal freedom and independence.

Over time, automobiles have represented much more than convenient transportation; however; cars, and more recently trucks and recreational vehicles, are a status symbol. The type of car a person could afford and then the style chosen communicated status. In this way the automobile became a symbol of success, much like owning a house. If one worked hard enough, everything, including a beautiful house in the suburbs and a fine automobile with a garage, would be the reward. A car in the driveway was a tangible statement to one's community that they belonged in the mainstream of American life, and the brand and model type, such as a luxury or sports car, often helped to place an exclamation point on that statement.

The Automobile in the Early Twentieth Century

The early twentieth century ushered in a new era that was fueled by the public's imagination and desire for efficient and speedy land transportation. The aspirations of the inventors and industrialists who shaped the automotive culture changed the landscape of America and the world forever. The *cultural lag* (e.g., technological advances often have unforeseen negative consequences, such as the need for increasingly sophisticated safety devices in cars and trucks to reduce injuries and fatalities) that came about reflected an industry that addressed issues pertaining to driver, passenger, and pedestrian safety, negative environmental consequences, and vehicle reliability as an afterthought and only when the public demanded greater accountability. Industrialists driven by a vision of widespread adoption of motor vehicles had to be willing and able to adapt to the changing needs of the growing worker and consumer bases. Building increasingly reliable, safe, and affordable motor vehicles ultimately helped capture the public's collective imagination, win their trust, and most importantly, their belief that the benefits associated with motor vehicles outweighed the costs.

One of the most influential figures in automotive history was Henry Ford. He offered the world more than a vision of ingenuity and a blueprint for a profitable automotive manufacturer. He influenced the methods and means of production that helped drive the industrial revolution and pave the way for workers on assembly lines in the United States and eventually around the world to afford the cars they were building with an investment of sweat, energy, and determination. Workers' pride was associated with sound workmanship and ownership. The impact of motor vehicles on public life also was pronounced in other ways.

The automobile soon influenced the speed and efficiency in which city services were carried out, leading to an improved quality of life, health, and well-being of the general population. Streets were cleaner and safer thanks to mechanized street cleaners and motorized police cars; fires were much less destructive because the horse-drawn or steam-powered fire wagons were replaced with speedy and reliable gasoline-powered rigs; and a person or animal with an injury or illness was better served thanks to ambulances and automobiles that transported sick and injured patients to hospitals and clinics or brought professionals to the patients in any number of diverse locations within a community or the outlying rural countryside. Irrespective of the situation, from transporting a pregnant woman in an ambulance to the hospital or carrying the deceased in a hearse to a cemetery, automobiles have played a key role in helping people as they experience what are often considered to be defining moments in any person's life.

Henry Ford: An Industrial Giant and Forbearer of the Emerging Car Culture

One name that is synonymous with serving as a catalyst in cultivating the seeds of a car culture when the auto industry was in its infancy is Henry Ford. Ford did not invent the automobile, design the internal combustion engine, or originate the creative and revolutionary methods of assembling automobiles on wheeled platforms that resulted in a quantum leap toward greater work efficiency and ultimately to the efficient and profitable mass production of automobiles. It was his competitor Ransom E. Olds who first introduced mass-production techniques after he founded the Olds Motor Works in 1899 in Detroit, Michigan (Sandler, 2003). However, Henry Ford is responsible for something much more important than achieving any of these early and important automotive milestones; he built the most popular car in history and improved on the mass-production techniques that were initially pioneered by Olds. By moving parts along a conveyor belt, Ford was able to maximize efficiency that led to greater output. It was these production methods that perhaps first exemplified ergonomic and human factor principles being efficiently applied in the industrial work setting.

Most importantly Ford paid his Ford Motor Company employees who were working on the assembly line a wage that enabled them to purchase the products they were building. The five dollar per day wage was a bold and revolutionary step taken by Ford that affected worker retention, loyalty, and empowerment that continues to influence modern labor relations and consumer spending. Henry Ford, like Olds, was a visionary who understood that once automobiles were affordable for the average citizen, they would radically alter the ways in which people moved within and between communities (Sandler, 2003). Ford wrote that he would build an automobile that would be an important staple in North American culture, and economically accessible (Ford, 2003).

The Model T fulfilled Ford's goal and set the industry standard because most adults could drive it and maintain it with minimal skills and resources. The Model T provided its owner with a strong and durable chassis that was mounted higher than the vehicles that were being built by other manufacturers competing for the finite number of buyers at that time. The Model T's higher profile helped its owner to traverse the poorly maintained dirt roads, cow pastures, dry riverbeds, and any number of other pathways that were not initially designed with automobiles in mind. Given that there were no dedicated automotive garages complete with certified automotive mechanics, owners of the Model T had to make any needed repairs themselves, and parts for the car could soon be found in 'five-and-ten cent' stores throughout the country. It was not long before roads and bridges were expanding at an exponential rate to support the growing numbers of motorists who had given up their horse-drawn carriages, bicycles, steamships, and trains as their preferred methods of community mobility.

Henry Ford and the other industrial giants may have influenced American culture and the economy of the early 20th century more than anyone else working within the private sector. Ford was an individual with vision and imagination that transformed not only American culture and economy but also forever impacted how people around the world move from place to place. Perhaps his greatest achievements were paying his workers a wage that enabled them to purchase the products they were creating and offering those high-quality products at an accessible price to the general population, which moved them closer to realizing the American Dream. Although Henry Ford could not have imagined all of the ways his vision has impacted American culture, there is no question that he has left an indelible mark on global transportation for decades to come.

The American Dream after World War II: From Factories to Suburbs

The impact of the automobile was felt most acutely after World War II. The economic boom years after World War II provided a growing middle class eager to buy a car and buy into the American Dream. In addition, vast regions of the country were suddenly accessible to the average American through a system of new interstate highways that extended personal travel over greater distances than ever before. Technologic developments of this time also made cars more comfortable and stylish. The automobile was therefore useful and efficient for commuting from home in the suburbs to work in the city. In time the automobile became the primary means by which families spent their leisure time. Although air travel has transformed personal travel over longer distances, the automobile nonetheless remains an overwhelmingly practical method of transportation and a symbol of personal success.

The motorcar was one of the major contributors if not *the* major contributor to suburbanization of America during the years 1920 to 1960. By sheer force of numbers, utility, and aesthetic appeal the automobile irrevocably transformed the geographic and socioeconomic landscape. In 1900, there were only 8,000 cars in the entire country, owned naturally enough by the very rich. However, by 1925, a new Model T was rolling off the assembly line every 15 seconds, and by 1930 there were 26 million cars used by about one-half the U.S. population. Today, estimates account for more cars on the road in the United States than there are Americans under the age of 21. Indeed, there is a registered automobile for every 1.3 persons in the United States, and the average American household has twice as many vehicles than it does children under the age of 20 (Wachs & Crawford, 1992). In 2003, it was reported in *Salon* magazine that there were 107 million U.S. households, each with an average of 1.9 cars, trucks, or sport utility vehicles (SUVs) and 1.8 drivers. That equaled 204 million vehicles and 191 million drivers (Miller, 2003).

In large part, the explosion of automobile ownership owes a debt of gratitude to Henry Ford's use of standardized parts and the widespread adoption of his revolutionary production methods such as the assembly line. This meant the purchase price of a car decreased even as wages increased throughout the country. Before World War I, an automobile cost the average American worker the equivalent of 24 months' wages. By the late 1920s, a vehicle could be purchased for about three months' wages (Berger, 2001). However, since then the cost of automobiles has increased significantly in conjunction with American's demands for bigger and more comfortable cars. The automobile industry estimates the average car today is purchased for about $25,000. This represents far more than 3 months' wages. This accounts for an internalized relationship between individuals and automobiles that exceeds financial cost.

Suburbanization: A Transformation in American Life

The force of suburbanization has significantly reshaped American work and leisure. The 1950s and 1960s saw the birth of a new class of professional and managerial workers. Likewise, the economy saw a transformation from industrial labor and blue-collar jobs to white-collar professional and management jobs. This new class of worker was distributed among the various strata of the corporation to transmit instructions and information and to supervise directly the work process. The work process itself was broken down into numerous separate tasks and synchronized through the scientific management of individual and group worker behavior, which in many ways mimicked the technologic innovation of automated assembly line decades earlier. As the work process intensified, the length of the workday was shortened, and wage rates increased. Furthermore as manufacturing declined in central cities, the proportion of communications, finance, management, clerical, and professional services located there increased.

Moreover, the socio-economic relationship between suburbs and the central city changed. Many formerly centralized institutions and services were relocated in the suburbs. As downtown shopping districts were transformed into central government and corporate headquarters, small retail services that could not afford skyrocketing rents and were losing customers unwilling to face downtown traffic snarls relocated in the suburbs near their customers. As a result, large department stores set up branch stores in these satellite communities. Mail-order firms like Sears, Roebuck and Company and Montgomery Ward turned into suburban chains. Banks also established branches in suburban communities. Dentists, doctors, and a variety of other professional service providers opened offices near their clients' (and their own) homes. Popular forms of arts and entertainment and most professional sports teams eventually abandoned the heart of many American cities, leaving behind decaying shells of what were once attractive entertainment venues.

Automobiles also had a profound impact on the architecture and housing that continues to be built along the roads and highways that exist in every town, village, and city. The car culture created these roadways, as well as one-, two-, three-, and even four plus-car garages that are like small houses built to protect and preserve the beloved automobile. Wachs and Crawford (1992) in their book *The Car and City*, describe the unique relationship that has been cast between the automobile and American cities like Los Angeles, which embraced the automobile as a symbol of cultural liberation. Gas stations, motels, hotels, shopping malls, drive-in movie theaters, suburbia, and traffic jams would probably not exist, or not exist as we know them, if not for the automobile. Auto racing has become the most popular sport in America, and automobiles continue to serve as a highly desired status symbol by much of the population.

More than one century ago and up to and including present day motorists, persons began to identify with their automobiles differently than with other modes of transportation; drive-in movie theaters gave way to drive-in banking, restaurants, pharmacies, and even wedding chapels (Sandler, 2003). Historically, the personal mobility facilitated by the automobile has not only played a key role in improving overall personal and public health and well-being but also it has had a significant impact on the collective ability to express personal individuality.

The Proliferation of Roads and Highways in America

In 1904, there were only 250 paved and gravel roads in the United States. During the first decade of the 1900s, the pressure for more roads initially came from the 10 million registered bicyclists who were members of influential clubs such as the League of American Wheelman, who persuaded Congress to establish the Bureau of Road Inquiry to investigate how the government could build a network of roads and highways (Sandler, 2003). Bicycles eventually were replaced with motorized vehicles, and local automobile clubs throughout the country that eventually merged to become the American Automobile Association (AAA), which along with automobile manufacturers and oil companies, began to advocate for better and more numerous roads.

In 1904, Congress approved the formation of the U.S. Office of Public Roads that provided financial assistance to the states for building new and improved roads. The Federal Highway Act was passed in 1909 and provided taxpayer dollars to begin building federal highways, organizing the country's roads into federal and state systems, and creating a system of numbering and marking the roads and highways; a system of paved roads that could accommodate millions of motorists by the 1920s (Sandler, 2003). As the affluent middle class grew, automobiles became much more important in terms of leisure and recreation rather than only for driving to work. The 1950s and 1960s brought the opening of the national park system, and camping became a financially accessible vacation option for the average suburban family. The automobile offered the opportunity to see what was exciting and new that only 20 years earlier was accessible only to the wealthy elite. The car was instrumental in helping forge familial relationships.

Interstates: Branches of the Car Culture

That the rise of the automobile and suburbanization coincided with the building of freeways and interstates should be no surprise. There also is evidence that the car industry developed in the cities with the greatest number of paved miles, such as Cleveland and Detroit, but not Chicago, Philadelphia, or Washington, DC. Large-scale national projects, many of which began in the Depression era to stimulate the economy, funded by the government, eventually provided a massive system of interconnected roads and highways across the United States. The interstates were the cathedrals of the car culture, and their social implications were staggering. Within a decade they would alter where and how Americans lived and worked. (Goddard, 1994).

The interstate system took several decades to complete. Interstate designers followed the *'form follows function'* architecture typical of the 1950s (e.g., Albert Kahn who built the General Motors Building, the River Rouge factory, and others; Ludwig Mies van der Rohe whose spare clean lines inspired countless office towers; and modernist French architect Le Corbusier who designed buildings and furniture designer). There was sameness in the architecture of this period, but this sameness in design was the perfect metaphor for generations who welcomed consistency and quality control in their hotels, restaurants, and service stations.

The 1950s saw a massive growth of motels, drive-ins, and roadside diners to support interstate travel. McShane (1994) describes how influential key automobile industrialists were in influencing transportation policy to their advantage. Laws were passed and changed to favor the car companies who argued their industry was fueling the American economy. Early industrialists enjoyed significant success in altering the landscape to accommodate the automobile. The shopping centers of the 1950s became malls in the 1960s. Car design and urban design moved in tandem. Cities and towns began to reshape themselves around the potential of the car to take people greater distances from home (Goddard, 1994). The *'main streets'* of America in the present continue in sharp decline as the shopping malls with ample free parking pull consumers into the suburbs.

The Automobile's Influence on Work and Daily Life: Historical Roots

Sociologists Robert and Helen Lynd (1929) conducted a major study of American society during the 1920s. '*Middletown*' was the name used to disguise Muncie, Indiana, the actual place where they conducted their research. One of their findings was that the automobile had transformed the lives of people living in Middletown and by extension virtually everywhere else in the United States. The Lynds found that the automobile became so important to Middletown residents that many families expressed a willingness to go without food and shelter, mortgage their homes, and deplete their bank savings rather than lose their cars. Other observers found that rural families were similarly attached to their cars. When a U.S. Department of Agriculture inspector asked a farmwoman, during the 1920s why her family had purchased an automobile before equipping their home with indoor plumbing, she replied, "*Why, you can't go to town in a bathtub!*" (Lynd, 1929). For these urban and rural Americans alike, the car had become a basic social necessity.

Although the Lynds may not have fully appreciated it at the time, consumer goods, including the automobile, were slowly eroding class differences, actually leveling the socioeconomic playing field. Automobile ownership brought its own kind of democracy to American life. Automobility also was a strong contributor to women's liberation. Although the automobile did not lessen women's work, it nonetheless offered new possibilities for personal movement. It especially liberated women from the home. The automobile was a private vehicle, and that characteristic made it safer and more acceptable than public streetcars or trains. Even the most genteel women began traveling alone; some wealthier women took cross-country trips together unescorted by male relatives. This freedom, as many women described the experience of driving, was the positive side to the transformation of women's lives.

Historically, however, the primary use of the automobile was for husbands' transportation, primarily to work from home. Many workers had careers downtown, and family life at home was in the suburbs. Decades ago, the traditional family consisted of two-parent households with a stay-at-home mom. Fathers were typically the sole breadwinner and really the only one to need a car. Grocery shopping did not always demand a car because groceries were often delivered directly to suburban homes. There were also many stores within walking distance of the family home. Children walked to school. Families walked to church. Thus mothers and children lived in their local neighborhoods and only used the automobile as part of family outings on weekends.

The Automobile and Its Role in Changing Personal and Professional Networks

Car culture has profoundly affected personal and professional networks. Reflection on the past 50 years confirms radical shifts in the ways we communicate with others and move through physical and social space. Most certainly our social and professional networks have expanded well beyond Cooley's (1902) description of traditional primary and secondary groups that were synonymous with one's family, neighborhood, and self-contained communities that Ferdinand Toennies (1935) referred to as *gemeinschaft*. The automobile industry helped fuel the rapid industrialization of the United States and much of Europe, which greatly influenced how and where people interacted. Pastoral *gemeinschaft* communities of place, belonging, and social reciprocity disintegrated, and societies emerged that reflected a *gesellschaft* existence (Toennies, 1935). Group members that previously interacted within smaller, tight-knit, and cohesive geographic communities now comprised citizens that no longer associated solely with a single primary community located in physical space but began interacting in and between multiple communities in which secondary or weak ties played an increasingly important role in defining social life (Granovetter, 1983).

The automobile was originally designed to transport workers and goods, although it was soon after marketed as a means for the entire family to travel together. Recall the Lynd's research in Muncie, Indiana and the access to town that the automobile provided for relatively isolated rural families. Historically then the place of automobile in *gemeinschaft*-type communities was to provide efficient transportation of goods and people and sometimes to provide a means for family locomotion for leisure purposes. In contrast, in contemporary society, the use of the automobile is primarily a solitary activity. The automobile provides utility and functionality related to helping people fulfill their work and family obligations, fostering strong and weak ties, and meeting daily functional needs, but the car also serves as a dynamic (albeit expensive) form of self-expression of one's identity and even worldview.

Born to Be Wild: Car Culture and the American Teen

In the United States, the automobile has become a symbol of freedom and mobility. Not only do teenagers anxiously wait for the day they can obtain their driver's licenses so they can be mobile and free, but also many elderly perceive driving cessation with a loss of independence, mobility and freedom.

This identifies the importance of the automobile in American life and its relationship to individual identity throughout the life cycle.

It must also be recognized that buying one's own first car and getting a license to drive may be two of the most significant moments in a young person's life after marriage and children. At the cusp of adulthood teenagers are exploring their identities and their futures. This accounts for the concerted interest the automobile industry places on it. Research shows that brand loyalty occurs early in life. Therefore there is a great motivation on the part of the automotive industry to get a new driver for life. The success of that campaign rests largely with advertising. Ford is one of the nation's largest advertisers. According to *Advertising Age*, an industry trade magazine, Ford's advertising budget has grown from about $13,500 in 1904 to an estimated $2.4 billion in 2001.

In part due to aggressive advertising, the automobile has come to pervade American culture not only on the streets and in local drive-ins but also in entertainment. In films, the stars were often a combination of character and car. James Dean and his anti-establishment motorbike epitomized the '*Rebel Without a Cause*.' The blonde in her white T-Bird (Suzanne Somers' character in the film '*American Graffiti*') was not even given a name, just credited '*Blonde in T-Bird*.' Even the hit songs of the 1960s captured a generation and lifestyle focused on cars and girls. From the little Deuce Coupe to the 1934 wagon, '*Woody*' to the little GTO, cars became centralized symbols of American culture.

Contemporary teens are still a key market for advertisers, but marketing efforts and car buyers themselves are more diverse. Advertisers, as well as automobile designers, have also become much more cognizant of the unique needs of various segments of the driving market, including older drivers and drivers with disabilities, enhancing their automobiles with more safety and convenience features, such as on-board navigation and security systems.

Irrespective of car design, consumers continue to personalize and customize their cars to meet their individual needs. One example of car customization is the bumper sticker and personalized license plates. Bumper stickers and other decals on motor vehicles proclaim any number of value statements, such as a driver's opinion about the pro-life versus pro-choice debate and endorsements of political candidates. Vehicle license plates are another example of personal expression. Vehicle plates originated during the Roman Empire, when anyone who owned a chariot was required to register his vehicle and affix an identification tag to it. Today, thousands of people subscribe to license plate catalogs, collect and trade license plates at conventions, and pay a premium for vanity plates that communicate creative personalized messages in a few letters or include images that reflect a driver's school or organizational affiliation.

The Automobile and the American Public: Identity Sells

The type of motor vehicle a consumer chooses to drive is influenced by the brand image that is the result of a manufacturer's carefully orchestrated media campaign. For generations the vehicle type has provided consumers with a kind of symbol or badge designed to communicate a not-so-subtle message about one's perceived status, role, personal aesthetic (e.g., taste), or financial situation. Functionality and form also influenced who was able to drive the earliest automobiles. In 1911, Charles F. Kettering introduced the electric starter that was sold to the Cadillac Motor Company in 1912, facilitating women's ability to sit the driver's seat because hand-cranking the engine was no longer required. However, it would take generations, a growing public concern, and legislation to begin effecting sufficient attitudinal change to achieve greater vehicle accessibility and adapted driving solutions for people with disabilities.

Moline, Illinois banker Wallace Ames stated in 1925 *"The paramount ambition of the average man a few years ago was to own a home and have a bank account. The ambition of the same man today is to own and drive a car..."* People have benefited from owning an automobile, and the automobile industry was instrumental in creating a large middle class within North America and other industrialized regions of the world. However, industry also contributed to myriad social problems that emerged as cities throughout North America matured. During the second half of the 20th century in the United States access to affordable and reliable automobiles facilitated an efficient means for the mass exodus of people and industry away from tired urban centers, turning pastoral and rural settings into suburban America and further reinforcing dependence on the automobile and the proliferation of urban sprawl.

In contemporary society, gentrification of varying degrees has taken place in the previously abandoned centers of many American cities. The reclamation of urban America by individuals, families, businesses, corporations, and institutions continues to largely depend on the existence of a viable infrastructure that enables efficient, reliable, and cost-effective transportation of people and the delivery of essential goods and services. Urban renewal has helped to expand and improve alternative transportation infrastructure (e.g., mass transit systems that offer citizens a variety of transportation options that are dependable, efficient, and economical) in a few major metropolitan areas (e.g., Washington, DC, New York City, Boston, and San Francisco) but not in most urban or rural locations in the United States. For generations automobiles also have continued to be the way people prefer to move from place to place within and between their communities (Molnar et al., 2003; U.S. Department of Transportation, 2003). Individuals who possess the skills necessary to drive and the financial resources to own or lease a vehicle have helped to sustain the necessity in many parts of the world to possess a motor vehicle.

Driving: A Rite (of Passage) or a Right?

In contemporary industrialized societies in the United States and abroad, driving is not considered an inalienable right but a privilege that is granted by the government and defined in legal terms (Wang et al., 2003). However, driving is much more than a privilege, luxury, or *instrumental activity of daily living (IADL)* as some would suggest; it is an *activity of daily living (ADL) (Miller, 2003)* that is necessary for a full and productive social life in urban and rural areas around the world. Many people equate the possession of a driver's license with choice, freedom, and self-identity (Gillens, 1990). The European Conference of Ministers for Transport (1994) studied the social costs of driving and reported that like most Americans, the adult European population largely held the belief that they possess a right to use a vehicle to meet their transportation needs.

One contributing factor may be that the rite of passage associated with earning and keeping a driver's license is a universal symbol of autonomy and independence. A significant sector of American society views driving to be essential to their independence and quality of life (Molnar et al., 2003). Further, it is apparent that many Americans have developed a fascination with the automobile to the extent that is has become a celebrated image or dominant theme for television programs, movies, music, books and magazines, poetry, and even theatrical productions.

Unlike the European model that has facilitated efficient and cost-effective methods for moving people (e.g.,the masses) within self-contained and vibrant urban areas, the American model has helped to foster the exponential growth of sprawling suburban communities that to some symbolize America's wealth and prosperity. To others suburbia represents unwarranted sprawl that necessarily dilutes municipal resources as city officials work to provide a range of public services to ever growing but much less densely populated suburban areas. The critical infrastructure required to support cities includes fire and police services, garbage collection, public transportation, school systems, and so on. Many cities in America today face a tremendous challenge in providing such services with a dwindling tax base. It is useful to note that U.S. highways, roads, and bridges that crisscross and dot the once pastoral American landscape provide transportation arteries for approximately 140 million vehicles that move people and goods and facilitate the delivery of myriad services every day.

Although the car culture around the world may differ in some important ways from the situation in the United States, nonetheless there is still a ubiquitous car culture and a complex infrastructure that supports it. Global transportation infrastructure has grown exponentially to facilitate the transfer of people and goods. However, the negative consequences that are associated with the auto industry and the embrace of the personal automobile globally are significant, for example the potential effect vehicles have on global warming, diminished air quality, expanding health concerns and depleted natural resources. These factors and others have caused some people to promote the need for developing alternative and renewable energy sources, improved mass transit systems, and the next generation of clean vehicles.

The car culture in modern U.S. society demands that normative adult behavior include driving as the primary means for community mobility. Driving is an extraordinarily complex activity requiring complementary cognitive, sensor perceptual, psychomotor, and functional abilities especially as vehicles continue to be engineered to move at higher rates of speed (Molnar, 2003; Freund, 2002; Steinfeld et al, 1999). Individuals no longer capable of fulfilling societal expectations, including being able to independently and safely perform the tasks associated with driving, are sometimes seen as incompetent and are often stigmatized (Goffman, 1963). Driving cessation can lead to diminished spontaneity (Korner-Bitensky et al., 1994), feelings of being a burden on family members (Cook & Semmler, 1991), and a perceived loss of social status (Barnes & Hoyle, 1995; Cynkin & Robinson, 1990).

Luborsky (Luborsky, 1998) used the cultural context as a backdrop against which he described popular cultural ideas of full adulthood and how they affect the social experiences, interpersonal interactions, and self-esteem of people with recently acquired disabilities. He asserted that every culture's model of adulthood includes the notion that the realization of competence and mastery occurs when language and the ability to achieve and maintain willful movement is successfully acquired. Duggan (2000) expanded this idea and described how the loss of independent motor control threatens the experiences of full adulthood because social interaction and roles are negatively affected. People that comprise the geriatric population are all too familiar with being marginalized and disenfranchised as a result of diminished personal and community mobility. Thus, for the elderly, contending with disabilities, driving or the resumption of driving is a major goal toward maintaining *community integration* (Ranney & Hunt, 1997) and *quality of life.*

American Modernity and the Open Road

During the 20th century automobiles became part of our daily lives and an extension of ourselves: symbols of who we are as a people (or at least the image of people we wish to be). There are many indicators of the importance, meaning, and role of the automobile in our society; the fact that we have dedicated more land to cars (roads, parking, etc.) than to housing, for example, identifies their importance to the broader society. Other indicators include the number of magazines devoted to cars and car cultures, the use of automobiles in film and television, in literature and media. The automobile has deeply penetrated our psyche and our everyday language. Consider for example the phrases '*Sunday driver*', '*backseat driver*', '*joy ride*', '*hitchhiking*', and '*the information superhighway*', that have become part of the American culture.

The automobile has also been important to music, reminding us of the freedom, excitement, and promise of the open road. As early as 1899, Tin Pan Alley was turning out car-related hits such as *Fifteen Kisses on a Gallon of Gas* and *I'm Going to Park Myself in Your Arms*. The tradition of cars in songs continued throughout the 20th century. In the 1960s, in what was to become one of the most productive musical decades ever, we heard *Ramblin' Man* by the Allman Brothers Band, *Take Me Home* by Woody Guthrie, *Country Roads* by John Denver, and *America* by Simon and Garfunkel. However, no form of popular expression has celebrated the automobile with more passion and attention to nuance than rock and roll. From Chuck Berry to the Beach Boys and Bruce Springsteen to Steppenwolf, the glories and tragedies of the car culture are well documented. In *Ballad of Betsy* the Beach Boys described a car as '*more loyal than any friend can be.*' Two of Bruce Springsteen's hit songs about cars include *Born to Run* and *Cadillac Ranch*. Finally music played in automobiles includes *Route 66*, composed by Bobby Troup and first recorded by the Nat King Cole Trio in 1946. This song has been recorded by every generation since, from the Andrew Sisters and Bing Crosby to Chuck Berry and the Rolling Stones.

The automobile has similarly influenced American literature and film. Perhaps John Steinbeck's classic *The Grapes of Wrath* is most well known. In the film version Henry Fonda stars as Tom Joad. In a most memorable scene Fonda is seen driving his family's run-down pickup truck away from their Midwestern farm after being evicted by their landlord driving his new, luxury Duesenberg. The integration of narrative and material possession is seamless, the luxury car serving as an adjective describing social place and material wealth and power, and the old truck, the lack thereof. Thus cars in film, just as in music and literature before it, were used to reinforce the notion that dreams are possible. Perhaps going where you wanted and when you wanted was even an idea that evolved from our romantic notions of the cowboy and the West. The car in all forms of popular culture underscores the idea of self-determination and self-reliance, fundamental values in the American cultural tradition.

The Car and Family Life

Expanding economies in China and India are providing new markets for the consumption and production of automobiles. The challenge of automobility is *sustainability* (of the world's resources in the form of fossil fuels and raw materials) but also *social*. Does the organization of our world around the automobile really make economic sense, environmental sense, and social sense? Although new technologies and advances in automobile engineering abound, contemporary society is diverse. The limitations of auto mobility are becoming clearer. On one hand it appears life is virtually impossible without the automobile, although an increasingly vocal minority suggests it is precisely the automobile industry and politic lobby surrounding the car industry that has put us in the situation we are now in (Holtz, 1997).

Much of the reliance on cars today reflects the way that two-worker and single-parent households juggle the complicated responsibilities of home and work. The car offers the convenience and flexibility essential to working parents, particularly mothers who often carry the double burden of working at work and home. The car is essential in nearly every city and suburb and small town. In most urban areas and certainly in rural America, there may be no other efficient way of arriving to work and school on time. Public transit service is not always available to connect suburbs and city, let alone suburb to suburb. Related issues include the other ways automobiles are utilized. Driving is increasingly linking work travel with family leisure and household errands, intensifying the need to have a car that offers this form of transportation flexibility.

Modern life is much more fragmented than in earlier decades. It was said that the 1970s were the '*now generation*,' but it seems much truer today. North American society at least demands everything '*right now*' and '*on demand*.' From e-mail and instant text messaging on cell phones to ubiquitous drive-through banking, pharmacies, and fast food restaurants, we have grown accustomed to and dependent on efficient access to goods and services without having to leave the safety and comfort of our motor vehicles.

Marginalization and the Automobile: Who is Left Behind?

Ever since the advent of the automobile, there have been disenfranchised groups (e.g., lower socio-economic groups) who could not afford an automobile and thus could not take part in its major economic and social transformations. One sector that was negatively impacted was small family-run businesses. Small, independent businesses simply could not afford off-ramp locations adjacent to freeways, leaving mostly nationwide chains like Holiday Inn and McDonald's to flourish. Main Street America gave way to drive-through pickup windows on the off-ramps of interstates and freeways.

Others have lost out too, including entire towns that have suffered downturns in the automobile industry. One of the best-known examples is Flint, Michigan, made famous in Michael Moore's film *Roger and Me*. Flint experienced unprecedented economic growth with the automotive production, and was left devastated after General Motors laid off 30,000 workers from its assembly plants in the early 1980s. Flint continues to experience significant unemployment and economic disparity.

Others have analyzed the auto industry and its role in contributing to, not ameliorating, urban decay. Thomas Sugrue for example writes about Detroit as symbolic of rust-belt cities to show how deindustrialization and racial discrimination helped maintain and deepen the social and economic differences between blacks and whites living in and around Detroit (Berger, 2001). Unsurprisingly Sugrue found that much of the postwar planning of the city (e.g., highways, land clearance for urban renewal projects, retail development, etc.) had a negative and disproportionate impact on poor blacks living in Detroit.

At the individual level many people never had a car and did not participate in the American Dream; this is consistent in contemporary times. Jane Holtz Kay (Holtz, 1997) reports in *Asphalt Nation* that in larger cities 60% of mass transit riders are women, and 48% are African American or Hispanic, more than twice their number in the population. Although many 'haves' get good service, 38% of transit riders are 'have-nots,' surviving at just about the poverty level with family incomes of less than $15,000, according to a study by the American Transit Authority.

The automobile has become a critical aspect of modernity. Not only is the ability to drive an expression of autonomy and independence but also it contributes to the maintenance of our family and social ties, the daily operation of households, and the pursuit of a variety of recreational activities. Thus, it can be argued that for aging individuals and people with disabilities, driving or the resumption of driving is a major goal toward achieving and maintaining optimal community integration.

The Absence of Automobility Brings Isolation and Stigma

Persons who are carless are often viewed as aberrant and excluded from mainstream American life. Absence of automobility as a result of poverty and/or cessation of driving accentuate societal stigmatization. The choice not to drive can be perceived as stigmatic insofar as the variety of social disadvantages presumed attached. The absence of automobility, places due limitations on economic mobility. It also makes it far more difficult to live independently because automobile transportation is a necessity to enable all one's routine community activities (work, sports and leisure) and routine processes such as grocery shopping, church participation, and social activities. Automobility enhances reliability, flexibility, and especially efficiency of intercommunity mobility and intercommunity travel. Individuals who cannot drive (irrespective of the reason) are placed in a disadvantageous position insofar as public transportation is often unavailable or inconvenient, and workplaces may be significantly far from homes to make walking or other methods of transportation practical.

Older drivers and drivers with disabilities are at an even more pronounced disadvantage. Already marginalized by a society that devalues those who are '*different*' or '*less able*,' disabled persons face the additional challenge of obtaining the requisite skills and technologies to enable them to drive. The impact of cessation of driving from the elderly is particularly pronounced through time trends. In 1983, one of every 15 licensed drivers in America was over the age of 70. By 2020, however, one of every five Americans is expected to be over 65 years of age, and most of them will probably be licensed to drive (Reno, 1988). What such drivers need and demand as they confront limitations to their ability to continue to drive raise fundamental concerns.

It can be argued that factors influencing a resistance to cessation of driving include the negative implications that are correlated with it.

Voluntary or involuntary driving cessation places limitations on individual social integration. In essence, the removal from mainstream cultural component also suggests that the individual is also marginalized. The reduced participation in society may be a contributing factor in limiting individual autonomy.

Conclusion

Driving and the infrastructure that supports a worldwide automobile culture influence how we interact with others, view the world, imagine how others perceive us, and how that image influences the way we perceive ourselves (Lyman & Vidich, 2000). The automobile and the generations of motor vehicles that have evolved from the early steam- and electric-powered horseless carriages have also profoundly influenced an American culture, which in turn has promoted a global car culture and impacted social integration. Individuals who possess the necessary resources to own or lease a vehicle have more than an efficient means for intercommunity and intercommunity mobility; cars and trucks are tangible symbols that remind us individually and collectively that with ownership comes the message that we are fully engaged in mainstream American life.

The cultural transition of automobility from privilege to right is paramount in understanding its link to individual autonomy. Entrenched values in society over generations helps define '*fundamental rights*.' The value of the automobile to American culture has shifted from basic transportation to a myriad of symbolism which includes *social status*, *freedom*, and *identity*. Access to mobility becomes an integral process by which individuals become part of society, and in turn, accentuate individual autonomy. Group integration is therefore connected to, and central to individual identity.

Limitations to mobility may serve to broaden marginalization of sectors of society that are already disenfranchised. If mobility is considered a *fundamental right*, its inaccessibility may be perceived as a *denied* fundamental right. Perceived marginalization becomes more powerful than actual disenfranchisement because of the cultural framework with which it operates within. Whether or not automobility is a fundamental right matters less than if it is identified culturally to be a fundamental right. In this vein, limitations to automobility serve as hindrances to individual autonomy, social integration and self-actualization.

References

Barnes, M. & Hoyle, E. (1995). Driving Assessment: A Case of Need. *Clinical Rehabilitation.* 9:115-120.

Berger M. (2001). *The Automobile in American History and Culture: A Reference Guide,* Westport, CT: Greenwood Publishing.

Cook, C. & Semmler, C. (1991). Ethical Dilemmas in Driver Re-education. *American Journal of Occupational Therapy.* 45:517-22.

Cooley, C. (1902). *Human Nature and the Social Order,* New York, NY: Charles Scribner's Sons.

Cynkin, S., Robinson, A. (1990). Occupational Therapy and Activities. *Health: Toward Health Through Activities.* Boston, MA: Little, Brown and Co.

Duggan C.H. (2000). God, If You're Real, and You Hear Me, Send Me a Sign: Dewey's Story of Living with a Spinal Cord Injury. *Journal of Religion Disability Health,* 4(1).

European Conference of Ministers for Transport. (1994). *Benefits of Different Transport Modes: Report of the 93rd Round Table on Transport Economics (ECMT Round Table).*

Ford, H. & Crowther, S. (2003). *My Life and Work (1922).* Whitefish, MT: Kessinger Publishing.

Freund, B. & Szinovacz, M. (2002). Effects of Cognition on Driving Involvement Among the Oldest Old: Variations by Gener and Alternative Transportation Opportunities. *Gerontologist,* 42: 621-633.

Gillens, L. (1990). Yielding to Age: When the Elderly can no Longer Drive. *Journal of Gerentological Nursing,* 16(11): 12-15.

Goddard, S. (1994). *Getting There: The Epic Struggle between Road and Rail in the American Century,* New York, NY: Basic Books.

Goffman, E. (1963). *The Presentation of Self in Everyday Life.* Garden City, NY: Anchor.

Granovetter, M. (1983). The Strength of Weak Ties: A Network Theory Revisited. *Sociological Theory* (1).

Holtz, K. (1997). *Asphalt Nation: How the Automobile Took Over America and How We can Take It Back.* New York, NY: Crown Publishers.

Korner-Bitensky, N., Sofer, S., Kaizer, F., et al (1994). Assessing Ability to Drive Following an Acute Neurological Event: Are We on the Right Road. Revue *Canadienne d'Ergotherapie,* 61, 141-148.

Luborsky, M. (1998). Creative Challenges and the Construction of Meaningful Life Narratives. In Adams-Price CE (Ed.) *Creativity and Successful Aging,* New York, NY: Springer Publishing Company.

Lynd R.S. & Lynd, H.M. (1929). *Middletown: A Study in Modern American Culture.* Orlando, FL: Harcourt Brace.

McShane, C. (1994). *Down the Asphalt Path: The Automobile and the American City,* New York, NY: Columbia University Press.

Miller, L. Cars, Trucks Now Outnumber Drivers. *Salon,* August 29, 2003.

Molnar, L., Eby, D. & Miller, L. Promoting Independence and Well-being: Successful Approaches to Enhancing Elderly Driving Mobility. International Conference on Aging, Disability, and Independence, Washington, DC: 2003.

Olson, B. & Cabadas, J. (2002). *The American Auto Factory.* St. Paul, MN: MBI Publishing.

Ranney, T. & Hunt, L. (1997). Researchers and Occupational Therapists can Help Each Other to Better Understand What Makes a Good Driver: Two Perspectives, *Work: A Journal of Prevention, Assessment Rehabilitation,* 8: 293-7.

Reno, A. (1988). *Personal Mobility in the United States, In a Look Ahead: Year 2020.* Washington, DC: 1988, Transportation Research Board, National Research Council.

Sandler, M. (2003). *Driving Around the USA: Automobiles in American Life.* New York, NY: Oxford University Press.

Toennies, F. (1935) *Geist der Neuzeit.* Leipzig, Germany: Buske.

U.S. Department of Transportation. (2003). *Safe Mobility for a Maturing Society: Challenges and Opportunities.* Washington, DC: 2003, Government Printing Office.

Vidich, A. & Lyman, S. (1994). Qualitative Methods: Their History in Sociology and Anthropology. In Denzin, N., Lincoln Y., (Eds.) *Handbook of Qualitative Research.* Thousand Oaks, CA: Sage.

Wachs, M. & Crawford, M., (Eds.). (1992). *The Car and the City: The Automobile, the Built Environment, and Daily Urban Life.* Ann Arbor, MI: University of Michigan Press.

Wang, C., Kosinski, C. & Schwartzberg J. (2003). *Physician's Guide to Assessing and Counseling Older Drivers.* Washington, DC: National Highway Traffic Safety.

CHAPTER 6
PUBLIC SPACE AND CRIMINAL JUSTICE

Charles E. Crawford

Abstract: *Although public spaces such as parks, urban centers, and sidewalks are viewed as open to all residents, history reveals that they have been managed, controlled, and restricted. This chapter explores the meanings and conflicts over public space as cities attempt to control, and in some extreme cases make undesirables, such as the homeless disappear. Urban revitalization projects come into conflict with groups who assert their counterclaims and counter-uses of the same public space. It is within these battles over public space that the criminal justice system is used in a dramatic fashion to carry out sweeps of homeless encampments, and enforces laws that restrict public sleeping, and feeding the homeless. After reviewing the anti-homeless actions in key American cities and the role police and courts play in this process, we assess how some cities addressed the conflict over access and use of public space.*

Once we leave the control and safety of our homes and enter the public sphere we may have certain assumptions about our access to this space and what activities are allowed. The idealized public space is one in which every citizen feels invited to engage in a wide variety of activities with their fellows. Such a notion may be best visualized with the ancient Greek agora, the Roman forum, the coffee houses of Paris and Vienna, and in more recent times the suburban shopping mall, and the revitalized downtown spaces in many of our nation's cities. It is in these locations ideas were exchanged, commerce took place, and in some cases new philosophies and resolutions were launched. In theory, these spaces were the hallmarks of freedom and were sites of spatial democracy as they were open to all citizens and social and class differences could be set aside.

However, as Margaret Crawford (1995) shows, a closer examination of history reveals that this notion of an open and welcoming public arena may have been more idealized than real. These supposed sites of public space and democracy such as the agora, piazza, and the New England town squares in practice excluded several classes of citizens. Consider for a moment the groups throughout history that have been marginalized and barred from the public realm and discourse: women, slaves, working-class men, and racial and ethnic minorities. Each of these groups at different points in time and in different locations have found their presence unwelcomed, and in some cases threatening to city elites. This exclusion and struggle over access to public space continues today. This chapter seeks to explore the conflict over public space that many citizens take for granted as being open to all, and the role of the criminal justice system in regulating this space and people within.

Public Space

Before undertaking the journey through the contested public space and the role the criminal justice system plays in its regulation, it is important to clarify what a public space is. Although it may seem straightforward to define public space, each part of the term has numerous meanings. For example, what is public? From a political standpoint 'public' may refer to the citizenry. For many citizens public simply means anyone and everyone (Chua & Edwards, 1992). However, urban planners, architects, geographers, and sociologist among others have debated space as a concept extensively. Defining space can be complex; space for some may be a physical quantity such as abstract geometries, size, and volume (Hillier & Hanson, 1984). Others, such as Gieryn (2000) make a clear distinction between place and space. He suggests that space becomes a place when it is filled with meaningful objects, practices, and people. A place is a specific spot in a space; a place may be a home, campsite, beach, a village, or a nation.

Rather than attempting to resolve the space debate with an all-encompassing definition, throughout the remainder of this chapter space is best defined through Gans' (2000) use-centered view. From the use-centered view, space becomes more than just the physical dimensions of place. This perspective allows us to examine how individuals, groups, and governments transform the abstract or natural space into social space through economic, political, and legal forces.

When most people envision a public space it may simply be thought of as something that is publicly owned and shared with fellow citizens: spaces such as a sidewalk, a plaza, or a park. However, as Blomley (2001) points out, these are the spaces where the public sphere is created, challenged, and most importantly for this discussion, policed. Public space is a dynamic object that is fashioned from various competing groups in society. For this chapter the term public space is best illustrated by Roger Scruton's (1984) description. According to Scruton, public space is a location that is designed, all people have access rights to it with unplanned encounters with fellow citizens, and these encounters are subject to the norms of courtesy in that given society.

The common elements in the definitions of space and public space are at their core they should be open to all citizens. Not only is the public space necessary for economic and cultural life, it plays a vital role in the creation of democracy. Consider the public protests around the globe as the summits of the World Trade Organization, the Group of 8, and European Union took place. On February 15, 2003, more than 30 million people in 600 cities around the world entered the public space in a coordinated protest against the war in Iraq (Irazábal, 2008: 13-14). The creation of a vibrant democracy and cultural space is only possible when we are allowed to have spontaneous or at least self-directed encounters with our fellow citizens. Interestingly, it is within these encounters that we may come upon the homeless, panhandlers, and protesters all of whom represent unique challenges to public space. It is these unplanned encounters with groups that push the boundaries of public space that lead to calls of greater regulation and enforcement of orderly behavior.

Regulating Space

The battles over public space are well documented throughout history and the current news in our nation's cities. These struggles are intense and in many cases may appear to be justifiable. Consider the behavior of an aggressive panhandler, or bench squatter. According to Yale property and urban law professor Robert Ellickson (1996) this type of chronic misconduct must be controlled and regulated in accordance with local community wants and desires. It is these behaviors and spatial signals such as graffiti that may indicate a loss of control or breakdown in the social order, which in turn leads to declining usage of public space. Even a sensitive regulation of space as suggested by Ellickson is not without contention. Don Mitchell (2003) for example views these attempts at regulating public space little more than class warfare as they attempt to restrict the actions of marginalized groups such as the homeless.

As cities and urban centers in the United States attempt to attract businesses and residents into revitalized downtown areas there is often a friction as competing interests collide. The activities that take place in public spaces by the homeless, and the poor, may not align with the intended purposes of designers, local politicians, and middle class suburbanites. Specifically, the actions of the homeless push the limits of the use of public space; sleeping, bathing, or changing clothes are all activities that most citizens consider private and should not be viewed in the public sphere. These behaviors along with aggressive panhandling, and public drunkenness may be labeled chronic misconduct or nuisances.

Although some may view these behaviors as minor annoyances that can simply be avoided if we divert our eyes or cross the street to an adjacent sidewalk, this does not suggest that such actions do not impact people's lives. Given that these behaviors take place in public, they may affect hundreds and in some cases thousands of people per hour. As the hours move into days and weeks, certain public spaces may appear to lack social control and become a "broken window" signal that other more insidious behavior such as petty crime, prostitution, and drug sales are allowed.

Advocates of street control such as urbanologist Jane Jacobs (1961) and criminologist Wesley Skogan (1990) suggest that maintaining open and inviting sidewalks and parks are essential for neighborhood survival. The highly influential *Atlantic Monthly* article by James Q. Wilson and George F. Kelling (1982) titled '*Broken Windows: The Police and Neighborhood Safety*' clearly illustrates how these seemingly minor annoyances can transform a neighborhood. According to the authors, persistent minor disorder begins to disturb a neighborhood and is like a single broken window. The signal of an unrepaired broken window is that of a loss of control. Passersby will sense this loss and be encouraged to commit other acts of disorder since breaking other windows cost nothing. Once this process has begun, citizens start to avoid each other and more serious crime may flourish. The initial signal of a broken window has a compounding effect. If order and control of public space is to be established and maintained, the initial signal of disorder such as the single broken window must be addressed.

Despite the egalitarian views of public space that would allow a mix of conflicting usage, and overlook some chronic misconduct, when we review history and examine the current state of public spaces in our nation's cities the fact remains that public spaces are, and have always been regulated, gendered, managed, and controlled. Control has taken different forms over time, from Augustus' (63 B.C- 14 A.D.) Vigiles that fought street crime and protected property in Rome's 14 administrative districts (Stead, 1983), to the staggering number of CCTV surveillance cameras employed throughout the United Kingdom resulting in one camera for every 14 people (Marx, 2006). Surveillance, control, and management of space may be accomplished through a variety of tools, but some of the most invasive and divisive actions over controlling public space have come from the use of the criminal justice system to regulate the actions of the homeless.

The Law and the Homeless

Jeremy Waldron (1991: 296) has suggested that the use of laws to control property and space at their roots are about determining who is allowed to be in certain locations. Over the last two decades numerous American cities have sought to reclaim public space by passing dozens of laws restricting the actions of the homeless. Legal restraints on the actions of the poor and homeless have a lengthy history. For more than six centuries vagrancy laws were passed making it a crime to wander without visible means of support (Simon, 1991). However, in *Papachristou v. Jacksonville* (1972) the Supreme Court ruled such laws in the United States impermissible. In *Papachristou*, eight individuals were charged with various acts of vagrancy and convicted under the Jacksonville, Florida statute that prohibited rogues and vagabonds from strolling, wandering without any lawful purpose, or object. The court ruled the law impermissible as it criminalized an innocent act of wandering and strolling, and placed an undue amount of discretion in the hands of the police. Furthermore, the Court rejected the rationale that vagrancy laws prevented crime (Kelling & Coles, 1998: 55-56).

Essentially, the statute lacked clarity on how a reasonable person could avoid the prohibited behavior that is such a part of American life. After the Papachristou decision other courts began to overturn vagrancy laws as they failed to meet constitutional test and were often in violation of the Due Process Clause under the Fourteenth Amendment. This sent a message to other cities and states that existing loitering laws would more than likely not withstand close legal scrutiny leaving an opening to create new laws designed to accomplish the goals of controlling the displaced poor within public spaces. Don Mitchell (2001: 8) offers a more critical interpretation of such recent changes in the law, suggesting that such legal maneuvering serves a nervous middle class as they grapple with the insecurities of the economy. Perhaps his most stinging criticism of the use of law to regulate public space and the homeless is his proposition that not only do these laws attempt to annihilate public space, but the people that live within them.

There are less critical interpretations of the creation of anti-homeless laws, however even supporters of the current policies reach a very similar conclusion about the history and creation of modern laws that restrict public space and target the poor. Robert Tier (1993) for example sees such laws that target the actions of the homeless not as a war against the group but a way to satisfy the needs of social order, defend the culture of work and responsibility, and maintain public safety and courtesy. There have been numerous creative attempts to regulate the use of public space, from prohibitions on sidewalk sitting, bans on panhandling, to aggressively enforcing neutral laws such as open containers and loitering against the homeless. Tier (1993: 287) provides an interesting justification for such creative legal boundaries on the homeless by suggesting that limitations on the actions of street people are necessary if we are to promote and preserve a vibrant and diverse urban life.

Although anti-homeless laws may take different forms across the nation, there are certain ordinances that are commonly used. A 2006 report by The National Coalition for the Homeless and The National Law Center on Homelessness and Poverty surveyed 224 American cities to gain insight into the types of activities that are being targeted. Of the 224 cities surveyed:

- 28% prohibit "camping" in particular public places in the city and 16% had citywide prohibitions on "camping".
- 27% prohibit sitting/lying in certain public places.
- 39% prohibit loitering in particular public areas.
- 43% prohibit begging in particular public places; 45% prohibit aggressive panhandling, and 21% have city-wide prohibitions on begging.

The prohibitions against camping, sitting/loitering, and panhandling each represent unique legal and social challenges for cities as well as the homeless. Consider for a moment that the result of each of these prohibitions is criminalizing what the homeless may have to do for simple survival while the purported crime prevention efforts may be dubious at best (Smith, 1994). Mitchell (2001: 9) offers a more critical assessment of passages of such laws. Perhaps the goal that some cities hope to achieve is simply to have the homeless disappear in an attempt to sustain prosperity and social harmony, and these legal efforts prove to be less about crime prevention and more about crime invention.

Prohibitions against Sleeping in Public

Of all the anti-homeless laws that have been issued, the prohibition against public sleeping and urban camping get to the heart of the conflict over public space and survival for the homeless as there may be few alternatives for a safe place to sleep. A 2007 report from the National Law Center on Homelessness and Poverty reveals sobering statistics in light of the legal restrictions on public sleeping:

- Over the course of a year, between 2.3 and 3.5 million individuals, including over 1.35 million children will experience homelessness.
- On any given night, there are approximately 840,000 homeless people in the United States.
- In 2006, 29% of shelter requests by homeless families went unmet, an increase of 5% from the previous year.

Declining numbers of shelter beds results in an increase in the number of people sleeping on the streets, sidewalks, and parks which puts the homeless on a collision course with business owners, city officials, and citizens who are simply fed up with seeing downtown areas turned into campsites. One highly publicized legal battle over sleeping in public came during the early 1990s from the city of Santa Ana, California. Santa Ana was the first in the state of California to prohibit outright sleeping in public, and due to its success it prompted other cities in the state such as West Hollywood, Laguna Beach, and Santa Barbra to pass similar laws. Santa Ana had been pursuing an urban revitalization plan including a $60 million civic center and office complexes in the downtown area (Takahashi, 1999: 156).

In 1992 the city council of Santa Ana began targeting what was viewed as one of the worst problems of the city by passing an ordinance essentially designed to remove the homeless from public spaces by making camping on public property a crime. The ordinance was prompted by people who work in the courthouse, City Hall, and other

Civic Center offices who complained that they were being harassed and were afraid to walk in the area due to large numbers of homeless citizens camping (Cone, 1992).

The ordinance passed despite warnings from the Legal Aid Society of Orange County who informed the counsel that the city could be held in contempt of a Circuit Court ruling that prohibited the city from taken efforts to drive homeless individuals from Santa Ana (Martinez, 1992). Within hours of the ordinance being passed the enforcement began by posting flyers informing homeless residents that if they were in violation of the new law a citation would be issued requiring a court appearance. Failure to appear in court would result in an arrest warrant being issued and the violator would face up to six months in jail. The impact was immediate as nearly half of the homeless individuals in the targeted area departed.

Despite the initial success there was immediate opposition. In 1992 the Legal Aid Society, the American Civil Liberties Union, and the National Lawyers Guild filed suits against Santa Ana and four other cities in California who passed similar laws prohibiting camping on public property arguing the ordinances amounted to cruel and unusual punishment and violated constitutional rights of travel and movement (Takahashi, 1999: 158). This first action was only the beginning of numerous challenges to the ordinance that continued for several years and drew the attention of the U.S. Attorney General, State Supreme Court justices, and constitutional law professors who joined the side of the homeless plaintiffs while the city of Santa Ana was represented by more than 90 cities' attorneys from across the state of California, and numerous conservative legal foundations (Takahashi, 1999: 163). In 1995, the California State Supreme Court ruled the ordinance was constitutional declaring that there is no right to use public property for living accommodations or storage of personal items unless permitted by government ordinance (Dolan, 1995: A1).

Although the verdict appeared to settle the use of an anti-camping ordinance, one homeless man named James Eichorn raised an interesting argument in 1996. Eichorn was ticketed in 1993 for violating Santa Ana's anti-camping ordinance, but unlike most of his 72 co-defendants that were ticketed who pled guilty, Eichorn waived his right to a speedy trial and challenged the law in court. The argument raised by Eichorn's attorneys was essentially a necessity defense stating their client had no choice but to violate the ordinance in order to survive. The lower courts upheld the initial conviction with the judge asking Eichorn why he couldn't just walk a mile to a neighboring city and find a cushy spot in a park and make that his home. However, the appellate court overturned the conviction, and rejected the lower court judge's thinking saying that the city could not solve its social problems by forcing them into nearby communities (Marosi, 1999).

The initial support of the ordinance from the lower court did in fact provide an impetus for other cities across the country to use local ordinances to deal with large homeless populations and the issue of public sleeping. In addition to the survey of 224 cities and their criminalization of homelessness efforts, the 2006 report by The National Coalition for the Homeless and The National Law Center on Homelessness and Poverty also ranked the top 20 meanest cities based on the number of anti-homeless laws, intensity of enforcement, and severity of penalties. Although the Santa Ana case provides insight into one of the early battles over public sleeping/camping, a review of the 20 meanest cities reveals anti-camping ordinances are common tools used to target the homeless.

Sarasota Florida was listed number one on the top 20 meanest cities list. In February of 2005 the City Commission passed an ordinance prohibiting lodging out of doors. The city has shown its commitment to ending sleeping in public, as the current manifestation of the law was created in response to the previous anti-camping law being ruled unconstitutional for vagueness. The 2005 implementation of the ordinance required police officers to offer violators a ride to a shelter versus jail at least once a year. Even this ordinance was short-lived as it was overturned in June of 2005 for vagueness since the law did not specifically state what constituted a lodging violation. It failed to address questions such as whether it entailed putting a blanket on the ground, building a fire, pitching a tent, or a combination of these activities.

Assistant public defender Chris Cosden admonished the City Commission pointing out that they had tried twice and failed on both occasions and that time and money may be better spent dealing with the root causes of homelessness (The National Coalition for the Homeless & The National Law Center on Homelessness and Poverty, 2006). Nonetheless, two months later the City Commission passed a third ordinance making it a crime to sleep on public or private property without permission. This version of the ordinance clearly detailed what constituted '*camping*' with one or more of the following five elements being present:

- Numerous items of personal belongings are present.
- The person is engaged in cooking activities.
- The person has built or is maintaining a fire.
- The person has engaged in digging or earth-breaking activities.
- The person is asleep and when awakened states that he or she has no other place to live (The National Coalition for the Homeless & The National Law Center on Homelessness and Poverty, 2006: 25).

This new version of the ordinance has moved beyond targeting activities and has essentially criminalized the state of being homeless. The law has been challenged, and met with protest actions such as sleep-outs from homeless rights advocates and college students (Saewitz, 2006: BS1). Ultimately the courts found the ordinance to be constitutional. At year-end 2007, Sarasota police had made 131 arrests under the anti-lodging ordinance, including a one-month high of 34 arrests ("Records Reveal 131 Camping Arrests", 2007).

Other notable cities with severe penalties for public sleeping include Flagstaff, Arizona in which anyone caught sleeping in a car or in public may face $2,500 in fines and up to six months in jail, in San Antonio camping without a license or sleeping in a car will result in up to a $500 fine, and Bradenton, Florida in which sleeping in public after sunset and before sunrise, may result in up to a $500 fine and up to 60 days in jail (The National Coalition for the Homeless & The National Law Center on Homelessness and Poverty, 2006).

Feeding the Homeless

A fascinating extension of the control of public spaces can be found with the targeting of those who assist the homeless by providing food. In 2007 the city of Orlando Florida estimated there were more than 8,500 homeless people in its jurisdiction and only 2,000 shelter beds (Lewan, 2007). The site of controversy was Lake Eola Park in downtown Orlando that became a haven for the homeless. Like other cities discussed in this section, Orlando passed and began aggressive enforcement of an anti-camping ordinance that prohibited lying, sleeping, or being in a

horizontal position on benches, shrubs, or flowerbeds. After issuing hundreds of citations the city took a novel supply side approach to dealing with homeless populations by passing an ordinance in 2006 regulating the feeding of large groups in the downtown park. Under the new ordinance those wishing to feed a group of 25 or more would have to obtain a permit and no one would be allowed to have more than two permits a year, essentially criminalizing the feeding of homeless people and punishing those who attempt to help despite the lack of public services offered by the city (Lewan, 2007).

Such restrictions on feeding and providing food appear to be a new approach to controlling homeless populations in public space. Cities across the United States such as Las Vegas, Dallas, Atlanta, and Santa Monica all have restrictions or outright bans on feeding the homeless. However the enforcement effort in Orlando has received national attention with the arrest of Eric Montanez. Undercover officers from the Orlando Police Department observed and counted Montanez feeding 30 homeless people in the park, and seized a portion of the stew he was serving as evidence. Montanez was charged with the misdemeanor of feeding a large group in a city-owned park (Amber, 2007).

The American Civil Liberties Union has threatened to sue the city of Orlando as the ordinance interferes with religious groups and their mission to feed homeless populations (Komp, 2006). For cities that have passed ordinances restricting public sleeping and feeding the homeless, it is not the nuisance behaviors themselves that is the issue; it is the spatial context in which these actions occur. To paraphrase Don Mitchell (2001), once laws are used to annihilate public space, the annihilation of people is soon to follow.

Sweeps of Homeless Encampments

The prohibitions of public sleeping, urban camping, and feeding appear to be drastic measures to regulate homeless populations. However the most invasive and bitterly contested actions involving the criminal justice system and the control of public space is police sweeps of homeless encampments. The past 15 years have witnessed an expansion of the number of homeless individuals living in encampments across the United States. Across the country homeless advocacy groups and city agencies are reporting the most visible rise in homeless encampments in a generation (MSNBC, 2008). Recently, homeless encampments such as

Sacramento's 200-person tent city have attracted international media attention (Hubert, 2009).

Even as compassion poured out across the country in the form of donations and pressure to legalize the homeless camp in Sacramento, the underlying battle over the use of public space remained. Prior to recent attempts to remake the city, affluent classes moved to the suburbs effectively disconnecting themselves from urban centers and the plight of the homeless and impoverished citizens. As discussed earlier, as cities have attempted to revitalize their downtown areas and former factory waterfronts the affluent have been drawn back to the city center pushing the homeless to the fringes. The homeless have become recast as a dangerous group that needs to be removed from the sight of this newly affluent class. It is this preoccupation with sanitizing the city that drives officials to pass anti-camping laws and reflects the discomfort of having to visibly face poverty while strolling through newly renovated urban centers.

Cities do have a right to keep public spaces safe, and officials often cite homeless encampments as hot spots for crime such as the 2008 unsolved quintuple murder in a Long Beach, California homeless camp (Moore, 2008), and potential health hazards. For example the city of Oakland, California's Division of Housing and Community Development states the following on their webpage on homelessness: "*The City of Oakland is committed to mitigating the public nuisance, blight, and public health hazards associated with homeless encampments, and conducts regularly scheduled sweeps to maintain affected areas in a clean and orderly condition*" (Housing and Community Development, 2009).

On the opposite end of the spectrum, one group of advocates for the homeless in Tampa has proposed constructing and operating a tent city to provide temporary shelter. Catholic Charities suggested the tent city would be modeled after Pinellas Hope, a temporary shelter site in Pinellas Park that has had success at finding permanent housing for its members and support from the community. There would be an on-site manager and security, counselors would help people find jobs, and access social services, and area churches would donate food. The proposed plan was met with vehement opposition from residents near the proposed site who argued that crime and prostitution would flourish while property values and business expansion would plummet (Steele, 2009).

City officials find themselves in the middle of this battle over space trying to appease property owners and advocacy groups, while attempting to appear compassionate to the condition of the homeless. Ultimately the conclusion many city officials and supporters of anti-homeless laws reach is that it is far more efficient to employ rigid policing of public space (such as sweeps) to create a livable city (Mitchell, 2001b: 66). Sweeps of encampments essentially bring the full force of the criminal justice system down upon the homeless. Case in point, Los Angeles 2004, at 5:30 a.m. a caravan of police cars rolled into the intersection of Golden Avenue and James M. Wood Boulevard while most homeless residents were sleeping. Witnesses claimed the police ordered everyone out of their tents and began handcuffing them, tore down the structures, and informed the homeless residents they were being taken to jail for sleeping and sitting on the sidewalk. All of those in the encampment were taken into custody as other homeless people began to scavenge the remainder of the previous group's belongings (Chong, 2004).

The action appeared to be a targeted strike based on space, as one homeless rights advocate pointed out, homelessness occurs all over Los Angeles but the location of the current sweep is a highly visible area near a trendy loft district. Chong (2004) contends that some residents in the area cheered the actions of the police. He accounted that one business owner stated that since the police have a right to keep sidewalks safe, right of ways clear, homeless encampments should not be tolerated. These actions divide communities as advocates view it as a scene of intolerance and destruction while other residents feel welcomed relief.

Consider the recent attempts to regulate the space of the well-known Los Angeles Skid Row. Skid Row covers roughly a 50-block area of downtown with a history going back over 100 years. Today, Skid Row contains between 8,000-11,000 homeless people who live in cardboard boxes, tents, sleep in the backseat of automobiles, or cheap hotels. Skid Row is a troubled area where drugs, crime, and prostitution flourish, while the mentally ill are simply left to battle their own demons. Los Angeles Police Department (LAPD) Chief William Bratton refers to the area as *"Dante's Inferno"* (The National Coalition for the Homeless & The National Law Center on Homelessness and Poverty, 2006: 41). Despite this spatial and historical context, the surrounding downtown area is booming with developers making plans to convert rundown hotels into expensive high-rise condominiums and lofts. The holdup in creating nearly 5,000 new high-end housing units is Skid Row and its homeless residents (LeDuff, 2003).

The conflict and concern over Skid Row has resulted in criminal justice actions in the past. For example, more than 20 years ago controversial LAPD Chief Daryl Gates announced to the press that the homeless people of Skid Row had seven days to get off the streets or face arrest (Blasi, 2007: 22). In September of 2006, the LAPD with a new Police Chief, and the city of Los Angeles led a by a mayor who was former president of the Southern California ACLU, vowed to clean up Skid Row through a new program titled the Safer Cities Initiative. Chief Bratton essentially applied a broken windows strategy targeting quality of life issues that he successfully employed while he was Chief of Police of the New York City Police Department during the 1990s. The LAPD deployed an additional 50 patrol officers to a 20 block area of Skid Row along with an additional 25-30 narcotics officers, and mounted patrol resulting in one of the highest sustained concentrations of police officers outside of Baghdad (Blasi & Stuart, 2008: 1).

Although Chief Bratton stated his department does not target homeless people, and they would never arrest their way out of homelessness, nor would they intend to (Blasi, 2007: 22), the results of police saturation and targeting quality of life issues were seen immediately. Within the first year of the program, officers issued more than 12,000 citations and averaged 750 arrests per month. Although the Safer Cities Initiative has a 'Streets or Services' component aimed at finding temporary shelter for up to 21 days, of the more than 7,500 arrests made in the first 10 months of the program only 34 homeless arrestees completed the transition (Blasi, 2007: 6). A snapshot of funding allocations reveals the priority of the city. The cost of the 50 police officers drawn from other areas of the city was $6 million, furthermore the Mayor requested additional funding for the City Attorney of $175,000, to pay for one Deputy City Attorney and a paralegal, but there was no accompanying funding request for housing services (Blasi, 2007: 27).

Some permanent residents and the homeless of Skid Row have praised the officers and the aggressive enforcement tactics suggesting that the heavy police presence has improved life in the community (MacDonald, 2007). In early September of 2006, there were more than 2,300 people sleeping on the sidewalks and in tents. By October, there were fewer than 1,000. In addition to the reduction of the number of people sleeping on the sidewalks, reports revealed an 18% reduction in crime with a 32% reduction in major felonies (MacDonald, 2007; Winton & DiMassa, 2007). However, a more critical inspection of the reported crime reduction casts doubt on the claimed success. Blasi & Stuart (2008) examined detailed crime data before and after the launch of the Safer Cities Initiative as well as the crime in Skid Row and the surrounding Central Area. The authors found reductions in serious or violent crime in the Safer Cities Initiative areas were not statistically significant from the reduction in non-Safer Cities Initiative areas.

Despite some support from community residents, the actions of the LAPD have not gone without challenges. Chief Bratton attempted to clean up Skid Row in 2002 with a similar broken windows strategy prior to implementing the Safer Cities Initiative. In turn, the ACLU of Southern California filed two lawsuits to block what they viewed as harassment of the homeless and a violation of the Eighth Amendment by enforcing the anti-public and sidewalk sleeping bans (MacDonald, 2007). After the Safer Cities Initiative was launched, the ACLU filed additional lawsuits ultimately winning a settlement from the city of Los Angeles banning LAPD officers from conducting unconstitutional searches of homeless individuals and for officers patrolling Skid Row to undergo additional scenario-based training in order to protect the rights of the homeless (ACLU of Southern California, 2008).

It is important to note that crime reduction statistics may not be the best way to measure the effectiveness of a policing program. As Kelling and Coles (1998: 22-23) illustrate in keeping with the broken windows theory, the use of street sweeps and targeting undesirables is antithetical to the concept. What is desired under the broken windows strategy is a close collaboration with the police and citizens including the homeless, to develop and enforce neighborhood level rules of order; this is best accomplished through persuasion, discussion, and ordering with arrests as a last resort. Thus, it is the rules of the neighborhood and not the state that are the most important for shaping police activity in this area.

The perspectives involved in the battles over public space are as intense as the actions of prohibiting public sleeping and sweeps of homeless encampments. It is a delicate balancing act for criminal justice practitioners, as they must enforce controversial laws, and face pressures from business and property owners to increase aggressiveness in their policing actions with the homeless, all while homeless rights advocacy groups push for reforms and compassionate handling of a vulnerable population. What is needed in these war zones of public space it is a balanced, objective, and well-planned responses, rather than strategies that have proven to be ineffective in public policy.

Conclusion

As we examine the public spaces of our nation's cities and towns, it becomes apparent that they are not open to all citizens. This realization ultimately leads us to view the public realm differently as they are not locations of *spatial democracy*, but areas of *conflict* as differing groups clash and attempt to impose their visions of appropriate use and who is desirable within the space. Anthropologist James Holston (1995) calls these struggles and conflicts *"spaces of insurgent citizenship"*. These struggles occur in urban centers, public parks, and on Skid Row as the homeless assert and claim rights to public space and redefine citizenship all while living outside the norms and legal codes of the city.

As battles over public space escalate they can take on intense forms and the criminal justice system is often employed in an attempt to regulate the actions and people within them. Laws may be passed to sanitize the city. Jeff Ferrell (2001) illustrates this in his examination of the battle over space in Tempe Arizona as the city attempted to create a type of urban Disneyland that has a uniform commercial appeal welcoming to tourist, business, and nightlife. In other words, officials seek to create a downtown theme park minus the view of groups of people that may make those that are welcomed in the space uncomfortable. To achieve this end, cities can bring the full force of the legal and policing system down upon those who resist the change or imposition of the plans of designers, officials, and property owners.

Although it is easy to characterize the involvement of the criminal justice system in regulating public space as unwelcomed and intrusive, like many other social issues in life such as homelessness it is multifaceted. To reiterate, cities do have the right to maintain order and keep public areas safe. Even in an area such as Skid Row that has become synonymous with disorder and crime, Officer Deon Joseph assigned to the Safer Cities Initiative reminds us: *"The idea that because people were homeless, they had a right to break 'minor' laws...has led to nothing but death, disease and despair"* (MacDonald, 2007). However, the concern is that once laws are set in motion and police are called in to enforce order, the actions will exacerbate homelessness with citations and fines accumulating hundreds of dollars and a criminal record that may restrict future housing opportunities and programs.

Advocacy groups for the homeless are equally diverse as not all have sought to end policing of public spaces where the homeless may be targeted, but have tried in many cases to create a partnership with the criminal justice system to achieve a balance of access to public space and ensuring the rights of all citizens. For example, the Ft. Lauderdale Police Department has partnered with the nonprofit agency Taskforce for Ending Homelessness to create an outreach team made up of officers and a civilian outreach worker who was formerly homeless. In its five years of operation in Broward County, the partnership has had over 23,000 contacts with homeless individuals, placed 11,384 people in shelters, and estimates suggest that there are at least 2,400 fewer arrests each year.

There have been other successful alternatives to criminalization efforts against the homeless across the country such as the partnership between the Pasadena Police Department and the Los Angeles Department of Health to provide mental services to those in need, and the nation's first Homeless Court Program in San Diego designed to assist the homeless in dealing with outstanding warrants and criminal offenses (The National Coalition for the Homeless & The National Law Center on Homelessness and Poverty, 2006). It is efforts like these that take into account local neighborhood norms while attempting to administer justice and maintain order that may be more faithful renditions of the broken windows concept than the heavy handed, street sweeping tactics that result in lawsuits.

Conflict over public space will probably exist in any diverse society, and it may be revisionist history to view the golden ages and golden sites such as the Greek agora and the New England town square as open and welcoming to all citizens and somehow different from the challenges faced today in the spaces of our modern cities. Laws, codes, and force have been used throughout history to determine which groups were allowed to take part in public discourse in the golden sites. Today, no group challenges the boundaries of public space like the homeless, and it is the modern criminal justice system that is often used to accomplish the goal of restricting their presence in the public sphere. As Mitchell (2001) illustrates, we have reached a point where we attempt to reorder our cities in such a manner to neutralize homelessness as we convince ourselves that they are not really citizens with the same rights as those that work hard, and it is through legislation and police actions that public space for the homeless is annihilated.

The issues of homelessness are complex and solving the associated problems is well beyond the capacity of most agencies within the criminal justice system. The people that make up the homeless are equally multifaceted with some needing affordable housing, others mental health and drug counseling, and those who simply wish to be left alone. Aggressive law enforcement practices and anti-homeless legislation does little to solve the problem other than making public spaces exclusive. The criminal justice system does have a role to play in the conflict over public space as practitioners are on the frontlines of these battles and there is a need for order and safety for all citizens regardless of their ownership of private property. The access to public space is essential for freedom in any society, and this access to the public sphere and protections of rights can only be achieved through a balanced response from the police, courts, city officials, business owners, and all residents of the city.

References

ACLU of Southern California. (2008). LAPD Skid Row officers banned from unlawful searches under settlement with the ACLU/SC and National Lawyers Guild. Retrieved May 29, 2009. http://www.aclu-sc.org/releases/view/102919

Amber, A. (2007, April 05). Florida Homeless Advocate Arrested for Feeding the Homeless at City Park. Retrieved May 26, 2009. hhttp://www.associatedcontent.com/article/205132/florida_homeless_advocate_arrested.html?cat=8

Blasi, G. (2007). Policing Our Way Out of Homelessness? The First Year of the Safer Cities Initiative on Skid Row. Retrieved May 28, 2009. http://college.usc.edu/geography/ESPE/publications/policing_homelessness.html

Blasi, G., & Stuart, F. (2008). Research Report: Has the Safer Cities Initiative in Skid Row reduced serious crime? Retrieved May 28, 2009. www.law.ucla.edu/docs/did_safer_cities_reduce_crime_in_skid_row.pdf

Blomley, N., Delaney, D., & Ford, R. (2001). Introduction. In N. Blomley, D. Delaney, & R. Ford (Eds.) *The Legal Geographies Reader: Law, Power, and Space* (p. 1-5). Oxford, UK: Blackwell.

Chong, J. (2004, January, 17). 25 held after police clear encampment. *Los Angeles Times*. Retrieved May 27, 2009. http://articles.latimes.com/2004/jan/17/local/me-homeless17

Chua, B., & Edwards, N. (1992). Public Space, Design, Use and Management. In B. Chua & N. Edwards (Eds.) *Public Space, Design, Use and Management* (p. 1-10). Philadelphia, PA: Cornet Books.

Cone, M. (1992, September, 08). Police waiting to enforce ban on camping: Homeless people still at the civic center despite warnings from authorities say they have no place to go and plan to stay until they are removed. *The LA Times*. Retrieved May 18, 2009. http://articles.latimes.com/1992-09-08/local/me-166_1_civic-center

Crawford, M. (1995). Contesting the public realm: Struggles over public space in Los Angeles. *Journal of Architectural Education, 49(1)*, 4-9.

Dolan, M. (1995, April). State justices uphold tough homeless law. *Los Angeles Times*, A1.

Ellickson, R. (1996). Controlling Chronic Misconduct in City Spaces: Of Panhandlers, Skid Rows, and Public-space Zoning. *Yale Law Journal*, 105: 1165-1248.

Ferrell, J. (2001). Remapping the City: Public Identity, Cultural Space, and Social Justice. *Contemporary Justice Review*, 4(2), 161–180.

Gieryn, T. (2000). A Place for Space. *Annual Review of Sociology*, 26, 463-496.

Hillier, B., & Hanson J. (1984). *The Social Logic of Space*. Cambridge, MA: Cambridge University Press.

Housing & Urban Development. (2009). Homelessness & Hunger. Retrieved May 27, 2009. http://www.oaklandnet.com/government/hcd/homeless/encampments.html

Hubert, C. (2009, March 14). Some feel burned as media spotlight falls on capital's homeless camp. *The Sacramento Bee*.

Irazábal, C. (2008). Citizenship, Democracy and Public Space in Latin American. In C. Irazábal (Ed.) *Ordinary Place/ Extraordinary Events: Democracy Citizenship, and Public Space in Latin America* (p. 11-34). New York, NY: Routledge.

Jacobs, J. (1961). *The Death and Life of Great American Cities.* New York, NY: Vintage Books.

Kelling, G., & Coles. K. (1998). *Fixing Broken Windows: Restoring Order and Reducing Crime in our Communities.* New York, NY: Free Press.

Komp, C. (2006, August 4). Bans on feeding homeless spread, face challenges. Retrieved May 26, 2009.
http://newstandardnews.net/content/index.cfm/items/3503

LeDuff, C. (2003, July 15). In Los Angeles, Skid Row resists an upgrade. *The New York Times.* Retrieved May 19, 2009.
http://www.nytimes.com/2003/07/15/us/in-los-angeles-skid-row-resists-an-upgrade.html

Lewan, T. (2007, February 3). Orlando homeless laws stir heated debate. Retrieved May 25, 2009.
http://www.redorbit.com/news/general/826094/orlando_homeles s_laws_stir_heated_debate/index.html

Marosi, R. (1999, March 01). Ruling sides with homeless. *The LA Times.* Retrieved May 18, 2009.
http://articles.latimes.com/1999/mar/01/news/mn-12917?pg=1

Martinez, G. (1992, May 19). Santa Ana ban on camping by homeless gets initial OK - Law: Effort to oust growing tent communities could spur legal challenges. *The LA Times.* Retrieved May 20' 2009.
http://articles.latimes.com/1992-05-19/local/me-336_1_santa-ana

Marx, G. (2006). Surveillance cameras. In W. Staples (Ed.) *Encyclopedia of Privacy* (p. 544-549). Santa Barbara, CA: Greenwood Press.

McDonald, H. (2007, November 02). Tough love on Skid Row. *Wall Street Journal.* Retrieved May 29, 2009.
http://online.wsj.com/article/SB119397065225780165.html

Mitchell, D. (2001). The Annihilation of Space by Law: The Roots and Implications of Anti-Homelessness Laws in the United States. In N. Blomley, D. Delaney, & R. Ford (Eds.) *The Legal Geographies Reader: Law, Power, and Space* (p. 6-18). Oxford, UK: Blackwell.

Mitchell, D. (2001b). Postmodern Geographical Praxis? The Postmodern Impulse and the War against the Homeless People in the Post-Justice City. In C. Minca (Ed.) *Postmodern geography* (p. 57-92). Oxford, UK: Blackwell.

Mitchell, D. (2003). *The Right to the City: Social Justice and the Fight for Public Space.* NewYork, NY: Guilford Press.

Moore, S. (2008, November 3). Few Clues in Killing of 5 in California. *The New York Times.* Retrieved May 27, 2009.
http://www.nytimes.com/2008/11/04/us/04slay.html

MSNBC (2008, September 18). In hard times, tent cities rise across the country since foreclosure mess, homeless advocates report rise in encampments. Retrieved May 27, 2009.
http://www.msnbc.msn.com/id/26776283/

National Law Center on Homelessness and Poverty. (2007). Changing laws, changing lives: Lawyers working to end homelessness. Retrieved May 29, 2009.
http://www.nlchp.org/view_report.cfm?id=285

Records Reveal 131 Camping Arrests. (2007, November 11). Retrieved May 26, 2009.
http://sarasota.indymedia.org/local/records-reveal-131-camping-arrests

Saewitz, M (2006, December, 8). Sleep-out to protest ban on camping. *Herald Tribune.* Retrieved May 24, 2009.
http://www.heraldtribune.com/apps/pbcs.dll/article?AID=/20061208/NEWS/612080314/1270/NEWS0101

Scruton, R. (1984). Public Space and the Classical Vernacular. *The Public Interest, 74,* 5-16.

Simon, H. (1991). Towns without Pity: A Constitutional and Historical Analysis of Official Efforts to Drive Homeless Persons from American Cities. *Tulane Law Review,* 66(4), 631-675.

Skogan, W. (1990). *Disorder and Decline: Crime and the Spiral of Decay in American Neighborhoods.* Berkeley, CA: University of California Press.

Smith, D. (1994). A Theoretical and Legal Challenge to Homeless Criminalization as Public Policy. *Yale Law and Public Policy Review,* 12, 487-517.

Stead, P. (1983). The Roman police. *Policing: An International Journal of Police Strategies & Management,* 6, 3–7.

Steele, K. (2009, May 20). Advocates for homeless, residents square off on 'tent city'. *The Tampa Tribune.* Retrieved May 27, 2009.
http://centraltampa2.tbo.com/content/2009/may/20/tentcity

Takahashi, L. (1999). *Homelessness, AIDS, and Stigmatization: The NIMBY Syndrome in the United States at the End of the Twentieth Century*. Oxford, UK: Oxford University Press.

The National Coalition for the Homeless &The National Law Center on Homelessness and Poverty. (2006). *A Dream Denied: The Criminalization of Homelessness in U.S. Cities*. Retrieved May 18, 2009.
http://www.nationalhomeless.org/publications/reports.html

Tier, R. (1993). Maintaining Safety and Civility in Public Spaces: A Constitutional Approach to Aggressive Begging. *Louisiana Law Review*, 54, 285-338.

Waldron, J. (1991). *The Right to Private Property*. Oxford, UK: Oxford University Press.

Wilson, J., & Kelling, G. (1982, March). Broken windows: The police and neighborhood safety. *Atlantic Monthly*. Retrieved May 15, 2009.
http://www.theatlantic.com/ doc/198203/broken-windows

Winton, R., & DiMassa, C. (2007, March 03). Skid row cleanup is challenged. *Lost Angeles,Times*. Retrieved May 29, 2009.
http://articles.latimes.com/2007/mar/03/local/me-skidrow3?pg=1

CHAPTER 7
STATE EXPENDITURES ON THE CRIMINAL JUSTICE SYSTEM

George P. Mason

Abstract: *Crime is regularly assumed to occur disproportionately within U.S. inner cities due to poverty. This chapter challenges this assumption by examining state criminal justice expenditures. The main supposition is higher crime rates in the inner city reflect a disproportionate amount of per capita expenditures on the criminal justice system. The specific crime rates in Detroit, Michigan are examined to demonstrate the causal effects of an expanded state financed criminal justice system. Data for this study was obtained through the United States Department of Justice (Federal Bureau of Investigation and Bureau of Justice Statistics) and the United States Department of Commerce (Bureau of the Census). Regression analyses utilize semi-logarithmic transformations to estimate criminal justice system expenditure trends over time. The chapter concludes with an examination of overall state expenditures. Findings suggest that the current war on drugs may be nothing more than a euphemism for a concentrated state sponsored repression of urban African American populations.*

In both the urban poverty and criminology literature, it is regularly assumed that crime disproportionately occurs within United States urban cities, or inner cities, as a result of high poverty levels. Although U.S. crime rates have declined since 1994, it is still assumed by some that the rate of crime is higher in the inner city due to the poverty and racial characteristics of those living there (Herrnstein, 1995; Herrnstein & Murray, 1994; Wilson & Herrnstein, 1985; Murray, 1984). In fact, it is commonly suggested by more liberal research that relatively high U.S. inner city crime rates are directly attributable to problems of racial housing segregation, economic poverty, unemployment and underemployment, and even single parenthood (for example Wilson, 1987; Murray, 1984; Lewis, 1969; Moynihan, 1969).

From this body of research, the growth of the '*culture of poverty*' and '*underclass*' theses has reinforced the causal relationship of higher crime rates to various social pathologies. This body of research makes the assertion that the relationship between the socio-demographic characteristics of urban city residents and crime levels is accurately reflected within the '*official*' crime rates. These official crime statistics are generally drawn from data published annually by the US Federal Bureau of Investigation Uniform Crime Reports (UCR). These statistics vary considerably from the actual amount of crime in society, irrespective of detection or arrest.

The following examines whether the higher official rates of crime in the inner city are simply a function of state expenditures on the criminal justice system. The main supposition of this paper is that urban city crime rates primarily reflect higher per capita criminal justice expenditures in those geographic areas. In other words, the higher per capita criminal justice system expenditures in the inner city result in higher crime detection rates. Higher crime rates are the direct result of the increasing concentration of all criminal justice resources within urban cities and not a 'culture of poverty' or higher criminality of inner city residents.

The official rates of crime are quite different from the actual rates of crime. Victimization surveys and criminal self-report studies have repeatedly demonstrated that the criminal justice system accounts for very little crime (Conklin, 2001). Another reason for this difference is that most crimes are not reported to nor even known by the police (Cromwell & Dunham, 1997; DeKeseredy & Schwartz, 1996; Evans & Himelfarb, 1996). Rates of crime, as reported by the Federal Bureau of Investigation's Uniform Crime Reports (UCR), primarily and categorically reflect street crime and exclude crimes associated with wealthier members of society (Coleman, 1998; Reiman, 1998; Ermann & Lundman, 1987; Quinney, 1979, 1977; Chambliss, 1975; Sutherland, 1949).

Official detection of crime is problematic at the best of times and, depending on the type of crime, estimates of the '*dark-figure of crime*' can be as high as 90 percent. Thus, it must be assumed that crime is committed at all socioeconomic levels of society but the form it takes varies based upon one's opportunities. Although actual crime is difficult to determine, criminal justice officials, the media, and many social scientists continually reinforce the fear of crime for both *ideological* and *financial* purposes (MacLean, 1996; DeKeseredy & Schwartz, 1996; Krisberg, 1994; Gebotys et al., 1988). It can also be added that the assumptions about the relationship between poverty and general social pathologies reflects similar ideological purposes (Valentine, 1971).

The fear of crime has penetrated inner city life in the United States for numerous years. Although the fear of crime is *real* in its effects, media and academia have perpetuated these fears through presenting UCR data simply to further specific agendas through *uncritical* reliance upon official data sources (Epstein, 1997). Moreover, the causes of crime, as represented by UCR data, have historically been attributed to factors such as *poverty* and *race*. Today, the main causal antecedent to crime is considered to be poverty, particularly the poverty found in the urban city. Racially segregated poverty within U.S. cities, and the criminal justice system responses to it, is simply a euphemism today for continued systemic and structural racism against African Americans. Fainstein (1996: 218) has suggested that, irrespective of political and theoretical perspectives, contemporary discourse of the underclass represents a social science coding schema for the ghetto, black ghetto, or simply a euphemism for black.

The current study demonstrates the extent to which higher urban city crime rates are affected by state criminal justice expenditures. It seeks to test the assumption that poverty causes crime holds up to statistical inspection. As the amount of money spent on the criminal justice system is considerable, its allocation requires scrutiny to understand how the state polices inner city residents. In general, the state *'polices'* the U.S. inner city while *'protecting'* suburbs and more affluent areas. The hypothesis to be tested is whether increases in per capita criminal justice system expenditures in the inner city of Detroit result in higher crime detection rates than in the surrounding suburban communities. In other words, higher UCR crime rates, as the representative measure of *'official crime,'* are the direct result of the increasing concentration of all criminal justice resources within the inner city rather than changes in criminality.

The relationship between measures of crime and expenditures for policing, courts, and corrections are examined with governmental data for Detroit, Wayne County, Michigan, and the federal government. The following will provide a statistical and conceptual test to determine whether increases in inner city crime rates represent the development of state repression.

Theoretical and Conceptual Framework

President Lyndon B. Johnson launched two initiatives in the mid-1960s to ostentatiously combat rising poverty and crime in the U.S. In his 1965 Presidential State of the Union Message, President Johnson declared a state of war; the enemies in this war were poverty and crime. The first of these initiatives was the '*war on poverty*' and the second was the '*war on crime*' (Quinney, 1977; Moynihan, 1969). The two initiatives were systematically linked in their creation and intention. Yet, both initiatives can clearly be considered failures in social policy to achieve the publicly stated goals; the war on poverty was significantly underfunded and had little hope of success from the onset (Axinn & Levin, 1997). The actual intention of these two initiatives must be questioned concurrently, as neither has made inroads into either poverty or crime.

The Johnson Administration's initiatives signified important changes within society. Rather than eliminating the problems of poverty or crime, the changes of the 1960s resulted in a new form of *social control*. The enemy was not new according to the President but rather an ancient evil that tempts all people and threatened the social character established during the 1950s (Quinney, 1979). The result was the ideological creation and social impression that crime was rampant in U.S. society. Similar populist rhetoric was used in the development of the war on poverty. However, the stated enemy in this war was juvenile delinquency which apparently resulted from the socialization of poor families (Moynihan, 1969). The initiatives created within Johnson's New Deal have very different implications when they are considered simultaneously.

One of the most important implications was the development of a '*conventional wisdom*' in society surrounding the relationship between poverty and crime (Axinn & Levin, 1997; McDonald, 1979). The conventional wisdom which developed fostered the notion that the U.S. had an extremely generous and liberal social welfare system (for example, see Murray, 1984). With respect to crime, the conventional wisdom developed under Johnson's New Deal continues to suggest today that most adolescents do not respect authority, are lazy, have low moral standards, and are increasingly dealt with leniently by liberal law makers (McDonald, 1979:58).

The politics of the 1960s resulted in a new form of social control which was an ideological, pedagogic, and cultural transformation about the extent of crime in society. This is further exacerbated by contemporary mass media sensationalism of crime and portrayal of specific criminal offender characteristics such as race and poverty.

The mass media exposure of crime and poverty portrays very specific ideological images which connect both crime and poverty within a single framework. In particular, media images of crime are portrayed as violent acts primarily committed by African American men living within inner city poverty or the 'ghetto' (DeKeseredy & Schwartz, 1996). Moreover, media images emphasize crimes committed in urban cities over those occurring in the more affluent suburban areas, particularly crimes which are infrequent, very violent, and related to illegal drugs or narcotics in some manner. Inner city African American women living in poverty are increasingly portrayed as 'typical' criminals within the media when arrested for drug usage and trafficking, particularly if the woman is pregnant (Conklin, 1998).

It is clear that the correspondence between official crime rate statistics and the crimes represented within crime news is minimal and unsubstantiated (Katz, 1987). Yet, as Herman & Chomsky (1988) noted over twenty years ago, the social effects of media reports have broader ideological and social effects in the development of racist and classist public attitudes. The result is the creation of public attitudes which do not reflect the realities of crime but nevertheless impact upon public perceptions, governmental policy initiatives, and criminal legislation.

Those segments of society (the 'underclass') which cannot be controlled through economic coercion alone are controlled both through the direct physical force of the state *and* the ideological construction of a negative racial social stereotype: one from which individuals strive to distance themselves (West, 1994). It is the reliance upon economic inequity which creates the possible conditions necessary for a class and race based division within society (Burawoy, 1985). In U.S. society, the middle-class is the group in which ideological consent is most necessary for the continuation of capitalism, including the more affluent African American middle-class (West, 1994). In effect, direct economic coercion becomes displaced by a hegemonic regime and the organization of consent at the level of economic class (Burawoy, 1979). In Detroit, this direct economic coercion in 1995 translated into a conservatively estimated poverty rate at one-third (33.1%) of the population (U.S. Bureau of the Census, 1999).

The notion of deterrence is central to the argument that state criminal justice system expenditures at current levels are necessary to prevent more crime from occurring. The notion of deterrence is directly related to the poverty causes crime thesis. However, it is clear from the literature that general deterrence through increased criminal justice expenditures is unlikely to lead to less crime: particularly when there are not accurate measures of the actual amounts of crime (Sacco & Kennedy, 1998). In fact, the notion of general deterrence may be another euphemism or code for the continued ideological justification for the development of a police state in the inner city to control African Americans.

While the ideological development of criminal images misrepresent the extent of crime committed by poor inner city African Americans, governmental policies have coincided with the images portrayed within mass medium. The war on crime has increased substantially since Johnson and Congress enacted the *Omnibus Crime Control and Safe Streets Act*. State criminal justice system expenditures had increased to a dramatic $15 billion by 1974 (Quinney, 1977). In 1992, the direct expenditures for the U.S. criminal justice system approximately totaled $94 billion (Bureau of Justice Statistics, 1996).

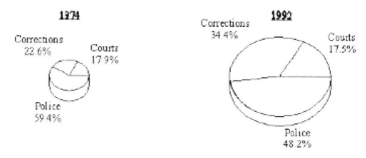

Figure I

The 1992, state criminal justice expenditures represent an increase of 627.12% compared to 1974. Figure I demonstrates the magnitude to which criminal justice system expenditures have increased in spending between 1974 and 1992 (in constant 1982 dollars). The increase in state criminal justice expenditures has been 220.37% since 1974. Figure I also illustrates that the allocation of funding to each area within the criminal justice system had increased substantially by 1992. In 1992, the police expenditures accounted for $41.327 billion or 44 percent of the total state criminal justice system; judicial and legal expenditures were $20.949 billion or 22 percent; and, correctional costs were $31.461 billion or 34 percent. The comparable expenditures in 1974 were $8.512 billion for policing, $2.569 billion for judicial and legal, and $3.240 billion for corrections.

The distribution of criminal justice expenditures has dramatically changed in two distinct ways between 1974 and 1992. First, the state has allocated a greater proportion of resources to corrections and a lower proportion to policing. It should also be noted that each of the three areas have increased in real dollar amounts and based upon per capita expenditures. In effect, the overall proportional decrease in policing expenditures is more than compensated by the magnitude of per capita expenditures. Moreover, the relative changes in criminal justice expenditures reflect the substantial increases of drug related incarcerations of African American men (Cayley, 1998; National Criminal Justice Information and Statistics Service, 1998).

Second, in the explosion of correction spending during the 1980s, there was also a corresponding shift of fiscal burden towards the state level. Municipalities such as Detroit have had court and correctional expenditures reduced while police expenditures have correspondingly increased: the burden for corrections and courts has shifted slightly to the county level but more dramatically to the state level. The Wayne County correctional expenditures have increased by about 14 percent from 1982 to 1992. Over the same time period, criminal justice expenditures in Michigan nearly expanded by 242% (in constant dollars).

The conclusion that 'war on crime' advocates would reach, such as the FBI, is that increased state criminal justice expenditures have caused the decrease in crime since 1994: the main premise behind the war on crime and populist explanation for over two million people incarcerated today. In fact, the FBI has suggested that any relationship of this nature would be explained by the increased "*strength and the aggressiveness of a jurisdiction's law enforcement agency*" and not as a result of a 'net-widening' or relative increase in the overall criminal justice system (Federal Bureau of Investigation, 1995: iv).

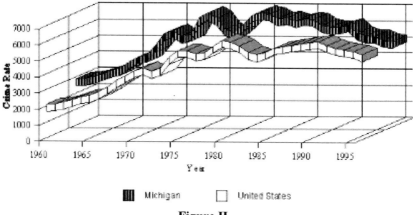

Figure II

In fact, the official UCR crime rates have dramatically increased in the U.S. since the war on crime was declared. Figure II presents a comparison of U.S. and Michigan UCR index crime rates between 1960 and 1996. Clearly, the UCR index crime rates have increased dramatically since the early 1960s across the nation and within Michigan. From the data presented in Figure II, it would be a simple conclusion to suggest that all crime has uniformly increased across the nation. However, there are specific relationships one can observe from the UCR crime rates.

While possibly an anecdotal correlation, there was a dramatic increase in the crime rates for all the categories within the UCR in the period corresponding with and immediately after the enactment of the *Civil Rights Act* of 1964. Although it has been suggested that crime rates in the United States dramatically increased until 1994 (Rand et al., 1997), the argument is based upon a shorter time series analyses which exclude long term trends. The UCR data demonstrate that overall U.S. crime rates continued to increase until the peak years of 1980 and until 1981 within Michigan.

A careful delineation of the UCR official crime rates reveals some interesting information about crime rates. First, the national UCR crime rates reached peak levels in 1979, 1980, and 1981 with rates per 100,000 people of 5565.5, 5950.0, and 5858.2 respectively. As well, two other peak periods in the national UCR index crime rates occurred during 1975 (5298.5) and 1991 (5897.8). In Michigan, the UCR index crime rates peaked in 1975 (6800.0) and 1981 (6854.0) and have steadily declined since 1981.

Notwithstanding the numerous methodological and ideological problems of utilizing the UCR crime rates as indicators of criminality and their comparisons with other geographical regions (see Conklin, 2001; Maxfield & Babbie, 2001), the trends clearly demonstrate that the most serious of street crimes has decreased nationwide. Data from the National Crime Survey and National Crime Victimization Survey also demonstrate that victimization rates for general violent and property crimes have decreased steadily since 1979. The reported overall victimization rate decrease of five percent between 1973 and 1995 does not correspond with the 116 percent increase in crimes reported by police over the same period of time (Rand et. al., 1997). This would suggest that the police are simply decreasing the number of unknown crimesBwhat is referred to in the criminology literature as the '*dark-figure of crime*.' The exploration of crime rates within the inner city of Detroit between 1982 and 1992 may provide some insight into the underlying political and economic nature of how the criminal justice system is structured.

Methodology

Data for this paper were collected as part of a larger research project currently underway examines issues surrounding social justice and inequality. The methodological approach of this paper is based upon an investigation conducted into Canadian state criminal justice system expenditures by MacLean (1996) and McDonald (1979). The data for the current study were obtained through the United States Department of Justice (Federal Bureau of Investigation and Bureau of Justice Statistics) and the United States Department of Commerce (Bureau of the Census).

Published statistical documents and more recent Internet data resources were both used in the collection of data. While there may be considerable limitations to the UCR crime reporting data, it is clear that they conservatively under-represent the extent of actual crime. Nevertheless, the UCR index crimes can serve as an adequate dependent variable within the exploratory study of state criminal justice system expenditures. Moreover, the poverty causes crime advocates discussed above have used UCR data as representative of crime. As such, it creates a methodological congruence to utilize UCR data in challenging that particular ontology.

The above hypothesis postulated that crime rates will increase with state criminal justice system expenditures. In contrast, it is possible under a null hypothesis that there is an inverse relationship or even no relationship. To test this hypothesis, it was necessary to utilize a regression analysis with a semi-logarithmic transformation to account for a number of methodological issues (Pedhazur, 1982).

Among the methodological issues to address, the two most important are inflationary trends and comparable crime rates. First, the state criminal justice expenditures needed to be standardized for comparison. Although actual expenditures are presented for replication purposes, each of the dollar values were converted to standard 1982 values. The values are calculated according to the Consumer Price Index for 1950 to 1996 (Bureau of the Census, 1997). Second, the state criminal justice expenditures had to be standardized to account for population and compound growth in the criminal justice system. The simple regression analysis does not account for changes over time while the semi-logarithmic transformation allows for temporal standardization. As well, crime rates must be equivalent for comparative purposes. Thus, both state criminal justice expenditures and crime rates were recoded as rates per hundred thousand people.

Dependent Variable

The dependent variable is the frequency of crimes known to policing agencies as reported by the Federal Bureau of Investigation Uniform Crime Reports. The UCR is a national collection of municipal, county, and state law enforcement agencies which report data on crimes known or detected by those agencies. For the ten year period between 1982 and 1992 inclusive, the eight UCR index crimes remained constant. The reporting categories are '*murder and non-negligent manslaughter*,' '*forcible rape*,' '*robbery*,' '*aggravated assault*,' '*burglary*,' '*larceny-theft*,' '*motor vehicle theft*,' and '*arson*.'

The eight UCR index crime categories were collapsed into two types of offences to facilitate the statistical analysis of the data. The two types of offences correspond to offences which are violence against the person and offences against property. The first group of offences was designated as Violent Offences and included the index crime categories of 'murder and non-negligent manslaughter,' 'forcible rape,' '*robbery*,' and '*aggravated assault*.' The second classification of offences was denoted as Property Offences and included the UCR crime index data for '*burglary*,' '*larceny-theft*,' '*motor vehicle theft*,' and '*arson*.' Finally, the total crime index offences were created in the variable Total Offences for comparative purposes. Each variable was calculated in rates per one hundred thousand persons.

Independent Variable

The independent variable for the study is state criminal justice system expenditures. There are four indicators of state criminal justice system expenditures which are used. The four indicators correspond to four specific areas of analysis: (i) court and legal expenditures, (ii) corrections expenditures, (iii) policing expenditures, and (iv) total criminal justice system expenditures. Each of the indicators measure direct costs such as salaries, wages, equipment, capital, and other expenses. The dollar amounts have been reported by the criminal justice system agency as expenditures made to provide the service within the jurisdiction of which the agency was responsible. As well, the measurement of state criminal justice system expenditures included the subtraction of intergovernmental costs which are the resources provided by one level of government to another to offset the costs of the particular service. These intergovernmental costs include such things as grants-in-aid, shared revenues, fiscal assistance, and programs delivered under cost-sharing arrangements. The calculation of both direct and intergovernmental costs is the total criminal justice system expenditures for the particular level of government (Bureau of Justice Statistics, 1996).

The years 1982 through 1986 and 1992 have been chosen due to methodological and access limitations of the data. The Bureau of Justice Statistics (1996) delineated the comparability problems with the *Expenditure and Employment* series with other state criminal justice system expenditure measures. The variable Total Expenditures represents the combination of expenditures for court and legal, corrections, and police services.

Court and legal expenditures are combined together to create the variable Court Expenditures. The expenditures are reported by the Bureau of Justice Statistics. The data for the variable Court Expenditures includes total court costs, legal service and prosecution functions, and public defense activities. The variable includes data for both criminal and civil justice activities as source documents, for many governments do not separate these activities. Data on expenditures may also include probation costs when the cost was unrecognizable from the source documents (Bureau of Justice Statistics, 1996).

Correction expenditures are the reported values of all corrections by the Bureau of Justice Statistics. The correctional facilities included every public institution used to incarcerate individuals after passage of court sentencing or while awaiting a court trial (Bureau of Justice Statistics, 1996). State hospitals for the criminally insane, jails, prisons, reformatories, and all other institutions for the correction of illegal behavior (such as drug and alcohol treatment and rehabilitation) are included within the collection of correction expenditures. The total cost of corrections is represented by the variable Correction Expenditures.

Police expenditures are the reported costs of all law enforcement agencies. The police expenditures may represent costs for providing traffic enforcement, crime prevention activities and programs, regular policing services, and other such functions of the police (Bureau of Justice Statistics, 1996). Data on expenditures include all sworn and non-sworn, either full or part-time law enforcement officers. The total expenditures for law enforcement are included in the variable Police Expenditures.

One purpose of examining the three areas of state criminal justice system expenditures as separate independent variables is to demonstrate the degree to which expenditures have been relocated from one area to another. In Figure I, the state criminal justice system expenditure allocations were demonstrated to have increased somewhat since 1974. Thus, it was necessary to separate the three areas to make the changes explicit rather than simply using total expenditures as a measure of the state criminal justice system.

Findings and Discussion

Figure II demonstrated the UCR crime rates for the United States and Michigan. Clearly, the notion that violent crime rates continue to increase across the nation is a misconception of even the official crime rate. In fact, it would be appropriate to suggest that media and academic reports calling for increased state criminal justice expenditures are neither based upon increasing UCR crime rates nor the principles of general deterrence. Therefore, it has been suggested that an alternative explanation may be best suited to understand the '*conventional wisdom*' of poverty and crime in the inner city.

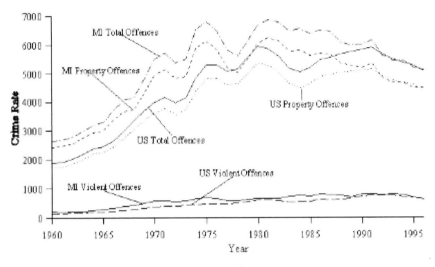

Figure III

Figure III represents the trends in the UCR crime rates for the United States and Michigan between 1960 and 1996. While the earlier UCR crime rates for Michigan are somewhat higher than the nation, the more recent crime rates reflect the national average. The separation of the UCR categories of crime demonstrates that increases between 1960 and 1996 primarily reflect property offences. However, the application of the semi-logarithmic equation demonstrates the trends by estimating the data more accurately within a model which accounts for temporal changes.

Figure IV

Figure IV represents the semi-logarithmic transformation of the data to provide the best-fit for estimation purposes. It is clear from Figure IV that the Detroit property offences have decreased from 1982 to 1992. The semi-logarithmic transformation demonstrates a trend towards substantially lower property offences in the 1980s which continued well into the 1990s. Intuitively, this would not be expected because of the increasing state criminal justice expenditures. In other words, one could reasonably expect that the number of property offences should increase as a result of increased resources to detect crimes against property. Furthermore, if it is assumed that poverty causes crime, it would be expected that property offences in Detroit would have either increased or remained constant: particularly since the estimated poverty rates increased to almost 40 percent (39.6%) by 1993 (Bureau of the Census, 1993). Moreover, the level of poverty in Detroit steadily increased from 1970 to 1993 while the quality of life declined (Housing and Urban Development, 1997). Yet, neither pattern is evident from the UCR data for Detroit.

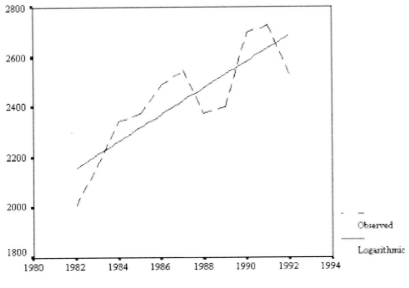

Figure V

Figure V presents the violent offences for Detroit between 1982 and 1992. Similar to the property offences, a semi-logarithmic transformation of the data was performed to examine the trends for violent offences over the time period. The UCR violent offences have increased from 1982 to 1992 and the trend would suggest that violent crimes will continue to increase. According to the assumption that increased state criminal justice expenditures will lead to increased detection, it could be logically concluded that either more violent crime is occurring as a result of poverty or that more violent offenders are being detected by the law enforcement agencies. However, if Sugrue's (1996) analysis is fairly accurate, one could conclude that the increased racial segregation in Detroit, and the relationship the '*underclass*' has with the police, is creating the conditions which have led to an urban crisis between inner city residents and the police. Further examination of the UCR categories reveals some interesting information about violence in Detroit.

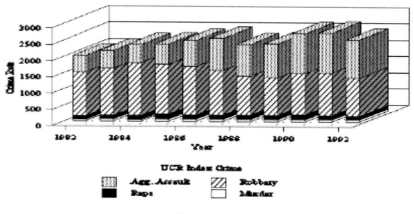

Figure VI

The UCR data demonstrate that the most serious violent crimes in Detroit continue to decrease and all crime categories except aggravated assault have fallen since 1975. Figure VI presents the actual differences in crime rate trends among UCR violent offences for Detroit between 1982 and 1992. Clearly, there are three specific trends which become evident from the data. First, the UCR violent offence categories of *'murder and non-negligent manslaughter'* and *'forcible rape'* have remained fairly constant within the population between 1982 and 1992. Second, the category of *'robbery'* has dramatically decreased over the 1982 to 1992 period. According to the *'poverty causes crime thesis,'* it would be logically expected that robbery would have increased substantially in this period, particularly as it is a fairly straightforward and expedient method to procure money. The third trend which becomes apparent is the dramatic increase in the *'aggravated assault'* category.

The dramatic increase in aggravated assaults could easily be explained according to the cultural theories discussed above. In essence, the cultural theories would suggest that the increasing racial segregation, poverty, and lack of employment opportunities for African Americans in Detroit may lead to more frustration and acts of violence against others in the community (Sugrue, 1996). However, if that were the case, then it would be logically expected that all (or at least some) categories of violent offences or property offences would show similar trends to the aggravated assault category: a theoretical presumption which is not supported in the data. Therefore, another explanation which examines the state criminal justice system expenditures needs to be pursued.

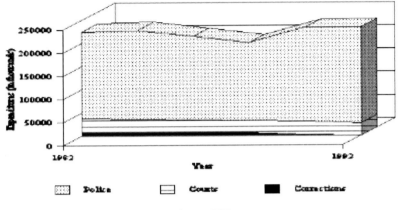

Figure VII

In the examination of state criminal justice expenditures over the 1982 to 1992 period, a different set of trends becomes apparent. Figure VII presents the state criminal justice expenditures for Detroit between 1982 to 1986 and the year 1992. Data for the years 1987 through 1991 are not available in the *Justice Expenditure and Employment Extracts* (due to *'government cutbacks'*) and comparison with other data sources would introduce bias. The total Detroit expenditures in constant 1982 dollars were \$224.537 million in 1982 and increased slightly to \$233.811 million by 1992. While the overall state criminal justice expenditures have remained fairly constant (as has the population of Detroit), the proportion of expenditures borne within the respective criminal justice system areas have changed slightly.

After standardizing the yearly expenditures for population growth and inflationary trends, the pattern in the changes become evident when calculated in constant dollars. First, the court and legal criminal justice expenditures in Detroit have decreased by approximately 11 percent in real terms from 1982 (\$30.228 million) to 1992 (\$26.885 million). Second, the proportion of state criminal justice system expenditures within Detroit devoted to corrections has decreased substantially from almost eight million dollars in 1982 (\$7.866 million) to less than one-half million in 1992 (\$0.467 million). Finally, the amount of state criminal justice system expenditures devoted to policing in Detroit has increased by over eleven percent from 1982 (\$186.442 million) to 1992 (\$206.458 million). Clearly, the small overall state criminal justice system expenditure increases and the substantial decreases to the correctional and court sectors have been added to policing budgets in the Detroit inner city.

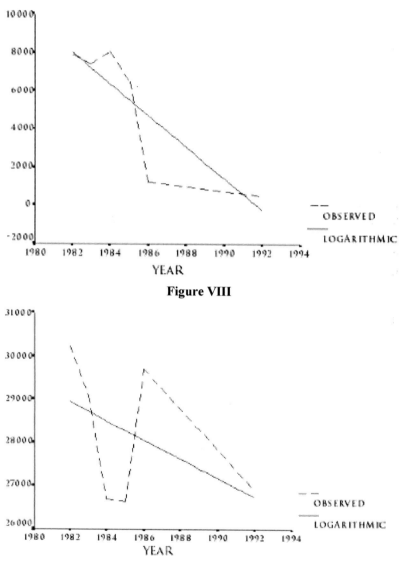

Figure VIII

Figure IX

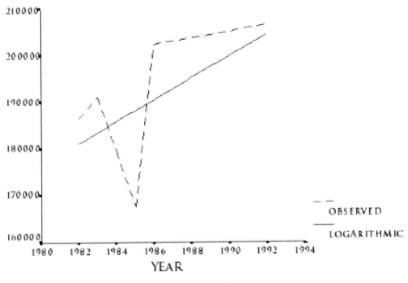

Figure X

Figure VIII, Figure IX, and Figure X provide semi-logarithmic transformations of each area within the Detroit criminal justice system. Figure VIII demonstrates that the state criminal justice expenditures for corrections have decreased substantially and, according to the trend, will eventually become an insignificant expenditure for the criminal justice system within Detroit. Without considering the trends within Wayne County and all of Michigan, the data would be suspect at the very least. However, the decline in correctional spending in the Detroit area has been more than made up by increased spending by the county and state levels (Bureau of Justice Statistics, 1987-1996).

In constant 1982 dollars, the Wayne County correctional expenditures have increased by about fourteen percent from 1982 ($81.155 million) to 1992 ($92.574 million). More importantly, the increase in Michigan correctional expenditures offers some insight: Michigan correctional expenditures nearly expanded by 242 percent in constant dollars from 1982 ($252.712 million) to 1992 ($609.501 million). In other words, the burden for correctional facilities has become centered at the county and state levels of government outside of Detroit which has enabled the state criminal justice system to allocate more resources to policing the inner city of Detroit.

Figure IX represents the actual expenditures and semi-logarithmic trend in state criminal justice system expenditures for the courts and legal system in Detroit from 1982 to 1992. A pattern similar to correctional spending is apparent from the expenditure data. Overall, court and legal expenditures have decreased in constant 1982 dollars within Detroit from 1982 ($30.228 million) to 1992 ($26.886 million). Wayne County judicial and legal expenditures decreased in terms of constant dollars very slightly between 1982 ($40.038 million) to 1992 ($39.389 million). However, the Michigan court and legal system increased expenditures in constant dollars by more than eleven percent from 1982 ($123.890 million) to 1992 ($138.001 million).

While the trend clearly indicates that inner city state criminal justice system expenditures are increasingly directed towards policing functions, it should be noted that overall, the smallest increases were in the court and legal expenditures. The complete state criminal justice system courts and legal expenditures increased by only five percent (5.38%) in the period between 1982 and 1992. This might suggest, combined with the other data presented, that the court and legal system are providing less resources for defense of offenders as prosecution, incarceration rates, and prison populations in Detroit and across the nation have reached unprecedented levels in U.S. history (Conklin, 1998).

Figure X provides the semi-logarithmic transformation and actual state criminal justice system expenditures on policing for Detroit between 1982 and 1992. The actual and trend in policing expenditures within the inner city definitively supports the hypothesis that the inner city is policed while the suburbs are protected. In constant 1982 dollars, police expenditures in Detroit increased by over twenty million dollars from 1982 ($186.443 million) to 1992 ($206.458 million). While the percentage increase represents just slightly over 10 percent (10.74%), the increases reflect similar patterns in Wayne County and the State of Michigan. Wayne County increased expenditures on policing by 96.24% from 1982 to 1992. The State of Michigan also increased policing expenditures (albeit at a substantially smaller percentage) by 17.88% from 1982 to 1992 in constant 1982 dollars.

Table I

State Criminal Justice System Expenditures in Detroit: Analysis of Expenditures Explained by Time, 1982-1992

Indicator	Pearson Correlation	Annual Growth Rate (%)	r^2	t-Statistic	Significance of t-value
Total court and legal expenditures	-0.105	-12.8	0	0.547	0.601
Total correction expenditures	0.531	3.5	0	-0.121	0.907
Total police expenditures	-0.821	8.77	0.77	-2.92	0.022
Total Model State CJS Expenditures			0.69	4.89	0.002

Table I provides a summary of the statistical calculations for state criminal justice system expenditures. As the criminal justice system has experienced an overall increase in its surveillance of the inner city, it was necessary to determine the relative statistical significance of these changes in expenditure levels. This is extremely important: comparing graphical information may be useful, but it may also be somewhat limited as a result of the different scales used in the presentation of the data. Table I examines the relationship found in Figures VIII through X and demonstrates that the relationship between the criminal justice expenditures and crime rates is significant for the entire regression model (F-statistic=6.671, df=4) and the probability of rejection is considerably low (p=0.021).

Conclusion

The increase in state criminal justice policing expenditures within the Detroit inner city is a phenomenon worth noting and continued study. Unfortunately, the relationship between the criminal justice system and poverty has been neglected by many critical researchers in the United States. The results of the current study demonstrated some interesting findings pertaining to state criminal justices system expenditures. Obviously, the null hypothesis of no relationship between crime rates and criminal justice expenditures must be rejected. However, there are limitations to the data which must be noted and substantive issues which must be included in future research.

The measurement of the relationship between state criminal justice expenditures and crime rates is only as efficient as the data permit. First, the UCR index crime rates only represent known offences for the most serious offences. The UCR crime rates do not reflect all law enforcement agencies within the criminal justice system, and if they did, they would still not record the actual rates of crime. However, the criminal justice expenditures tend to have been somewhat more reflective of the resources devoted by the state for maintaining and developing particular relations in society. This is particularly important when considering that UCR crime levels have decreased overall and in most categories. The exception was noted to be the aggravated assault index crime for Detroit. The current study, and the literature discussed above, would suggest that this category of crime increase is not representative of rising violent crimes. If they were, other crimes of violence would correspond with the increases but represent the increased presence of law enforcement in the inner city and against African Americans, today under the pretext of a 'war on drugs.'

By every available measure of the criminal justice system, African Americans have not increased illegal actions or activities more so than any other group since at least the early 1970s, if at all (DeKeseredy & Schwartz, 1996). However, arrest rates and admission rates to state prisons for young African American men have increased substantially since the early 1980s and continue to today. The 'war on drugs' is so 'successful' that the percentage of state and federal prisoners incarcerated for drug offences surpassed the number of property offenders by 1991 (Conklin, 1998). It should come as no surprise that the majority of drug arrests are for simple possession of illegal substances. In 1996, 75% of all national drug arrests were for possession, which had decreased from 80% in 1982 (National Criminal Justice Information and Statistics Service, 1998). Finally, the majority of arrests were for the 'soft' drugs such as marijuana and hashish, contrary to public perceptions about drug crimes.

Essentially, the 'war on drugs' equates to a war on the inner city, poverty, and African Americans--nothing less than the manufacture of an ideological enemy which keeps the relations of poverty and an increasing police state strikingly absent from media, research, and even everyday discourse. Today, the targeting of High Intensity Drug Trafficking Areas (HIDTAs) by law enforcement agencies are the latest euphemism for suppressing visible minorities under the guise of drug enforcement.

Although the premise of the paper is that African Americans have been targeted in the inner cities through a war on drugs, it is clear from the latest White House Drug Policy, under the Office of National Drug Control Policy, that the poorest Latino, African American, and European American communities are also being targeted in the war on drugs. The result is that the U.S. system of criminal justice is premised upon *structured* and *systemic racism*, and not predicated upon *individual actions of racism*, which control the inner city through definitions of the 'underclass' and the resulting 'social pathologies' such as drugs. The result of increased policing is already occurring in the streets of Detroit and other large U.S. cities: violence between the policed and police. The question that must be asked is whether criminal justice expenditures should be allowed to increase while providing diminished returns or should society deal with the inner cities by engaging in preventative economic programs to deal with real social problems.

References

Axinn, J., & Levin, H. (1997). *Social Welfare: A History of the American Response to Need. 4th ed.* New York, NY: Longman.

Burawoy, M. (1979). *Manufacturing Consent: Changes in the Labor Process under Monopoly Capitalism.* Chicago, IL: The University of Chicago Press.

_____1985 *The Politics of Production: Factory Regimes under Capitalism and Socialism.* London, ON: Verso.

Cayley, D. (1998). *The Expanding Prison: The Crisis in Crime and Punishment and the Search for Alternatives.* Toronto, ON: House of Anansi Press Limited.

Chambliss, W. (1975) Toward a Political Economy of Crime. *Theory and Society*, 2: 149-170.

Coleman, J. (1998). *The Criminal Elite: Understanding White-Collar Crim,. 4th ed.* New York, NY: St. Martin's Press.

Conklin, J. (1998). *Criminology, 6th ed.* Boston, MA: Allyn and Bacon.

_____(2001). *Criminology, 7th ed.* Boston, MA: Allyn and Bacon.

Cromwell, P. & Dunham, R. (1997). *Crime and Justice in America: Present Realities and Future Prospects.* Upper Saddle River, NJ: Prentice Hall.

DeKeseredy, W. & Schwartz, M. (1996). *Contemporary Criminology.* New York: Wadsworth. Epstein, W. M. (1997). *Welfare in America: How Social Science Fails the Poor.* Madison, WI: The University of Wisconsin Press.

Ermann, M. D. & R. J. Lundman (1987). *Corporate and Governmental Deviance: Problems of Organizational Behavior in Contemporary Society,* 3rd ed. New York, NY: Oxford University Press.

Evans, J. & Himelfarb, A. (1996). Counting Crime. In *Criminology: A Canadian Perspective,* 3rd ed., Linden, R. (Ed.) Toronto, ON: Harcourt Brace.

Fainstein, N. (1996). Race, Class, and Segregation: Discourses about African Americans. In *Readings in Urban Theory,* Fainstein, S & Campbell, S (EDS.): 216-45. Cambridge, MA: Blackwell.

Gebotys, R., Roberts, J. & DasGupta, B. (1988). News Media Use and Public Perceptions of Crime Seriousness. *Canadian Journal of Criminology,* 30:3-16.

Herman, E. & Chomsky, N. (1988). *Manufacturing Consent: The Political Economy of the Mass Media.* New York, NY: Pantheon Books.

Herrnstein, R. (1995) Criminogenic Traits. In *Crime,* Wilson, J & Petersilia, J. (Eds.): 39-63. San Francisco: Institute for Contemporary Studies Press.

Herrnstein, R. & Murray, C. (1994). The *Bell Curve: Intelligence and Class Structure in American Life.* New York, NY: Free Press.

Katz, J. (1987). What Makes Crime 'News'. *Media, Culture and Society,* 9:47-75.

Krisberg, B. (1994). Distorted by Fear: The Make Believe War on Crime. *Social Justice,* 21:38-49.

Lewis, O. (1969) The Culture of Poverty. In On Understanding Poverty: Perspectives from the Social Sciences, Moynihan, D. (Ed.): 187-201. New York, NY: Basic Books.

MacLean, B. (1996). State Expenditures on Canadian Criminal Justice. In Crime and Society: Readings in Critical Criminology: 117-54. Toronto, ON: Copp Clark.

Maxfield, M. & Babbie, E. (2001). *Research Methods for Criminal Justice and Criminology. 3rd ed.* New York, NY: Wadsworth.

McDonald, L. (1979). Crime and Punishment in Canada: A Statistical Test of the Conventional Wisdom. In *Crime and Delinquency in Canada*, Vaz, E. & Lodhi, A. (Eds.): 57-85. Scarborough, ON: Prentice-Hall.

Moynihan, D. (1969). The Professors and the Poor. In *On Understanding Poverty: Perspectives From the Social Sciences*, Moynihan, D. (ED.): 3-35. New York, NY: Basic Books.

Murray, C. (1984). *Losing Ground: American Social Policy, 1950-1980.* New York, NY: Basic Books.

Pedhazur, E. (1982). *Multiple Regression in Behavioral Research: Explanation and Prediction. 2nd ed.* New York, NY: Holt, Rinehart and Winston.

Quinney, R. (1977). *Class, State, and Crime: On the Theory and Practice of Criminal Justice.* New York, NY: David McKay.

_____1979 *Criminology. 2nd edition.* Boston, MA: Little Brown.

Reiman, J. (1998). *The Rich Get Richer and the Poor Get Prison: Ideology, Class, and Criminal Justice. 5th ed.* Boston, MA: Allyn and Bacon.

Sacco, V. & Kennedy, L. (1998). *The Criminal Event. An Introduction to Criminology. 2nd ed.* Scarborough, ON: International Thomson Publishing.

Sugrue, T. (1996). *The Origins of The Urban Crisis: Race And Inequality In Postwar Detroit.* Princeton, NJ: Princeton University Press.

Sutherland, E. (1949). *White Collar Crime: The Uncut Version.* New Haven, CT: Yale University Press.

Valentine, C. (1971). The "Culture of Poverty": Its Scientific Significance and Its Implications for Action. In *Culture and Poverty*, Leacock, E. (Ed.): 193-225. New York, NY: Simon and Schuster.

West, C. (1994). *Race Matters.* New York, NY: Vintage Books.

Wilson, J. & Herrnstein, R. (1985). *Crime and Human Nature.* New York, NY: Simon and Schuster.

Wilson, W. (1987). *The Truly Disadvantaged: The Inner City, the Underclass, and Public Policy.* Chicago, IL: University of Chicago Press.

Government and Data Sources Cited

Rand, M., Lynch, J. & Cantor, D. (1997). Criminal Victimization, 1973-95. United States Department of Justice, Bureau of Justice Statistics. Washington, DC: U.S. Government Printing Office.

United States Department of Commerce, Bureau of the Census (1993). Small Area Income and Poverty Estimates Program. Washington, DC: U.S. Government Printing Office.

_____1997 Statistical Abstract of the United States: 1997. Washington: U.S. Government Printing Office.

_____1998 Current Population Reports, Series P-25. Washington: U.S. Government Printing Office.

_____1999 Small Area Income and Poverty Estimates Program. Washington, DC: U.S. Government Printing Office.

United States Department of Housing and Urban Development (1997). The State of the Cities. Washington, DC: U.S. Govt. Printing Office.

United States Department of Justice, Bureau of Justice Statistics (1987). Justice Expenditure and Employment Extracts: 1982 and 1983 Data from the Annual General Finance and Employment Surveys. Washington, DC: U.S. Government Printing Office.

_____1991 Justice Expenditure and Employment Extracts: 1984, 1985, and 1986 Data from the Annual Gen. Finance & Employment Surveys. Washington, DC: U.S. Govt. Printing Office.

_____1996 Justice Expenditure and Employment Extracts: 1992 Data from the Annual General Finance and Employment Surveys. Washington, DC: U.S. Government Printing Office.

United States Department of Justice, Federal Bureau of Investigation (1982-1986, 1992, 1995-1997). Uniform Crime Reports for the United States. Washington, DC: U.S. Govt. Printing Office.

United States National Criminal Justice Information and Statistics Service (1976). Expenditure and Employment Data for the Criminal Justice System, 1974. Washington, DC: U.S. Government Printing Office.

_____1998 Sourcebook of Criminal Justice Statistics. Washington, DC: U.S. Government Printing Office.

CHAPTER 8
MINORITY WOMEN IN VIOLENT
RELATIONSHIPS

Krim K. Lacey

Abstract: *It is estimated that there are approximately 4.8 million women annually who experience an incidence of rape and physical assault by an intimate partner. While violence against women occurs across class, culture, ethnicity, race and socioeconomic lines, minority and immigrant women are at increased risk for intimate partner violence. A large percentage of abused women stay with or return to their abuser. Using data from the National Violence against Women Survey (NVAWS), this research examines the contribution of socioeconomic, family structure and emotional abuse on minority women's decision to stay in or leave violent relationships. The study revealed that these factors influence minority women's decisions. However, some of the factors that influenced women's decision were contrary to previous findings. This study attempts to identify misconceptions and further understanding of the issue. Recommendations and implications of the study are discussed.*

Objective of the Study

Historically, society has paid limited attention to domestic violence. The lack of attention can be attributed to a number of reasons. First, it was not until after the 1960s that women's perspectives were becoming addressed in our society. Secondly, violence against women in the confines of the home was viewed as a private matter and was arguably a common practice in the past (Gelles, 1985). During the Roman era, men had the legal right to beat their wives for things such as drinking or walking outdoors without their faces being covered, while adultery was punishable by death (Siegel & McCormic, 2003). Thirdly, in the past, women were seen as the property of men (Pleck, 1983). This gave men a tremendous amount of power and control over women and their well being. Although this view has since become disfavored, there are men who continue to hold onto the notion that women are their property, allowing them the right to do with them as they please. It is presumed that this notion has contributed to a problem that is prevalent in our society today.

It is estimated that there are approximately 4.8 million women annually who experience an incidence of rape and physical assault by an intimate partner (Tjaden & Thoennes, 2000). While violence against women occurs across class, culture, ethnicity, race and socioeconomic lines, for certain segments of the population the reality appears to be much harsher. Minority and immigrant women are among those who are *most vulnerable* to abuse (Unicef, 2000).

Studies indicate that at least 60 percent of immigrant Korean women had been battered by their husbands (Tjaden & Thoennes, 2000). About 48 percent of Latinos reported an increase in violence against them since immigrating to the United States (Dutton et al., 2000). For Black females, the occurrence of intimate partner violence appears to be much more prevalent when compared to other racial/ethnic groups. Black females were found to have experienced intimate partner violence at a rate that is 35% higher than their white female counterparts and about 2.5 times the rate of women of other races (BJS, 2000).

When a woman is abused she is faced with decisions on how to prevent future occurrences. Deciding what to do in these circumstances can be difficult. The fact that women may have developed close intimate bonds, have dire economical circumstances, have invested many years of their lives in the relationship and have uncertainties about the violence their partners may be capable of after they leave the relationship, are just some of the things a woman may consider before making a decision. Despite the threat that the abuse poses to their health and welfare, a large number of women often choose to remain in or return to the relationship. Approximately two-thirds (65.5%) of intimate partner victims reported being victimized on more than one occasion (Tjaden & Thoennes, 2000). Though reasons for remaining in violent relationships are not fully understood, choosing to stay in such relationships, increase the risks of physical injury or death. In 1999, intimate partner violence accounted for approximately 1,218 deaths among women (BJS, 2001).

Over the years research has provided valuable insight on the impact of intimate partner violence on women and society in general. As issues relating to class, socioeconomic status, culture and race/ethnicity are more a focal point of these studies, it is evident that not all women experience violence at the same rate, nor is women's response to abuse the similar across groups. Given that research has provided indications that minority women are more affected by intimate partner violence than other ethnic groups, it is of importance to further understand whether their status as minority women coupled with other factors, increases their susceptibility to abuse and further prevents them from leaving their abusers.

This study therefore examines the contribution of socioeconomic, family structure, and emotional abuse on minority women's decision to stay in or leave violent relationships. This study also aims to examine whether these influence operate in similar or different manner for persons of different racial and ethnic groups (e.g., Hispanic, Black and Non-Minority).

Review of Literature

Studies have discussed the role of socioeconomic factors in intimates leaving/staying in abusive relationships. It can be argued that some women may be dependent on their partner for financial support and may have fewer alternatives to staying. Such a theory especially holds true for stay-at-home spouses with children where the partner is the sole provider, as well as for individuals who lack the education and skills to survive in our society. Their inability to be self-sufficient may create barriers that keep them from freeing themselves from their abusers. Accordingly, the fewer resources a woman has, the more 'entrapped' she is (Gelles, 1976). This dependency may prevent women from being able to negotiate change in their lives (Kalmuss & Straus, 1982).

Interviews with 41 families in which the women had been abused by their husbands found women that were least likely to seek intervention were those who were less likely to have completed high school and more likely to be unemployed (Gelles, 1976). Kalmuss and Straus (1982) found in their nationally representative study consisting of 2,134 adults, that women's dependency was related to abuse. Women with fewer resources were less capable of making change in their lives. Hence, economic and not psychological dependency was found to keep women in severely abusive relationships.

Strube and Barbour (1983) also provided valuable insights into the effects of socioeconomic influences on women's decision. In examining both *objective* (e.g., economic) and *subjective* (e.g., psychological) factors in women's decision to leave abusive relationships, economic dependency was found to be a significant factor in battered women's decision to leave.

Later studies conducted on 251 women in counseling provided further indication of the influence of economic status on their decision to leave their relationships. Findings from the study indicated that women who left their relationships were more likely to be employed and to have been in their relationships for a shorter period of time than those who remained (Strube & Barbour, 1984). Aguirre (1985) found in a study on shelter victims of abuse that women who were economically dependent on their husbands were more likely to return to the violent relationship. In studying chronically and formerly battered women from Waco and Austin, Texas, Frisch and MacKenzie (1991) found that less educated and unemployed individuals may have difficulty leaving because of their economic dependency and the lack of options for supporting themselves and their children. Johnson's (1992) study on 426 battered shelter women found that unemployed battered women who had been living with their spouses and had high family incomes were likely to return to the abusive relationship.

Studies specifically geared to ethnic populations further support the influence of socioeconomic factors on the decision of women to leave or remain in violent relationships. In-depth interviews conducted on women from a Vietnamese community suggested that economic hardship could prevent women from leaving abusive relationships (Bui & Morash, 1999). A more recent qualitative study conducted on battered women in rural China also yielded similar results. Along with other sub themes, deficiency of personal resources was found to impede women's tendencies to leave their abusive partners (Liu & Chan, 1999). As such, those found to be economically dependent tended to remain in relationships. Furthermore, studies conducted on Latino immigrant women found that the lack of money was one of most frequently cited obstacles for remaining in violent relationships (Dutton et al., 2000).

While studies have consistently pointed to socioeconomic factors as significant predictors in women's decision to remain with their abusive partners, there are other factors found to be consistently influential. Strube and Barbour (1984) found in their study that a greater percentage of women who remained in abusive relationships were married and had children in the household. Studies further indicate that Black abuse victims were more likely to remain in a marital relationship at the time of interview than White victims (Schwartz, 1988).

Research further suggests that emotional/psychological abuse can be just as harmful and can affect women in different ways. For some women, it can be the impetus to leave, for others that might not be the case. Herbert, Silver, and Ellard (1991) found that verbal/emotional abuse was just as, or more difficult for abused women to deal with than physical abuse. Studies indicate that separated abused women experienced higher levels of emotional abuse (Hilbert et al., 1997; Jacobson et al., 1996).

With the influx of immigrants from patriarchal societies entering the United States on a yearly basis, it is not odd that they carry these beliefs and attitudes with them. Even with the 'melting pot' philosophy, individuals are not prevented from maintaining their cultural ideals. Hence, although abuse against women has become disfavored in U.S. society and culture, certain immigrant or minority groups still view some physical contact as an acceptable behavior from their partner. Also, some immigrant and minority groups see matters of the home as a private, family issue (as cited in Raj & Silverman, 2002). As a result, they may choose neither to seek outside help nor leave abusive relationships.

For other immigrant women, going to refuges such as shelters are a culturally unacceptable option. Seeking outside assistance is not only frowned upon, but it also implies shame and provides criticism of that particular culture (as cited in Raj & Silverman, 2002). Moreover, within some communities, instead of helping women to leave, community leaders encourage the women's silence and place more emphasis on the maintenance of the relationship with the abuser (as cited in Raj and Silverman, 2002).

Perilla (1999) suggests that wife beating is an acceptable part of marriage where women have lower status than men, particularly among minority and immigrant women. Among Latin women, the tendency to abide by such cultural scripts has had a profound influence over their decision to stay in the relationship. For Blacks, Moss and Company (1997) found that along with being socialized not to go outside the family and friends network, seeking assistance is seen as a "put down" of Black men by Black women. Furthermore, seeking outside assistance such as calling the police is culturally unacceptable. African American women are socialized to appear in control in the presence of Anglo Americans, especially when dealing with the legal system where there tends to be some mistrust.

Among minority and immigrant groups, the legal system is often perceived as oppressive. Blacks tend to see the legal system as more punitive towards Blacks (Moss et. al, 1997). As result, Black women's reluctance to involve police in personal matters or assistance is based on their perception of the unfair treatment of Black men and other minority men in the legal system. Rather than turn to social or law enforcement agencies, African American women are more inclined to endure the abuse until it becomes too intense for them to withstand (Hampton et al., 2003).

Bui and Morash (1999) suggest that Vietnamese women's reasons for not seeking protection from the criminal justice system surround the fear of their husbands being arrested and subjected to racial discrimination. Further, ethnic women's reluctance to leave stems from their limited language skills that impede their ability to communicate with agencies. Even when immigrants and undocumented immigrants seek assistance from shelters, the language barrier continues to pose a problem, as well as not having the appropriate documentation to be admitted into the shelters (Raj & Silverman, 2002).

Methods

Sample
Data for analysis was drawn from the National Violence Against Women (NVAW) survey which was jointly sponsored by the National Institute of Justice (NIJ), the National Center for Injury Prevention and Control (NCIPC) and the Center for Disease Control (CDC) (Tjaden & Thoennes, 1998). The sample was based on a random digit-dialing sample of households within the United States, including all 50 states and the District of Columbia. Prior to data collection, a number of steps were taken to ensure validity, confidentiality, safety of respondents and prevention against research bias. For instance, interviewers involved in the study were trained to recognize respondents' concerns (e.g. overhearing). To protect participants from any foreseeable harm, respondents were given access to hotlines, local support and shelters.

Additional measures were taken to control for differential response rates. The sample was stratified by regions and within each region a simple random sample was drawn. Contact was made to the household of eligible participants that represented the numbers selected from the random sample. In instances where there was more than one member per household who may have qualified for the study, preference was given to the respondent with the most recent birthday.

After all measures were taken, approximately 8000 women over the age of 18 were included in the sample. For the purpose of this study, however, attention will be given to a subset of respondents representing the minority who had experienced violence (e.g., threats, physical assault, rape, stalking) at some point of the relationship and had provided response to having stayed or left a violent relationship.

Measures
Stay/leave: The dependent variable for the study was stay/leave. To measure stay or leave participants were asked: *"Did you ever leave your current husband/partner because he/she was violent towards you?"* Respondents were given the option of yes or no. The '*yes*' category represents leaving violent relationships and '*no*' represents staying in violent relationships.

There were several socioeconomic, family structure and emotional abuse independent variables. There are as follows:

Employment: Employment was measured by asking participants: "Are you currently (1) employed full-time; (2) employed part-time; (3) in the military; (4) unemployed and looking for work, (5) retired and not working; (6) a student; (7) a homemaker; (8) something else?"

Education Level: Education level was measured by asking participants: *"What is the highest level of education you have completed?"* Respondents were given several options that include: (1) no schooling; (2) 1st-8th grade; (3) some high school; (4) high school graduate; (5) some college; (6) 4 year college degree; (7) post-graduate?"

Income: Respondent's and Partner's income level was ascertained by asking how much income did they personally receive in 1995 before taxes? Was it: (1) Less than $5,000; (2) $5,000 to $10,000; (3) $10,000 to $15,000; (4) $15,000 to $20,000; (5) $20,000 to $25,000; (6) $25,000 to $35,000; (7) $35,000 to $50,000; (08) $50,000 to $80,000; (09) $80,000 to $100,000; (10) over $ 100,000; or (11) none?

Marital Status: To measure marital status, participants were asked if they are currently: (1) married; (2) common law relationship (VOL); (3) divorced; (4) separated; (5) widowed; 6) single and never married.

Number of Years Known Partner: The length of time the respondent knew their partner was measured by asking participants the question: *"How many years have you known him/her?"* The length of time respondents knew their partner ranged from less than one year to 75 years.

Years Lived With Partner: Years lived with partner is a scale level variable that reflects the question: *"How many years have you lived with your husband/partner?"* The amount of years respondents lived with their partner ranged from less than one year to 74 years.

Number of Years Married: The length of time respondents were married was measured by asking the question: *"How long have you been married?"* This scale variable ranged from less than one year to 69 years.

Number of Persons 18 and Older Live in Household: Number of persons 18 years and older live in the household reflects the question: *"Including yourself, how many persons 18 years and older live in this household?"* This scale variable ranged from one to six persons.

Number of Children under 18 years Live in Household: Number of children 18 years of age and under living in the household reflects the question: *"How many children under 18 years of age live in this household?"* This scale variable ranged from zero to ten children.

Emotional Abuse: Emotional abuse was measured by several variables. Participants were asked: Thinking about your current husband (wife)/ partner would you say he/she 'makes you feel inadequate'; 'shouts or swears at you'; 'calls you names or puts you down in front of others?' These answers included responses of: (1) Yes; (2) No.

Data Analysis

Statistical Package for the Social Sciences (SPSS) was used to conduct the analysis. Univariate and bivariate analyses were conducted. Univariate provided an overview of the sample distribution for each variable. Cross-tabulations with chi-square test of significance was used to assess the relationships between the independent and dependent variables. An apha of .05 was used to assess significance.

Sub sample

Due to the nature of the study, a subset of the sample was drawn to reflect the minority population (see Table 1). The subset was comprised of 108 minority female participants. The composition consisted of Black (41.7%), Asian (4.6%), Indian (2.8%), Hispanic (43.5%), and Mixed (7.4%). The majority (57.4%) of respondents was either married or in common-law relationships. The education level of participants within the sample was also diverse and included individuals who had as low as a 1st grade education to as high as a post-graduate degree. Within this category, the most frequent response of the participants was that of high school graduate (32.4%) followed by those who had received some (29.6%) college education. Approximately half (52.8%) of the sample had high school or less education.

Univariate analysis further revealed that a majority of the respondents were employed full-time (50.0%), followed by those who were homemakers (19.4%) and participants who were unemployed/looking for work (13.0%). Based on the analysis, a majority (58.3%) of the participants had some form of employment (whether part-time or full-time) or was in the military.

In reference to the income level of the respondents, the analysis showed an almost even distribution among the categories. However, most (16.7%) respondents indicated that they earned under $5,000 annually. Further, more than half (60.2%) of the sample had incomes that were less than $25,000. Most participants also indicated that their partner had earned between $5,000-$10,000 and between $35,000-$50,000.

The length of time the participants' had *known* their partner ranged from one to 60 years with an average time of 19.2 years and a standard deviation of 14.9 years. Participants also tended to have *lived* with their partners for less than a year to as much as 60 years. Respondents had lived with their partners an average of 17.2 years with a standard deviation of 18. 3 years. Moreover, the number of years that some respondents and their spouse had been *married* ranged from less than a year to 40 years, with a mean of 17.2 years and standard deviation 18.2 years.

Data was collected on individuals residing in these households. They include other persons, as well as children. There was an average of 2.2 persons 18 and *older* living in the household with a standard deviation of 1.1 persons. When it came to the actual number of children *under* the age of 18 that resided in the household, there was a range of zero children to as many as six children. The average number of children was 1.6 with a standard deviation of 1.3 children.

Information obtained on emotional abuse (see Table 3) revealed that when "H/W/P calls respondents names in front of others", an overwhelming majority (72%) of respondents indicated '*no*' while 28 percent said '*yes*.' When examining the item "makes respondents feel inadequate", again a majority (62.7%) of respondents provided a response of '*no*'and 36 percent said '*yes*.' Finally, respondents were almost split when it came to whether H/W/P shouts or swears at the respondents. Still, according to the analysis, the majority (52.0%) of respondents indicated '*yes*', while 48 percent said '*no*' to this question.

Finally, when assessing the dependent variable (e.g. stay/leave violent relationships), the analysis indicates that independent of all factors the majority (63.9%) of respondents provided a response of '*no*' indicating they were still in the relationship at the time of survey as compared to 36.1 percent of minority respondents who had left the relationship." (see Table 4)

Table 1

Demographic Characteristics of Participants

Characteristics	Minority Women		Overall Sample	
	n	**%**	**n**	**%**
Gender of participants				
Female	108	100.0	8000	100.0
Race of participants				
White	---	---	6452	80.7
Black/African American	45	41.7	780	9.8
Asian/Pacific Islander	5	4.6	133	1.7
Indian/Alaskan Native	3	2.8	88	1.1
Mixed Race	8	7.4	397	5.0
Participants of Hispanic Origin				
Yes	47	43.5	628	7.9
No	---	---	7317	91.5
Marital Status of participants				
Married	60	55.6	4976	62.1
Common-law relationship	2	1.9	32	.4
Divorced	3	2.8	867	10.8
Separated	17	15.7	185	2.3
Widowed	7	6.5	678	8.5
Single & never married	19	17.6	1224	15.3
Employment status of participants				
Employed full-time	54	50.0	3678	46.0
Employed part-time	8	7.4	1009	12.6
In the military	1	.9	21	.3
Unemployed/looking for work	14	13.0	278	3.5
Retired/not working	4	3.7	1176	14.7
Student	2	1.9	357	4.5
Homemaker	21	19.4	1233	15.4
Education Level of participants				
No schooling	---	---	11	.1

Characteristics	Minority Women		Overall Sample	
	n	**%**	**n**	**%**
1st- 8th grade	10	9.3	245	3.1
Some high School	12	11.1	600	7.5
HS graduate	35	32.4	2752	34.4
Some college	32	29.2	2336	29.2
4 yr college degree	13	12.0	1360	17.0
Postgraduate	4	3.7	659	8.2
Income R received before taxes				
Under $5,000	18	16.7	1005	12.6
$5,000-$10,000	12	11.1	812	10.2
$10,000-$15,000	15	13.9	842	10.5
$15,000-$20,000	12	11.1	736	9.2
$20,000-$25,000	8	7.4	597	7.5
$25,000-$35,000	11	10.2	826	10.3
$35,000-$50,000	10	9.3	719	9.0
$50,000-$80,000	2	1.9	329	4.1
$80,000-$100,000	2	1.9	51	.6
Over $100,000	---	---	73	.9
None	4	3.7	326	4.1
Income Spouse/Partner received before taxes				
Under $5,000	7	9.3	153	2.8
$5,000-$10,000	9	12.0	250	4.6
$10,000-$15,000	8	10.7	353	6.5
$15,000-$20,000	6	8.0	418	7.7
$20,000-$25,000	8	10.7	496	9.1
$25,000-$35,000	2	2.7	739	13.5
$35,000-$50,000	9	12.0	783	14.3
$50,000-$80,000	5	6.7	489	9.0
$80,000-$100,000	1	1.3	96	1.8
Over $100,000	1	1.3	142	2.6
None	---	---	47	.9

Note: The scale used to collect income information is not a customary measure and may impact the outcome due to overlapping categories. This could not be avoided due to the original manner in which the data was collected.

Table 2

Demographic Characteristics of Participants

Characteristics	Minority Women			Overall Sample		
	n	m	std	n	m	std
Respondent's Age	108	38.38	12.9	8000	45.19	12.9
Number of persons 18 years and older live in HH	108	6.87	7.7	8000	2.08	7.7
Number of children under 18 years old live in HH	107	1.63	1.3	7991	1.25	5.9
Number of years R known husband/partner	75	19.16	14.9	5459	22.81	17.0
Number of years R lived with husband/partner	75	16.35	17.4	5459	19.27	16.0
Number of years R and spouse been married	60	17.20	18.3	4931	20.24	15.6

Table 3

Emotional Abuse: Response by the Overall Sample and Minority Participants

Characteristics	Minority Women		Overall Sample	
	n	**%**	**n**	**%**
H/W/P calls R names in front of others				
Yes	21	28.0	203	3.7
No	54	72.0	5236	95.9
H/W/P makes R feel inadequate				
Yes	27	36.0	328	6.0
No	47	62.7	5071	92.9
H/W/P shouts or swears at R				
Yes	39	52.0	518	9.5
No	36	48.0	4916	90.0

Table 4

Participants Response to Staying/Leaving Violent Relationships

Characteristics	Minority Women		Overall Sample	
	n	**%**	**n**	**%**
Did you ever leave your current partner because he/she was violent towards you				
Yes (leaving)	39	36.1	36.1	132
No (staying)	69	63.9	63.9	250

Results

Socioeconomic Influences

Findings from the bivariate analysis reveal that over two-thirds of employed minority women stayed in a violent relationship at the time of the survey as compared to over one half of respondents who were not employed (69.8% vs. 55.6%). Furthermore, when examining the effects of respondents education level on staying/leaving, the results show that respondents with a high school diploma or less education [$\chi^2 = 3.44$, p > .05] were less likely to stay with their abuser when compared to their college educated counterparts (56.1% vs. 73.5%). Additionally, participants with higher income levels were found to have stayed with their abuser at a higher rate than respondents with low income levels, though marginally significant. Specifically, participants who earned $25,000 or more were over 20 percentage points more likely to stay in the relationship than respondents who earned $25,000 or less (80.0% vs. 58.8%). When it came to the income level of the respondent's partner, the rate at which respondents stayed in violent relationships differed between groups. Respondents with partners that earned $35,000 or more continued in the relationship at a higher rate than respondents whose partners earned $35,000 or less (81.2% vs. 65.0%).

Family Structure Influences

The impact of family structure influences was also assessed (see Table 5). The results show that almost three-quarters of married and common law respondents [$\chi^2 = 3.16$, p > .05] were more likely to continue in the violent relationship compared to over half of single respondents (e.g. divorced, separated, widowed, single and never married) (71.0% vs. 54.3%).

Respondents were also found to stay with their abuser at a higher rate as the relationship developed and as they began to intertwine their lives more with the other person. More respondents who *lived* with their partner for six years and beyond stayed in the relationship than those who had lived with each other for less than five years (67.2% vs. 60.0%). Similarly, respondents who had been *married* for nine years or more were more likely to stay in the relationship than respondents who had been married for less than nine years (69.2% vs. 60.9%). Furthermore, respondents who had *known* their partner for six years or beyond continued in the relationship at a higher rate than those who had known their partner for five years or less (68.7% vs. 56.1%).

Analysis of residents within the household indicated that when respondents had more children (e.g. one or more children) *under* the age of 18 living in the household, the rate at which they stayed with their abuser was about nine points (8.7%) lower than for those with no children under the age of 18 living in the household (61.7% vs. 70.4%). When it came to persons *over* the age of 18 living in the household [χ^2 = 6.91, p < .05], almost three-quarters of respondents with two or more individuals residing in the household stayed in the relationship compared to less than half of respondents living in households with one or less persons over the age of 18 living in the household (70.7% vs. 42.3%).

Emotional Abuse

Analyses of the emotional abuse items showed that in all cases these factors significantly influenced the decisions made by minority women (see Table 6). Specifically, effects were detected for: "calls respondents names in front of others" [χ^2 = 7.47, p < .05]; "shouts or swears at respondents" [χ^2 = 5.36, p < .05]; and "makes respondents feel inadequate" [χ^2 = 13.74, p < .01]. Although these items were found to be significant, the data also shows that experiencing emotional abuse did not necessarily result in participants' staying in abusive relationships. In fact, the opposite was true. Respondents, who were called names, were shouted or sworn at and were made to feel inadequate by their partners exited the relationship at higher rates than respondents who did not have such experiences. The rate at which individuals who had been emotionally abused exited relationships was more than twice the rate of those who had not been emotionally abused [e.g. respondents who were called names (52.4% vs. 20.4%), respondents who were shouted or swore at (41.0% vs. 16.7%) and respondents who felt inadequate (51.9% vs. 14.9%)].

Table 5

Socioeconomic and Family Structure Influences on Stay/Leave Relationship for Minority Female Respondents (n = 108)

Characteristics	Leave %	Stay %	χ^2 (1)	p
Socioeconomic Influences				
Employment Status				
Employed	30.2	69.8	2.32	.128
Not Employed	44.4	55.6		
Education				
High School or Less	43.9	56.1	3.44	.064
College	26.5	73.5		
Income				
R Income (25k or Less)	41.5	58.5	3.66	.056
R Income (25k or Above)	20.0	80.0		
P Income (35k or Above)	18.8	81.2	1.43	.232
P Income (35k or Less)	35.0	65.0		
Family Structure Influences				
Marital Status				
Married & Common Law	29.0	71.0	3.16	.075
Single	45.7	54.3		
Years Known Partner				
Six Years and Beyond	31.3	68.7	1.74	.187
Five Years or Less	43.9	56.1		
Years Lived With Partner				
Six Years or Beyond	32.8	67.2	.610	.435
Five Years or Less	40.0	60.0		
Number of Years Married				
Above Nine Years	30.8	69.2	.755	.385
Nine Years or Less	39.1	60.9		

Characteristics	Leave %	Stay %	χ^2 (1)	p
Number of Persons > 18 in HH				
Two or Beyond	29.3	70.7	6.91	.009
One or Less	57.7	42.3		
Number of Children <18 in HH				
One or Greater	38.3	61.7	.656	.418
No Children	29.6	70.4		

Table 6

Emotional Abuse on Stay/Leave Relationship for Minority Female Respondents (n = 75)

Characteristics	Leave %	Stay %	χ^2 (1)	p
Emotional Abuse				
Shouts or Swears at R				
Yes	41.0	59.0	5.36	.021
No	16.7	83.3		
Calls R Names in Front of Others				
Yes	52.4	47.6	7.47	.006
No	20.4	79.6		
Makes R Feel Inadequate				
Yes	51.9	48.1	13.74	.001
No	14.9	85.1		

Black/African American Women and Staying/Leaving Violent Relationships

Socioeconomic Influences

In assessing the influence of socioeconomic indicators (see Table 7) among Black females (n = 45), it was found that employed respondents were more likely to continue in a relationship with their abuser than those who were not employed (70.0% vs. 60.0%), though not significant. Furthermore, 59 percent of high school or less educated respondents stayed in the relationship as compared to 77 percent of college educated respondents (59.1% vs. 77.3%).

While it was assumed that respondents' income would significantly influence staying or leaving abusive relationships, the direction of effects was opposite than what was expected. In fact, respondents who earned $25,000 or less exited the relationship at more than three times the rate of their counterpart (37.5% vs. 11.1%). Analysis conducted on the income level of the respondent's partner further indicates that Black females whose partner made more than $35,000 tended to stay in the relationship at a higher rate than those whose partners earned $35,000 or less (100.0% vs. 73.7%).

Family Structure Influences
Among family structure influences, only individuals over the age of 18 residing in household [$\chi^2 = 18.41$, $p < .01$] and marital status [$\chi^2 = 4.56$, $p < .05$] significantly influenced Black females decision (see Table 7). For instance, Black females tended to remain in the relationship at about five times the rate when two or more individuals over the age of 18 years resided in the household compared to households with one or less individuals over the age of 18 years (84.4% vs. 16.7%). Additionally, four in five married and common law respondents stayed with their abuser compared to just over half of single respondents (84.2% vs. 53.8%).

There were several family structure variables for which significance was not obtained, including years respondents lived with partner, years been married to partner, and number of children under 18 years living in the household. But even though these comparisons did not reach statistical significance, for some of these variables the percentages were quite meaningful. Almost three-quarters of respondents that lived with their partner for more than six years stayed in the relationship compared to over half of respondents that lived with their partner for five years or less (73.9% vs. 59.1%). Respondents who had been married for more than nine years were more likely to stay with their abuser than those who had been married for fewer years (83.3% vs. 60.6%). Finally, respondents with no children *under* the age of 18 living in the household were seven percentage points (6.9) more likely to stay in the relationship when compared to respondents living in the household with one or more children (71.4% vs. 64.5%).

Emotional Abuse

In examining emotional abuse on leaving/staying (see Table 8), effects were detected for items: "calls respondents names in front of others" $[\chi^2 = 4.34, p < .05]$ and "shouts or swears at respondents" $[\chi^2 = 3.85, p < .05]$. An inspection of the significant items found that respondents were more likely to stay in the relationship if they had not experienced emotional abuse as compared to respondents who had been abused. For those who were called names in front of others about half stayed in the relationship as compared to more than three-quarters of respondents who had not experienced such abuse (50.0% vs. 86.4%). Furthermore, respondents who had not experienced shouts or swear remain in the relationship compared to two-thirds of respondents who did experience such an ordeal (92.9% vs. 62.5%). Although respondents' feelings of inadequacy did not significantly predict staying or leaving, the findings indicate that a smaller percentage of participants stayed with their abuser when these feelings occurred than if they had not experienced them at all (55.6% vs. 85.7%).

Table 7

Socioeconomic and Family Structure Influences on Stay/Leave Relationship for Black/African American Female Respondents (n = 45)

Characteristics	Leave %	Stay %	χ^2 (1)	p
Socioeconomic Influences				
Employment Status				
Employed	30.0	70.0	.450	.502
Not Employed	40.0	60.0		
Education				
High School or Less	40.9	59.1	1.68	.195
College	22.7	77.3		
Income				
R Income (25k or Less)	37.5	62.5	2.26	.133
R Income (25k or Above	11.1	88.9		
P Income (35k or Above)	0.0	100.0	.166	.197
P Income (35k or Less)	26.3	73.7		

Characteristics	Leave %	Stay %	χ^2 (1)	p
Family Structure Influences				
Marital Status				
Married & Common Law	15.8	84.2	4.56	.033
Single	46.2	53.8		
Years Known Partner				
Six Years and Beyond	25.0	75.0	2.32	.128
Five Years or Less	47.1	52.9		
Years Lived With Partner				
Six Years or Beyond	26.1	73.9	1.11	.292
Five Years or Less	40.9	59.1		
Number of Years Married				
Above Nine Years	16.7	83.3	2.05	.153
Nine Years or Less	39.4	60.6		
Number of Persons > 18 in HH				
Two or Beyond	15.2	84.8	18.41	.000
One or Less	83.3	16.7		
Number of Children <18 in HH				
One or Greater	35.5	64.5	.207	.649
No Children	28.6	71.4		

Table 8

Emotional Abuse on Stay/Leave Relationship for Black/African American Female Respondents (n = 30)

Characteristics	Leave %	Stay %	χ^2 (1)	p
Emotional Abuse				
Shouts or Swears at R				
Yes	37.5	62.5	3.85	.050
No	7.1	92.9		
Calls R Names in Front of Others				
Yes	50.0	50.0	4.34	.037
No	13.6	86.4		
Makes R Feel Inadequate				
Yes	44.4	55.6	3.20	.073
No	14.3	85.7		

Hispanic Women and Staying/Leaving Violent Relationships

Socioeconomic Influences
Similar procedures were undertaken with the Hispanic population (n=47) to assess the association of the predictors on leaving and staying in violent relationships (see Table 9). According to the results, no significant effects were detected among the socio-economic influences. However, the percentages indicate that most employed Hispanic females leaned towards staying with their abuser when compared to respondents who were not employed (69.6% vs. 50.0%).

In other analyses, the contribution of respondents' educational level on their continuance in violent relationships did not hold as expected. Respondents with a high school education or less also stayed in the relationship at a lower rate than college educated respondents (53.3% vs. 70.6%).

The income levels of the respondents [χ^2 = 3.18, p > .05] and their partners were also assessed. Respondents with lower income levels (e.g. $25,000 or less) exited the relationships at more than twice the rate of higher income respondents (46.4% vs. 16.7%). Respondents whose partner earned more than $35,000 were 25 points more likely to stay with their abuser than respondents whose partner had income levels of $35,000 or less (75.0% vs. 50.0%).

Family Structure Influences

The number of years respondents had known their partner, had lived with their husband or had been married also did not significantly contribute to the relationship-related decision-making of Hispanic females. Still, differences in raw percentages indicate that when respondents had *lived* with, *known* and/or were *married* to their partner for a shorter period of time, the likelihood of staying in the relationship with their abuser increased. Specifically, respondents who lived with their partner for five or less years stayed in the relationship at a higher rate than those who lived with their respondents for more than six years or beyond (63.3% vs. 56.0%). More respondents who had known their partner for five years or less stayed in the relationship than respondents who had known their partner for six years or beyond (63.2% vs. 57.1%). Respondents who had been married for nine years or less stayed in violent relationships at a higher rate when compared to respondents who had been married for more than nine years (63.3% vs. 52.9%). The results from these analyses suggest that Hispanic women were more likely to stay in abusive relationships when they had fewer years of involvement with their spouse or an intimate partner.

Further analysis indicates that three-quarters of respondents who resided in households with one individual *over* the age of 18 stayed in the relationship compared to more than half of the homes with two or more such individuals (75.0% vs. 54.3%). For those respondents who have children living in the household *under* the age of 18, it was found that participants were more likely to stay in the relationship when they had no children in the household compared to respondents with one or more children (75.0% vs. 56.4%). The rate at which married and common law respondents stayed with their partner was almost equal to that of single respondents (58.6% vs. 61.1%). Therefore, the likelihood of staying in abusive relationships by women of Hispanic descent increases when fewer people over or under the age of 18 years live in the household.

Emotional Abuse

Unlike socioeconomic and family structure influences, emotional abuse such as whether respondents were shouted or swore at [$\chi^2 = 3.97$, p < .05] and respondents' feelings of inadequacy [$\chi^2 = 8.31$, p < .05] significantly influenced the choices made by Hispanic females. In both cases, the rate at which women who encountered these types of abuse exited relationships far exceeded the rate of those who did not have such experiences. While effects were not found for those respondents who were called names in front of others, the raw percentages indicate that they also exited relationships at almost twice the rate of those who did not experience this form of emotional abuse (60.0% vs. 31.8%).

Table 9

Socioeconomic and Family Structure Influences on Stay/Leave Relationship for Hispanic Female Respondents (n = 47)

Characteristics	Leave %	Stay %	χ^2 (1)	p
Socioeconomic Influences				
Employment Status				
Employed	30.4	69.6	1.87	.172
Not Employed	50.0	50.0		
Education				
High School or Less	46.7	53.3	1.34	.247
College	29.4	70.6		
Income				
R Income (25k or Less)	46.4	53.6	3.18	.075
R Income (25k or Above	16.7	83.3		
P Income (35k or Above)	25.0	75.0	.825	.364
P Income (35k or Less)	50.0	50.0		
Family Structure Influences				
Marital Status				
Married & Common Law	41.4	58.6	.029	.866
Single	38.9	61.1		
Years Known Partner				
Six Years and Beyond	42.9	57.1	.170	.680
Five Years or Less	36.8	63.2		

Characteristics	Leave %	Stay %	χ^2 (1)	p
Years Lived With Partner				
Six Years or Beyond	44.0	56.0	.283	.595
Five Years or Less	36.4	63.6		
Number of Years Married				
Above Nine Years	47.1	52.9	.487	.485
Nine Years or Less	38.5	61.5		
Number of Persons > 18 in HH				
Two or Beyond	45.7	54.3	1.59	.207
One or Less	25.0	75.0		
Number of Children <18 in HH				
One or Greater	43.6	56.4	.953	.329
No Children	25.0	75.0		

Table 10

Emotional Abuse on Stay/Leave Relationship for Hispanic Female Respondents (n = 32)

Characteristics	Leave %	Stay %	χ^2 (1)	p
Emotional Abuse				
Shouts or Swears at R				
Yes	61.5	38.8	3.97	.046
No	26.3	73.7		
Calls R Names in Front of Others				
Yes	60.0	40.0	2.26	.132
No	31.8	68.2		
Makes R Feel Inadequate				
Yes	72.7	27.3	8.31	.004
No	20.0	80.0		

Comparing Minority and Non-Minority Women's Staying in Violent Relationships

The findings among minority groups provide some indication of the importance of socioeconomic, family structure and emotional abuse on minority women staying/leaving violent relationships. While it is evident that these factors are influential when it comes to minority groups, it raises the question of whether these same factors impact the choices made by non-minority respondents (n=270). Results of the study indicate that the factors that influence non-minority females' decision to stay with their abuser are different in some cases, yet similar in others when compared to their minority counterparts.

Socioeconomic Influences
For instance, there is a marginal relationship between education and leaving/staying for minority respondents (p = .064), this was not the case for non-minority women. In spite of this, the raw percentage within both groups indicated that higher education women are more likely to stay in the relationship.

Family Structure and Influences
Among family structure influences, respondents' marital status [χ^2 = 6.00, p < .05] affected the choices made by non-minority female respondents. Married and common law respondents were about 17 (16.7) points more likely to stay with their partners than respondents who were single (69.8% vs. 53.1%). This finding was different than their minority counterparts for whom such influence was found to be marginally significant.

Among the minority population, a possible explanation for this difference may be due to a smaller sample size that could have had an effect on the outcome. Still, a common trend in the data was found in women's decision to stay or leave the relationship for both groups. Minority and non-minority married and common law respondents stayed in violent relationships at a higher rate than single participants.

Additional influences found to impact non-minority female respondents' staying/leaving in violent relationships included the number of years the respondents had known their partner [χ^2 = 5.02, p < .05] and the number of children *under* the age of 18 living in the household [χ^2 = 9.48, p < .01]. The data shows that non-minority respondents who knew their partner for a longer period of time (e.g. six years or more) remained with their abuser at a higher rate compared to non-minority respondents that knew their partner for less time (e.g., five years or less) (69.9% vs. 55.4%). Moreover, the rate at which respondents with one or more children exited relationships was almost twice the rate of respondents with no children (41.7% vs. 23.7%). These findings again differed from their minority counterparts due to the absence of significance. Despite the lack of significance, the raw percentages indicate a similar direction in women's decision to stay on the basis of these characteristics.

Emotional Abuse

Similar to their minority counterparts, emotional abuse were found to significantly impact non-minority women's decisions. With the exception of respondents who felt inadequate, the findings indicate that when women experienced these types of abuse (e.g., called names in front of others; shouted or sworn at) there was a greater tendency to discontinue the relationship. These findings also proved to be the same for their minority counterpart. As such, respondents who were called names in front of others were about 17 (16.5) points more likely to exit the relationship than those who did not experience this (42.9% vs. 26.4%). Respondents who were shouted or sworn at exited the relationship at a slightly higher rate than those who did not experience such abuse (37.1% vs. 34.6%).

Therefore, from the comparisons made between non-minority and minority respondents, it is evident that socioeconomics, family structure and emotional abuse significantly impact women's decision to stay or exit relationships. However, the direction in which they significantly impact women's decision to stay or leave a violent relationship differs between racial/ethnic groups when it comes to some of the socioeconomic and family structure influences than for emotional abuse. Unexpectedly, participants were more likely to discontinue the relationship when they experienced emotional abuse rather than stay with their abuser.

Discussion

The aim of this study was to examine the relative contribution of family structure, socioeconomic and emotional abuse on minority women's decision to stay in or leave violent relationships. Previous studies have provided evidence of the importance of such factors on women's response to abuse. For instance, when addressing the impact of socioeconomic influences, studies have suggested that individuals with limited resources are more susceptible to staying with their abusers (Gelles, 1976). In other words, it is implied that having a low socioeconomic standing limits alternatives and therefore creates dependency. Dependence on the partner for support leads to vulnerability that causes victims to accept further abuse.

The findings of this study indicated that minority women were significantly more likely to stay in the relationship when they had more people (e.g., two and beyond) rather than fewer people over the age of 18 in the household. Individuals in the household may provide protection, and in other cases guilt for considering to leave the relationships. Another possible explanation could be that the risk is much greater for those who have other members in the family that could be affected (e.g., whether financially or physically) if they choose to leave their abuser.

Other significant findings indicate that participants are exiting relationships when they experience emotional abuse. While socioeconomic factors such as income and education were marginally significant, it also worked in the opposite direction than what was expected. Respondents with high socioeconomic standing tended to stay in the relationship when compared to those with low standing.

Among specific minority groups, the predictors varied in their significance to staying or leaving violent relationships. For Black respondents, marital status, education, having persons over the age of 18 years in the household and emotional well-being was all influential factors. Participants who were married and had more people in the household were more likely to stay in the relationship. For women of Hispanic descent, only emotional factors significantly influenced staying or leaving violent relationships. Hispanic females tended to exit relationships when they experienced episodes of shouts or swears, and when they were made to feel inadequate.

The comparison between minority women in general and non-minority women revealed that there were some differences as well as similarities; particularly when it came to emotional abuse, where the tendency was for the women to leave their abuser. This was evident when participants were shouted or sworn at and when they were called names in front of others.

Limitations of Study

It is without question that there are many limitations to this study. While one of the strengths of this study was that it was based on a representative sample, it is unfortunate that the sample size (e.g. n =108) for the population of interest made it rather difficult to draw comprehensive conclusions or conduct analysis (e.g. multivariate) to test for interaction effects. A more adequate sample size would have added more substance and knowledge to the body of literature regarding the impact of predictors on minority women's decision to stay or leave in violent relationships.

Another problem that is also data related pertains to the use of secondary data. The availability of extant data made it feasible and convenient to conduct studies of this sensitive nature. However, using such datasets often lead to questions about the collection and the data entry process. Further, the fact that the variables were predetermined made it rather difficult to test concepts (e.g., culture, religion) that may have added immensely to this study. Further, the time frame in which the data was collected is also another limitation to this study. Since data was fielded from November 1995 to May 1996, findings from this study may not be reflective of current trends. It has been almost ten years since the data was collected.

Finally, it should be noted that the overall results obtained from the income status of the participants and their partners were based on categories that were not mutually exclusive and exhaustive (e.g., over $25k and under $25k). As a result, the findings based on these categories should be interpreted cautiously.

Implications of the Study

Despite the limitations, findings of the study have implications for intervention and prevention against intimate partner violence. A focus of intervention and prevention among this population should be specific and family centered. The outcome provided evidence that a *'one size fits all'* approach is not always the most rational way of determining how some groups will respond in certain situations, or the approach to take when treating women from various ethnic/racial backgrounds. The results of this study may be viewed as a lesson to professionals such as social workers, who are urged to rethink some of their methods in counseling and treating women who are faced with similar dilemmas. Especially among minority women, it may be time for these professionals to become more aware of their client's cultural heritage before attempting to address their situation. The key to effective treatment may actually lie in awareness.

It would also be advantageous to develop interventions that aim to empower minority women by providing women with a positive outlook on their on lives without an abusive partner. Secondly, the intervention and prevention should be designed to educate women about the potential ill effects of intimate partner violence and the impact it may have on the lives of others as well as themselves. Thus, interventions should have a step-by-step approach to severing ties with an abusive partner.

Additionally, perhaps it is time to refocus and direct more resources and attention in maintaining the family unit and improving relationships since women are staying in relationships in cases when the expectations are that they would leave. Efforts geared to the abuser getting help to address anger should also be a focus. These efforts at intervention or prevention should be culturally based or specific.

References

Aguirre, B.E. (1985). Why do They Return: Abused Wives in Shelters. *Social Workers*, 350-354.

Bourg, S., & Stock, H.V. (1994). A Review of Domestic Violence Arrest Statistics in a Police Department using a Pro-arrest Policy: Are Pro-arrest Policies Enough? *Journal of Family Violence, 9*(2), 177-189.

Buchanna, D.R., Perry, P.A. (1985). Attitudes of Police Recruits Towards Domestic Disturbances: An Evaluation of Family Crisis Intervention Training. *Journal of Criminal Justice, 13*, 516-572.

Bui, H., & Morash, M. (1999). Domestic Violence in the Vietnamese Immigrant Community: An Exploratory Study. *Violence Against Women, 5*(7), 769-795.

Bureau of Justice Statistics. (2001). Intimate Partner Violence and Age of Victim, 1993-99. Retrieved March 3, 2002. http://www.ojp.usdoj gov/bjs/abstract/ipva99.htm

Bureau of Justice Statistics. (2000). Intimate Partner Violence. Retrieved March 3, 2002. http://www.ojp.usdoj.gov/bjs/abstract/ipv.htm

Cate, R.M., Henton, J.M., Koval, J., Christopher, F.S., & Lloyd, S. (1982). Premarital Abuse: A Social Psychological Perspective. *Journal of Family Issues, 3*(1), 79-90.

Dutton, M.A., Orloff, L.E., & Hass, G.A. (2000). Characteristics of Help-seeking Behaviors, Resources and Service Needs of Battered Immigrant Latinas: Legal and Policy Implications. *Georgetown Journal on Poverty Law and Policy, 12*(2), 245-305.

Frisch, M.B., & MacKenzie, C.J. (1991). A Comparison of Formerly and Chronically Battered Women on Cognitive and Situational Dimension. *Psychotherapy, 28*(2), 339-344.

Gelles, R.J. (1976) Abused Wives: Why do They Stay. *Journal of Marriage and the Family, 38*(4), 659-668.

Hampton, R.L, Oliver, W., & Magarian, L. (2003). Domestic Violence in the African American Community: An Analysis of Social and Structural Factors. *Violence Against Women, 9*(5), 533-557.

Herbert, T.R., Silver, R.C., & Ellard, J.H. (1991). Coping with an Abusive Relationship: How and Why Woman Stay. *Journal of Marriage and the Family* 53(2), 311-325.

Hilbert, J.C., Kolia, R., & VanLeewan, D.M. (1997). Abused Women in New Mexican Shelters: Factors that Influenced Independence on Discharge. *Affilia, 12,* 391-406.

Jacobson, N.S., Gottman, J.M., Gortner, E., Berns, S., & Wu Shortt, J. (1996). Psychological Factors in the Longitudinal Course of Battering: When do the Couples Split Up? When does the Abuse Decrease? *Violence and Victims, 11(4),* 371-392.

Johnson, I.M. (1992). Economic, Situational, and Psychological Correlates of the Decision-making Process of Battered Women. *Families in Society: The Journal of Contemporary Human Services,* 168-176.

Kalmuss, D.S., & Straus, M.A. (1982). Wife's Marital Dependency and Wife Abuse. *Journal of Marriage and Family*, *44*(2), 277-286.

Moss, V.A., Pituala, C.R., Campbell, J.C., & Halstead, L. (1997). The Experience of Terminating an Abusive Relationship from an Anglo and African American Perspective: A Qualitative Descriptive Study. *Issues in Mental Health Nursing, 18,* 433-454.

National Center for Injury Prevention and Control, CDC. (2003). Intimate Partner Violence Fact Sheet. Retrieved October 10, 2005. http://www.cdc.gov/ncipc/factsheets/ipvfacts.htm

Perilla, J.L. (1999). Domestic Violence as a Human Rights Issue: The Case of Immigrant Latinos. *Hispanic Journal of Behavioral Sciences, 21*(2), 107-133.

Pleck, E. (1983). Feminist Response to "Crimes against Women," 1868-1896. *Journal of Women in Culture and Society, 8*(3), 451-469.

Raj, A. & Silverman, J. (2002). Violence Against Immigrant Women: The role of Culture, Context, and Legal Immigrant Status on Intimate Partner Violence. *Violence Against Women, 18*(3), 367-398.

Rhodes, N.R., & McKenzie, E.B. (1998). Why do Battered Women Stay: Three Decades of Research. *Aggression and Violent Behavior, 3*(4), 391-406.

Rusbult, C.E., & Martz, J.M. (1995). Remaining in an Abusive Relationship: An Investment Model Analysis of Nonvoluntary Dependency. *Personality and Social Psychology Bulletin, 21*(6), 558-571.

Siegel, L., & McCormick. (2003). *Criminology in Canada; Theories, Patterns, & Typologies, 2nd Edition*. Canada: Thomson.

Strube, M., & Barbour, L.S. (1984). Factors Related to the Decision to Leave Abusive Relationship. *Journal of Marriage and the Family*, 837-844.

Strube, M., & Barbour, L.S. (1983). The Decision to Leave an Abusive Relationship: Economic Dependence and Psychological Commitment. *Journal of Marriage and the Family, 45*(4) 785-793.

Schwartz, M.D. (1988). Marital Status and Woman Abuse Theory. *Journal of Family Violence, 3*(3), 239-248.

UNICEF. (2000). Domestic Violence Against Women and Girls. *Innocenti Digest, 6, 1-28.*

Tjaden, P., & Thoennes, N. Violence and Threats of Violence Against Women and Men in the United States, 1994-1996 [Computer file], ICPSR version. Denver, CO: Center for Policy Research [producer], 1998. Ann Arbor, MI: Inter-university Consortium for Political and Social Research [distributor], 1999.

Tjaden, P.G., & Thoennes, N. (2000). *Extent, Nature, and Consequences of Intimate Partner Violence*. Washington, DC: U.S. Department of Justice, Office of Justice Program, National Institute of Justice.

CHAPTER 9
COLLECTIVE BEHAVIOR AND MODELS OF CONFLICT

Frank Tridico and Charles E. Crawford

Abstract: *Every social movement is unique in its organizational structure, strategies and tactics it employs, its goals and the nature of collective action it undertakes. There are however, themes that can be discerned that make some social movements similar to one another. This helps bring some understanding to the phenomena but it does not serve as a comprehensive analysis. For example, some collective movements have similar themes yet the nature of their struggles is bound by different criteria. Internal and external constraints play significant roles in how the social movement organization fares against its adversary. In this chapter, various models of collective action and the dynamics of social movement are examined individually and through comparative analysis. Through both analyses, we examine how collective identity is strengthened through conflict rather than consensus, and how dissent is a fundamental medium for change in various contexts.*

Five models will be examined in this study. These include: (1) World Trade Organization (WTO) protests, (2) Fascist Italy and Communist Eastern Europe in the 1930s, (3) military coups in Africa, (4) the sit-in movement and bus boycotts in the 1950s, and (5) the prisoner rights movement. While the nature and extent of conflicts contained therein are unique, common themes can be discerned through comparative analysis. In challenging a more powerful adversary, the dissenting faction operates from a disadvantage. Hence, in-group hegemony and collective identity are likely to be enhanced through conflict, or it may be exhausted along with the social movement's tenure.

In faring against more powerful adversaries, social movements often must enter the realm in which the adversary is situated. In some models, the dissenter is able to engage its adversary within its own jurisdiction. Regardless of its location, conflict will either result in the dissenter's goals being realized (to varying extents) or being rebuked through resistance. Legitimacy plays an important factor in the struggles (Canel, 1992; Scott, 1990), with the more legitimate faction having an advantage prior to, and during conflict. Legitimacy, whether it is real or perceived, is a crucial element in a faction's ascent to power.

The models will be examined in terms of nature of conflicts, location of conflicts, internally analyzed through an historical lens and the social movement's organizational processes, and through comparative analyses. Jenkins (1981) asserts that central concerns are addressed including whether the movements are internal or external struggles, level of power attained, the degree of legitimacy attained, how the social movement organizations measure success/gains, and what has changed as a result of collective action.

The first model: World Trade Organization Protests

<u>Nature of conflict</u>: More powerful adversary (located within economic and political realms) v. less powerful but more aggressive dissenter (located within civil society)

<u>Location of conflict</u>: Social cultural realm

One important criterion in measuring the dynamics of a social movement is its tenure. The power to engage in a series of collective action is not the same as the power to sustain them over time. Some social movements are able to utilize members to engage in social action without having control over them or resources to reward their efforts (Oberschall, 1992; McCarthy & Zald, 1988). This loose structure puts the movement in a quandary because the autonomy of its adherents leaves it open to defection, conflict and competition.

Internal dissent becomes a challenge for loosely organized social movements. One manner in which they seek to build solidarity between adherents is to embark in aggressive attack against an adversary. For example, opponents of the World Trade Organization often form protests where member nation representatives meet to discuss trade. Here, the adversary is the World Trade Organization. The social movement makes a number of calculated assessments before engaging in protest. These include:

(1) Leaders of the movement may or may not take part in the actual protest. Their main contribution is to organize the protest and devise strategy.

(2) Leaders of the movement utilize large numbers of protestors as a strategy to bring attention to their cause.

(3) Leaders of the movement may not encourage violence or aggressive acts but they do not condemn it. Such protests often end up in direct confrontation with the adversary and ultimately law enforcement.

(4) Adherents to the movement focus on the *cause*, or group or movement interests and put those in front of their own individual interests.

(5) Adherents to the movement usually belong to multiple social movement organizations. It is not uncommon to have the same persons involved in other causes and protests.

(6) The more radical adherents are more likely to have had direct confrontation with law enforcement, been arrested and/or charged. Such conflict has only fueled their motivation for dissent.

(7) The social movement does not wish to negotiate. It seeks to dismantle the cause they combat against while conceding nothing.

(8) The social movement organization has few committed members long-term and many short-term recruits. Its message seems to resonate with a core group within society but not enough to sustain the movement over a long period of time.

(9) Conflict is absolutely necessary to mobilize the social movement. Without conflict, it is not organized sufficiently to combat its adversary by other means.

The World Trade Organization, as an adversary, will thrive despite being confronted with angry protestors. The social movement goes into remission almost immediately after the conflict. It will resurface at another date and location. What then is the purpose of collective action if it changes little? Moreover, how is it that collected action that appears so organized and so spirited reaches levels of impotence after limited time?

The social scientist does well to look beyond the actual sensationalism of conflict between aggressor and adversary and focus on a number of critical areas. Questions that need address include:

(1) Was the social movement an internal or external struggle?

(2) Who has greater power?

(3) Who has greater legitimacy?

(4) How does the social movement organization measure success/gains?

(5) What has changed as a result of the collective action?

The first question: Was the social movement an internal or external struggle?

In this case, protestors were clearly outside of the realm the World Trade Organization exists. Indeed, one can posit that the WTO exists partially in the economic realm and partially in the political realm. It has therefore, greater legitimacy than its aggressor. The dissenting party comes from the social/cultural realm where access to power and influence is the least likely to be found in. The social movement is thus an external struggle, where outsiders attempt to influence the internal dynamics of the adversary. This makes it difficult to enhance change from within the structure of the adversary. The adversary can either resist and/or wait until the cycle of protest exhausts itself. It is not bound to change.

The second question: Who has greater power?

If we define power as having access to influencing change and enforcing such change, then it clearly distinguishes adversary and aggressor. The adversary in most conflicts tends to be the one that is more powerful. The dissenting faction seeks to challenge the more powerful adversary to instigate reform in unconventional manners. In many cases, it either refuses to enter a legitimized field of dissent (e.g., the political arena) or does not know how to enter the field. In taking the battle to its own playing field (e.g., civil society) it maintains some advantage for a limited period of time. Once its prowess is exhausted within the cycle of protest, and the more powerful adversary leaves the aggressor's playing field, the dissenter returns to its original position. The social movement organization has not replaced its adversary with greater power. The more powerful adversary maintains its stronger position.

The third question: Who has greater legitimacy?

Power and legitimacy usually are synonymous concepts. The adversary (in this case the World Trade Organization) continues to thrive despite short-term setbacks when engaging in aggressive protests by the dissenter. However, its power is restored once it returns to its own playing field. Moreover, the adversary being on the receiving end of violent protest many times restores or regains added legitimacy. Through its own victimization, it redefines its own civility. The aggressor, particularly if it comes into direct confrontation with the law, is discredited. It loses much of its legitimacy because of its enduring utilization of unlawful means to achieve its ends.

The fourth question: How does the social movement organization measure success/gains?

Erroneous assessments are usually made in the definition of success. Different social movement organizations define success differently. Sometimes, what may appear to be a setback may indeed constitute a perverted gain for the dissenter. Some social movements may have the message of protest to resonate nationally or internationally as its chief goal. Conflict then becomes important in bringing the cause exposure. If this is what matters to a social movement organization, then it can achieve success through these means. Its utilization of large numbers of volunteer adherents is limited to a specific area and time. They are not needed for later negotiation with the adversary because there is no plan for discourse.

The fifth question: What has changed as a result of the collective action?

In this example, both the adversary and the aggressor win some advantage through conflict. They achieve this of course for different reasons. The adversary is conveniently placed in a position of victim. Here, the spotlight ignores what platform the organization may have that may or may not be detrimental to other parties. The spotlight is shone upon it as a victim of lawlessness and mob aggression. While it may lose its power in that it cannot retaliate, its legitimacy is not only restored but in some ways, enhanced. It returns to its sphere and assumes its development.

The aggressor is confronted with an odd mix of success and failure. On one hand, its protest wins it initial favor from sympathizers who share consensus with their cause. This initial favor quickly dissolves from many sympathizers that denounce illegal action. Once it moves from the legal to illegal parameters, the social movement loses much of its legitimacy as a movement. However, radical sympathizers identify with its plight and it strengthens their resolve. This creates a new pool or more radical adherents to the cause. This is a necessary component in its next cycle of protest. Each successive protest is necessary to maintain the cause's sustenance. Since it only exists in the social/cultural realm it must continue to exercise its dominance within it. Whether it is perceived as legitimate or illegitimate; matters *less*. Whether it as a social movement organization can continue to thrive and reconstitute itself in more aggressive cycles matters *more*.

This model suggests that strange developments occur after conflict between the two factions. On the one hand, it serves to elevate the legitimacy and power of the adversary (World Trade Organization). On the other hand, it actually decreases the legitimacy of the aggressor (WTO protestors) but it re-affirms its power by attracting new, more radical sympathizers to its movement. In this vein, it guarantees its emergence as a more aggressive and committed force against the adversary. Such power is only wielded within civil society in the social/cultural realm and it does not extend outside of its parameters.

The second model: Fascist Italy and Communist Eastern Europe

<u>Nature of conflict</u>: More powerful adversary (located within political realms) v. less powerful but more organized and committed dissenter (located within civil society)

<u>Location of conflict</u>: Political realm

Two historical examples to assess this model of collective action are used: These include:

(1) Fascist Italy, where groups such as Italian Catholic Action organized for resistance under the legitimate umbrella of the Fascist-Vatican Concordat (Webster, 1960).
(2) Eastern Europe after 1989, where centralization of power in repressive states offered dissidents a unified collective and a specific common target to attack (Bunce, 1990).

Both of these historical periods share similarities. These include:

(1) Italy had a fascist regime during the early to mid-20th Century. Much of Eastern Europe was under Communist dominion in the

1980s. Both systems were similar in that they were repressive, authoritarian states.

(2) Both Italy and Eastern Europe in their respective periods restricted civil liberties in an effort to minimize dissent.

(3) Both systems incorporated huge bureaucracies to expand the power and authority of the state.

(4) The individual in both systems was subordinate to the regimes. Autonomy and individualism was discouraged.

Although they were in different eras and in different geographic regions, both Italians and Eastern Europeans were governed under repressive regimes. These authoritative systems specifically suppressed interaction of collective actors that is integral in the organization stages of social movements. However, not all repression quells dissent. Repression itself can produce a radicalization of collective action and a more effective organization of adversaries.

While it crushes resistance under many circumstances, the centralization of power and influence in repressive states offers dissidents several advantages in the process. These include (i) a renewed consciousness of identity, (ii) commitment to a cause, (iii) a centralized target to attack, and (iv) solidarity among adherents.

While the authoritarian regimes in both Italy and Eastern Europe crushed external dissent, they facilitated internal hegemony within the oppressed. The very nature of oppressive states makes it difficult to build trust. They rule with iron fists in an effort to discourage collective actors from challenging its authority of rule. Its self-preservationist ideals actually serve to be the seeds of their own destruction. This was the case in both historical examples. Here, the disenfranchised have a crucial weapon; they have a great deal in common (Bunce, 1990).

Strong leadership, organization and well-defined goals are the base components of social movements. Without them, they will not enjoy tenure as social movement organizations. However, these three criteria are not enough to overcome the power of a stronger adversary. In the contexts of both Italy and Eastern Europe, it was necessary to have effective strategies and tactics and to exercise these in the opportune moment. Mobilization then, becomes crucial in waging successful attack on the intended target. If the target is more powerful and more legitimate and has more resources, it retains the advantage.

In both examples, dissidents organized effectively over years, waiting for the states to become vulnerable. In fascist Italy, growing disillusionment with Dictator Benito Mussolini coupled with his weakening relationships with the monarchy, the Church and former bureaucratic alliances opened glaring weaknesses and opportunity for mobilization to occur. The repressive state began to loosen its domestic grip due to its imperialist dalliances. Mussolini was eventually deposed in a coup d'état and replaced immediately through the political system.

In Eastern Europe, state socialism began to weaken and eventually collapse in the late 1980s. Russia was the exception in this course. It was President Gorbachev who brought major reforms to Communism that specifically opened opportunity for new freedoms. Russian society moved from repressive system that raises the contender's cost of collective action to a facilitating system that lowered the contender's cost (Tilly, 1978).

The right of dissent, when introduced is a powerful weapon to afford to an adversary. In Italy, dissidents mobilized when the system was vulnerable. In Eastern Europe, dissenters moved forward when the system was collapsing. In Russia, contenders mobilized under new reforms from within the system itself. In these examples, organization occurs within civil society; mobilization begins in the social/cultural realm and eventually attains power within the political realm.

Where the first and second models differ

In the first model, the more powerful adversary was the World Trade Organization. Although it yields great influence in a global economy, it is not a government. As such, it does not have the power and authority to repress dissent. Its two central strengths include:

(1) It operates outside of the social/cultural where dissidents (WTO protestors) have more control of the playing field.
(2) It is afforded greater legitimacy by not engaging in retaliatory behavior. The added legitimacy comes at the expense of the social movement organization that opposes it.

In the second model, the more powerful adversary was the State itself. Here, it controls all access to power. This includes the powers to: (i) enact legislation, (ii) enforce its own laws, (iii) disband all opposition parties, (iv) disband constitutions at will, (v) suspend civil liberties, (vi) expand bureaucracy, (vii) eliminate or limit religion, (viii) eliminate or limit freedom of expression and freedom of the press, (ix) control the courts, (x) control the economy, and (xi) control social mobility.

These authoritarian systems operated within the political realm but their tentacles spread to all other areas of society: the legal, economic and social/cultural. The latter afforded some refuge from such control but only through effective mobilization at the opportune moment of greatest vulnerability could dissenters overcome these systems.

Clearly there are more differences between the more powerful adversaries in each model. There are great differences between the less powerful dissenters in each model. Dissidents in the first model have at their disposal the opportunity to attack the more powerful opponent in other areas: the political, legal and economic spheres. Yet for some reason, they take revolutionary tactics and remain concentrated in civil society. They cannot overcome a more powerful adversary in large part, because they choose not to alter their strategies to acclimate them to new ideas and new challenges.

Presented is a visual display of the characteristics of dissidents for both models. It affords the reader what makes the dissidents similar and what makes them different in their respective struggles against more powerful opponents.

Model 1: WTO Protestors	**Model 2: Italian/ Eastern Europeans**
• a renewed consciousness of identity • commitment to cause is *limited* to protest • a centralized target to attack • adherents come and go; solidarity is limited to protests • *many* battles with no victory in *civil society*	• a renewed consciousness of identity • strong commitment to the cause • a centralized target to attack • solidarity among adherents • calculated strategies *one* final victory is in *political realm*

The third model: Military coups in Africa

<u>Nature of conflict</u>: Powerful adversary (located within political realm) v. more powerful and committed dissenter (located within civil society)

<u>Location of conflict</u>: Political realm through military insurgency in African states

Africa has a history of military intervention in political affairs. This has given rise to a number of violent military coups in various nations within the continent. For over three decades, from 1960 to the 1990s, coups were practically the only means by which changes of government were achieved in Africa.

There were widespread movements for expanding the base of political parties. This was one sharp shift to working *within* the system itself. Initial successes afforded the masses a voice in their own affairs. It allowed the masses to change policies at the political level and help charter a course for their futures. Important to note was that it involved *politicization* and not *military intervention.*

Once politicization became the medium to bring forth change, leaders within movements in the social/cultural and political realms recognized that there was a key danger in new abuses of power and influence that could mimic its predecessors' policies. Demanding accountability on multiple levels, the *new systems* sought to inject checks and balances that would prevent history from repeating itself. It would repeat itself.

The masses initially believed that they could hold political figures accountable. Few political officials believed that they could. Indeed, corruption began to embed itself *within* more sophisticated forms of organizational structural dynamics. The bureaucratic structures of the *new* Africa would only serve as legitimized forms of corruption.

There was one difference. The military was used to *enforce* such legitimacy. Elites would rule with legitimacy *and* force. This gave rise to military coups. These new social movements would be seen as injecting more violence, resistance to established governments, aggressive dissent and eventual corruption within their own factions, and more so once they assumed greater power and influence through military coups. It also meant increased suffrage for the civilian populations.

Military coups are not unique aberrations. Indeed, they appear to be a *norm* in a systematic cyclical pattern of addressing corruption with escalating violence and further corruption. Important to demarcate are the conditions that make such political corruption thrive and revolutionary movements to develop.

This phenomenon develops and thrives in states that have all the right preconditions. These include one, several or all of the following:

(1) political elites who base their claim to power on ethnic, regional or religious rather than national constituencies
(2) the lack of effective and independent established and external institutions to operate as a system of checks and balances
(3) varying limits, or complete denial of freedom of expression or of the press, in an effort to minimize dissent
(4) collaboration of both the political and military to maintain corruption through both legitimacy of law and enforcement of such policies
(5) the use of systematic terror and violence against the civilian masses to instill fear and to dissuade forms of potential dissent

What is ironic is that dissenting factions, including but not limited to, rebel factions or parts of the military, usually present themselves as guardians of the national interest who will cleanse politics of corruption. History usually repeats the same cycles of violence, abuse and corruption. Once power is seized within the State, the emergent elites become similar or worse violators than their predecessors.

This cycle of corruption, coups, and counter-coups has proved difficult to break. What is important is that we identify what the conditions are that continue this process of cyclical abuse. Once we identify these, it becomes possible to address these in an effective manner.

This model differs greatly from the first model in a number of ways. These include:

(1) Dissenters in the third model are committed rebel forces that remain through the conflict and the development of a new regime. WTO protesters do not do this. They tend to disperse quickly after the collective action is exhausted.

(2) Dissenters in the third model (rebel forces) are organized, with a sophisticated chain of hierarchal command. They are structured like the national military but they are smaller in number. WTO protesters organization quickly disperses in conflict with law enforcement.

(3) Rebel forces have a calculated strategy with a clear set goal: forced removal of the adversary through deadly action and immediate insurgency. They do not *demand* change from the adversary. They *make* change by removing the adversary from its command.

(4) Rebel forces are concerned with the attainment of power. They are less concerned about causes or the plight of the disenfranchised. Their motivation is self-serving and to expand their power base within the society.

This model is *similar* from the first model in a number of ways. These include:

(1) Individuals of both social movement organizations place the larger group's interests ahead of their own individual ones. The level of commitment to the many enables individual units to ignore personal risks in the engagement.

(2) Rebel forces and WTO protesters may view violence (levels of course will vary) as an acceptable, and perhaps even necessary, course of action in confrontation with the adversary.

(3) Both models focus on significant change. Both dissenters in each model want absolute change without negotiation or compromise.

(4) Both models attract radical members to their causes.

The third model *differs* greatly from the second model in a number of ways. These include:

(1) Dissenters in the third model are rebel forces that stage a military coup to resolve their dispute. Dissenters in the second model depose the adversary through legitimate channels in the political system.

(2) Dissenters in the third model use violence as a means to an end. Dissenters of the second model retain the use of force as an option of last resort.

(3) Dissenters in the third model are motivated by the pursuit of power. They are not committed to a cause to rectify the abuses

and injustices of the current regime. Political dissidents of the second model want to initiate positive change; their pursuit is a *cause*.

(4) Dissenters in the third model replace the leadership in the political realm with the military (legitimate or rebel forces). Dissenters in the third model replace the leadership whom they opposed but do not bring forward a better, more egalitarian system. In most cases, it becomes worse than the previous regime. Political dissidents in the second model replace the leadership but with a less *authoritarian* one.

The third model is similar to the second model in several ways. These similarities between rebel forces in Africa and former political dissidents in fascist Italy and communist Eastern Europe include:

(1) They all have a centralized target: the government. In both models, dissidents calculate strategies to completely depose the ruling party.

(2) Committed members are patient in their strategy. They engage in conflict with the adversary on their own terms. When the adversary is vulnerable or when they are at their strongest, they initiate combat.

(3) After deposing the previous regime or government, the ascent to power brings with it legitimacy. The new leadership can enforce these new laws. The new leadership subordinates the wider society to its will.

The fourth model: The sit-in movement and bus boycotts in the 1950s

Nature of conflict: Powerful adversary (the State) v. large, organized and committed dissenters (located within civil society)

Location of conflict: Social/cultural realm

Morris (1981: 764) argues that during the sit-in movement of 1960 that it was the pre-existing social structures that gave the movement the resources and communication networks to foster and sustain their tenure. This argument refutes the more traditional approach that had the Congress for Racial Equality (CORE), the Southern Christian Leadership

Conference (SCLC) and the National Association for the Advancement of Colored People (NAACP) operating in spontaneous unity to forward the civil rights movement. The existence of sophisticated organization network, calculated strategies and long-term goals runs contrary to the argument that the Movement was spontaneous and had limited tenure. The pre-existing internal organizations were centered on the Baptist Church as a coordinating unit. The Church did four specific things:

(1) It acted as a catalyst for identity formation and building for disenfranchised African-Americans.
(2) It served as protection for the Movement to avoid reprisals from the State.
(3) It collected and re-distributed resources for the Movement in order for it to mobilize.
(4) It specifically perfected strategy and directed action between 1955 and 1960.

Many civil rights movement scholars concur that the black Southern student sit-in movement of 1960 was both a crucial development and the next stage of tests against the State after the bus boycotts between 1955 and 1960 (Matthews and Prothro, 1966; McAdam, 1979; Meier and Rudwick, 1973; Oppenheimer, 1964; Zinn, 1964). The sit-in movement revitalized the civil rights movement and afforded it greater victories against the State. One specific threat it posed to the State was that it was perceived to possibly turn into militant action (Obear, 1970; Sale, 1973).

The sit-in movement was important because its rapid spread across southern states gave it momentum as well as strength. It directly pulled many people directly into the movement. Morris (1981: 362) traces sit-ins being conducted between 1957 and 1960 in at least fifteen cities in 10 states.

Rational planning was part of the early waves of sit-ins. In the late 1950s, the Nashville Christian Leadership Council formed non-violent workshops. These workshops taught local college students the strategies and tactics of non-violent protest and dealing with more powerful opponents in law enforcement and the State (Bracey et al., 1971). Meier & Rudwick (1973) argue that careful planning of up to one year in advance afforded the movement effective results. Such evidence refutes traditional analyses of the sit-in movements as unplanned, spontaneous and limited in ineffectiveness. They specifically challenged the State's legitimacy. They were protesting unjust policies that were legitimized through laws but their dissent was public, organized and peaceful. This created a dilemma for the State as it could not exercise its power to control peaceful and lawful dissent through aggressive action. Such action could affect the State in three specific manners:

(1) It would come at some expense of its legitimacy.
(2) It could initiate further peaceful protests.
(3) It could escalate peaceful protests into more aggressive forms of dissent.

Organizational and personal networks produced what are termed *clusters* of sit-ins in Oklahoma in 1958. These quickly spread through effective networking and organization within a one hundred mile radius of Oklahoma. The spread of clusters brought peaceful protests into the national and international media spotlight. The State was presented with a viable threat it could not ignore. Its legitimacy was being directly *challenged*. The clusters enabled an aggressive but peaceful and lawful confrontation with the State.

In Nashville, the first signs of change within civil society began to emerge. Segregation laws continued to be in effect, but the sit-in movement coupled with peaceful bus boycotts directly influenced the desegregation of a number of private establishments and public transportation facilities (Morris, 1981: 377). Both the sit-ins and boycotts were the initial collective action that was used as a model for the mobilization stages of the civil rights movement in the 1960s. While the 1960s presented new challenges because it expanded its mobilization to a national context and directly brought the movement into direct legal confrontation with the State, it served as the model for effective strategy. Although on its own, it had limited change in both the legal and political realms, it did bring the movement national exposure, affording it the legitimacy it needed to challenge the State directly.

The fifth model: The Prisoner Rights Movement

<u>Nature of conflict</u>: More powerful adversary (correctional officials and administrators) v. prison inmates aided by activist judges and attorneys

<u>Location of conflict</u>: The legal realm through the correctional system. The final model we explore takes place in our nation's prisons and

courts. Prisoner rights raises many questions and issues, at their core they challenge the authority of correctional officials as they attempt to manage and control what appears to many citizens to be an increasingly violent and organized group of inmates. The subject of prisoner rights often angers citizens as they consider the irony of how a convicted criminal who has victimized a fellow citizen could be given rights and protection of the laws that they violated. Like other movements, to gain insight into prisoner rights they must be examined within their social and temporal contexts.

Historically, a convicted criminal suffered physically and legally. For example, in ancient Rome the criminal was stripped of citizenship, property, and his wife was declared a widow unable to remarry; he essentially became a slave. This view was upheld in the United States in the landmark case *Ruffin v. Commonwealth* (1871) in which the counsel for defendant Ruffin applied for a writ of error, arguing that his client was not tried by a jury of his vicinage. Justice Christian of the Virginia court delivered the majority opinion that an inmate is civilly dead ever entrapped in restraints and regulations; the criminal is no longer a person but a slave of the State (Sarat and Kearns, 2002: 225). The impact of this decision would last for nearly a century.

Although the courts were not completely uninvolved in inmate complaints and conditions, the decades of the 1940s, and 1950s were a time when the courts could be described as having a '*hands off doctrine*' when it came to prisoner's rights. The belief of the courts during this time period was that they lacked expertise in the area of corrections and judicial intervention would only lead to excessive litigation undermining correctional officials' discipline and authority (Wallace, 1994). However, the 1960s brought changes not only to the social structure of society through the civil rights movement as discussed earlier in this chapter, but was a decade in which the courts began to retreat from this doctrine.

The civil rights movement was instrumental in laying the foundation of the prison rights movement. Ultimately it was the Warren Court (1953-1969) that set the tone for judicial activism through broad interpretations of the Constitution. The Court was committed to extending constitutional protections to minorities and was deeply involved in jails and prisons. As Kenneth Pye (1968) points out, the Court's interest and concern with criminal procedure and prison policy can only be understood in the context of the civil rights struggle.

With the assistance of activist judges, a cadre of informed prison lawyers, and a public disillusioned with the notion of rehabilitation the prisoner rights movement was born and the courts made it clear an inmate does not check their constitutional rights (though limited) at the prison gates. The prisoner rights movement during the 1960s stands in stark contrast to the other examples of social movements outlined in this chapter. Rather than utilizing organized or aggressive protest as a tool it began with simple legal challenges to practice religion, which in-turn cleared the path for greater access to the legal machinery that would embolden the movement leading to a politicization of inmates and instability in correctional management. Were it not for the context of social upheaval of the civil rights movement that challenged the legitimacy of the social order, the prisoner rights movement would not have been able to create the changes that would shape the nature of correctional practices for decades to come.

Prisoner Rights and Civil Rights as a Combined Movement

One of the early connections of the civil rights movement and the beginnings of prisoner rights as a social movement began in the early 1960s as members of the Nation of Islam were incarcerated and introduced African American inmates to Islamic religious and cultural/political education. These efforts were viewed as a threat inside of prisons that were becoming increasingly hostile and polarized by race. Correctional staff harassed Islamic ministers, their meetings were disrupted, and their communications were often censored (Lucken & Blomberg, 2000). As inmates became activists the correctional system responded with aggression isolating inmates, denying parole, and destroying personal property (Wald, 1980).

The early victories of the prisoner rights movement centered on religion and the practice of Islam demonstrating a key linkage to the broader civil rights struggle and social movements outside the prison walls and may have mobilized the prison rights movement during the 1960s and 1970s. Jacobs (1997) points out that between 1961 and 1978 there were 66 federal court decisions related to the practice of Islam in prison. In fact the early cases such as *Fullwood v Clemmer* (1962) that forced the Washington D.C. department of corrections to permit Muslim activities in the prison and the ruling in *Cooper v Pate* (1964) that allowed Muslim inmates access to the Koran and a place to worship, essentially affirmed the First Amendment rights of inmates to practice their religion effectively overturning the Ruffin decision giving inmates protection under the Civil Rights Act of 1871.

The parallels between the civil rights movement and the prisoner rights movement were not simply coincidence. Many of the key litigators for the civil rights movement were active in prisoner rights. For these legal activist, civil and inmate rights were intimately connected, and making prisoner rights a part of the agenda of the civil rights movement was a natural extension as prisons in America during the 1960s and 1970s were housing more African American and Hispanic inmates. In many ways the prisoner rights movement was the civil rights movement extended to the prison setting. Civil and prisoner rights movements shared commonalities. Members of each movement often faced violent resistance. Both were seeking the rights of citizenship, launching a fight against inhumane treatment, and as discussed earlier those who fought for civil rights often found themselves incarcerated leading to a natural progression of participation in prisoner rights. In many ways the prison had become a reflection of the larger society.

Organized Violence and Prisoner Rights

As the civil rights movement gained greater momentum and successes it also began to change for some, from non-violent protest to Black Nationalism. The change was startling to many in American cities as the country appeared to be consumed by hate and rage as race riots took center stage during the mid to late 1960s. For example, the Watts Riots of 1965 lasted for more than six days with more than 1,000 injuries and 34 deaths, and numerous rioters were reported to have been shouting, "*get whitey*" (Roberts and Kilbanoff, 2007). This anger was now moving into previously non-violent civil rights organizations such as the Student Non-violent Coordination Committee (SNCC) who began distributing the writings of Malcolm X and Frantz Fanon over Mahatma Gandhi. The change in tactics and taking an anti-war stance on Vietnam split SNCC into those that did not believe in black separatism and those that wanted to purge all whites from the organization and seize power.

This radicalization and politicization of the civil rights movement would eventually spill over into the prisoner rights movement particularly with the growth of the Black Panthers in the California prison system. Despite its growing radicalization it is during this stage of the prisoner rights movement that it gains support beyond the African American community and civil rights, and became a larger movement as inmates were at times compared to political prisoners. Inmates suddenly found a diverse group of supporters for their cause: white college students with an anti-establishment mentality, Vietnam veterans, and feminist protestors. The result of this support was a greater solidarity among inmates of all races who viewed themselves as a unified class (Lucken and Blomberg, 2000). These multiple factors would all combine and lead to one of the most famous correctional uprisings in American history: Attica.

The Attica Prison Riot

The riot at Attica Correctional Facility in New York took place between September 9th and 13th, 1971. Thirty-nine people were killed and more than 80 others were wounded during the state police attempt to retake the prison. Attica was an overcrowded prison holding more than 2,200 inmates with few meaningful programs. In addition, the inmate population was increasingly urban and had become 54% African American. The correctional staff however was nearly all white conservative officers from rural New York. Minority inmates were being influenced by the Black Panthers and Black Muslims. For example, one year after Black Panther member George Jackson published his critically acclaimed book *Soledad Brother* he was fatally shot during an alleged escape attempt from a California prison. In reaction to the shooting, African American inmates in Attica demonstrated a collective action and consciousness the next day by moving silently in rows of twos while wearing black armbands. The infamous prison riot would take place a few weeks later.

The 1971 McKay Commission described the conditions in Attica, the food was barely edible, recreation was minimal, and treatment of the inmates was often degrading. However, these conditions existed in other New York prisons of the time and even some prisons today. In many ways as the McKay Commission put it, Attica was every prison (Attica: The Official Report, 1972). This leads to asking the question why did the uprising take place at this institution? Again the social context of the civil rights movement must be considered. As discussed earlier, the civil rights movement and the prisoner rights movements were both being radicalized. These radical nationalist and leftist ideologies were the strongest in New York City with California's San Francisco Bay a close second. Sentenced offenders who were seen as part of the radical movement in New York City were often transported to Attica due to its remote location. The result of these actions would create an unprecedented concentration of prison revolutionaries and activists in one setting (Useem and Kimbal, 1991).

Any inmate who was politically aware or had their consciousness raised, was viewed suspiciously and found themselves in direct conflict with prison officials. Although the Attica riot was a spontaneous outburst of violence, it was the development of a negotiation team and plan that gripped the nation and transformed Attica from a simple prison riot to a metaphor for the social problems that plagued America. The inmate leaders prepared a list of demands including better food, medical treatment, and freedom to practice their religion. Ultimately the peaceful negotiations deteriorated due to several factors: poor negotiating conditions, the use of an observers' committee, an impasse on the list of demands and immunity, and prison officials leaking false rumors of the correctional officers turned hostages being tortured (Welch, 2004). Eventually the state police would be ordered to retake the prison resulting in one out of every 10 people in the yard being struck by gunfire (Attica: The Official Report, 1972).

Why was a Violent Assault Ordered?

Unsubstantiated fear may have been one of the factors that led to a forceful takeover, as police officers outside the prison walls were under the impression that hostages were being tortured, and that inmates were fortifying their position and possibly constructing bombs. Furthermore, Commissioner Oswald and Governor Rockefeller were concerned the intense press coverage of the riot would lend support to revolutionary movements across the country. A more direct answer comes from Commissioner Oswald himself and demonstrates the frustration of the correctional system in dealing with the most powerful expression of the prisoner rights movement to date. Essentially he stated that they were not simply dealing with an uprising over conditions or grievances, he felt they were dealing with organized revolutionaries attempting to gain public support and undermine authority everywhere. Governor Rockefeller went one step further and suggested the use of violence to retake the prison was a public statement of the state's sovereignty and power and that social change through violent means would be rejected to preserve lawful society (Useem and Kimbal, 1991).

The Attica uprising resonated throughout the country as the images, statements of the inmates and film footage were disseminated worldwide. In this instance, the prisoner rights movement flowed into the community and infused other social movements. For some, Attica became an example of how the government could not be trusted, and reshaped the political ideology of the time, and influenced social movements for Hispanics, students, women, as well as prisoners in other institutions.

The Outcomes of Prisoner Rights Movement

The impact of the Attica prison riot and more generally the prisoner rights movement was felt immediately by correctional officers and administrators and did end some of the most damaging prison practices such as starving inmates and routine beatings. The Texas and Arkansas departments of corrections stand as two of the most startling examples of correctional practices that were ended through sustained legal challenges from inmates. The Texas Department of Corrections employed a trustee system using building tenders (BT): hardened convicts who were essentially functioning as quasi-correctional officers. The BTs carried clubs, protected officers, issued commands to inmates, and beatings to control others (Marquart and Crouch, 1985).

The Arkansas prison system employed equally brutal methods to control inmates such as the Tucker telephone. Inmates were punished by being restrained to a bed in the Tucker hospital where a correctional officer would administer shocks to the inmate by attaching electrodes from a crank style telephone generator (Murton and Hyams, 1969). Scandals such as these along with the atrocities and corruption at institutions such as the Cummins prison farm in Arkansas were well documented and proof to activists of the need to have legal intervention in prisons to protect inmates from constitutional violations and abuse.

The prisoner rights movement ultimately increased inmate's access to the courts, and brought about much needed reforms. Outside of dismantling specific egregious practices there was a significant overall impact on correctional administration and management. Prisons could no longer rely on coercive tactics to control inmates and had to develop bureaucratic procedures to hear grievances. Another interesting outcome of the prisoner rights movement was that it brought about a new type of administrator: one that was expected to understand the law and be able to resolve conflicts before they turned into lawsuits (Welch, 2004). In addition to bringing about a new breed of administrator, the prisoner rights movement had a lasting impact on the inmates themselves as they became highly aware of their constitutional rights and legal protections.

The Backlash

There were also unintended consequences of the prisoner rights movement. Critics of judicial activism felt that the courts may have overstepped their bounds and undermined correctional authority in matters of operating the prison. With greater access to courts and the willingness of the judiciary to hear such cases there was a dramatic increase in the number of lawsuits filed by inmates. The last 40 years has witnessed an onslaught of prison litigations that in turn has infuriated citizens. It may be misleading to characterize prison litigation as legal pollution, since prior to the 1960s prison lawsuits were limited at best (Thomas et al., 1986). More recently, the public attention has been focused on frivolous lawsuits from inmates bringing about a major change in prison litigation with the passage of the Prison Litigation Reform Act in 1996.

The Prison Litigation Reform Act was driven by the public perception of inmates' abuse of the legal system and that prisoners now possessed more rights than crime victims. The act essentially limited the actions of courts in prison cases and created punitive sanctions for filing what were deemed to be frivolous lawsuits. The Prison Litigation Reform Act according to critics may serve to make prisons tougher and to keep poor conditions and mistreatment out of the public view (Robertson, 2002). The current conservative position of the courts is a major departure from the activist jurists of the 1960s and 1970s. It is clear that the trend is to curtail prisoner rights rather than uphold them as well as reversing previous decisions (Lucken & Blomberg, 2000).

The Prisoner Rights Movement Today and Beyond

There appears to be an end to the prisoner rights movement from the nature and form it took in the 1960s and 1970s. The unique social context of the time period infused both civil rights and the prisoner rights movement with hostility towards government and a level of radicalization and politicization that has yet to be matched today. As social activism outside of prison subsided, it began to retreat on behalf of inmates as well. As Wald (1980) points out, the romanticized notions of inmates as political prisoners and leaders that was held by activist and scores of uncompensated attorneys gave way to a more conservative view that the inmates were simply criminals. Prisoner rights as a social movement have lost its mass appeal, and may have exhausted itself. The challenge remaining today for jailhouse lawyers and prison rights advocates is to keep from losing the gains made during the height of this highly influential movement.

Establishing links between the five models

An examination of the five models is offered in visual display:

The first model: World Trade Organization Protests

<u>Nature of conflict</u>: More powerful adversary (located within economic and political realms) v. less powerful but more aggressive dissenter (located within civil society)

<u>Location of conflict</u>: Social/cultural realm

<u>Dynamics of conflict</u>: Aggressive protesting escalating into possible violence

<u>Outcome of conflict</u>:
(1) World Trade Organization gains added legitimacy.
(2) WTO Protestors lose legitimacy but gain new committed radical members ensuring the social movement organization continuity.

The second model: Fascist Italy and Communist Eastern Europe

<u>Nature of conflict</u>: More powerful adversary (located within political realms) v. less powerful but more organized and committed dissenter (located within civil society)

<u>Location of conflict</u>: Political realm

<u>Dynamics of conflict</u>: Calculated, patient and committed dissenter attacks at opportune moment and deposes the adversary of leadership (with or without violence)

<u>Outcome of conflict</u>: Patience pays off and dissenter deposes former leader and gains power legitimacy

The third model: Military coups in Africa

Nature of conflict: Powerful adversary (located within political realm) v. more powerful and committed dissenter (located within civil society)

Location of conflict: political realm through military insurgency in African states

Dynamics of conflict: Aggressive and violent military coup leading to multiple deaths

Outcome of conflict: former leadership is deposed and replaced by a military rebel group who may be more ruthless than the former leadership

The fourth model: The sit-in movement and bus boycotts in the 1950s

Nature of conflict: Powerful adversary (the State) v. large, organized and committed dissenters (located within civil society)

Location of conflict: Social/cultural realm

Dynamics of conflict: Non-violent smaller protests sparking additional organized clusters and spreading to several states

Outcome of conflict:
  (1) The State's power is minimized because it cannot respond aggressively because laws have not been broken.
  (2) Some desegregation occurs prior to Civil Rights laws
  (3) Used as a model for Civil Rights Movement of the 1960s

The fifth model: Prisoner Rights

<u>Nature of conflict</u>: More powerful adversary (correctional officials and administrators) v. prison inmates aided by activist judges and attorneys

<u>Location of conflict</u>: The legal realm through the correctional system

<u>Dynamics of conflict</u>: Pursuing constitutional rights and protections through federal courts with occasional violent clashes with correctional authorities escalating into riots.

<u>Outcome of conflict</u>:
  (1) Affirmed the constitutional rights and protections of prisoners overturning the '*slave of the state*' doctrine.
  (2) Ended degrading and abusive practices in numerous prisons and ushered in a new type of prison administrator.
  (3) Became a part of the radicalized and confrontational forms of social protest during the 1960s and 1970s.
  (4) Gave rise to a collective consciousness and politicalization of inmates.

Each model has been used as an analysis of the nature of the conflict between social movement organizations. Each model is different than another, noting smaller or significant variations in strategies and tactics employed, levels of power, degrees of organization and goals factions seek to attain as a result of such conflict.

The following themes can be discerned from a comparative analysis of all five models. These include:

  (1) In all cases, a rise in power for one faction comes at the expense of the other. This strengthens the argument of conflict theory because it posits change as a central component of conflict.
  (2) In most cases, violence was not a necessary process to achieve dramatic change and to attain goals for the dissenting faction. The sit-in movement and the Bush v. Gore models were consistent with this theme and the Italian/Eastern European model maintained violence as an option but chose non-violent political processes as preferred alternatives. Only the WTO

protestor and the African military coup models had violence as central components in achieving their respective objectives.

(3) In most cases, dissenters were less powerful challengers against a more powerful adversary.

(4) In all cases, except for the WTO protestor models, the less powerful challenger eventually wins in a conflict with a more powerful adversary.

(5) While conflict gives rise to eventual equilibrium after the process is exhausted, in all cases, some change occurs.

(6) In all cases, emergent equilibrium does not guarantee that conflict will not return. In all cases, conflict is likely to ensue when new challengers emerge.

The comparative analysis of these five models shows several common themes despite their different organizational dynamics. It is important for the social scientist to use both critical and comparative analyses in attempting to explain the nature and dynamics of social movements and their conflicts with other factions. In the examination of conflict, the social scientist should not exhaust her/his analysis on what makes factions *different*. We learn just as much, if not more, when we examine what makes factions *similar*.

References

Attica: The Official Report of the New York State Commission (1972). New York, NY: Bantam Books.

Bracey, H., Meier, A., Rudwick, E. (Eds.). (1971). *Conflict and Competition: Studies in the Recent Black Protest Movement, A Wadsworth Series: Explorations in the Black Experience*. Belmont, CA: Wadsworth.

Bunce, V. (1990). Democracy, Stalinism and the Management of Uncertainty in Gregory Szoboszlai (Ed.), *Democracy and Political Transformation*. Budapest: Hungarian Political Science Association (138-164).

Canel, E. (1992). New Social Movement Theory and Resource Mobilization: The Need for Integration. In William K. Carroll (ed.), *Organizing Dissent: Contemporary Social Movements in Theory and Practice*. Victoria, BC: Garamond Press.

Jacobs, J. (1997). The Prisoner Rights Movement and its Impact. In J. Marquart and J. Sorenson (Eds.), *Correctional Contexts* (p. 231-47). Los Angeles, CA: Roxbury.

Jenkins, J.C. (1981). Sociopolitical Movements. *The Handbook of Political Behavior*. 4: 81-153.

Lucken, K. and Blomberg, T. (2000). *American Penology: A History of Control*. Edison, NJ: Aldine Transaction.

Marquart, J., and Crouch, B. (1985). Judicial Reform and Prisoner Control: The Impact of *Ruiz v. Estelle* on a Texas Penitentiary. *Law and Society Review*, 19(4), 557-586.

Matthews, D. and Prothro, J. (1966). *Negroes and the New Southern Politics*. New York, NY: Harcourt, Brace and World.

McAdam, D. (1979). 'Political process and the civil rights movement 1948-1962. Ph.D. dissertation. Department of Sociology, State University of New York at Stony Brook.

McCarthy, J.D., Zald, M. N. (1987). 'Resource Mobilization and Social Movements: A Partial Theory.' In Zald and McCarthy (eds.). *Social Movements in an Organizational Society*. New Brunswick, NJ: Transaction Books.

Meier, A. & Rudwick, E. (1973). *CORE: A Study in the civil rights movement 1942-1968*. New York, NY: Oxford University Press.

Morris, A. (1981). Black Southern Student Sit-In Movement: An Analysis of Internal Organization. *American Sociological Review*. December, 46: 744-767.

Murtan, T., and Hyams, J. (1969). *Accomplices to Crime: The Arkansas Prison Scandal*. New York: Grove.

Obear, F. (1970). Student Activism in the Sixties. In Julian Foster and Durward Lon (eds.), in *Protest: Student Activism in America 1970*. New York, NY: William Morrow (11-26).

Oberschall, A. (1992). *Social Movements: Ideologies, Interests and Identities*. Englewood Cliffs, NJ: Transaction Publishers.

Oppenheimer, M. (1964). The Southern Student Movement: Year 1. *Journal of Negro Education* (33) 396-403.

Pye, K. (1968). The Warren Court and Criminal Procedure. 67 *Michigan Law Review* 67, 249-256.

Roberts, G. and Kilbanoff, H. (2007) *The Race Beat: The Press, the Civil Rights Struggle, and the Awakening of a Nation*. New York, NY: Vintage.

Robertson, J. (2002). The Jurisprudence of the P.L.R.A.: Inmates as "Outsiders" and the Consequence of Countermajoritarian Difficulty. *Journal of Criminal Law and Criminology*, 92(1), 187-210.

Sale, K. (1973). *SDS*. New York, NY: Vintage.

Sarat, A. and Kearns, T. (2002). *History, Memory and the Law*. Ann Arbor, MI: University of Michigan Press.

Scott, A. (1990). *Ideology and the New Social Movements*. London, ON: Unwin Hyman Ltd.

Thomas, J., Keeler, D., and Harris, K. (1986). Issues and Misconceptions in Prisoner Litigation: A Critical View. *Criminology*, 24(4): 775-798.

Tilly, C. (1978). *From Mobilization to Revolution*. Reading, MA: Addison-Wesley.

Useem, B., and Kimbal, P. (1991). *States of Siege: U.S. Prison Riots, 1971-1986*. New York, NY: Oxford University Press.

Wald, K. (1980). The San Quentin Six Case: Perspective and Analysis. In T. Platt and P. Tagaki (Eds.), *Punishment and Penal Discipline: Essays on the Prison and the Prisoners' Movement* (pp 165-175). Crime and Social Justice Associates.

Wallace, D. (1994). The Eighth Amendment and Prison Deprivation: Historical Revisions. *Criminal Law Bulletin*, 30(1), 5-9.

Webster, R. (1960). *The Cross and the Fasces: Christian Deomocracy and Fascism in Italy*. Stanford, CT: Stanford University Press.

Welch, Michael (2004). *Corrections: A Critical Approach*. New York, NY: McGraw Hill.

Zinn, H. (1964). *SNCC: The New Abolitionists*. Boston, MA: Boston Beacon Press.

CHAPTER 10
TERRORISM

Charles Quist-Adade, David Barry and Meghan Kenney

Abstract: Acts of terrorism taking place both internationally and domestically in the last decade of the 20th century and into the 21st century can be examined to demonstrate how modern terrorism is both similar and different from the terrorism of previous centuries. Understanding how terrorism has evolved provides insight into the role that terrorism has played in changing people's way of life throughout the world, and a greater understanding of the ongoing influence modern terrorism will have in subsequent eras. The sophisticated organizational structure and devastating tactics used by such groups make a study of the phenomenon imperative. The chapter forwards definitions and forms of terrorism, comparatively analyzes groups organizational structures and level of sophistication and threat they pose, examines strategies and tactics utilized, and extent of mobilization. International and national legislative policy trends are examined, and their implications to society are addressed. If organized terror is to be combated, the amalgamation of political, legal, economic and social initiatives may serve as an effective process.

Types of Terrorism

The concept of terrorism is not simple to define, and a great deal of confusion has emerged as governments, academics, and the mass media have applied the concept to individuals, groups, events, and acts of violence that have occurred in modern times. For example, suicide bombings, political assassinations, mass killings of civilians by a military, and many other violent acts have been classified as terrorism. Assaults on civilian, military, and/or infrastructure in an attempt to disrupt continuity and create internal chaos within the State serve as objectives for dissenting factions. Whether they are domestically initiated or foreign factions abroad, acts of terrorism are overt, tangible processes of dissent in its rawest form.

Terrorism is an act composed of at least four crucial processes. These include: (i) violence, (ii) a political motive or goal, (iii) perpetuated largely against innocent persons, and (iv) committed before large audiences in order to instill fear and chaos (Combs, 2009: 11). While terrorism has historic roots and its fundamental characteristics of terrorist acts have not changed, the associated tactics and strategies, weapons, network links and support systems, and even motivations have been subject to change in recent years (Combs, 2009; 14).

The rationalization of violence is embedded in (i) rebellion to a perceived foreign authority and (ii) a declared right of self-determination. Terrorism has found itself fostered by causes of the extremist wings of left and right political wings through historical processes such as anarchism, Nazism, nationalism, separatism, and religious fanaticism. Combs (2009: 42) offers examples of each from political left to right, including the Japanese Red Army (anarchist), the Provisional Irish Republican Army (nationalist), ETA (Basque) (separatist), Aryan Nations (neo-Nazi), and al-Qaeda (religious zealot). These examples illustrate a broader spectrum of organizations and causes, each with political objectives and the instrument of terror and chaos used as its specific strategy. In this vein, the political axes of left to right can be questioned because such organizations have as many similarities as differences, particularly through objectives, strategies, organizational structure and method of mobilization.

While there are numerous approaches toward defining the concept of terrorism, there are also multiple types. This section furthers the discussion and attempt to understand modern-day terrorism in comparison to terrorism in the past by exploring the various types of terrorism. This is accomplished by first addressing the conceptual distinctions between five types of terrorist-acts. Then, these types are exemplified by examining actual acts of terrorism. Feliks Gross (1990) offers five types of terror-violence. These include:

(1) *Mass terror*. This refers to state terrorism administered by the reigning governmental regime in order to instill social order through the limiting and/or cessation of dissent.
(2) *Dynastic assassination*. This includes acts of violence against political leaders and elite with the objective of challenging their legitimacy, deposing them and/or instilling chaos.

(3) *Random terror.* This accounts for violent acts upon public places (e.g., bombs in post offices, shootings in airports, etc.). Here, the objective is to attain maximum damage to accentuate attention to the act and its underlying message.

(4) *Focused random terror.* This form focuses on violent acts on the specific agents of oppression. Here, the numbers of victims within the acts come secondary to (i) increasing the likelihood of impacting valued targets and (ii) accentuating the likelihood that the message is more pronounced than the numbers of casualties.

(5) *Tactical terror.* Here, violent acts are systemized toward the controlling government as part of a larger plan. Gross's typologies of terrorism aids in categorizing actual acts of terrorism in history so as to establish a better understanding of this complicated concept.

As Combs (2009) noted, one aspect that these five types of terrorism have in common is the inclusion of some form of state terrorism. This is similar to what Gross (1990) called '*mass terrorism*', Thornton (1964) named '*enforcement terror*', and Wilkinson (1974) termed '*repressive terror*'. The terming of groups and organizations as terrorists is difficult at best. For instance, acts of violence by organized crime in the United States are not necessarily included within the same conceptual framework as guerrilla fighters in Colombia or parts of Africa. Combs (2009) simplified how groups are understood as terrorists by focusing on the targeted audience. It is the audience targeted by acts of terror that determines who is labeled as a terrorist or not.

Once different types of terrorism have been categorized, actual processes of terror can be embedded within constructs. Gross (1990) argues that State terrorism as particularly crucial in understanding historic roots and expansions of organized dissent. Three forms of terror include internal State terrorism, external terrorism, and internal-external terrorism.

Internal State Terrorism

In terms of Gross's typologies of terrorism, state terrorism is best understood as mass terrorism, or the application of violent acts to ensure social order and restrict opposition. Examples of state terrorism are vast and reach far back in history. The Roman emperor Nero, for instance, illustrated the process of ruling by fear and terror A.D. 64 (Milton, 1983). Unlike the other four types of terrorism, state terrorism is unique because the instigating entity is a large and organized unit in society: the ruling government. Therefore, dissimilar to small terrorist groups and organizations, states employing terrorism can have an enormous scope of influence.

State terrorism can be applied *internally*, on a state's own citizens, or *externally*, on another state's citizens (Combs, 2009). Internal state terrorism can include intimidation, coercion, or genocide (Combs, 2009). *Intimidation* occurs when the state attempts to predict and dissuade opposing forces. *Coercion* refers to the direct involvement of governmental agencies to restrict opposition. *Genocide* refers to the intentional elimination of entire groups thought to oppose the ruling agenda (Combs, 2009).

Examples of each form of internal state terrorism can be found throughout history. For instance, Nazi Germany used all three tactics of internal state terrorism so as to ensure civic obedience. Thousands of cases of imprisonment, torture, and death account for Hitler's reign of terror; which eventually lead to the mass genocide of ethnic Jews and opposing forces (Combs, 2009). Coercion and genocide are also exemplified in the Soviet Union. Acts of coercion ensued as individuals opposing the Soviet agenda were imprisoned in Siberian Gulags (prison camps). In addition, millions died due to execution, hunger, and disease (Combs, 2009; Quist-Adade, 2001).

National Socialism in Nazi Germany

Serving to illustrate State instilled terror, it should be noted that it has longer tenure and widespread effects when it is legitimized through political power. Tridico (2003) accounts that National Socialism, a form of political fascism, won wide support among the unemployed, the impoverished middle class, and industrialists who feared socialism and communism. To fully comprehend Nazi intelligentsia, its underlying principles must be clearly delineated. The New Nazi State of 1933, as its hidden objectives were progressively revealed, would stir up many enemies: enemies of the regime and of the German race. The foundation of the future Third Reich would require the elimination of these undesirable elements. To accomplish this, there would have to be a rigorous purification, both mental and biological.

Racism was not only pervasive in the social/cultural realm of Nazi Germany through rhetoric and propaganda but reinforced and legitimized by State law. On September 15, 1935, thirteen decrees deprived Jews of their civil rights, including the forbidding of sexual intercourse and marriage with Aryans and a covert and systematic exclusion from public function and other positions or avenues of influence. Operating on a continuum, the Nazi regime sought more aggressive strategies to demoralize their targets. Such actions included confiscating possessions to ensure that Jews remained poor and eventually, relocating thousands of them in specific places for more effective suppression (Aziz, 1976).

The Nazi plan was organized on a continuum over time to ensure more overt acts of discrimination against their Jewish targets. What was necessary for such strategy to be realized was that the social, cultural and political climate of the time coincided with their racist sentiments.

Anti-Semitism in the social/cultural realm through rhetoric and propaganda afforded the political realm to legitimize discriminatory policies against Jews. Once certain policies were enacted and enforced with little resistance by either their targets or the German population, the Nazi regime moved forward aggressively. Rhetoric and propaganda along with an accentuated level of anti-Semitism helped to legitimize discriminatory policies and the enforcement of these policies served to demoralize Jews and perpetuate anti-Semitism (Tridico, 2004). The Nazi strategy was to convince the population that such oppression was justifiable, that Jewish influence of any kind was a threat to Germany and its people and that this problem had to be addressed forcefully, directly and without regret.

The breadth of the Nazi regime is perhaps best illustrated by the participation of German citizens in the Nazi mission. In German industry, concentration camp laborers were used on the railroads, German staff conducted death convoys to crematoriums and from the field of medicine, experiments were conducted in the concentration camps (Aziz, 1976). The underlying motivation for the citizen participation in these acts is inconsequential. Whether they participated out of acceptance of the Nazi imposed anti-Semitic beliefs or out of fear of consequence, the Nazi mission was accomplished by the state of chaos and fear brought about by Nazi terrorist tactics.

This affirmation of the Nazi regime's true racist agenda was hauntingly underscored by Adolf Hitler who gave the orders for the final solution program. Reinhard Heydrich (Lieutenant-General) would develop the plan for the assembly and extermination of European Jews, while Himmler would carry out the plan in the concentration camps. Once Heydrich's plan was formalized, a conference would be called to ensure the cooperation of the top administrators of the Third Reich. Hitler recognized the importance of secrecy as to avoid any resistance by the German population and insisted on keeping the entire operation private.

The power of absolute rule

National Socialists in Germany used rhetoric and propaganda used effectively to gain control for the implementation of their plan for world conquest. Tridico (2004) accounts that the campaign allowed both factions to do the following:

(1) gain access to the political arena where they could challenge for State control
(2) replace the media, education and mediums of information with their message
(3) rile the masses emotionally and garner their attention
(4) forge a common identity through nationalism
(5) forge a common ideology through a common enemy (e.g., aliens, socialists etc.)
(6) slowly enact laws to legitimize their programs
(7) forge a common identity through a common enemy from within one's own group (e.g., citizens who dissented were enemies of the State)

The sophisticated organizational structure of the State affords internal terror to be organized and systematically applied with limited resistance. While rhetoric and propaganda were used by Nazis as a softer, covert form of social control, the regime eventually attained enough power to significantly alter its society through absolute control. Such control included: (i) enacting new legislation and enforcing its laws with aggression, (ii) limiting civil liberties, (iii) limiting religious freedom (iv) controlling free speech by gaining control of the press.

Evidence of intimidation and coercion by a state can be difficult to locate until after the fall of the ruling regime. Evidence of genocide, on the other hand, can be easier to confirm. The act of genocide, for whatever reason (e.g., ethnic cleansing, political opposition, etc.), has occurred throughout human history. Contemporary examples include over a million deaths in Cambodia during the Khmer Rouge reign, hundreds of thousands of deaths in Rwanda during the 1990s, and over a million Armenian deaths by Turks during the beginning of the twentieth century (Combs, 2009).

From Africa to Australia, from the Middle East to the Far East, in India and Pakistan, in Sri Lanka, and from Chechnya to Columbia, ethnic strife rages (Human Rights Watch, 2003). In Africa, not only were whites arrayed against blacks in Apartheid South Africa, but also Indian minorities were expelled from Uganda in 1975, and African ethnic and religious disputes in Rwanda, Sudan, Somalia, Ethiopia, Liberia, Sierra Leone, Nigeria, and elsewhere have erupted in bloody massacres (Heisler, 1977). More than 800 thousand Rwandese lost their lives in one of Africa's worst genocides. In the immediate aftermath of the disintegration of the Soviet Union, a sizeable percentage of the population was caught up in a fit of inter-ethnic rebellions and massacres. The fall of communist Yugoslavia left in its trail ethnic massacres now euphemistically called 'ethnic cleansing' (Quist-Adade, 2001).

If internal terror is not State sponsored in terms of the State targeting its citizens, it can also be initiated against the State and/or citizens by a domestic faction. As described by Gurr (1984) and Smith (1998), domestic terrorism can be categorized into three types: (i) vigilante, or right-wing extremism, (ii) insurgent, or left-wing terrorism, and (iii) transnational, or international terrorism. Right-wing extremist terrorism can include anti-government militia groups like the ones who orchestrated the Oklahoma City bombing in 1995 and the shoot-out in Waco, Texas in 1993 as well as religious fanatics like the Christian Identity Movement. Transnational terrorism, a form of terrorism most ignored until recent years due to the isolated geographical location of the United States, was made poignant in the first bombing of the World Trade Center in 1993.

Left-wing terrorism, while having results not as large in scope as right-wing extremism or transnational terrorism, has orchestrated events of terror throughout history as well. Specifically, eco-terrorism, groups with single-issue focuses pertaining to the treatment of animals and the environment, has had a dramatic effect regarding the way humans treat the planet. The Earth Liberation Front, for example, has caused millions of dollars worth of damage to corporations and businesses they believed were damaging to the environment. The Animal Liberation Front has a violent history of property destruction, death threats, and arson for animal rights.

External Terror

As pernicious as internal terror can be insofar as it uses the State as a medium for achieving its objectives, external terror strikes at the very structure of nation states because it comes from the outside. This is usually administered in one of two ways: either state-directed or state-supported. State-directed terrorism refers to the formal involvement of a state in the actual acts of terror. State-supported terrorism refers to the informal involvement by supplying aid and information to the actual groups committing terror (Combs, 2009). Distinguishing between the two, of course, can be complicated until well after the deeds have been done.

Examples of external state terrorism are also many. The Central Intelligence Agency (CIA) supported efforts in Chile during the 1970s to eliminate Salvador Allende from office which eventually included the assassination of Rene Schneider, the commander in chief of the Chilean Army. Like efforts were offered in Nicaragua during the early 1980s to destabilize the Sandinista regime. There is also some indication that some Middle Eastern states have supported various factions in other states in order to cause havoc, promote fear, and destabilize rivaling regimes. The Soviet Union is another example that supported various communist groups throughout the world in order to create revolutionary outcomes (Sterling, 1981).

Internal-External Terror

This categorization accounts for organized violence against civilians or military because such targets are more readily accessible than preferred targets which are not. In an effort to attack a larger target (e.g., external governments), terrorist organizations channel their objectives within domestic jurisdiction. The callous disregard for human lives, national law and/or international law makes them both difficult to combat, and more likely to ascend to power.

The insurgency in Iraq serves as an applicable case study in such form of terror. More than 140 foreigners have been kidnapped in Iraq, and at least 28 of them have been executed. Iraqis have also faced an epidemic of kidnappings in the chaos since the fall of Saddam Hussein. Insurgents have used kidnappings and bombings as their signature weapons in a campaign to undermine the interim government and force the U.S. and its allies out of Iraq.

Particularly heinous are the tactics and strategies insurgents and terrorists are using to spread a message of hatred and terror to those they oppose. In the process, various terror groups are targeting soft targets such as foreign contract workers, poorly trained Iraqi police and national guards, as well as Iraqi civilians. The acts are growing more desperate, cruel and sensationalistic.

Insurgent and terrorist groups are cognizant that terror has now become a marketable commodity. In this vein, the currency is not necessarily money but the transference of hatred, terror and chaos. In videotaping and transmitting of such barbaric acts, a smaller, less-equipped insurgency is able to wreck havoc within a fragile Iraqi State.

Discernable themes

In attacking the legitimacy of State law and order, insurgents and terrorists in Iraq have concentrated on clear objective. However, the complexity of this phenomenon is that it is multi-faceted. While some argue that the tactics of the insurgency cannot sustain itself over time and that this process will eventually exhaust itself, it is posited that the level of sophistication is accentuated by the fact that chaos is, in its very essence, a realized measure of success. There are a number of discernable themes that demonstrate that the insurgency will adapt itself to numerous methods to secure instability within the region. These include:

(1) The dismantled Iraqi political and legal systems have created lack of State legitimacy and power; there appears to be no identifiable and enforceable rule of law. This has empowered and emboldened the insurgency.

(2) The current interim government is not perceived as a legitimate council but a puppet regime put in place and controlled by the

United States. Insurgents have used this lack of legitimacy to exert fear among Iraqi citizens.

(3) Since the declaration of victory by former President Bush, there have been thousands of deaths and significant injuries to U.S. and coalition soldiers and to civilians. Insurgencies (both domestic and foreign) have formed small pockets of regional organized militias of terror aimed at creating chaos and fear.

(4) Initial targets have been U.S. and coalition forces through street-to-street armed battles. This has waned considerably due to increased intelligence, superior military strength and technology by coalition forces.

(5) The next wave of terror included suicide attacks by committed domestic and foreign insurgents. This created confusion to coalition forces that were unprepared for this form of ground warfare. This tactic appears to be a concerted strategy by insurgents.

(6) Photographs of humiliating treatment of detainees at Abu Ghraib prison were effective in riling the masses of both insurgents and foreign and domestic terrorists. Intelligence suggests that since this time, they have been more organized, more committed and more brutal in their tactics and strategies.

(7) Kidnapping of non-military persons appear to be the most recent form of terror tactics used to instill fear and act as leverage to make demands. U.S., Britain, Poland and Australia have not been deterred and have refused to make concessions. Kidnappers have been successful at having other governments pull out of the region in exchange for the lives of the abducted. Spain, the Philippines and Japan withdrew their forces almost immediately after such developments, marking specific successes for the insurgency.

(8) Both kidnappings and the brutal murders of abducted civilians are tactics to instill fear to coalition governments and to their populations at home. The beheading of victims purposely memorialized on video and then immediately distributed via the Internet suggests that they are meant to force coalition

governments' home populations put pressure on their governments to withdraw from the region.

(9) It is clear that whatever tactics and strategies are being employed by insurgents and domestic and foreign terrorists, that the main coalition forces are not negotiating with them and are not being deterred. It is the position of coalition governments to not negotiate with insurgents and terrorists. This suggests that unless the strategies and tactics used by insurgents and terrorists shift to new forms or exhaust themselves, the immediate form of terror (kidnapping and taped murders of non-military civilians) will be the main tactic.

Instilling Fear through Brutality

Terrorists have not used kidnapping and taped beheadings historically, but they have been utilized by rebel forces in waves of genocidal massacres in Africa and during the Khmer Rouge Canon in Cambodia. In shifting to new tactics and strategies, Islamic terrorists and insurgents appear to be growing more desperate and brutal.

It would appear that coalition forces may have underestimated the resilience of the insurgency. However, past dalliances in Korea, Vietnam, Somalia and other African and Middle Eastern States have demonstrated that insurgencies retain tenure over time when there are perceived causes to fight for. Hatred is a pernicious motivation to resist a perceived oppressor. This is unsettling, but it has been consistent. Most wars of this kind do not end after military victory. Rather, they begin when such victory has been declared.

Current Policy Trends

Perl (2003: 7-12) forwards five methods used by the United States to curtail terrorism. These include:

(1) *Diplomacy or constructive engagement.* International groups such as the United Nations (U.N.) or the North American Treaty Organization can enact legislation to prohibit states from forming alliances with groups suspected of harboring terrorism. Diplomatic negotiations with nation states can serve as effective processes to lobby for sovereign governments to deal with

terrorist organizations through their own legislative efforts (Schmierbach et al., 2005).

(2) *Economic sanctions and inducements.* Economic sanctions have been a proactive method of denying terrorist states or groups the funds needed to act. Economic manipulations can be effective methods to dissuade states or groups to assist terrorist organizations. Economic inducements attempt to solve terrorism through loss of recruitment. It is hypothesized that improving economic conditions through education and assistance problems can dissuade potential adherents of terrorist organizations from joining (Morales & Asthappan, 2009; Perl, 2003; Cullen & Agnew, 1999).

(3) *Covert actions or rewards for information programs.* Similar to the policies of crime control and confidential informants, terrorist organizations may be infiltrated by teams through covert operations (Morales & Asthappan, 2009). Here, the process entails gaining knowledge of the internal dynamics of terrorist groups including strategies and tactics utilized, organizational structure, short and/or long term goals, and methods of mobilization (Tridico, 2003; Oberschall, 1992). Operations include the interception of unlawful processes or preemptive striking of organizations before an event can occur.

(4) *Law enforcement cooperation.* This process serves as useful, proactive measures in specifically combating groups that cross jurisdictions (Morales & Asthappan, 2009). Active shared intelligence by international, national, state and local law enforcement and government agencies enhance the quality of information gathering, shared resources and level of mobilization.

(5) *Military force.* This policy can entail overt aggression or covert force. Each act becomes potentially problematic insofar as the targets involve terrorist organizations that may be operating within sovereign nations. Nation-states may make cooperation difficult since it involves foreign governments to utilize military action on domestic soil. Further, the risks to civilian casualties are accentuated particularly because terrorists have, particularly in recent years, shown disregard to international laws regarding

the treatment of civilians. Military acts against terrorists may need to involve ground warfare, which also increases the likelihood of added civilian injury and death. Military force has been deemed to be a system of last resort but one that provides the most tangible results insofar as it engages terrorists directly.

Civil Liberties and Terrorism

While terrorism continues to be more regularly pronounced in nations facing internal turmoil and disarray (e.g., Afghanistan, Iraq, Somalia, etc.) as well as regions of historic conflict (e.g., Israel, Palestine, etc.), it has had implications on the State power-civil liberty dichotomy in the United States. A common consequence of a government's response to terrorism has historically involved the infringement of civil liberties. During the formative years of the United States, James Madison wrote extensively about how to respond to threatening factions.

For Madison (2002), eliminating such groups is accomplished by controlling either the causes or effects of such actions. However, as Jurgensen noted (2004), in order not to infringe on the American moral bedrock of freedom and civil liberties, Madison believed that only efforts to control the effects of factioning groups, not their causes, should ensue. Madison admitted that civil freedom guaranteed in a society like the United States would inevitably attract small collections of discontent and threatening individuals against the majority. But, in order not to withdraw this guarantee of civil liberties, the state should not aim in controlling the unavoidable creation of such groups, but instead, grapple with its effects (2002).

Although a democratic government like the United States aims to protect its people while at the same time preserving civil liberties, serious safety threats can make this goal unbalanced. To date, infringements on civil rights have regularly occurred during times of war. The recent War on Terror exemplifies this. Viscusi and Zeckhauser (2003) found that overall, respondents in their study were more inclined to sacrifice civil liberties in order to reduce the risk of terrorism. Specifically, their study focused on whether individuals in airports were willing to be screened, as long as this did not affect their waiting time. To make matters more complicated, however, nonwhites were less likely to agree to the screening that whites (2003). Therefore, further scrutiny into the manner of profiling is necessary.

Hardin (2004) also explored civil rights infringements during times of war by focusing on the rate of growth for surveillance technology in comparison to the speed of surveillance policy. In short, Hardin posited that the growth of technology is too fast for the policy makers to keep up (2004). Therefore, the use of such technologies is regularly allowed not because policy makers permit it, but because policy makers have yet to review it. Still, for Hardin, the best course of action is for the courts to continue assessing the use of such surveillance technologies, despite their rapid growth in development (2004).

The infringements of civil rights have notably occurred during times of war as illustrated in studies on the War on Terror. Despite Madisonian suggestions regarding the proper response to threatening factions as controlling the effects; policy during the War on Terror appears to instead focus on the causes, by restricting civil liberties. One hypothesis for this is posited by Jurgensen (2004), who pointed out a major difference between threatening groups today in comparison to the eighteenth century is the scope of their influence. Unlike Madison's time, contemporary threatening groups can have access to large-impact weaponry and means of mass communications, not yet created two hundred years ago. Unlike the factioning groups during Madison's time, today's groups have a larger scope of influence and are therefore, more threatening. This major difference requires a different interpretation regarding the protocol for dealing with such threats.

The impact of terrorism has great consequences regarding the way attitudes and policies around civil liberties are established. In addition, changes in terrorism over time have influenced the way governments respond and, accordingly, the need to infringe on civil rights for the sake of protection. As described above, these issues have been discussed since the beginning of American policy-making, and continue to impact the way we balance the need for protection and the rights we have as citizens. However, changes in technology and the scope of threats from such factioning groups presents new dangers and requires new ways of responding to these threats.

It can be argued that the USA PATRIOT Act has weakened the Fourth Amendment protections by permitting the 'sneak and peek' warrants (through section 218) and delayed notification of the search warrant's execution (through section 213). These two sections of the Act provide law enforcement accentuated authority. There are two fundamental concerns with such added power. First, the Act permits through an executed warrant to have investigating officers secretly enter a premises, conduct a search, potentially obtain photographic evidence but not physically confiscate physical objects and leave without giving notice. This directly challenges provisions within the Fourth Amendment and landmark cases set forth therein. As a result of such cases, when search warrants are executed, due process regularly entails law enforcement to leave a copy of the warrant if the premises were unoccupied, and to file an inventory with the court.

Shulman (2003) accounts that Section 213 of the Act allows agents to *delay* notification of the search warrant's execution if the Stated can effectively submit that the following criteria can be met:

(1) that doing so would endanger an individual's physical safety
(2) that doing so may cause evidence to be compromised
(3) that doing so may cause someone to flee prosecution
(4) that doing so could compromise the investigation or unduly delay trial

International and national legislative efforts have been proactive measures in addressing and combating terrorism. Both processes have involved a shift in power from civil liberties to greater State power. This shift has been accentuated since the attacks on American soil in 2001. The USA PATRIOT Act, readily passed with minimal dissent months thereafter, has largely not been placed under constitutional oversight through Supreme Court challenges. This is due in part to the fact that many of its powers afforded to government and law enforcement have either not been fully utilized or there have been few abridgments to civilian parties. Internationally, nation states are operating collaboratively despite varying constitutions, legislations and political systems.

While terrorism continues to be pervasive and pronounced in various areas globally, it is the underlying causes contained therein that must be addressed if it is to be effectively curtailed. Terror, and the hatred that fuels it, cannot be separated. Without hatred, terrorism lacks the systemic components that drive its mobilization. We conclude the chapter not only on policy trends and civil libertarian concerns, but through a socio-psychological lens of the roots of intolerance and how conflict emerges in both sporadic and organized manners.

Explaining Conflict

Two theoretical approaches (the social construction of reality and critical constructivism) serve to explore the roots of intolerance. Two concepts (ethnocentrism and dialectics) assist in elucidating the origin and the complex nature of tolerance and intolerance, and conflict that emerges as a result.

Ethnocentrism: The 'Mother' of All Sentiments and Impulses

The term combines the Greek word '*ethnos,*' which means '*people*' or '*folk*' and the Latin word '*centrum*' or '*center.*' Thus, when individuals account for an individualistic perspective, all external norms and values are judged in comparison to its internal ones. Ethnocentrism, the wellspring of all human sentiments both vile and noble, is both the balm and the bane of human societies. The tendency of people to do this engenders collective self-assurance, solidarity, and self-worth. Ethnocentrism can also have devastating consequences for both the in-group itself and the targeted out-group. While ethnocentrism promotes in-group centrality, its antithetical opposite, 'reverse ethnocentrism,' engenders out-group denigration, aversion, and marginalization.

For the in-group, ethnocentrism may breed collective ignorance and self-delusion, which may in turn lead to a false sense of superiority and invincibility. Ethnocentrism forges in-group hegemony through internalization of collective identity and through out-group rejection and hostility. It also gives birth to several other attitudes, including prejudice, stereotyping, intolerance and, ironically, tolerance.

So then what causes ethnocentrism? Scholars from diverse fields have offered a plethora of theoretical explanations. The social sciences, sociology and psychology, in particular, have offered both individual-focused and structural-focused theories, including authoritarian personality, self-identity, group conflict, symbolic interactionism, social exchange and functionalism. While most of these theories access some causes of ethnocentrism, the conflict perspective, which locates prejudice in socio-economic praxis (the struggle over scarce resources), offers a more nuanced and hence more applicable explanation. The conflict theory is rooted in the human tendency to seek to advance and protect self-interest. In our attempt to meet basic needs of food, shelter, and clothing, which are attained through social integration, individuals operate in competition with other groups for resources that are always relatively scarce.

Winners in this struggle must create social institutions to protect the resources they have gained, so they develop ideologies to justify why they won and the losers lost. The losers are portrayed in demeaning and degrading terms, dismissed as genetically inferior, lazy, deficiently endowed, etc. The losers' religion, ethnicity, race, class, sexuality, biological or genetic predispositions are invoked as reasons for their alleged inferiority and low socio-economic status. These characteristics are further exploited by the winners, utilizing them as points of comparative evaluation and exclusion from the in-group. The ideologies of the winning group, regarding the out-group, manifest themselves as prejudice, stereotypes, and sometimes outright propaganda, which are disseminated via the various agents of socialization and the knowledge industry as a whole. Additionally, ideologies and attitudes of the in-group, about themselves, are both developed and strengthened through this process to subsequently be promulgated through interpersonal interactions and socialization.

Symbolic Interactionism, as described by Herbert Blumer, also offers a possible explanation for ethnocentrism and subsequently for tolerance and intolerance. Integrationists believe that humans are pragmatic actors who must continually adjust their behaviors in reaction to other humans' behavior. Utilizing this perspective, neither the actors nor the actions of a society possess any meaning until one is ascribed to them and this meaning is only ascribed through the evaluation of another actor in that society.

Through this process, each actor associates meaning and value to material and actions. When individuals present interactions that are evaluated as helpful or neutral to the actor he, viewing himself as another symbolic object in society, will imaginatively rehearse the possible outcomes of his actions, finally choosing those he believes will allow him to negotiate a socially constructed relationship through tolerance Conversely, when another individual in society interacts with an actor seeking to perform or obtain these now meaningful materials or actions the actor must assess the situation and alter his behavior accordingly. When the behavior of the intervening individual is defined as in opposition to the behaviors of the actor, the actor reacts through intolerance, labeling both the action and the individual who performed, it as negative. This negative trademark, carried into future social interactions, leads to stereotyping and prejudice.

When prejudice is sufficiently widespread, it fosters a fertile soil for hatred, intolerance, and ultimately discrimination against identifiable groups. Stereotyping reflects and reinforces prejudice by creating a system of uniformed social evaluation. Stereotypes, like prejudice, are socially learned, often being handed down from one generation to another and through association with members of various social groups. The stereotypes that people learn not only provide justification for prejudice and discrimination; they also produce stereotypical behavior in those who are stereotyped, leading to a self-fulfilling prophecy. In this way, a fertile ground is prepared for the seeds of intolerance to germinate and grow. In short, intolerance is a symptom; a manifestation of an ongoing tug-of-war between groups over economic, political and social resources. Intolerance persists because of real or imagined threats to dominants' material standing, through competition for jobs, housing, schools, etc.

The Social Construction of [In]tolerance

Thus, intolerance like its antithetical corollary, tolerance, is a social construct. The social construction view of [in]tolerance derives from the theory of the social construction of reality, which posits that there is nothing natural or normal about the world we inhabit. Rather, social reality is created by individuals to reflect certain interests in a world not necessarily of their making. Tolerance and intolerance emerge together from the womb of the social construction of reality, as it were. They are both learned in the social context and designed to protect vested interests of the group to which an individual belongs.

While sociobiologists and some behavioral psychologists would want to persuade us that intolerance and its benign corollary, tolerance, are genetic or biological traits, there is overwhelming evidence that humans acquire the capacity to tolerate or '*intolerate*' in a social context. Humans may have incipient urges or natural proclivities toward tolerance or aversion, but these proclivities must first be nudged into action, nurtured and directed through the various agents of socialization.

The idea that tolerance and intolerance are learned is especially poignant when one considers that the premise for such behaviors is most often constructed upon other socially created characteristics. For example, the Nazi's did not lack tolerance for dark haired, dark eyed individuals. Rather, this biological trait was merely a convenient, observable, associated characteristic of Jewish people. Thus, the Nazi's did not lack tolerance for a dark features, they harbored excessive intolerance for Jews. In this case, the intolerable trait for the Nazi, in-group was that of religion, a purely social construct. The case of the Nazi's is not unique in this way. Even racial intolerance is founded on the social construction of race itself; what it means in the world to be black, white, Asian, etc. rather than the genetic differences between various groups of people.

Blessing [In]tolerance: The Legitimization of Tolerance and Intolerance

Human behavior such as [in]tolerance is simply behavior. However, whether a specific behavior is perceived to be tolerable or intolerable depends on who is describing the behavior, and where the describer is in relation to the ideological fence; this accounts for religious, political, moral and ethical divides. Almost invariably, the members of the group on the other side of the fence are categorized as having a propensity or proclivity to act or behave intolerably by virtue of their membership of that group. From the critical constructivist perspective, [in]tolerance is not only a human creation; it is also created by the power elite within societies.

Critical constructivism is a theoretical framework based on the assumption that the way social reality is constructed, perceived and presented usually reflects the interests of society's elite more than those of the mainstream, and often at the expense of those with the least power in society. Crudely put, the critical constructivist perspective posits that while human reality is collectively constructed by all members of society, what becomes acceptable reality must first be sanctioned, sanctified, and legitimized by the power or ruling elite.

Through this perspective, terrorism and the tactics employed by terrorists is best understood. Constructively, the terrorist or terrorist group must always posses less power and stand in opposition to the ruling elite. It is true that by opposing the outstanding ruling elite, terrorist groups do not seek to obtain sanction or legitimization from the ruling elite. Quite contrary, they seek to create a new ruling elite, through propaganda. Terrorist propaganda seeks to recruit those on the fringes of the ruling group and those in other opposing groups. This recruitment of societal resources allows the terrorist group to first, gain a social foothold in the constructed reality through which groups will then progress to implementing legal and economic footings thus overturning the aforementioned ruling elite.

It is in this way that critical constructivism differs from social constructivism. Critical constructivism emphasizes the role of *elite* interests in the process of reality construction. It combines conflict theory and social constructivism, providing a construct in which terrorist groups must first create a class of ruling elite before their acts can achieve systemic change.

Tolerance and intolerance are decidedly human inventions rather than natural or genetic conditions. Both entities are the products of social interactions and therefore are found not in the impulses or even in the psyche of individuals, but in the actions and inactions of collectives. This is to say that one cannot be intolerant when there is not another to intolerate. Similarly, one mad Hitler could not have enacted the Holocaust alone. He required his henchmen and the legions of the German masses and the presence of the German Jewry. Intolerance and intolerance are *social constructions built out of social interactions*. Thus, the solution to intolerance is to be found within the social, collective condition. It is also useful to recognize that tolerance and intolerance are dialectical, rather than binary opposites or dichotomies of good and evil. The two cannot be separated.

The roots of terrorism have been entrenched historically through rationalized hatred. Terrorism must be understood as organized social movements operating as dissenting factions against state or international authority. It is the self-determination component that serves as a rationalized process that fosters and sustains hatred, eventually leading to conflict. It is imperative then, that any discourse on this malady should not dismiss its root causes. If organized terror is to be combated, a paradigm shift must occur in which the foci of this political, legal, economic and social battle are those of causation. Group-think and the collective identities of groups both in power and opposing those in power must be carefully segmented, examined and understood with regard to the political, legal, economic and social resources and agendas of such groups. Only after one is able to ascertain a deep understanding of both groups alone but of their interactions together will progress be made in combating the issue.

References

Aziz, P. (1976). *Doctors of Death*. Geneva: Ferni Publishers.

Combs, C. (2009). *Terrorism in the Twenty-First Century* (5th ed.). New York, NY: Pearson Education, Inc.

Cullen, F. & R. Agnew. (1999). *Criminological Theory Past to Present*. Los Angeles, CA: Roxbury Publishing Company.

Gurr, T. (1988). Political Terrorism in the United States: Historical Antecedents and Contemporary Trends. In Michael Stohl (Ed.), *The Politics of Terrorism*. New York, NY: Dekker.

Hardin, R. (2004). Civil Liberties in the Era of Mass Terrorism. *The Journal of Ethics*, 8, p. 77-95.

Heisler, M.O. (1977, September). Ethnic Conflicts in the World Today: An Introduction, *Annals of the American Academy of Political and Social Sciences*. p. 433.

Human Rights Watch. Monthly E-mail Update, November 2002. http://www.hrw.org/update/2002/11.html

Jurgensen, A. (2004). Terrorism, Civil Liberties, and Preventive Approaches to Technology: The Difficult Choices Western Societies Face in the War on Terrorism. *Bulletin of Science Technology Society*, 24(55), p. 55-59.

Madison, J., Hamilton, A., & Jay, L. (2002). The Federalist papers (based on the original McLean edition of 1778), No. 10. In T.J. Lowi, B. Ginsburg, & K. Shepsle (Eds.), *American government: Power and purpose 7th Ed*, pp. A35-A36). New York, NY: Norton.

Milton, M. (1983). *The Terrorists*. New York, NY: Harper & Row.

Morales, D. and J. Asthappan. (2009). Looking Back: Self-Interest and U.S. Terrorism Policy. In R. Muraskin and A. Roberts (Eds.) *Visions for Change: Crime and Justice in the Twenty-First Century, 5th Ed*. Upper Saddle River, NJ: Pearson Education, Inc.

Oberschall, A. (1992). *Social Movements: Ideologies, Interests and Identities*. Englewood Cliffs, NJ: Transaction Publishers.

Perl, R. (2003). *Terrorism, the Future, and U.S. Foreign Policy (Order Code IB95112)*. Washington, DC: Congressional Research Service.

Quist-Adade, C. (2001). *In the Shadows of the Kremlin and the White House: Africa Media Image from Communism to Post-Communism*. Lanham, MD: University Press of America.

Schmierbach, M., M. Boyle, & McLeod, D. (2005). Civic Attachment in the Aftermath of September 11. *Mass Communication & Society*, 8(4): 323-346.

Shulman, S. (2003) Note: USA Patriot Act: Granting the U.S. Government the Unprecedented Power to Circumvent American Civil Liberties in the Name of National Security, *University of Detroit Mercy Law Review* 80:427-444.

Smith, B. (1994). *Terrorism in America: Pipe Bombs and Pipe Dreams*. Albany, NY: State University of New York Press.

Sterling, C. (1981). *The Terror Network*. New York, NY: Holt, Rinehart, and Winston.

Thornton, T. (1964). Terror as a Weapon of Political Agitation. In H. Eckstein (Ed.), *Internal War* (p. 77-78). London, UK: International Institute for Strategic Studies.

Tridico, F. (2004) *Contemporary Issues in Law and Society*. Sault Ste. Marie, ON: Landon Elsemere Press.

Tridico, F. (2004) *The Social Construction of Reality*. Sault Ste. Marie, ON: Landon Elsemere Press.

Viscusi, W., Kip, & Zeckhauser, R. (2003). Sacrificing Civil Liberties to Reduce Terrorism Risks. *The Journal of Risk and Uncertainty*, 26(2/3), p. 99-120.

Wilkinson, P. (1974). *Political Terrorism*. Cambridge, MA: Harvard University Press.

CHAPTER 11
IS HOUSING DISCRIMINATION A RELEVANT SOCIAL JUSTICE ISSUE?

George P. Mason

Abstract: Statistics routinely establish that African Americans, more than any other minority, are still the most residentially segregated group in the United States. In this chapter, the social justice issue of residential segregation is examined using a comparison of 1990 and 2000 Census data for 331 Metropolitan Statistical Areas. Evidence demonstrates that residential segregation has declined slightly for blacks across the United States but has increased substantially for Latinos, while remaining relatively unchanged for Asian/Pacific Islanders. A combination of sociological approaches is employed to develop a unique social justice approach to the issue: a historical sociology of law framework of housing discrimination and desegregation illustrated with case study research using Metropolitan Detroit. Also included is a review of residential preferences of black and whites, indicating that both structural and individual factors must be considered in understanding contemporary residential segregation. While black-white residential segregation has decreased very slightly, patterns of overall residential segregation have increased.

In a country that advocates social justice and equality for all, segregation of people based on one's race or ethnicity seems simply out of place. Equality is a concept that does not provide distinctions between individuals based on any physical or group characteristic, especially that of race. Discrimination based upon race goes against the very foundations of an equal society, particularly because race is such an arbitrary social construction. The very notion of dividing the United States into '*us*' and '*them*' is incompatible with the idea of equality and social justice. Although one would like to believe and hope that racial inequality does not exist in present day society, there is no place that it is more striking than in housing discrimination of African Americans.

Housing discrimination is a process in which individuals within the community, property realtors, and even lawmakers engage to keep one group of individuals (most often blacks) from integrating into specific neighborhoods (typically white). It can be argued that contemporary social discrimination is the historical product of slavery as is the treatment of blacks as second-class citizens, inferior to whites. Current prejudices in society have a strong historical origin. After slavery was abolished, a new era of '*equality*' emerged in that blacks had '*separate but equal*' rights, even though separate was anything other than equal. Separate but equal under Jim Crow kept blacks and whites segregated in public places to the extent that a "*hardening color line in employment, education, and especially housing*" developed following Reconstruction (Massey & Denton, 1993:30). The 1960s Civil Rights movement redefined equality in the passage of laws that recognized African Americans as equal citizens.

One of the most important pieces of legislation that came out of this redefinition of equality was the *Civil Rights Act*. Under Title VIII, the *Fair Housing Act of 1968*, discrimination based on race in housing was made illegal throughout the United States. The continued advancement towards social justice in our society, including the complete integration of blacks and whites, would seem to make sense and one could have reasonably believed that housing segregation would no longer be a relevant social justice issue in the twenty-first century. However, research and experience demonstrates that this is not the case; residential segregation by race continues to exist at extremely high levels and is a key social justice issue today.

The question to be addressed in this chapter is why residential segregation should continue to be a focus of research. The problem of housing discrimination in the form of residential segregation should be addressed because it is a reflection of the overall inequality of individuals within society as a whole. Robert Park and Ernest Burgess noted in their 1925 book *The City* (1967) that what takes place in U.S. cities is a representation of the collective morals and habits of the individuals that reside within, and the state of the nation in general. The early sociologists of the Chicago School realized this and their study of urban populations became one of the foundations for social problems research.

The first section of this chapter will demonstrate specific patterns of housing discrimination in the form of residential segregation in the United States. Residential segregation is examined with specific attention towards African Americans, Latino Americans, and Asian/Pacific Islanders across urban areas throughout the United States. African Americans, more than any other minority, are still the most segregated and discriminated against group in society. However, recent changes in black-white residential segregation patterns reflect increases in residential segregation between whites and other groups of people. It can be said that the color line is now becoming *diversified* into *different* and *multi-layered* color lines. It is because of these realities that the second and third sections of the chapter focus specifically on the issue of housing discrimination and residential segregation as they affect African Americans.

After examining data on residential segregation, the mechanisms which perpetuate this inequality in U.S. society are assessed. Legal actions taken by government meant to reduce housing discrimination have not effectively combated the problem. The second section of the chapter will focus on the legal decisions that have established and defined acts of housing discrimination based on race to be illegal. The efficiency of the legislation is limited because it only deals with federal property, relies heavily on individual complaints, and often ignores individual actions such as *steering* within the broader framework of society. While there is no attempt to delineate the entire legislative framework, key events must be identified to gain a broader conceptualization. This approach from within sociology of law moves the analysis beyond the rigid confines of jurisprudence and empiricism towards a more nuanced racial discrimination analysis.

It can be argued that housing discrimination cannot be completely explained by structural factors such as economic and legal disparities. Thus, it is important to consider the impact of individual attitudes and preferences held collectively by the members of a society. It is equally important to consider how these individual attitudes and preferences affect the structural aspects of racism within U.S. society. The third section of the chapter will focus on the role of individual beliefs and preferences of both blacks and whites as it impacts upon levels of residential segregation and racial integration. A review of the individual factors is important because, even if structural improvements are made in the areas of economics, politics or jurisprudence, prejudices and attitudes of individuals and groups of individuals will very well still exert a lot of influence over actual neighborhood makeup.

Residential Segregation in the United States

Ecological theory is one of the foundations that social justice practitioners use when researching race-based residential segregation within U.S. cities. According to Park (1967) and Burgess (1967), the spatial relationships between groups of humans are the product of particular geographical and socio-spatial competition, domination, invasion, and succession between out groups. According to this approach, the result of the changes in the urban environment may lead to social problems and social disorganization such as housing discrimination (Burgess, 1967). McKenzie (1967:64) noted in his elaboration of ecological theory that relationships between people in a community continually change and social and political problems can be the result. Housing segregation can be explained as the result of the countervailing forces as different groups and individuals compete for limited urban resources.

The United States has historically been an ethnically and racially diverse nation. The unintended consequence of this diversity has been widespread residential segregation into black ghettos, Latino barrios, Asian enclaves, and white slums. Many people continue to live in ethnically and racially disparate neighborhoods where enduring or meaningful interactions across racial and ethnic lines are rare. Residential segregation can limit the economic opportunities of non-white residents who disproportionately live in low-income, inner-city neighborhoods distant from economic opportunities. Since the late 1960s, the United States has faced two challenges to residential integration. The first is the persistent socio-spatial divide between whites and blacks. While residential segregation between whites and blacks has slightly decreased in recent years, the socio-spatial barrier between these two groups is still substantial and white-flight has continued to occur (Wilson, 1999). The second challenge is the integration of the two fastest growing minority groups (Latinos and Asian/Pacific Islanders) and the subsequent increase in segregation of both groups.

Changes in Residential Segregation, 1990-2000

This section describes changes in patterns of residential segregation in metropolitan areas within the U.S. for four major racial/ethnic groups. There is a comparison of African Americans, Latinos and Asian/Pacific Islanders with whites between 1990 and 2000. Several factors influence patterns of residential location including socioeconomic status, employment opportunities, housing availability and discrimination, and immigrant settlement patterns. This analysis controls for several of these factors in order to analyze the effects of demographic and economic changes, immigration flows, and housing stock on residential segregation.

The primary data source for this research is the United States Census 1990 and 2000 Redistricting and Demographic Data. Residential segregation is measured using the Dissimilarity Index calculated at the census tract level using the 2000 Census boundaries for Metropolitan Statistical Areas (MSAs). While there are various techniques to measure and theorize residential segregation (see Massey & Denton, 1988a), this measure is utilized in our analysis to demonstrate a temporal comparison and pattern of residential segregation for conceptual purposes. The Dissimilarity Index is examined for each of 331 MSAs in the United States and move beyond the Glaeser and Vigdor (2001) report by including more MSAs in the analysis.

In terms of scope and analysis, the prognosis differs as the analysis moves beyond the Glaeser and Vigdor report's optimism of decreasing segregation. Given this, multiple comparisons demonstrate that there is social change towards (albeit not yet reached) a *trichotomous hypersegregation* of Latino, black and white segregated communities. The Dissimilarity Index indicates the proportion of one racial/ethnic group that would have to relocate in order to be evenly distributed, given the theoretical maximum of that racial/ethnic group in the city, under conditions of maximum segregation (known as evenness): the higher the index, the greater the residential segregation (Massey & Denton, 1988a: 284).

Census data (United States Census of Population and Housing 1990a, 1990b, 2000a, 2000b) clearly indicate that African Americans remain the most widely residentially segregated group in the United States. Latinos and Asian/Pacific Islanders are also highly segregated, although not to the same extent as African Americans. Table 1 accounts for the Dissimilarity Index summary data measures for all 331 MSAs in 1990 and 2000, and the respective changes between the two Censuses within Table 2. The Dissimilarity Index data has been dichotomized into large MSAs with populations equal to or greater than one million persons and small MSAs of less than one million persons. The dichotomy allows the reader to account for and highlight the substantially higher rates of residential segregation in the 61 large urban centers with populations of one million and above.

Table 1: Residential Segregation in Census Metropolitan Statistical Areas, 1990-2000

		Non-Hispanic White	Black/ African American		Latino		Asian/Pacific Islander	
	Total Population	% of Total Population	% of Total Population	Dissimilarity Index	% of Total Population	Dissimilarity Index	% of Total Population	Dissimilarity Index
All MSAs								
1990	198,400,277	73.2%	12.9%	67.8	9.7%	49.7	3.5%	41.2
2000	225,981,477	66.0%	13.5%	64.3	13.6%	51.0	4.9%	41.4
+/-	27,581,200	-7.2%	0.6%	-3.5	3.9%	1.3	1.5%	0.2
Large MSAs								
1990	127,830,800	69.7%	14.6%	71.5	11.1%	52.5	4.1%	42.0
2000	146,733,822	61.7%	15.1%	67.9	15.4%	53.9	5.9%	42.7
+/-	18,903,022	-8.0%	0.5%	-3.5	4.3%	1.4	1.9%	0.7
Small MSAs								
1990	70,569,477	79.5%	9.9%	58.0	7.3%	42.1	2.4%	38.7
2000	79,247,655	73.9%	10.7%	54.9	10.3%	42.9	3.1%	36.7
+/-	8,678,178	-5.6%	0.8%	-3.1	3.0%	0.8	0.7%	-1.9

Source: United States Census of Population and Housing, 1990 and 2000 PL 94-171 Redistricting Data.

The data in Table 1 indicate that African Americans as a group experience high rates of residential segregation in both large and small MSAs. It is important to note that rates of residential segregation for African Americans have decreased from 1990 to 2000 by three and one-half points. Overall, African Americans had a Dissimilarity Index measure of 64.3 in 2000, down from 67.8 points in 1990. Residential segregation in large MSAs for African Americans decreased by 3.5 points and decreased by 3.1 points in small MSAs. With the increases in overall percentage of African Americans in both large and small MSAs and within the general population, it is cautioned that residential segregation may have decreased slightly more than simple Dissimilarity Index measures for blacks. However, it should be accounted that the 2000 levels are substantially high and illustrate the breadth of this social problem.

It is equally important to take notice that Latinos had an increase in residential segregation from 1990 to 2000. The Dissimilarity Index measures for Latinos increased in all the MSAs by 1.3 points, indicating an increase in the residential segregation of Latinos. In small MSAs, the

Dissimilarity Index increased by less than 1 point. In large MSAs, the Dissimilarity Index increased by 1.4 points. Both increases are indicative of a trend towards an increased residential segregation of Latinos. These increases are particularly noteworthy in absolute terms given the sizeable increases in the percentage of total population for Latinos. According to the Census data presented in Table 1, Latino populations in the 331 MSAs increased from slightly over 19 million persons in 1990 to almost 31 million persons in 2000.

Asian/Pacific Islanders had Dissimilarity Index measures which are somewhat contradictory. Asian/Pacific Islanders saw a very slight increase in the Dissimilarity Index measure for all 331 MSAs. In small MSAs, Asian/Pacific Islanders measured lower on the Dissimilarity Index by 1.9 points. Asian/Pacific Islanders measured 0.7 points higher for those living in the large MSAs. In both large and small MSAs there were increases in the percentage of Asian/Pacific Islanders of the total population. While the Dissimilarity Index does appear to decrease for Asian/Pacific Islanders, there should be no mistake that more actual individuals in this group would have to move from their current communities in 2000 than in 1990.

Table 2a: Residential Segregation in Ten Largest Census Metropolitan Statistical Areas, 1990-2000

	Total Population	Non-Hispanic White % of Total Population	Black/ African American % of Total Population	Dissimilarity Index	Latino % of Total Population	Dissimilarity Index	Asian/Pacific Islander % of Total Population	Dissimilarity Index
Atlanta, GA								
1990	2,959,950	71.0%	25.2%	67.1	1.8%	33.5	1.8%	41.5
2000	4,112,198	59.8%	29.2%	64.7	6.2%	51.1	3.6%	44.3
+/-	1,152,248	-11.2%	3.9%	-2.4	4.4%	17.6	1.8%	2.9
Boston, MA-NH								
1990	3,227,675	86.1%	6.6%	69.4	3.7%	53.4	3.0%	44.2
2000	3,406,829	80.0%	7.2%	66.1	5.4%	58.2	5.3%	44.9
+/-	179,154	-6.1%	0.6%	-3.3	1.7%	4.8	2.2%	0.7
Chicago, IL								
1990	7,410,858	66.1%	19.3%	83.8	10.9%	62.1	3.4%	44.3
2000	8,272,768	58.0%	19.1%	80.1	16.6%	61.4	5.0%	42.7
+/-	861,910	-8.1%	-0.2%	-3.7	5.7%	-0.7	1.6%	-1.6
Dallas, TX								
1990	2,676,248	67.6%	15.8%	62.5	13.5%	49.8	2.5%	42.0
2000	3,519,176	56.2%	15.3%	59.0	22.6%	53.9	4.4%	44.5
+/-	842,928	-11.4%	-0.5%	-3.5	9.1%	4.1	1.8%	2.4
Detroit, MI								
1990	4,266,654	74.3%	22.1%	87.4	1.8%	38.5	1.3%	42.8
2000	4,441,551	69.7%	23.2%	84.8	2.7%	45.1	2.6%	45.7
+/-	174,897	-4.6%	1.1%	-2.6	0.8%	6.5	1.3%	2.9

Table 2b: Residential Segregation in Ten Largest Census Metropolitan Statistical Areas, 1990-2000

Total Population	Non-Hispanic White % of Total Population	Black/ African American % of Total Population	Dissimilarity Index	Latino % of Total Population	Dissimilarity Index	Asian/Pacific Islander % of Total Population	Dissimilarity Index
Houston, TX							
1990 3,322,025	56.6%	18.5%	66.4	20.7%	49.4	3.8%	45.9
2000 4,177,646	46.1%	17.7%	66.7	29.3%	55.2	5.6%	48.8
+/- 855,621	-10.5%	-0.8%	0.3	8.6%	5.7	1.8%	2.9
Los Angeles-Long Beach, CA							
1990 8,863,164	40.8%	11.2%	72.7	36.4%	61.2	10.8%	46.3
2000 9,519,338	31.1%	10.0%	67.3	43.3%	63.3	12.9%	48.1
+/- 656,174	-9.7%	-1.2%	-5.4	6.9%	2.2	2.2%	1.9
New York, NY							
1990 8,546,846	47.9%	26.3%	81.5	18.6%	64.1	6.5%	48.4
2000 9,314,235	39.6%	25.0%	81.5	22.6%	66.0	9.5%	50.0
+/- 767,389	-8.4%	-1.4%	0.0	4.0%	2.0	3.0%	1.6
Philadelphia, PA-NJ							
1990 4,922,175	75.4%	19.1%	76.7	3.2%	61.6	2.1%	43.3
2000 5,100,931	70.2%	20.5%	72.3	4.6%	59.9	3.6%	43.4
+/- 178,756	-5.1%	1.4%	-4.5	1.4%	-1.8	1.5%	0.1
Washington, DC-MD-VA-WV							
1990 4,223,485	64.5%	25.4%	65.0	4.9%	41.9	4.8%	35.5
2000 4,923,153	56.1%	26.4%	62.8	8.3%	48.3	7.4%	38.5
+/- 699,668	-8.4%	1.1%	-2.2	3.4%	6.4	2.5%	3.0

Source: United States Census of Population and Housing, 1990 and 2000 PL 94-171 Redistricting Data.

Table 2 provides a detailed examination of the ten largest MSAs and the corresponding measures on the Dissimilarity Index. In all ten of the largest MSAs, non-Hispanic whites had decreased as a percentage of the total population. It was originally believed that this was indicative of white-flight from the heavily populated MSAs. However, on closer inspection four of the ten largest MSAs, Atlanta, Dallas, Houston, and Washington, had increases in the actual number of whites. Four MSAs, Boston, Chicago, Detroit, and Philadelphia, had very modest decreases in the number of whites living within the urban areas. Los Angeles and New York both had considerable decreases in the number of whites living in the MSA: Los Angeles saw a reduction of 655,657 whites whereas New York saw a reduction of 405,502 whites. While the latter two MSAs may indeed have recently experienced white-flight, the reader should be cautious in interpreting the data to come to this conclusion.

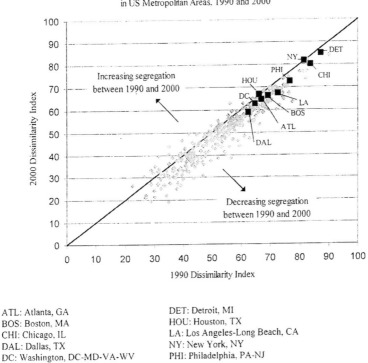

Figure 1: African American/Non-Hispanic White Dissimilarity in US Metropolitan Areas, 1990 and 2000

ATL: Atlanta, GA
BOS: Boston, MA
CHI: Chicago, IL
DAL: Dallas, TX
DC: Washington, DC-MD-VA-WV

DET: Detroit, MI
HOU: Houston, TX
LA: Los Angeles-Long Beach, CA
NY: New York, NY
PHI: Philadelphia, PA-NJ

Figure 1 plots each of the 331 MSAs in the United States and labels the ten MSAs in the country with the largest populations from Table 2. Figure 1 plots the absolute difference between the 1990 Dissimilarity Index against the 2000 Dissimilarity Index for African Americans. The 45-degree line is a hypothetical line representing no change in the Dissimilarity Index and segregation levels of the MSAs from 1990 to 2000. It can be seen from this graphical display that the residential segregation trends and level of residential segregation for African Americans over the past decade have slightly decreased.

Table 3: Highest and Lowest Levels of Residential Segregation for African Americans

Metropolitan Statistical Area[1]	2000 Index	Change 1990-2000
Overall Mean[2]	64.6	-2.8
Most Segregated		
Detroit, MI	84.8	-2.6
Gary, IN	84.1	-5.7
Milwaukee-Waukesha, WI	82.1	-0.5
New York, NY	81.5	0.0
Newark, NJ	80.3	-2.2
Chicago, IL	80.1	-3.7
Cleveland-Lorain-Elyria,.OH	77.0	-5.4
Buffalo-Niagara Falls, NY	76.8	-3.2
Flint, MI	76.7	-4.5
Cincinnati, OH	74.2	-2.0
Least Segregated		
Dover, DE	33.2	4.2
Bloomington, IN	33.0	-1.1
Greenville, NC	32.9	-7.2
Merced, CA	32.8	-3.7
Fayetteville, NC	32.6	1.3
Lawton, OK	31.2	-2.3
Enid, OK	30.1	-6.9
Lawrence, KS	26.9	-1.9
Jacksonville, NC	26.2	3.5
Fort Walton Beach, FL	19.8	-7.6

Source: United States Census of Population and Housing, 1990 and 2000 PL 94-171 Redistricting Data.
[1]Only the 247 MSAs with a substantial population of African Americans are included in the tabulations. The minimum threshold is 3% of the total MSA population or 20,000 persons.
[2]The overall mean Dissimilarity Index score is weighted by the size of the African American population in the MSA.

Reproduced in Table 3 is the most and least segregated MSAs for African Americans along with their 2000 Dissimilarity Index scores and the change in Dissimilarity Index from 1990 to 2000. Of the 331 MSAs, only 247 MSAs are included in the calculations presented in Table 3 as the study used a minimum threshold of either 20,000 individuals or three percent of the total population of African American residents in the respective MSA. This distinction controls for extreme fluctuations based on small population numbers, which would likely affect the analysis and conclusions.

As a whole, residential segregation for African Americans declined nearly 3 points from 1990 to 2000. The 247 MSAs had an overall mean change of -2.8 points on the Dissimilarity Index from 1990 to 2000. Despite the declines in segregation witnessed over the past few decades (Farley & Frey, 1994; Massey & Denton, 1987, 1993), several areas of the country remain decisively residentially segregated into white and black worlds. In large urban areas such as Detroit, Milwaukee, New York, and Chicago, *hypersegregation* exists and over 80% of African

Americans would need to relocate residence in order to be evenly distributed across the metropolitan area with non-Hispanic whites.

Residential segregation of blacks is, and will be in the foreseeable future, extremely high given the historical pattern of only modest declines over the last few decades. The metropolitan areas with the highest level of African American segregation are found in the Midwest and Northeast regions of the country, while the majority of the least segregated areas are found in the South. This finding is consistent with the historical findings and discussion by Massey and Denton (1993) which also indicated much higher residential segregation in the Midwest and Northeast.

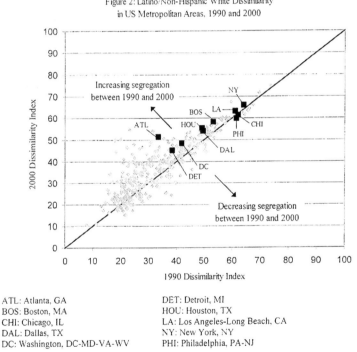

Figure 2: Latino/Non-Hispanic White Dissimilarity in US Metropolitan Areas, 1990 and 2000

ATL: Atlanta, GA
BOS: Boston, MA
CHI: Chicago, IL
DAL: Dallas, TX
DC: Washington, DC-MD-VA-WV

DET: Detroit, MI
HOU: Houston, TX
LA: Los Angeles-Long Beach, CA
NY: New York, NY
PHI: Philadelphia, PA-NJ

Source: United States Census of Population and Housing, 1990 and 2000 PL 94-171 Redistricting Data.

Latino residential segregation from non-Hispanic whites, while lower on average than African American residential segregation, increased in most MSAs over the period between 1990 and 2000. Figure 2 illustrates that the trend has been towards greater residential segregation of Latinos. The graphical illustration is in stark contrast to that of Figure 1 as residential segregation is substantially lower but would appear to be rising fairly rapidly. Accordingly, the data from Table 2 presented earlier reflects the pattern of increased residential segregation in all but two of the ten largest MSAs: Philadelphia and Chicago were the only MSAs among the ten largest MSAs having lower Dissimilarity Index scores in 2000 than in 1990 for Latinos.

In previous decades, Latino residential segregation remained relatively moderate in comparison with African American residential segregation, although substantial increases were witnessed in areas of rapid immigration (Massey & Denton, 1987, 1993). Previous research suggested that residential segregation for some groups may be driven by the settling patterns of immigrants. Some metropolitan areas serve as 'ports of entry,' which are common destinations for new immigrants due to existing immigrant communities that provide social and economic networks for those new to the United States (Newbold, 1999).

The findings evidenced in Figure 2 demonstrate that the rising Dissimilarity Index scores, combined with the dramatic increases in urban Latino populations, constitutes a second layer of residential segregation in addition to the historical pattern of African American residential segregation. In other words, it is argued that U.S. society is heading toward a trichotomous segregation rather than the historical black-white dichotomy of residential segregation.

Table 4: Highest and Lowest Levels of Residential Segregation for Latinos

Metropolitan Statistical Area[1]	2000 Index	Change 1990-2000
Overall Mean[2]	51.3	2.9
Most Segregated		
Lawrence, MA	75.3	1.2
Reading, PA	71.6	2.1
Providence-Fall River-Warwick, RI	67.6	8.1
Bridgeport, CT	66.4	-1.2
New York, NY	66.0	2.0
Newark, NJ	64.8	-1.4
Hartford, CT	63.6	-1.9
Los Angeles-Long Beach, CA	63.3	2.2
Springfield, MA	62.9	-0.7
Allentown-Bethlehem-Easton, PA	62.4	1.7
Least Segregated		
Bellingham, WA	22.1	1.9
Melbourne-Titusville-Palm Bay, FL	21.9	2.7
Bremerton, WA	21.9	3.2
Gainesville, FL	21.3	-0.4
Olympia, WA	20.4	5.3
Fort Collins-Loveland, CO	20.1	-1.7
Lawton, OK	19.8	-1.3
Pocatello, ID	17.8	-0.7
Casper, WY	17.1	-1.9
Redding, CA	10.7	3.0

Source: United States Census of Population and Housing, 1990 and 2000 PL 94-171 Redistricting Data.
[1]Only the 204 MSAs with a substantial population of Latinos are included in the tabulations. The minimum threshold is 3% of the total MSA population or 20,000 persons.
[2]The overall mean Dissimilarity Index score is weighted by the size of the Latino population in the MSA.

The most and least segregated MSAs for Latinos are presented within Table 4 along with corresponding Dissimilarity Index measures and the changes from 1990 to 2000. Using the same criteria as with the measures of MSAs by African American Dissimilarity Indices, analysis was based on the 204 MSAs which met the minimum threshold of either 20,000 Latinos or 3 percent of the total population in the respective MSA. The Dissimilarity Index and residential segregation of Latinos from non-Hispanic whites increased by an average of 2.9 points over the 204 MSAs. The increase in the overall mean most certainly indicates and provides evidence that metropolitan areas which contain larger proportions of the nation's Latino population have become more segregated from 1990 to 2000. All but one of the most segregated areas for Latinos is located in the Northeast: the one exception being Los Angeles.

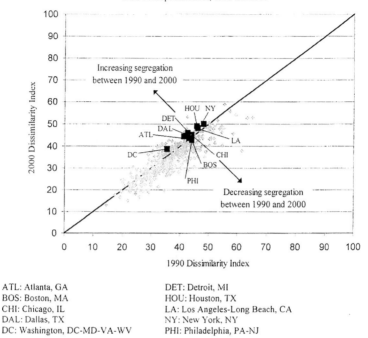

Figure 3: Asian-Pacific Islander/Non-Hispanic White Dissimilarity
in US Metropolitan Areas, 1990 and 2000

ATL: Atlanta, GA   DET: Detroit, MI
BOS: Boston, MA   HOU: Houston, TX
CHI: Chicago, IL   LA: Los Angeles-Long Beach, CA
DAL: Dallas, TX   NY: New York, NY
DC: Washington, DC-MD-VA-WV PHI: Philadelphia, PA-NJ

Source: United States Census of Population and Housing, 1990 and 2000 PL 94-171 Redistricting Data.

It was found that the residential segregation of Asian/Pacific Islanders is generally lower than African Americans and Latinos. The difference between the Dissimilarity Index measures of African Americans and Asian/Pacific Islanders is 22.6 points with a mean score of only 42.0 for Asian/Pacific Islanders. Figure 3 appears to illustrate that Dissimilarity Index scores and residential segregation have declined in most MSAs since 1990. However, Asian/Pacific Islanders residential segregation increased somewhat in the most populous metropolitan areas over the past decade. Historically, Asian/Pacific Islander residential segregation from non-Hispanic whites has been relatively low compared to the other ethnic groups, even in areas with large Asian populations (Massey & Denton, 1988b).

Table 5: **Highest and Lowest Levels of Residential Segregation for Asian/Pacific Islanders**

Metropolitan Statistical Area[1]	2000 Index	Change 1990-2000
Overall Mean[2]	42.0	1.1
Most Segregated		
Ann Arbor, MI	58.8	3.3
Lafayette, IN	55.4	-2.0
Atlantic-Cape May, NJ	53.2	10.6
Wausau, WI	52.8	-12.3
Lowell, MA-NH	51.5	-1.6
New York, NY	50.0	1.6
State College, PA	49.1	-3.2
Houston, TX	48.8	2.9
San Francisco, CA	48.6	-1.4
Sacramento, CA	48.6	-0.3
Least Segregated		
Santa Rosa, CA	25.6	0.6
Santa Cruz-Watsonville, CA	25.3	-5.8
Tucson, AZ	25.0	-1.5
San Luis Obispo-Atascadero-Paso Robles, CA	24.6	-5.3
Stamford-Norwalk, CT	24.5	4.6
Boulder-Longmont, CO	24.0	-3.0
Bellingham, WA	23.2	3.2
Colorado Springs, CO	22.4	-5.5
Lawton, OK	22.3	-0.1
Fort Walton Beach, FL	22.2	-2.3

Source: United States Census of Population and Housing, 1990 and 2000 PL 94-171 Redistricting Data.
[1] Only the 111 MSAs with a substantial population of Asian/Pacific Islanders are included in the tabulations. The minimum threshold is 3% of the total MSA population or 20,000 persons.
[2] The overall mean Dissimilarity Index score is weighted by the size of the Asian/Pacific Islander population in the MSA.

The mean Dissimilarity Index measure indicates that Asian/Pacific Islander residential segregation increased by 1.1 points from 1990 to 2000. This average increase occurred despite the finding of moderate declines in the majority of the most segregated MSAs in the country (refer back to Figure 3). As is the case with Latinos, areas with larger Asian/Pacific Islander populations are considerably more residentially segregated and thus contribute substantially to the increase in the weighted overall mean. This may be the result of excluding MSAs based on the criteria of having a population Asian/Pacific Islanders with 20,000 individuals or at least 3% of the total population. This study's analysis may be limited as only 111 of the 331 MSAs had Asian/Pacific Islander populations sufficiently large enough for inclusion in the calculations. However, it is argued that the criteria used strengthens the analysis by illustrating that as the proportion of people of color increase, there is an increased likelihood that residential segregation will result.

Frey and Farley (1996) have shown that areas with the highest levels of Asian residential segregation are clustered outside of the western region of the United States and include several university towns with large

Chinese student contingents. In 2000, many of the most segregated metropolitan areas for Asians are in regions with large universities. Table 5 includes MSAs which could be considered university towns such as Ann Arbor, Lafayette, and State College. Frey and Farley (1996) noted that Asians are often over-represented in university populations compared to their distribution in the general population. They also noted that increases in immigrant groups, such as the Vietnamese, Cambodian, and Laotian, has resulted in considerable concentration of these new immigrants into communities because there is a lack of economic means to reside in more integrated communities (Frey & Farley, 1996:38-9) .

To summarize this chapter thus far, as the United States has become more racially and ethnically diverse, it has become ever more important to look at how people of different racial/ethnic groups are living and working together. At the beginning of the twenty-first century, many neighborhoods in the United States remained divided along racial and ethnic lines, especially in the largest, most populous, urban centers. Several characteristics of metropolitan areas and attendant social problems are related to the level of residential segregation. Population size and region of the country exhibit strong and consistent relationships with segregation for all groups. The regional economic base and immigration flows to an area significantly impact residential segregation, but the effects differ based on the racial/ethnic group. New housing construction appears to lower residential segregation for all groups, although the reason for this relationship remains unclear from the data examined. To the extent that these factors can be influenced by policy mechanisms, areas and regions can address high levels of segregation and attempt to improve its negative impacts.

Legal Framework for Housing Discrimination and Residential Segregation

> *"No State shall make or enforce any law which shall abridge the privileges or immunities of citizens of the United States: nor shall any State deprive any person of life, liberty, or property, without due process of law; nor deny to any person within its jurisdiction the equal protection of the laws..."*

While these are the words found in the Fourteenth Amendment of the U.S. Constitution, it is commonplace that exception exists for African Americans trying to buy a house in many suburban neighborhoods. This criticism would seem to be very harsh as the United States prides itself within the international community by claiming equality for all under the law. Although racial equality has come a long way since Jim Crow and slavery, it is far from being realized: inequality along class, race and gender lines is the *de facto* law, and this is most poignant in the area of housing discrimination. Since the passage of the Equal Rights Amendment, the government has taken many steps to overcome the prejudices that African Americans face when trying to purchase homes in areas outside of the urban inner city. Yet more often the not, government does not or cannot deal effectively with housing discrimination.

The previous section provided empirical evidence that identifies residential segregation as a problem of housing discrimination within the United States. This section focuses on the legal framework of housing discrimination and demonstrates how current levels of residential segregation became enshrined in U.S. government policy and common law. Residential segregation continues to exist across the United States in part because governmental policy and legislation allows private organizations and state entities to act out racially motivated biases. Sitkoff (1993: 220-5) has noted in his discussion of the struggle for black equality that *de jure* legislative changes have not resulted in *de facto* changes to the variety of social problems the majority of African Americans face in the U.S. Sitkoff certainly recognized that there have been legal precedents in court rulings and enacted legislation outlawing discriminatory practices. However, he suggested that a Second Reconstruction after the *Civil Rights Act of 1964* was followed by a retreat of the Supreme Court so dramatic, that housing discrimination towards African Americans still exists today.

For almost a quarter century, it has been a policy of the United States to provide for fair and open housing throughout the country within specified constitutional limitations (Reed 1991). Senator Edward Kennedy stated in support of the *Civil Rights Act of 1968*:

> *"The private terror which has too often been a way of life for thousands of our citizens is not simply wanton violence. It is aimed precisely at the attempt by Americans to exercise their rights which the Fourteenth Amendment protects- to live as citizens as equally with their neighbors* "(Congressional Record, Vol. 114, Part 2, 90th Congress, Second Session: 2084).

It is with the above words that the *Civil Rights Act* became thought of as an extension of the Fourteenth Amendment. The *Civil Rights Act* included Title VII, a section that was groundbreaking in the terms of housing discrimination. Title VIII of the *Civil Rights Act of 1968* made discrimination in the rental or sale of housing on the basis of race, color, religion, or national origin a violation of federal law. This title along with its amendments, passed in 1988 to include women and the disabled, became known as the *Fair Housing Act* (Reed, 1994).

The *Fair Housing Act* prohibits discrimination in the terms and conditions, refusal to deal, discriminatory advertising, falsely representing availability, denying use of or participation in real estate services, and making representations regarding entry or prospective entry of a protected class into a neighborhood (Reed, 1991). The prohibitions of the *Fair Housing Act* only apply to federally owned, operated, or funded dwellings thus, leaving room for private owners to discriminate. Another problem with the *Fair Housing Act* is that it only mandates an investigation of discrimination if there is reasonable cause to believe that discrimination occurred, and the reasonable cause must be submitted in writing or over the telephone to the Department of Housing and Urban Development (HUD) by the complainant. The result is that the *Fair Housing Act* only provides for dealing with incidents of discrimination which are specifically brought to the attention of HUD through an individual who believes that they were discriminated against and ignores any type of primary prevention of housing discrimination.

In order for an individual to bring an act of housing discrimination to HUD's attention, the discrimination would have to be so blatant for someone to realize that they are being discriminated against. The *Fair Housing Amendments A*ct has been in effect since March of 1989 and after its enforcement commenced, the Housing Discrimination Study found that in 1989 the overall incidence of discrimination against black home seekers was 53 percent for renters and 59 percent for home buyers. Overall, there is little evidence that the strengthened enforcement mechanisms and increased penalties have had widespread impact on the extent of housing market discrimination (Reed, 1994).

Another problem with the legislation enacted to help aid in the problem of housing discrimination is the focus on income. Many programs such as the one implemented under Title VIII are premised on a mistaken belief that residential segregation can be combated solely through low-income housing. Evidence from housing audits in a wide range of locales confirms that discrimination does not cease upon black attainment of income parity with white home seekers (Newburger, 1984). Despite consistent evidence to the contrary, racial segregation is all too commonly equated with low income (Metcalf ,1988). Black access to good quality housing and neighborhoods is clearly separate from and broader than the simple question of the supply and distribution of low-income housing (Lake, 1979).

The *Fair Housing Act* applies to all federally owned, operated or funded property, leaving private institutions to do as they please. Sugrue (1996: 43) was more explicit in his research by providing evidence that residential segregation was the historical result of collusion between government, financial institutions and real estate agents. When a community goal of residential segregation between whites and blacks could not be obtained by legislation, whites entered into various private agreements such as restrictive covenants that were enforced under common law. Whites who favored the separation of blacks from whites in residential areas could simply rely upon equity courts to support the municipal ordinances and covenants mandating racial segregation.

From World War I to the early 1960s, privately adopted racially restrictive covenants provided an effective means of barring blacks from entering white sections of many cities. Unobtrusively and clandestinely, except for those against whom the covenants were directed, a legal means was developed to continue racial segregation despite constitutional and common law doctrines contrary to such intent (Vose, 1959). Turning to the contention that racially restrictive covenants were against the Fourteenth amendment, Judge Van Orsdel of the Supreme Court stated that the clause of the Fourteenth amendment inhibited only the power of the state. It did not he said, apply to individuals taking actions in regards to their own properties (Vose, 1959: 18). This line of legal reasoning was apparent in early cases dealing with residential segregation caused by racially restrictive covenants.

The Supreme Court of Louisiana supported, in *Queensborough Land Co. v. Cazeaux* (1915), a covenant prohibiting the sale of certain property to African Americans for twenty-five years. A little over ten years later, in *Schulte v. Starks* (1927) the Michigan Supreme Court upheld restrictive covenants, in a certain district where a consistent practice of exclusion of blacks had been followed, a somewhat indefinite covenant providing that property should not be transferred to any person *"whose ownership or occupancy would be injurious to the locality."*

Another Michigan case, *Kathan v. Stevenson* (1943), ruled that no racial restrictive agreement could be implied from the fact that building restrictions sought to maintain property values and a high-class residential character in the neighborhood. In this case, verbal assurances and years of exclusion of blacks made no difference because the recorded restrictions lacked specific words excluding *"Negroes."* These cases were brought to court long after all citizens were said to enjoy equal rights within the United States. In general then, to have a binding covenant, the parties must have made clear their desire to exclude blacks, although their use of racial terms did not need to be scientifically explicit (Vose, 1959).

These above examples set the historical framework for restrictive housing covenants in the United States and the government's avoidance of eliminating housing discrimination. The Federal Housing Authority routinely ignored housing discrimination and actually worked quite overtly to ensure racial segregation throughout the entire country. Sugrue (1996) explained that the Federal Housing Authority routinely refused underwriting loans for black residential construction while providing such assurances for comparably economically situated whites building literally within a few city blocks. Most certainly the government and financial complicity in residential segregation paved the way for the current levels of segregation we discussed above.

An example of the restrictive covenants used to promote structured racism through residential segregation is that of Grosse Pointes, Michigan. While this community has its own history and specific geopolitical circumstances, it can be held up, not as an anomaly but, as illustrative of residential *hypersegregation* patterns. The Grosse Pointes are a combination of six communities (Grosse Pointe, Grosse Pointe Township, Grosse Pointe Park, Grosse Pointe Farms, Grosse Pointe Woods, and Grosse Pointe Shores) on the north-eastern edge of Detroit with very lavish and opulent homes.

At first glance, one could easily intuitively conclude that class and not race is the primary determinant in residential patterns as the residents of the Grosse Pointes are amongst the highest economic strata in U.S. society. Yet, Grosse Pointe Farms was a community that in 1969, five years after the *Civil Rights Act of 1964* had been passed, defeated a municipal law to make housing discrimination illegal. The Grosse Pointes also did not have a single real estate broker sell any residential property to any African American prior to 1970 (Cosseboom, 1972).

The Grosse Pointes explicitly enforced a very strict housing covenant until the use of the Point system gained national attention in 1960 (Sugrue, 1996). This community went to the extent as to empower the Grosse Pointe Property Owner's Association, the Grosse Pointe Brokers Association, and Grosse Pointe realtors to screen prospective residents to see if they qualified for home ownership under very specific racial considerations (class and gender were also dimensions used for discrimination). Private investigators were employed to complete a questionnaire on prospective residents which asked questions relating to ancestry, country of origin, appearances, accents, dress, grammar, occupation, and generally questions relating to what was considered *'typically American.'*

Once the questionnaire was completed, each potential resident was given a score up to a maximum of 100 points. Home ownership was conditional upon whether the potential resident could score the prescribed number of points determined by the deemed race of that prospective resident. Many whites needed only to score 50 points, many eastern Europeans needed 55 points, southern Europeans needed anywhere from 65 to 75 points, Jews needed at least 85 points, and blacks and Asians could simply not buy property within Grosse Pointe (Cosseboom, 1972).

Grosse Pointe, like many Michigan metropolitan suburban areas and similar areas across the nation demonstrate that the degree of black-white residential segregation remains high due to deep-seated historical antecedents. Residential segregation remains high despite evidence of shifting white attitudes about race and despite successful court challenges to programs that perpetuated racial segregation. Metropolitan Detroit, home to about half of all Michigan residents, offers a particularly stark, although not unique, example of the persistence of black-white residential segregation. In the metropolitan Detroit area, the pattern of black-white segregation has fluctuated only slightly since 1940. In fact, rates of residential segregation in Detroit were higher in 1990 than they were in 1960, in spite of the liberalization of attitudes toward race, being a hotspot of social justice activism and the UAW, and the passage of the *Civil Rights Act of 1964* and *Fair Housing Act of 1968*.

Table 6: Residential Segregation in Grosse Pointe, Michigan, 1990-2000[1]

Total Population		Non-Hispanic White		Black/ African American		Latino		Asian/Pacific Islander	
		Number of Residents	% of Total Population	Number of Residents	% of Total Population	Number of Residents	% of Total Population	Number of Residents	% of Total Population
Grosse Pointe city									
1990	5,681	5,632	99.14%	7	0.12%	64	1.14%	42	0.74%
2000	5,670	5,510	97.18%	45	0.79%	83	1.46%	87	1.53%
Grosse Pointe township									
1990	2,850	2,630	92.28%	36	1.26%	18	0.63%	178	6.25%
2000	2,743	2,600	94.79%	16	0.58%	49	1.79%	124	4.52%
Grosse Pointe Farms city									
1990	10,092	9,915	98.25%	5	0.05%	64	0.63%	172	1.70%
2000	9,764	9,561	97.92%	78	0.80%	108	1.11%	120	1.23%
Grosse Pointe Park city									
1990	12,857	12,452	96.85%	53	0.41%	157	1.22%	267	2.08%
2000	12,443	11,735	94.31%	437	3.51%	217	1.74%	281	2.26%
Grosse Pointe Shores village									
1990	2,951	2,727	92.41%	36	1.22%	18	0.61%	178	6.03%
2000	2,823	2,671	94.62%	17	0.60%	49	1.74%	130	4.61%
Grosse Pointe Woods city									
1990	17,715	17,450	98.50%	7	0.04%	121	0.68%	246	1.39%
2000	17,080	16,562	96.97%	134	0.78%	167	0.98%	425	2.49%

Source: United States Census of Population and Housing: Social and Economic Characteristics, 1990, CP-2-24, Table 7 and United States Census of Population and Housing: Profiles of General Demographic Characteristics, 2000, Table DP-1.
[1]The 2000 Census allows respondents to declare more than one response for race. I have included all responses which may total more than 100% of the population. The non-white categories for 2000 may be overstated as a whole by a maximum of: Grosse Pointe city 34; Grosse Pointe Township 24; Grosse Pointe Farms city 41; Grosse Pointe Park city 246; Grosse Pointe Shores village 24; and, Grosse Pointe Woods city 139.

Table 6 presents a strong contrast to the earlier data which illustrated high Dissimilarity Index values. The Grosse Pointes are populated with a predominance of white residents with limited presence of blacks, Latinos, or Asian/Pacific Islanders. In all six municipalities, non-Hispanic white residents constitute well over ninety percent of the population. While four of the six municipalities became more integrated, the progress over ten years was less than resounding. In 2000, the most integrated community was Grosse Pointe Park and it had a non-Hispanic white population of 94.31%.

The above example, which illustrates only a small part of Michigan, and yet smaller part of the United States, indicates that racial segregation still exists and is the result of historical patterns of housing discrimination. According to the United States Constitution, restrictive housing covenants violate the Fourteenth Amendment: but when it concerns private property, how can discrimination be regulated? Communities like the Grosse Pointes were able to use their discriminatory practices because no one challenged the historical patterns of housing discrimination and the resulting residential segregation. It is unfortunate however that the only time discrimination is recognized is after it has already occurred.

One such challenge to residential segregation was *Shelley v. Kraemer* (1948) in which the United States Supreme Court ruled that racially restrictive housing covenants were unenforceable. *Hills v. Gautreaux* (1976) was another such case in which the United States Supreme Court ruled against racially isolated public housing projects.

The *Fair Housing Act of 1968* also forbade discrimination against minorities by real estate brokers, property owners and landlords. Yet, real estate agents developed more furtive tactics to preserve the racial homogeneity of neighborhoods. The most significant was and is the practice known as *steering*. Steering is the practice of directing white home buyers to all-white communities and black home buyers to predominantly black or racially transitional neighborhoods. Real estate brokers catered to what they believed were the prejudices of their white customers (DeMarco & Galster, 1993).

A 1979 study of real estate practices in metropolitan Detroit revealed the prevalence of racial steering by brokers who showed African Americans homes in black or racially mixed neighborhoods and seldom showed whites homes in racially diverse communities or in places that had any visible minority population (Pearce 1979). More recent audit studies of housing discrimination conducted by the Department of Housing and Urban Development and by local housing and non-profit agencies included matched pairs of black and white testers who are sent to randomly selected real estate offices. These studies consistently show the persistence of discriminatory treatment of black home seekers and renters (Massey & Denton, 1993). In short, discrimination by brokers has played a significant role in maintaining patterns of racial segregation throughout the United States. Despite the *Civil Rights Act of 1968* and the *Fair Housing Act* under Title VIII, this practice is very effective in creating and maintaining residential segregation.

The Fourteenth Amendment, the *Civil Rights Act of 1968* and Title VIII are all designed to help fight discrimination. The Department of Housing and Urban Development was created in 1965 as another agency which furthered the government's intervention into housing discrimination. HUD has the implicit mission to create a decent, safe, and sanitary home and suitable living environment for every individual and to enforce housing laws. Throughout the years since the creation of HUD there have been many Congressional and Presidential actions which established major HUD related programs. According to the HUD web site, these actions include such key events as:

- The passage of the *Civil Rights Act of 1968* and *Fair Housing Act*, which made the majority of housing discrimination illegal and gave HUD enforcement responsibility;
- The passage in 1988 of the *Fair Housing Amendments Act* which made it easier for individuals whom faced discrimination to sue and added more serious penalties for offenders.
- Public Housing reforms passed in 1998 by Congress to reduce segregation by race and income.

There are a number of different acts that were passed over the years but when it comes to the enforcement of housing discrimination, it is still the responsibility of the individual to file a complaint. The Ohio Civil Rights Commission (OCRC) provides an interesting illustration in the description of the process in Ohio as:

> "*An individual who feels he or she has been treated in a discriminatory manner must file a charge with the OCRC within one year of the alleged act of discrimination. The commission must complete its investigation of the charge of discrimination within one hundred days. During that time, the Commission will either negotiate a settlement of the charge or make a finding as to whether or not the evidence substantiates that the law has been violated. If the evidence is insufficient to meet the legal standards of proof to show a violation of the law, then the Commission will dismiss the charge*" (Ohio Civil Rights Commission Annual Report 1998).

It can be argued that the process under HUD is flawed in a few significant ways. First, it leaves the action up to the individual to recognize if they have been discriminated against. HUD is generally reactive rather than proactive. It is also very hard to prove discrimination when it is not an act by an individual against another which is clearly racist in intent. As mentioned in the examples of Michigan restrictive housing covenants, residents and real estate agents use tactics such as block busting and steering to circumvent laws. The complaint procedure requires that people report the discrimination, but as the National Crime Victimization Survey reports, most crimes go unreported, and discrimination is against the law, thus many acts of discrimination may also go unreported.

The legal jurisprudence of fighting racism has very important origins in the distant past but racism is still a problem of the United States in the twenty-first century. The government has established that acts of housing discrimination are illegal. However, as the evidence demonstrates, U.S. cities are still segregated. This indicates that past and current legislation has not been very effective to date. Housing covenants still implicitly exist within privately owned property in that real estate agencies still steer African Americans away from upper-class white neighborhoods. The biggest problem is that the government does not seek out issues of housing discrimination and it could only do so with proper enforcement and adequate levels of funding. Therefore, although there have been some advancements, more often than not, the government fails to address housing discrimination.

The Role of Preference in Residential Segregation

The previous sections have examined the overall patterns of black-white racial segregation that exist in housing as well as the history of government intervention and its lack of widespread effect. This section seeks to explore the role of personal preference in the perpetuation of residential segregation. The main question is whether the opinions of individuals about who should live where and what neighborhoods should look like can explain a significant portion of residential segregation. As well, it can help to understand whether housing discrimination based on race is simply a function of the structural elements of U.S. society. A survey of current literature and results of several studies confirm that the impact of individual preferences on residential segregation and certainly cannot be ignored (Harris, 1999, 2001; Bobo & Zubrinsky, 1996; Farley et al., 1994; Clark, 1991, 1992; Galster, 1990).

As the focus of the previous section on the lack of enforcement of laws and statutes argued, the loopholes and blind eyes turned to housing discrimination does much to keep residential segregation enduring. However, if there was a general consensus of citizens to not stand for such violations of fair housing laws, then more of these illegal discriminations would be detected and punished.

Economic factors are also a strong structural component of residential segregation. Separating the effects of race from class can be difficult even in the best analyses. In 1995 the median African American family income was only $25,970. This was substantially below the all-household median of $34,076 (Palen, 2001:74-75). It could simply be a matter of class keeping these races apart. However, despite some increases in integration there is still a substantial gap for blacks as incomes rises (Freeman, 2000).

Massey and Fischer (1999) found that black residential segregation remains at high levels across the spectrum of income levels and that the gap between blacks and other minority groups, such as Latinos and Asians, actually increases as income level rises. Massey and Denton (1993: 87) concluded in their research that the result of this is that the poorest Latinos are segregated from whites less than the wealthiest African Americans: a finding which is supported in the data presented earlier. It seems that citing economic differences between blacks and whites is not such a simple answer to explain residential segregation. There are certainly other factors at play which increases residential segregation. These factors perpetuate the economic inequality of minorities and especially that of African Americans. Among the many effects of residential segregation identified by researchers, the lack of home ownership was found by Flippen (2001) to be the most important in perpetuating residential segregation.

In discussing the structural elements of residential segregation it can be seen that there are other factors influencing how these elements operate. The attitudes and preferences of individuals throughout society may be the missing link. Opinion studies of racial preferences have been conducted nationally since the 1940s and have revealed some improvement in white racial attitudes (Clark, 1991). While only 36% surveyed in 1942 said it would not make a difference if a black person with the same income and education as themselves moved into their neighborhood, this number had risen to 85% by 1972 (Schuman & Bobo, 1988: 274).

The finding of changing racial preferences by itself may seem to nullify any notion that racial preference makes a difference in residential segregation but deeper study of historical preferences reveals this is not the case. Many whites may be willing to live in integrated neighborhoods but when the question of proportion is added, it draws much more conservative responses. Affirmative answers to the question '*Would you move if colored people came to live in your neighborhood in great numbers?*' has shown only very slow decrease since the 1950s (Clark, 1991: 2). Most specific questions such as these have shown that although whites are now more in favor of integration, they still do not want large numbers of blacks in their community. Harris (2001) has also shown that the pure race hypothesis does not apply to neighborhood satisfaction of the majority of blacks or whites. This shows that racial preference is still an issue worth talking about despite some positive attitudinal changes over time.

In analyzing the role of racial preference it is helpful to frame the discussion with some of the ideas of how racial attitudes affect housing segregation. Clark (1991) presented a number of such ideas which included a clear explanation of the Schelling segregation model. The Schelling segregation model suggested that small differences in choices taken as a whole aggregate can leads to structural patterns of segregation (Clark, 1991: 1). This means that very minor differences in the behaviors of individuals because of their racial preferences may actually result in highly segregated areas that are largely black or largely white. Clark also stated that variations in the model might alter findings including changes in preferred proportions of racial composition, proportion of the two preferencing populations, policies and laws affecting residential movement, and finally the neighborhood size encompassing the totality of individual choices (Clark, 1991: 5). Nonetheless, the Schelling segregation model proposed that even slight differences in the preferred proportions of neighborhood integration between blacks and white can in fact lead to high levels of segregation.

Other hypotheses of residential segregation and residential preference included three tested by Bobo and Zubrinsky (1996) on the nature of attitudes toward residential integration. The first idea, the perceived economic statue difference hypothesis, asserts that attitudes on integration stem from perceived group differences in socioeconomic characteristics like income, occupation, and associated differences in lifestyle (Bobo & Zubrinsky, 1996: 885). This hypothesis is based on class differences more than racial differences and, as was previously stated, Bobo and Zubrinsky found little evidence supporting this idea. Even controlling for class differences researchers like Flippen (2001) and Massey and Fischer (1999) have noted the independently continued effects of race on residential segregation.

The second hypothesis presented was the mere in-group preference or pure race hypothesis. This means that the primary mode for residential segregation is a belief that a natural ethnocentrism of one's own group affects residential choice rather than negative feelings for another group. Bobo and Zubrinsky (1996: 887) also found problems with this model and suggested that if in-group neighborhood preferences were equally distributed across varying groups, with equivalences in the quality of housing stock, these preferences may be a neutral factor.

The prejudice hypothesis was the final theory considered by Bobo and Zubrinsky (1996). This is closer to traditional notions of prejudice in that it stresses the importance of hostility towards other groups in shaping individual racial contact attitudes. As will be shown, this theory seems to be the most applicable of the three. Although overtly racist attitudes have diminished in the last thirty years, covert prejudices still remain and they have a noticeable effect on the patterns of residential segregation.

The inconsistencies in the racial preferences of whites in the United States have already been alluded to with the discussion of historical attitudes but the reasons for these variations are many. First, the idea of proportion of blacks in a neighborhood is quite revealing to the true racial attitudes of whites. In studies where white respondents were asked to choose the composition of neighborhood where they would be most comfortable, a large proportion of whites felt most comfortable when less than one-third of residents were black. However, as the proportion of blacks reached one-third to one-half the percentage of whites that said they would still feel comfortable living in the area dropped to 50% or less (Zubrinsky & Bobo, 1996, Massey & Denton, 1993: 92; Clark, 1991: 9). It is possible that this opposition to large numbers of blacks is based on the idea of maintaining status and not necessarily negative racist attitudes in general (Zubrinsky & Bobo 1996).

This is not to say that negative racial attitudes do not exist. Bobo and Zubrinsky (1996) delved directly into this issue by examining how measures of racial stereotypes related to attitudes about residential segregation. Respondents were asked to rate the four different target groups of whites, blacks, Hispanics, and Asians on areas such as intelligence, welfare preference, and ease with which a person could get along with each members of each group. The results of the study found that blacks had the most negative overall rating and whites received the best ratings (Bobo & Zubrinsky, 1996: 894). It would appear that negative racial attitudes are definitely manifest in white preferences of neighborhood compositions.

More examples of negative racial stereotypes are also found in Massey and Denton (1993). Some other negative stereotypes attributed to blacks include being less likely to take care of their homes and yards, were more prone to violence, and were not as quiet as whites. When findings like these are combined with the fact that blacks indeed face a greater amount of housing discrimination than do Hispanics or Asians (Massey & Fischer, 1999), a connection between negative racial stereotype ratings and attitudes about housing integration seems to be justified (Farley et al., 1994).

The hierarchy in the order of preferred neighbors with whites at the top and blacks at the bottom, provides more evidence against the theory of positive in-group feelings and ethnocentrisms being the basis of housing preferences. Residential preferences cannot be explained as the result of a race-specific, pure race hypothesis. If it were merely positive feelings for one's own group that dictated housing preferences, the level of residential segregation of all minorities from whites would be much more consistent across each minority group (Zubrinsky & Bobo, 1996: 358). However, this is not the case. Studies have shown black residential segregation to be higher (Harris, 2001; Freeman, 2000; Massey & Fischer 1999). Therefore, it can be concluded that negative attitudes towards blacks more than other minorities must be present within the framework of residential segregation across the United States.

A final area of white preference that impacts segregation research is the consistent trend for whites to stress the importance that blacks families in their neighborhood should have an equal class and income status as themselves. Many whites fear that blacks of lower-class status moving into their neighborhoods will depreciate their home values (Harris, 2001; Clark, 1991). It can be argued that this may be a simple extension of stereotypes of blacks. This is quite apparent in the cases whereby whites became extremely upset when HUD has attempted to build low-income, small-scale, and post-1970s housing projects integrated into middle or upper class areas of a city (Massey & Denton, 1993: 227-9). As stated previously, the intersection of race and class differences cannot be denied but the overall role of white discriminatory attitudes has quite an effect on the neighborhood composition preferences.

While white attitudes on housing preferences strongly manifest in many studies, they cannot totally explain the role of individual preference in residential segregation. Blacks too display distinct preferences as to their ideal neighborhood racial composition. Clark (1992), Massey and Denton (1993: 89), and Farley, Fielding and Krysan (1996) are among a number of researchers to assert that, when asked to choose their ideal neighborhood make-up, a majority of black survey respondents opt for an equal proportion of blacks and whites. This is distinct from whites whose most common preference is for a neighborhood that consists of one-third or less black inhabitants.

Though whites are willing to live in integrated neighborhoods, blacks prefer them. It seems there is variation between how whites and blacks understand the concept of what integration means (Clark, 1991). If Schelling's segregation model, discussed previously, is correct then this difference in preference for ideal neighborhood make-up between blacks and whites may be a large contributor to continued residential segregation. Another strong preference for many African Americans is their adamant unwillingness to be the first black family to move into an all white neighborhood as a *pioneer*. Zubrinsky and Bobo's (1996) survey showed that 64% of black respondents choose such a neighborhood as their last choice when asked to rate potential neighborhood combinations. This figure is consistent with the finding by Massey and Denton (1993: 90) in which 66% of black respondents in Detroit rated this scenario as their least preferred choice. Clearly, becoming a pioneering family is not an idea with which many blacks are comfortable.

The reasons for this discomfort have had some debate. African Americans are most likely to rate themselves as the group most likely of all minorities to upset the group of existing white residents in any community into which they move. Given that blacks have been shown to have accurate information about the housing market, it seems that perceptions of hostility towards blacks are an important part of their search for residence (Zubrinsky & Bobo, 1996: 351). Freeman (2000: 18-19) has suggested that blacks may feel more comfortable near other blacks because it serves as a buffer to the history of negative experiences with whites. He admits that the research on this subject is mixed and it cannot yet be considered a valid explanation for the residential preferences of blacks.

Finally, an aspect of black residential preference that must be addressed is the difference between preferential attitudes and actual living conditions. Though many surveys show a preference for living in more integrated neighborhoods only a small number of blacks are actually able to realize this level of racial integration (Bobo & Zubrinsky, 1996: 899). Clark (1992: 461) found that of the large number of those who choose racial parity most actually lived, or were constrained to live, in neighborhoods that were 80% black. Though blacks would prefer more integrated neighborhoods, they are not able to achieve this because of the differing attitudes of white racial preference.

Conclusion and Discussion

Research has shown that both blacks and whites have definite opinions on what constitutes integration and that each group shows distinct preferences for such integration. It can be argued that the role of individual preference in residential segregation cannot be ignored. Even though it seems that white preference may exert more of an influence upon residential segregation, black attitudes on residential integration are important as well. The status of whites in society as well as the history of individual and structured racism which characterizes the United States gives their individual preferences even more weight. However, the interaction between black and white preferences will dictate whether levels of residential segregation will remain steady or continue to decline. It is contended that residential segregation will decline but it will occur at a slow rate as it has without significant domestic policy intervention.

There is also the question of how these individual factors actually interact with the structural elements of residential segregation which we have demonstrated still exist. It cannot be stated for certain whether there is a causal ordering to their relationship. Do structural factors influence the individual attitudes and preferences of both blacks and whites or is it personal preferences that form the basis for structural discrimination? It can be argued that the relationship of the two dimensions is reciprocal and preferences affect, and are affected by, the structural constraints and history of institutionalized racism. Underestimating either dimension will hinder efforts to find solutions to the problem of housing discrimination and residential segregation.

The importance of realigning structural elements such as housing practices, education, economic opportunities, and the nature of the urban environment is beneficial. However, it is believed that much of the legal and government effort put forth will not make substantial differences until diversity and integration are pursued as just social and policy objectives in their own right. It is in the combination of improvement in these individual and structural elements that the best hope of creating a society free from residential segregation for all can be found.

African Americans, Latinos and Asian/Pacific Islanders are still highly discriminated against within the area of housing. This specific type of discrimination leads to other inequalities such as residential segregation. Since the majority of African Americans and Latinos are today confined mostly to inner city conditions, it is argued that they are denied the same opportunities as those who live in suburban communities. One of the largest impacts residential segregation has is upon education because of how funding is directly tied to residential areas. Lack of funding, less qualified teachers and an overall deficiency of resources due to residentially segregated communities simply perpetuates the existing inequalities and reproduces existing patterns of residential segregation and ultimately racism (Sitkoff, 1993). Therefore, the next generation is likely to find themselves in the same conditions as their parents. These facts lend themselves ultimately to the development of a *trichotomous hypersegregation* which must be addressed in future research studies on residential segregation.

Even as African Americans attain middle or upper class status, residential segregation is still extremely high. Prejudicial attitudes of some affluent whites maintain segregation through unwritten housing covenants, lending practices in financial institutions and steering practices. Even when African Americans are accepted into the community, many whites strongly prefer that their incomes are within the same class, thus keeping lower class individuals out: something that can be used as a socially acceptable euphemism for racial discrimination. Another aspect of housing segregation is the continued collapse of inner cities. Condemned buildings along with high rates of crime are typical characteristics of many inner cities. There are few individuals who are willing to take on renovation or renewal projects. Schools, churches, homes, and other sound structures remain standing to rot in the midst of segregated inner cities.

While we have shown that residential segregation is still a problem within the United States, it is not purely a *structural phenomenon*. Although African Americans have come a long way in achieving equal rights, the journey is far from over. Until policymakers develop programs and legislation to combat residential segregation that are strictly enforced, there will be a long road to end residential segregation. Justice Harlan of the Supreme Court once said that the Constitution was color-blind. What this implies is that every U. S. citizen is entitled to life, liberty, the pursuit of happiness, and equal protection, regardless of the color of their skin. It is unfortunate that in the arbitrary and socially constructed idea of race that this equality vanishes. William Julius Wilson (1999: 117) is correct when he suggested that we all need to think more about what we have in common rather than the differences that keep us divided.

References

Bobo, L. & Zubrinsky, C. (1996). Attitudes on Residential Integration: Perceived Status Differences, Mere In-Group Preference, or Racial Preference? *Social Forces,* 74:883-909.

Burgess, E. (1967). The Growth of the City: An Introduction to a Research Project. p. 47-62 in *The City,* edited by R. E. Park, E. W. Burgess, and R. D. McKenzie. Chicago, IL: University of Chicago Press.

Clark, W. (1991). Residential Preferences and Neighborhood Racial Segregation: A Test of the Schelling Segregation Model. *Demography,* 28:1-19.

Clark, W. (1992). Residential Preferences and Residential Choices in a Multiethnic Context. *Demography,* 29:451-66.

Cosseboom, K. (1972). *Grosse Pointe, Michigan: Race Against Race.* East Lansing, MI: Michigan State University Press.

DeMarco, D. & Galster, G. (1993). Prointegrative Policy: Theory and Practice. *Journal of Urban Affairs* 15:141-60.

Farley, R., E. Fielding & M. Krysan. (1996). The Residential Preferences of Blacks and Whites: A Four-Metropolis Analysis. Presented at the annual meeting of the Population Association of America, New Orleans, LA.

Farley, R. & Frey, W. (1994). Changes in the Segregation of Whites from Blacks During the 1980s: Small Steps Toward a More Integrated Society. *American Sociological Review,* 59:23-45.

Farley, R., Steeh, C., Krysan, M., Jackson, T., & Reeves, K. (1994). Stereotypes and Segregation: Neighborhoods in the Detroit Area. *American Journal of Sociology,* 100:750-80.

Flippen, C. (2001). Residential Segregation and Minority Home Ownership. *Social Science Research,* 30:337-62.

Freeman, L. (2000). Minority Housing Segregation: A Test of Three Perspectives. *Journal of Urban Affairs,* 22:15-35.

Frey, W. & Farley, R. (1996). Latino, Asian, and Black Segregation in U.S. Metropolitan Areas: Are Multi-ethnic Metros Different? *Demography,* 33:35-50.

Galster, G. C. (1990). White Flight from Racially Integrated Neighborhoods in the 1970s: The Cleveland Experience. *Urban Studies* 27:385-99.

Glaeser, E. L. & Vigdor, J. (2001). *Racial Segregation in the 2000 Census: Promising News.* Washington, DC: Brookings Institution.

Harris, D. R. (1999). "Property Values Drop When Blacks Move In, Because...": Racial and Socioeconomic Determinants of Neighborhood Desirability. *American Sociological Review* 64:461-79.

Harris, D. R. (2001). Why Are Whites and Blacks Averse to Black Neighbors? *Social Science Research* 30:100-16.

Hills v. Gautreaux 96 S.Ct. 1538 (1976).

Kathan v. Stevenson 307 Mich. 485 (1943).

Lake, R. W. (1979). *The New Suburbanites: Race and Housing in the Suburbs.* New Brunswick, NJ: Rutgers University Center for Urban Policy Research.

Massey, D. S., & Denton, N. (1987). Trends in the Residential Segregation of Blacks, Hispanics, and Asians: 1970-1980. *American Sociological Review,* 52:802-25.

Massey, D. S., & Denton, N. (1988a). The Dimensions of Residential Segregation. *Social Forces,* 67:281-315.

Massey, D. S., & Denton, N. (1988b). Suburbanization and Segregation in U.S. Metropolitan Areas. *American Journal of Sociology,* 94:592-626.

Massey, D. S., & Denton, N. (1993). *American Apartheid: Segregation and the Making of the Underclass.* Cambridge, MA: Harvard University Press.

Massey, D. & Fischer, M. (1999). Does Rising Income Bring Integration? New Results for Blacks, Hispanics, and Asians in 1990. *Social Science Research,* 28:316-26.

McKenzie, R. D. (1967). The Ecological Approach to the Study of the Human Community. p. 63-79 in *The City*, edited by R. E. Park, E. W. Burgess, and R. D. McKenzie. Chicago, IL: University of Chicago Press.

Metcalf, G. R. (1988). *Fair Housing Comes of Age*. Westport, CT: Greenwood Press.

Newbold, K. B. (1999). Spatial Distribution and Redistribution of Immigrants in the Metropolitan United States, 1980 and 1990. *Economic Geography,* 75:254-71.

Newburger, H. 1984. *Recent Evidence on Discrimination in Housing.* Washington, DC: United States Department of Housing and Urban Development.

Ohio Civil Rights Commission. 1998. *The Ohio Civil Rights Commission Annual Report*. Columbus, OH: Civil Rights Commission.

Palen, J. J. 2001. *Social Problems for the Twenty-First Century*. New York, NY: McGraw-Hill.

Park, R. E. (1967). The City: Suggestions for the Investigation of Human Behavior in the Urban Environment. p. 1-46 in *The City*, edited by R. E. Park, E. W. Burgess, and R. D. McKenzie. Chicago, IL: University of Chicago Press.

Pearce, D. M. (1979) Gatekeepers and Homeseekers: Institutional Patterns in Racial Steering. *Social Problems,* 26:325-42.

Queensborough Land Co. V. Cazeaux 136 La. 724 (1915).

Reed, V. M. (1991). Civil Rights Legislation and the Housing Status of Black Americans: Evidence From Fair Housing Audits and Segregation Indices. *Review of Black Political Economy,* 19:29-42.

Reed, V., ed. (1994). Fair Housing Enforcement: Is the Current System Adequate? Pp. 222-36 in *Residential Apartheid: The American Legacy*, edited by R. D. Bullard, J. E. Grigsby III, and C. Lee. Los Angeles, CA: CAAS Publications, University of California, Los Angeles.

Schulte v. Starks 238 Mich. 102 (1927).

Schuman, H. & Bobo, L. (1988). Survey-Based Experiments on White Racial Attitudes Towards Residential Integration. *American Journal of Sociology,* 94:273-99.

Shelley v. Kraemer 68 S.Ct. 836 (1948).

Sitkoff, H. (1993). *The Struggle for Black Equality 1954-1992*. Revised edition. New York, NY: Hill and Wang.

Sugrue, T. J. (1996). *The Origins of the Urban Crisis: Race and Inequality in Postwar Detroit*. Princeton, NJ: Princeton University Press.

United States Census of Population and Housing, 1990. PL 94-171 Redistricting Data.

United States Census of Population and Housing, 2000 PL 94-171 Redistricting Data.

United States Census of Population and Housing: Social and Economic Characteristics, 1990, CP-2-24.

United States Census of Population and Housing: Profiles of General Demographic Characteristics, 2000.

United States Congress. 1968. Congressional Record, Vol. 114, Part 2, 90th Congress, Second Session: 2084 [114 Cong. Rec. 2084 (1968)]. Washington, DC: United States Government Printing Office.

United States Department of Housing and Urban Development. 2005. *Mission and History*. www.hud.gov/library/bookshelf18/mission.cfm

Vose, C. (1959). *Caucasians Only: The Supreme Court, the NAACP, and the Restrictive Covenant Cases*. Berkeley, CA: University of California Press.

Wilson, W. J. (1999). *The Bridge over the Racial Divide: Rising Inequality and Coalition Politics*. Berkeley, CA: University of California Press.

Zubrinsky, C. L. and L. Bobo. 1996. Prismatic Metropolis: Race and Residential Segregation in the City of Angels. *Social Science Research*, 25:335-74.

CHAPTER 12
THE MYTH OF RACE AND THE REALITY OF RACISM

Charles Quist-Adade

Abstract: This chapter examines the enigma and destructive power of race and racism and contends that these twin notions, while illogical and irrational, have real, abiding influence on the collective human psyche. I propose that the farce of these notions be taught to children as early as at the primary school level, because children, especially White children, are the first victims of racism. In addition, it is contended that racism and anti-racism are a dialectical process. Therefore, anti-racist education in the new century must go beyond the moralism of the victim groups and the intellectual elite to include all, including victims, victimizers, racialized and the 'raceless', White and Non-Whites, young and old. Moreover, anti-racist education must be creatively and dialectically praxis-oriented, transcending the classrooms and lecture halls to communities and the lifeworlds of all constituent ethno-racial groups, and transforming social and political structures that distribute valued social goods and resources.

'*Race*' and '*racism*' are paradoxically different things. Race does not exist, at least in the scientific sense; it is a chimera, a phantom. Racism, however, is a powerful reality: an invention that is absurd, illogical, irrational, and nonsensical. Race is a figment of the collective imagination. Racism manifests itself in a destructively powerful way. Yet together the two are interdependent, feeding upon each other.

The twin notions of race and racism combine to make a powerful concoction, poisoning human relations, maiming, killing, and destroying people everywhere in both hidden and open ways. Sometimes people appear to understand both the absurdity and the power of the twin notions as expressed in the following trite phrases: '*Our differences are only skin deep*' and '*we all belong to the human race.*' These two phrases are often invoked across the '*color bar*' either to promote racial harmony or to expose the fallacy of racial exclusiveness. The truth in these two observations is beyond contest. Yet the history of the human race suggests that people use these terms without really meaning the idea behind them.

So, then, what is '*race*' and what is '*racism*'? What follows is an attempt to answer this and other related questions: How did race and racism happen? What are their effects? How can the notion of race be dislodged from popular consciousness? How can racism be dismantled? The question of race does not lend itself to easy answers, but must be fully assessed.

There is little scholarly consensus on the meaning of the term '*race*.' However, most social scientists, and indeed biological scientists and geneticists, are in agreement that '*race*' is a concept invented by humans. Thus, '*race*' can be defined as a grouping of human population characterized by *socially* selected physical traits. What this definition points to, is that race is a social construct (society's invention). What we see and know as race is based on a small set of physical characteristics (e.g., skin color, hair color and texture, facial features, etc.) which are superficial manifestations of eons of genetic mutations and gene-environment interactions (Davies, 2001; Kuper, 1965; UNESCO 1965). In other words, race is neither *natural* nor *biological*. Instead, the concept was artificially and arbitrarily created by human beings. It also suggests that '*race*' is not genetically predetermined or divinely created.

The physical differences we see are adaptations to geographic and climatic conditions and are a survival mechanism for everyone. Long periods of adaptation to geographic and climatic conditions ensure the interaction between genes and the environment. Mutation took place in the *original* Englishman and *original* Ibo man in their efforts to survive in the polar and tropical regions respectively. In time, they passed on these survival genes to their offspring. Thus, the Englishman and his offspring became paler in their complexions, while the Ibo man and his descendants became darker, but with no clinical way to pinpoint where the 'Black' race *ends* and where the 'White' race *begins*.

However, that does not explain why the Ibo man became a member of the so-called 'Black' race and the Englishman became a member of the so-called 'White' race. The Ibo man did not call himself a 'Black' man until others defined him so. This suggests that race is a social construct. It is those who called the Ibo man 'Black' man and the Englishman 'White' man who gave birth to the idea of racism: the systematic means of denying access to resources and opportunities to a group based on their skin color or ethnicity (Myers, 2006). In other words, people created the concept of race at one point in time and produced ideas to justify the concept. Race and racism are modern inventions.

According to another historian, Gary Nash (1999), when Jamestown colonist John Rolfe took his new bride, Pocahontas (who had converted to Christianity), back to London in 1616, they caused an uproar among nobility of the Court of King James. This conflict did not arise because Rolfe, an Englishman, had married an Indian, but because Pochahontas, a princess, had married a commoner (*Race,* 2003). Kupperman (2000) points out that as for physical distinctions, Native Americans were most struck by the English colonists' beards and scent. The colonists wore the same clothes for weeks, were covered with lice, and rarely bathed. The English did not describe the Indians' color as red in the early days, but rather as tanned or tawny.

Race as a Modern Idea

The concept of race has not always been with us (Johnson, 2006; Snowden, 1970). There was a time before concepts of race and racism existed (Johnson, 2006). The term, according to historians, was first used in the 15th century by an English poet to refer to a line of British kings. Other historians trace the beginnings of the term to about 1580, when it was used to denote a group of people with common descent. Increasingly, the term came to refer to various nations, such as the German, British and Russian '*races*'. The modern use of the term can be traced to the 19th century and the advent of the European Enlightenment movement. Enlightenment scholars, preoccupied with the application of science in the study of human society, paved the way for scientific racism. The classification of the humans into subgroups or categories is similar to the manner by which faunal and floral types were pigeon-holed by biological scientists.

The pioneer in this field was the Frenchman Francois Bernier, who classified the human '*race*' into four categories: Europeans, Far Easterners, Sub-Saharan African, and Lapps (Montagu, 1997, 1964; Spickard, 1992; Lasker & Tyzzer, 1982; Gosset, 1963). After Bernier, a long line of the so-called naturalists emerged, including Georges Cuveir, James Cowels Prichard, Louis Agassiz, Charles Pickering, and Johann Friederich Blumenbach, each with his own number of racial groups.

Not surprisingly, all these European race categorizers placed the European (White) '*race*' on top of the human pile (Gould, 1994). The European '*race*' was not only assigned the best human characteristics, it was also elevated to the apex of human civilization. Blumenbach allotted the first place on the human classificatory ladder to the Caucasian '*race*' by contending that this stock displays the most handsome features. The other '*races*' are believed to have been degenerates of the Caucasian stock. The Caucasian, White or European 'race' then was made the yardstick with which other '*races*' were measured. Several pseudo-scientific experiments were carried out aimed at proving the intellectual superiority of the European '*race*' (Pieterse, 1995). These '*scientific*' racists employed several techniques and theories, including Craniometry (the technique of measuring the bones of the skull) and Phrenology (a theory claiming to be able to determine character, personality traits, and criminality on the basis of the shape of the head), trying desperately to prove the intellectual, moral and ethic superiority of Whites to non-Whites.

Samuel Morton (1839), the first famous American scientist who claimed to have measured brain capacity through skull size, made systematic errors and skewed his data in favor of his biases. Thus, he concluded that their larger skulls indicated racial superiority (*Race,* 2003). Others measured brain sizes of the so-called races and not surprisingly, concluding that Europeans, particularly Nordic (northern and western European) men had the largest brain size and therefore superior intellect.

In The Eye of the Beholder: Your 'Black' Person is My 'White' Person

It is ironic that race scientists did not provide one standard definition of '*race.*' Even in contemporary times, there lacks a uniform definition of the concept and confusion is rife regarding racial identity in the global community. What constitutes a 'White' person in Brazil, Haiti or Ghana is different from what constitutes a 'White' person in the United States of America or England. In the United States, thanks to the one-drop laws , any degree of African ancestry has historically made a person Black (Rockquemore & Brunsma, 2001). Such is not the case in Latin America or the Caribbean. There, any degree of non-African ancestry means that a person is not Black (Winn, 1995). Thus, the same person defined as Black in the United States may be considered Colored in Jamaica or Martinique and White in the Dominican Republic (Hoetink, 1967).

In Brazil, one survey of Blacks generated forty different words to describe their race or color (Page, 1994). Degler (1971) reports that, some '*Blacks*' in Brazil change their designations as they move to different social classes. Davis (1991) has observed that three fifths of Puerto Ricans who come to the U.S. mainland and are identified as Black were defined differently in their homeland. To a West Indian or African '*Black*' is a literal description; one is Black if one's skin is black. If one is lighter, one would be described as 'middle-class brown' or 'a light chocolate' (Gladwell, 1996).

Even more absurd is the fact that at one point in time, some Europeans were not considered 'White'. The Irish, the Italians, and indeed Mediterranean Europeans were not considered 'White' in the USA; they had to earn their '*whiteness.*' Race was never just a matter of how you looked, it's about how people assign meaning to how you look (*Race*, 2003).

According to historian Robin D. G. Kelley, Africans came to the New World not as Black people, not as Negroes. They didn't see themselves that way. They saw themselves according to their own sort of ethnic identities. The same was true of Europeans who viewed themselves as Portuguese, or English, or Irish (*Race,* 2003). Larry Adelman, Executive Producer of *Race* (2003) adds that the American Indians didn't see themselves as Indians. Nor did the English see themselves as White. Neither saw themselves as a race. Amerindian nations such as the Algonquians differentiated themselves from the Iroquois or Cherokee by religion, language and customs just as Protestant, English-speaking Britain distinguished itself from Catholic, Spanish-speaking Spain. Further, there is no agreed upon way to determine what constitutes '*race.*' Some have used skin color; while others have used facial features, brain size, cranial capacity or skull shape. Some have delineated several '*geographic races*', including the Amerindian, Polynesian, Micronesian, Melanesian, Australian, African, Indian, European and the Asiatic '*races*' (Langone, 1993).

Even more intriguing includes the arbitrary numbers of races various race scientists have introduced. Arthur Gobinneau, who is regarded as the founder of ideological racism, identified three: the European or Caucasian (White) race, the Mongolian or Asiatic (Yellow) race, and the Ethiopian or African (Black) race. Linnaeus (1758) identified four races; Blumenbach (1781) delineated five; Hooton (1926) discovered three; and

Garn (1965) found nine races (Orbe, 2001; Bernasconi, 2000; West, 1982). Hindsight and two hundred years of science tells us that the race scientists were badly mistaken. All the frenetic attempts to categorize the human groups into distinctive '*racial*' groups were discredited with the passage of time. Despite all the efforts by the ideological and intellectual heirs of the race scientists today, it has been shown, due in large part to the completion of the Human Genome Project,that it is illogical to classify the human species into distinctive and separate races or to isolate one pure, unadulterated racial group.

We're All Mongrels!

There is no pure *race*; most people are *racially* mixed. Goodman (2003) notes that all individuals are 'mongrels'; that we are the biological products of mixed ancestry (Race). In fact, Europeans and Americans may be the most blended. Centuries ago, Moors from northern Africa overran Spain and moved to France. The Greeks, Romans, Barbarians and Normans, all occupied southern Italy at various times. Spanish and Native Americans have combined in Mexico and in southern and Central America. A Hawaiian may have a mixture of Caucasian, Chinese, Japanese, Portuguese and Polynesian blood. Angolans may be Black and Portuguese; Cubans and Puerto Ricans may be Black and Spanish. Polynesians are a mixture of Negroid, Mongoloid and Caucasoid blood (Langone, 1993). One in four White Americans have a Black ancestor; three in four Blacks have a White ancestor. These figures may be even higher for Native Americans (Feagin, 2000; Jacobson, 1998).

There are no genetic markers that set the so-called races apart and no objective reason for splitting or lumping at any lower taxonomic level. As Pilar Ossorio points out in *Race* (2003), it is impossible to locate any genetic markers "*that are in everybody of a particular race and in nobody of some other race.*" In fact, 96.8% of the genetic code in Blacks and Whites is shared, with only a maximum of 0.032 of the genes varying between any White or Black person. The variation between Whites and Asians is 0.019 (98.1% similarity), and the difference between Blacks and Asians is 0.047 (95.3% similarity). These differences are far too small to indicate subspeciation, as such phenomenon would typically be characterized by variation many times greater than the above numbers. There are no subspecies of a given phylum with this high a degree of genetic overlap, anywhere in nature (Orbe, 2001). Holmes (2003:5) observed that one is smart if she or he is able to determine her or his '*race*', but even smarter if the individual does *not* know what race she or he is. The findings of the Human Genome Project (Davies, 2001; Hawley & Mori, 1999) and a great number of scholars across the globe appear to have fully discredited scientific racism, at least for now.

Here are a few of the findings based on *Race* (2003):

(1) What has been called '*race*' has no genetic basis. The so-called races share a common gene pool and operate within an open gene system on the basis of what social scientists call "*genetic interchangeability*" (See Omni & Winant, 2001).

(2) Human subspecies don't exist. Unlike many animals modern humans simply have not been around long enough or been isolated enough to evolve into separate subspecies or races. Despite surface appearances, we are one of the most similar of all species.

(3) Most traits are inherited independently from one another. The genes influencing skin color have nothing to do with the genes influencing hair form, eye shape, blood type, musical talent, athletic ability or forms of intelligence.

(4) Most variation is within, not between, '*races*'. Of the small amount of total human variation, 85% exists within any local population. About 94% can be found within any continent.

(5) Slavery predates race. Throughout human history, societies have enslaved others, but due to a unique set of historical circumstances, the European enslavement of Africans was the first instance where all the slaves shared similar physical characteristics. Until then, slavery was '*colorless*'.

(6) Race and freedom evolved together. The United States was founded on the radical new principle that '*All men are created equal.*' However, the slavery based early economy was rationalized by the new idea of '*race*'. This concept justified the denial of rights and freedoms for one group.

(7) Race justified social inequalities as natural. In America, it justified not only slavery but also the extermination of Indians, exclusion of Asian immigrants, and the taking of Mexican lands by a nation that professed a belief in democracy. Racial practices were institutionalized within American government, laws, and society.

(8) Race is not biological, but racism is still real. Race is a powerful social idea that gives people differing access to opportunities and resources. Governments and social institutions have created advantages that disproportionately channel wealth, power, and resources to White people, affecting the whole population.

So why did race scientists go to such lengths to categorize the human groups and assign them different meanings and ranks? These attempts were born out of an ideology of White supremacy, which holds that the White race is superior to the non-White races. '*Scientific*' racism was invented to rationalize this ideology. The ideology of White supremacy itself stemmed from Social Darwinism: a racist, sexist, and classist theory based on the premise of '*survival of the fittest*.' This term, coined by the English sociologist Hebert Spencer, was a vulgarization of a more complex theory by his compatriot Charles Darwin, the theory of evolution by natural selection. Herbert Spencer (1857) perverted Darwinism which sought to explain the origin and evolution of the plant and animal species through natural selection and struggle.

Darwin, Smith, and Spencer: Race, Europe and Social Darwinism

The assumption of Social Darwinism is that some races are endowed with superior genes, while others inherit inferior genes. Those with superior genes are better able to survive, thrive and control their social environments, which include those with inferior genes. Social Darwinists drew on the idea of struggle and survival as natural mechanisms for improving human genetic characteristics. In fact, inferior races and societies, it was hypothesized, would '*naturally*' wither away. Attempts to save them were in defiance of the laws of nature. Subsequently, Adam Smith's laissez faire economic theory (Smith, 1999) which proposed non-governmental intervention in economic affairs of individuals and the promotion of free-market economy based on the '*invisible hands*' of the market, was incorporated into Social Darwinism. The aim was to let the '*natural laws*' of the market take their due course, during which the '*economically deficient*' peoples would be weeded out and the '*economically progressive*' would thrive.

According to Mills (2006), in the 19th century Europeans increasingly became preoccupied, even obsessed, with the concept of race. White European military superiority was attributed to racial superiority while at the same time advances in the biological sciences heavily influenced the social sciences where there was an attempt to perceive of human beings as members of different sub-species or species. This racist thinking contributed to exclusionist ideas of nationalism in which a *'nation'* constituted a *'race'* (e.g., British race, German race, etc.). Mills (2006) suggested that many of the homogenous characteristics (not only physical characteristics but also moral, intellectual and spiritual characteristics) were transmitted genetically, and were thus racial.

Mills (2006) outlines several consequences of Social Darwinism and ultimately, white supremacy. These include:

- Races could be ranked, primarily according to proficiency in subjugating or even exterminating one's opponents; someone who kills with a spear or bow and arrow is more primitive than someone who kills with machine guns and artillery.
- Morality was rejected as a criterion for survivability as nature was considered amoral. Strength became the rationalization for colonization.
- Social Darwinists saw competition and struggle as separating the efficient and able from those less evolved. The economic survival of the fittest was called for.

Mills (2006) contends that Social Darwinists often blamed the government, including policies which relieved unemployment and destitution, as the reason for the contrary outcome. They argued that social welfare measures preserved inferior racial stock and encouraged their reproduction, eventually arguing that society and government should ensure by biological engineering and selective breeding that the superior human species thrived. Eugenics was born, applying to humans practices developed for the breeding of domestic animals. In North America, eugenicists and Social Darwinists tended to focus on immigration policies which focused on passing anti-Asian legislation. Southern, Eastern and Central Europeans immigrants were also held to be inferior, threatening to reduce the quality of the racial stock in Canada.

Christianity, Eurocentrism and Race

The Bible was also used to sanctify race bigotry and social inequality. For example, the Bible's story of Ham's curse suggested that God had ordained Africans to be slaves of Europeans. Euro-Christians came to believe that Africans were descended from Ham who was '*Black*' (Allahar, 1995). This color symbolism in Christianity extended to the image of Christ, '*white*' male. This may also explain why Satan is symbolized by the color black. God created man in His image; Europeans created God in their image.

Two interrelated processes are at play here: (1) a self-fulfilling prophecy and (2) the social construction of reality. W. I. and Dorothy Thomas, positing what is now known as the Thomas Theorem, declared that: "*If men define situations as real, they become real in their consequences*" (Thomas, 1928: 572). Thus, the crucial issue is not so much the actual punishment meted out by Noah to Ham, but rather it is the fact that later Christians came to understand such punishment in a specific way and to act on the basis of that understanding (Allahar, 1995).

Thus, the '*Hamitic curse*' and the color black came to be equated with punishment, evil and sin in Christendom. In the Middle Ages, the tripartite division of the world into Africa, Asia and Europe, as well as the Three Kings or Wise men who came to worship the Christ child, were based on that biblical logic. Saint Simon, one of the founders of Western social thought argued that Europeans are the sons of Abel, and that Asia and Africa inhabited by descendants of Cain. He characterized Africans as '*bloodthirsty*' and Asiatics as '*indolent*' (Eze, 2001; Manuel, 1956).

The color symbolism and the imagery of Eurocentrism succeeded the color symbolism and imagery of Christendom and passed over into European colonialism and slavery. The images of Africans and Blacks in the minds of Euro-Americans were built on such phenomena as the European slave trade, slave-master relationships in the plantations of the Americas, European colonization of the countries of Africa, Asia and Latin America; and White-Anglo-Saxon domination of the social, economic, ideological and political directions of multi-ethnic/multi-racial society (Pieterse 1992).

According to Pieterse (1992), in each of these relationships, Europeans constructed the images of non-European people in general, and of Africans and blacks in particular, on the basis of selective perception, expedience, and second-hand information mingled with reconstructed biblical notions and folklore, along with a dash of scientific ideas that were popular at the time. European views of Africans and their continent are a crystallization of images distilled from the travelogues and accounts of European explorers, Christian missionaries, and colonial (European) administrators. Added to these was imagery taken from popular scientific literature, particularly fiction and yellow journalism. During the colonial period, H. Rider Haggard's type of romantic popular tales, coupled with yellow journalism and pseudo-scientific reportage, painted the image of a dark continent inhabited by rude savages and godless heathens. The colonial remedy to this myth was the civilizing and proselytizing mission of the Christian West (Mezler, 1989).

Although we have come a long way from these influences the mere passage of time is not a proof that things have changed for the better in race relations between people of African descent and their former oppressors, enslavers and exploiters. Time, it is said, heals. Racism, described by Montagu, (1997:1) as "*man's most dangerous myth*" and by Nkrumah (1980: 114) as "*the foulest invention by man*," has over time only managed to mutate into less visible and less reprehensible forms. Contemporary Euro-American society has only temporarily repressed bone-chilling forms of racist evil and aggression. Racism has ceased to be the avowed commitment of Southern white supremacists. It has gone beyond wearing hoods and burning crosses to a more complex, structural, systemic, subtle and insidious idea that has refused to die. In its insidious forms, racism has become an unconscious habit corrupting legions of Whites, including many well-meaning ones.

Racism Continues to Thrive

There are as many definitions of racism as there are scholars studying the subject. According to Fleras & Kunz (2003), the varied definitions of term reflect the following concepts: doctrines, power, structures, prejudice, discrimination, intent, biology and culture. For our purpose, racism is defined as a set of ideas and ideals (ideology) that asserts or implies the superiority of one social group over another on the basis of biological or cultural characteristics, together with the institutionalized power to put these racialized beliefs into practice in a way that has the intent or effect of denying or excluding minority men and women (Flears & Kunz, 2003).

Racism in North America and most of Western Europe today has ceased to be the overt racism of the past. The general consensus is that racism today is generally more subtle, subliminal, polite, sophisticated, and

318 ◄ Chapter 12

covert. It is termed *'colorblind racism'* (Myers, 2006; Mulinari & Neergaard, 2005; Fekete, 2005, 2001; Hansen, 2004; Feagin, 2001; Kundnani, 2001; Bonilla-Silva & Forman, 2000; Essed, 1991). In Canada, some scholars even call it *'democratic racism'* (Henry & Tator, 2006; Fleras, 2001) as if there could be anything democratic about racism.

Social scientists such as Michael Baton (1970) and William Julius Wilson (1978) have for different reasons, declared racism to be dead. In his book, *The Idea of Race*, Baton contended that since the ideas that formed the bedrock of scientific racism until the middle of the past century are now discredited, racism is dead. Wilson (1978) declared that there was a declining significance of race in the United States. The supporting evidence for his triumphant declaration was to be found in the improved living conditions of African Americans and the emergent Black middle class. Of course, both of these declarations were not only overly optimistic (Satzewitch, 1998) they smacked of denial. They seemed to have been misled or pacified by the new, benign form of racism of the immediate post-Civil Rights era.

Baton and Wilson are not alone in this culture of optimism and wishful thinking. The benign, smiling face of racism today has made people of all complexions complacent. They console themselves with the usual refrain: *'We have come a long way indeed'*. They take tokenism (e.g., the hiring of a handful of Blacks for window dressing by some White employers) as improved race relations. They take examples of a number of Black men and women such as Colin Powell and Condoleeza Rice ascent to powerful government positions and the emergent success and wealth of African American entertainers and athletes as clear indications of race relations having improved vastly. The election of Barack Obama as the first African American President of the United States; something I would call significant tokenism. It would however be premature to attribute Obama's ascendancy to the most powerful position in the American government to radically transform race relations.

The New Racisms: Racism in the 21st Century

The fact that racism has changed its appearance and form makes it more insidious and treacherous. As it is said in Ghana, *'the snake under the grass is more dangerous than the snake on the tree for you can see the snake on the tree and know how to handle it (kill it or run away) but you cannot avoid the snake under the grass since it cannot be seen and therefore bites you without your noticing it.*' No form of racism around the world is better than any another. In all cases, lives are destroyed. People are harmed physically, psychologically, and emotionally. Racism in any form, quantity, or shape must not be tolerated.

Victims of racism cannot fight this malady alone. The healing process must involve both Whites and Blacks. Like a parasite, racism needs a host to thrive. To heal society of the disease of racism, both the parasite and the host must be treated. Racism is *dialectical*; it affects the victimized and the victimizer, both of whom must also be conscious of and alert to history and the changing realities of today. Victims and victimizers must acknowledge that all humans harbor and manifest prejudices, and that prejudice whether backed by power (racism) or not (race prejudice) is destructive. It hurts, impacts economically, it offends, destroys and kills (Feagin & McKinney, 2003). All people, whether dominant, majority or minority, are culpable, and do hurt people through their prejudices. Therefore, as Orbe (2003) notes, before we tell others to get out of their boxes, we must be prepared to get out of our boxes first. This should not be interpreted as '*distributive racism.*'

It would be incorrect to apportion blame to the victims of racism and the perpetrators of racism equally. Prejudice should not be confused with racism. Prejudice and stereotyping are symptoms: manifestations of an ongoing tug-of-war between groups over economic, political and social resources. While all people harbor prejudices about other human groups and stereotype out-groups, not all people are in a position to discriminate on a systematic basis.

It is a universal human impulse to use stereotypes to rationalize primitive fears and suspicions (Berger, 1999). People, irrespective of race or ethnicity, use stereotypes as mental templates as they navigate the complex world. Thus, stereotypes and prejudice, while universal, cut across racial and ethnic lines and are not the real problems. The real issue is the translation of prejudices and stereotypes into acts of discrimination at the personal, state, and systemic levels.

Feagin and Vera (1995) rightly insist that racism was more than a matter of individual prejudice and scattered episodes of discrimination. Arguing that there was no black racism in the United States, Feagin and Vera (1995) contend that there is no centuries-old system of racialized subordination and discrimination designed by African Americans to exclude white Americans from full participation in the rights, privileges, and benefits of this society. Thus, for example, while Black Britons may harbor anti-White British prejudice and stereotype all Whites and even act out their race prejudice or exhibit race animus from time to time, it is White Britons who are in the position to discriminate systematically against their Black compatriots. While White British racists, generally speaking, have a panoply of supporting institutions and agencies (state, judicial system, law enforcement agencies, media, educational system and general culture) Black Britons do not have sufficient resources to act out their race prejudice on a systematic basis. The system simply crushes those who try. Racism transcends stereotypes and individual prejudice. It is systemic, built into the culture, social institutions, and social structures.

Combating Racism through Education and Praxis

French philosopher Jean Jacques Rousseau (2003) said that '*man is born free but is everywhere in chains.*' Infants tend to freely relate to children across the color line. However, the quickly learn the danger involved in playing and interacting with children beyond their racial pale. All too soon, the children's innate freedom is constricted with '*chains*' everywhere.

Thandeka (2000) alludes to the Rousseauian chains in her book *Learning to be White*. Calling the process abuse, she explains the socialization processes that children, particularly Euro-American children, go through to avoid the racial '*other*'. Thandeka begins with the premise that Euro-American children learn to be White and asserts that this process is a form of abuse. White America's racial victim is its own child, she writes caustically, noting that most very young Euro-American children, for example, have not yet learned to avoid making African American friends or to think of such people as inferior. They learn to think of themselves as White, however, and only play with those from within their own racial community in order to avoid emotional abandonment and even physical abuse from their caretakers.

Thandeka concludes that the internal nonwhite zone was the killing fields of desire, the place where impulses to community with persons beyond the pale are slaughtered. The child develops antipathy toward its own forbidden feelings and to the persons who are the objects of these forbidden desires: the racial other. The child and then the adult learns how to suppress such risky feelings of camaraderie with persons beyond the community's racial pale in order to decrease the possibility of being exiled from his or her own community.

From the discussion above, it is clear that any hope of fighting racism must begin with the future parents, workers, chief executive officers, politicians, teachers and journalists. For, as the first victims of racism, they are also the easiest to redeem. It is important to educate them very early on about the social policies and institutional practices that advantage some groups at the expense of others (Feagin & McKinney, 2003).

Many people know that racism is a negative bad, yet they do nothing to end it. In fact, their inaction contributes to and reinforces racism. Racism persists not just because people are powerless to challenge and end it, but because it is seen as legitimate in the eyes of many. As Myers (2006) notes in spite of its oppressive nature, oppressive structures, including racism are considered to be legitimate because people see them as unchangeable, a fact of reality that just is. Arguing that racism is hegemonic, Myers (2006) states that many people adopt a colorblind attitude toward racism because they have no viable alternatives, and they do not recognize that North American society as inherently unfair. When a system is hegemonic, it is so pervasive and taken for granted that people are unable to step back, see it for what it is, and challenge it. (Myers 2006; also see Gramsci (1975, 1932).

Anthony Giddens' (1984) theory of positionality sheds further light on how racism persists notwithstanding the fact that most people acknowledge its pernicious effects. The central premise of positionality is that people's positions affect their identities, access to resources, and range of possible actions. Giddens (1984) also posits that people carefully negotiate power and privilege in their everyday interactions via reflexivity. Thus, people benefit from acting in ways that insulate rather than threaten their privilege. Myers (2006) points out that, privileges are made possible by one's position in the structure. Thus, people act rationally when they reinforce structural power differentials, even though such actions help not only to reify but also support and reinforce racism. Racism persists because of real or imagined threats to dominants' material standing, through competition for jobs, housing, schools, etc.

(Feagin & Herman, 2001; Fleras, 2000; Doob, 1999; Takaki, 1994; Bell, 1992).

Myers (2006) argues that Whites have historically fought to insulate and protect themselves from outsiders. The outcome, she points out, was racist oppression. Racism persists because the sense of threat persists. She argues that racism is dialectical, existing at three levels: *structural* (hierarchical), *interactional* and *ideological*. Structural racism allocates differential opportunities on the basis of race. For a hierarchical structure to persist and affect people, they must buy into and subscribe to its procedures. People act; thus racism operates on the interactional level at which they engage in racist practices, both knowingly and unknowingly. People may not view their racist behavior as problematic even if they recognize it. This lack of antiracist-consciousness is explained by ideological racism, which is a belief system that legitimizes racist structures and practices. People are born into or migrate to this society in which racism has existed and mutated over centuries. Over time, differential treatment of people of color becomes normalized, expected, and de rigueur.

Thus, racism, Myers (2006) explains, is hegemonic in that it is so much part of the fabric of people's past and present lives that it is often invisible or appears to be inevitable. The hegemony of racism makes it difficult to recognize, discuss, and challenge (Myers, 2006; Gramsci, 1932, 1975). Bigotry is learned through the various agents of socialization (e.g., family, peers, the educational system, mass media). Individuals are products of the socio-cultural systems into which they are born. Thus, racism is learned in the social context. It is a social construct; it is not innate or biologically predetermined.

Persons do also posses and exercise agency or free will (Johnson, 2000). While individuals may be socialized through afore-mentioned areas, they are capable of unlearning racism through the usage of logic. Berger and Luckman (1966) and Giddens (1984) proposed theories of the duality of structure and agency, arguing that while individuals act on things, their actions take place within the context of social structures and that at the same time individuals are not hopelessly disempowered by social structures. They posit a dialectic between individual powerlessness in the face of powerful social forces and human agency; the ability to innovate, create, challenge and resist. Long before Berger, Luckman and Giddens, Marx (1852) had astutely noted the dialectic of structure and agency when he stated: *"While men are changed by circumstances, circumstances are changed precisely by men."*

How do people make the systems of social injustice and inequality, such as sexism, racism, and privilege, happen? People perpetuate systems of social injustice by adopting what Johnson (2000) refers to as 'paths *of least resistance,*' one of which is silence. To perpetuate a system of oppression and privilege, we do not have to do something consciously to support it. Our silence is enough to ensure its future. No system of social oppression can continue to exist without most people choosing to remain silent about it. Johnson posits that if most Whites spoke out about racism, it would be the first step toward a revolutionary change. Unfortunately, many individuals simply choose the paths of least resistance and remain silent on racism, and it is easy for ethnic/racial minorities to read their silence as support for the system (Johnson, 2000).

Conclusion

In this article, *'race'* is argued to be a compelling social construct. While *'race'* does not exist as a biological fact, racism, the practical manifestation of race exists. Further, although the idea of race has been discredited, at least in the scientific community, racism continues to be perpetuated. Racism is *structural*, that is, it is tied to social structures and institutions. Thus, until these structures are reconstituted or replaced, curtailing its spread will be difficult.

Given that social structures and institutions are created by people, it is plausible to posit that change is possible. The UNESCO constitution rightly notes that wars begin in the minds of [men], and that it is in the minds of [men] that the defenses of peace must be constructed. It is humans who create(d) and reinforce racism; it is precisely they who can dismantle it. Education is of paramount importance in combating racism. If the history of multicultural education in the past century is any guide, anti-racist pedagogy in the 21st century must take a radically different direction. Thus, the fight against racism requires multiple and evolving strategies. The ever-changing, elusive nature of racism requires unending, tireless and all-inclusive ant-racist strategies, policies and actions on all fronts: activist, intellectual, religious/spiritual, and the mundane. I do not share the pessimism and fatalism of those who see racism as immutable, and racist society as incorrigible.

The cardinal question that has for a long time exercised the minds of a number of scholars is, if '*race*' does not exist as a biological and even empirical fact, then why the continued use of the term? Segall (1999) has suggested that merely treating the social construct of '*race*' as if it were a biological reality is itself '*racist*' and should be resisted vigorously as one resists racial discrimination. This argument misses the point, to say the least. The fact that race is not a biological entity, does not mean it is not real. There are legions of social realities that are real and yet not biological. The context of race has influences on where individuals will live, what schools they will go to, what jobs they may attain, whether or not they will have health insurance (*Race,* 2003).

To underscore '*race*' as Segall suggests is not only myopic, it is dangerous for it leaves intact the structural and systemic bases that nourishes racism. Like colorblind racism, dismissing or downplaying race does a significant disservice to the discourse of justice and offers little to addressing its implications. As Esch and Reodiger (2007) remind us, the way to non-racialism is through race. In other words, racism can only be combated when people acknowledge the powerful and destructive reality of race. The racialized societies of the 21st century have been under construction for more than three centuries.

Racism, as has been amply shown, is a human invention. While combating racism is a daunting task, it can be argued that since society has *made* it, it can also *unmake* it. It took more than three centuries and a civil war, millions of lost lives to cure America of its virulent addiction: slavery. One should have no illusion that slaying the beast of racism, the child of slavery, will be even more difficult. Combating racism in the 21st century will requires more than academic discourse and political pontification. Anti-racist education must transcend the moralism of the victim groups and the intellectual elite to include all: victims, victimizers, racialized and the '*raceless*,' White and Non-Whites, young and old.

The fight against racism must leave no one behind, evolving around a rainbow coalition and more. Even more importantly, anti-racist education must begin in the formative years of children, in the primary schools and be reinforced throughout the school years. Anti-racism education should play an integral part of the educational curriculum if we hope to achieve social justice. Finally, anti-racist education must be creatively and dialectically praxis-oriented, transcending the classrooms and lecture halls to communities and the lifeworlds of all constituent ethno-racial groups, and transforming social and political structures that distribute valued social goods and resources.

References

Allahar, A.L. (1995). *Sociology and the Periphery: Theories and Issues.* Toronto,ON: Garamond Press.

Alderman, L. (Producer). (2003). *Race: the Power of an Illusion.: Episode I.* [Video Documentary] California Newsreel: Public Broadcasting Service

Baton, M. (1970). *The Idea of Race.* London: Tavistock.

Bell, D. (1992). *Faces at the Bottom of the Well.* New York, NY: Basic.

Begley, S. (1995). Three is not enough. *Newsweek.* Vo/7. Number 21, 67-69.

Berger, Maurice. (1999). *White Lies.* New York, NY: Farrar, Straus & Giroux.

Berger, P. and Luckman, T. (1966). *The Social Construction of Reality: A Treatise in the Sociology of Knowledge.* Garden City, NY: Doubleday.

Bernasconi, R.& Lott, T. (2000). *The Idea of Race.* Indianapolis, IN: Hackett.

Bober, M. (1965). *Karl Marx's Interpretation of History.* New York, NY: W.W. Norton & Company.

Boxill, B. (2001). *Race and Racism.* Oxford: Oxford University Press.

Chase, Allan. (1976). *The Legacy of Malthus: The Social Costs of the New Scientific Racism.* New York, NY: Alfred A. Knopf.

Davis, F. J. (1991). *Who's Black: One Nation's Definition.* University Park: University of Pennsylvania.

Davies, K. (2001). *Cracking the Genome: Inside the Race to Unlock Human DNA.* XX: Free Press.

Degler, C. N. (1971). *Neither Black nor White: Slavery and Race Relations in Brazil and the United States.* New York: McMillan.

Diamond, J. (1994 November). Race without Color. *Discovery,* 82-89.

Doob, C. B. (1999). *Racism: An American Cauldron.* New York, NY: Longman.

Ebenstein, W. (Ed.) (1960). *Modern Political Thought: The Great Issues 2nd ed.* New York, NY: Holt, Rinehart & Winston.

Esch and Roediger. (2006). Non-racialism through Race. *The New Socialist*. Retrieved December, 2006. http://newsocialist.org/newsite/index.php?id=848

Essed, P. (1991). *Understanding Everyday Racism: An Interdisciplinary Theory*. Newbury Park, CA: Sage.

Eze, E.C. (2001). *Race and the Enlightenment*. Massachusetts: Blackwell.

Feagin J.R. (2000). *Racist America: Roots, Current Realities and Future Reparations*. New York, NY: Basic.

Feagin, J.R. & Herman, V. (2001). *White Racism: The Basics*. New York, NY: Routledge.

Feagin, J.R. & Herman, V. (1995). *White Racism: The Basics*. New York, NY: Routledge.

Feagin, J.R. & McKinney, K.D. (2003). *The Many Costs of Racism*. Lanham: Rowan & Littlefield.

Fleras, A. & Kunz, J. L. (2001) *Media and Minorities: Representing Diversity in a Multicultural Canada*. Toronto, ON: Thompson Educational Publishing.

Fekete, L. (2005, July). The deportation machine: Europe, asylum and human rights. *Race & Class*. 47: 64-78.

_____(2001, October). The Emergence of Xeno-Racism. *Race & Class*. 43: 23-40.

Fredrickson, G. M. (1985). *The Black Image in the White Mind: The Debate on Afro-American Character and Destiny*. New York, NY: Harper & Row.

Giddens, A. (1984). *The Constitution of Society*. Berkeley: University of California Press.

Gladwell, M. (1996 April/May). Black like them. *The New Yorker*, 74-80.

Gosset, T. F. (1963). *Race: The History of an Idea in America*. New York, NY: Schoeken.

Gould, S. J. (1996). *The Mismeasure of Man.* New York: W.W. Norton & Company.Gramsci, A. (1932/1975. *Letters from Prison*: *Antonio Gramsci*. L. Lawner (ed.) New York, NY: Harper Colophon.

Hansen, P. (2004, January). In the Name of Europe. *Race & Class*. 45: 49-61.

Hawley, R. S., & Mori, C. A. (1999). *The Human Genome: A User's Guide*. New York: Academic Press.

Henry, F. & Tator, C. (2006). *The Colour of Democracy: Racism in Canadian Society*. Toronto: Thompson-Nelson .

Hoetink, H. (1967). *Caribbean Race Relations: A Study of Two Variants*. New York: Oxford University Press.

Jacobson, M. F. (1998). *Whiteness of a Different Color: European Immigrants and the Alchemy of Race*. Cambridge, MA: Harvard University Press.

Johnson, A. (2000). *Privilege, Power and Difference*. New York: McGraw-Hill.

Johnson, S. (2006). *The Sin of Racism: How to be Set Free*. Lanham: Rowan & Littlefield.

Kenworthy L.S. (1946, Spring). James K. Aggrey: Reconciler of Races. *The Journal of Negro Education*, 15, 2: 181-190.

Kundnani, A. (2001, October). In a Foreign Land: The New Popular Racism. *Race & Class*. 43: 41-60.

Kuper, L (1965). Levi-Strauss, Claude: Race and History, *Race, Science, and Society*. 95-134.

Kupperman, K.O. (2000). *Indians and English: Facing Off in North America*. Cornell University Press.

Langone, J. (1993). *Spreading Poison: Racism and Prejudice*. New York, NY: Little Brown.

Lasker, G. W. & Tyzzer, R. N. (1982). *Physical Anthropology*. New York, NY: Holt.

Manuel, F. E. (1956). *The New World of Henri Saint Simon*. Cambridge, MA: Havard University Press.

Marx, K. (1852). "The Eighteenth Brumaire of Louis Bonaparte." [Pamphlet]. *Die Revolution*. New York, NY: Weydemeyer.

Mezler, V. (1989). Africa through racist spectacles. *African Events*.12.

Mills, W.G. (2006) *Racism and Social Darwinism*, Lecture Notes. Retrieved September 30, 2006 http://stmarys.ca/~wmills/course203/8Racism.html

Montagu, A. (1997). *Man's Most Dangerous Myth: The Fallacy of Race*. (6th ed.) Walnut Creek, CA: Alta Mira.

Morton, S. G. (1839). *Crania Americana*. New York: John Penningon

Mulinari, D. & Neergaard, A. (2005, January). 'Black skull' consciousness: the new Swedish working class. *Race & Class*. 46: 55-72.

Myers, K. (2006). *Racetalk: Racism Hiding in Plain Sight*. Lanham: Rowan & Littlefield,

Nash, Gary. (1999). *Forbidden Love: The Secret History of Mixed Race America*. New York: Edge Books.

Nkrumah, K. (1980). *Axioms of Kwame Nkrumah*. London: PANAF.

Omni, M. & Winant, H. (2001). Racial Formations. In Rothenburg , P.S.(ed). *Race, Class, and Gender in the United States*. New York, NY: Worth.

Orbe, M. P. (2001). *Interracial Communication: Theory into Practice*. Belmont,CA: Wardsworth/Thompson.

Page, C. (1994, January 5). Uneasy Journey to Political Correctness. *Louisville Courier-Journal*, A. 19.

Pieterse, J.N. (1992). *White on Black: Images of Africa and Blacks in Western Popular Culture*. New Haven: Yale University Press.

Quist-Adade, C. (2005, December). What is Race? What is Racism? *New African*. 446.

Rocquemore, K.A.& Brunsma, D.L. (2001). *Beyond Black*. Thousand Oaks, CA: Sage.

Rousseau, J.J. (2003). *The Social Contract*. New York, NY: Dover .

Satzewitch, V. (1998). *Racism and Social Inequality in Canada*. Toronto, ON: Thompson.

Segall, M. (1999). Why is there racism if there is no such thing as "race"? Conference transcripts http://www.vtpu.org.au/pastactivities/conferences/crc.php

Smith, Adam. (1999). *The Wealth of Nations*. London: Penguin Books.

Snowden, F. (1970). *Blacks in Antiquity: Ethiopians in Greco-Roman Experience*. MA: Belknap.

Spencer, H. (1857, April). Progess: Its Law and Causes, *The Westminster Review*, 67.

Spickard, P.R. (1992). The illogic of American Race Categorization. In M.P.P.Rott (ed.) *Racially Mixed People in America* .12-23. Newbury Park, CA: Sage.

Takaki, R. (1994). *A Different Mirror*. Boston, MA: Little, Brown.

Thandeka. (2000). *Learning to Be White: Money, Race and God in America*. New York, NY: Continuum.

UNESCO (1965). "Four Statements on the Race Question," in *Race, Science, and Society*, supra, at 341-64.

West, Cornel, et al. (1982). *Theology in the Americas*: Detroit II Conference Papers, NY: Orbis Books.

Wilson, W.J. (1978). *The Declining Significance of Race, 2nd ed.* Chicago,IL: University of Chicago.

Winn, P. (1995). *Americans: The Changing Face of Latin America and the Caribbean*. New York, NY: Pantheon.

CHAPTER 13
THE EVOLUTION OF PRIVACY

Frank Tridico

Abstract: While privacy has been given Constitutional legitimacy through landmark cases, most of these have been limited in numbers and recently decided. The Supreme Court has historically maintained a conservative ideological structure, one which has largely resisted overtures for federal incorporation of the Bill of Rights. The Due Process Revolution of the 1960s was an exception, incorporating Fourth, Fifth and Sixth Amendments into landmark rulings that furthered civil liberties while specifically limiting the power of the State vis-à-vis prosecutors and law enforcement. Through this momentum, the Court then advanced a liberal agenda of contraception, abortion and sodomy. While landmark gains in the 1960s were attained through the textualist approach (specific rights entrenched in Amendments), liberal gains were won on the concept of privacy, which is not specifically mentioned in the document. This raises a number of concerns over the role of the Supreme Court and how justice is defined.

In his confirmation hearings to the Supreme Court, Judge Robert Bork criticized the general and undefined right of privacy he claimed was "*invented*" in *Griswold v. Connecticut.* Opponents of his confirmation charged that Bork did not think Americans should enjoy privacy. Although Bork was denied access to the Court, he did underscore a historical ideological divide on the concept of privacy. Conservative Justices have contended that privacy is not specifically found within the text of the Constitution. Libertarians have argued that privacy is found within the Fourth Amendment but limited in its scope. Liberals have contended that privacy, although not specifically mentioned, can be deemed to be a fundamental right within the context of the Fourteenth Amendment's Equal Protection Clause.

In order to fully address the context of the discourse, it is necessary to given an historical account of the cases, extract the exact words used by Justices in their decisions, and then analyze them within the contexts of Constitutional legitimacy and social justice.

Griswold v. Connecticut (The Right to Contraception)

Griswold v. Connecticut, 381 U.S. 479 (1965), served as the first instrumental step in other gains made on privacy issues. This was a U.S. Supreme Court landmark case that accorded Constitutional protection for privacy rights. The case examined a Connecticut law that prohibited the use of contraceptives. By a majority vote of 7-2, the Supreme Court invalidated the law on the grounds that it violated the right to marital privacy.

Background of the Case

Appellant Griswold was the Executive Director of the Planned Parenthood League of Connecticut. Appellant Buxton was a licensed physician and a professor at the Yale Medical School. Both Griswold and Buxton were arrested after they provided information, instruction, and medical advice to married parties to prevent pregnancy through contraception.

Connecticut statute 53-32 accounted: "*Any person who uses any drug, medicinal article or instrument for the purpose of preventing conception shall be fined not less than fifty dollars or imprisoned not less than sixty days nor more than one year or be both fined and imprisoned.*"

The General Statutes of Connecticut Section 54-196 provided that "*Any person who assists, abets, counsels, causes, hires or commands another to commit any offense may be prosecuted and punished as if he were the principal offender.*"

The appellants were found guilty as accessories and fined $100 each. This prompted the parties to appeal to the Supreme Court on the basis that the law violated their Fourteenth Amendment rights.

Written Opinion of the Court

Justice Douglas provided the majority opinion:

"(Sic) The association of people is not mentioned in the Constitution nor in the Bill of Rights. The right to educate a child in a school of the parents' choice - whether public or private or parochial - is also not mentioned. Nor is the right to study any particular subject or any foreign language. Yet the First Amendment has been construed to include certain of those rights.

By *Pierce v. Society of Sisters*, supra, the right to educate one's children as one chooses is made applicable to the States by the force of the First and Fourteenth Amendments. By Meyer v. Nebraska, supra, the same dignity is given the right to study the German language in a private school. In other words, the State may not, consistently with the spirit of the First Amendment, contract the spectrum of available knowledge...And so we reaffirm the principle of the Pierce and the Meyer cases.

In *NAACP v. Alabama* we protected the "freedom to associate and privacy in one's associations," noting that freedom of association was a peripheral First Amendment right. Disclosure of membership lists of a constitutionally valid association, we held, was invalid "as entailing the likelihood of a substantial restraint upon the exercise by petitioner's members of their right to freedom of association." Ibid.

In other words, the First Amendment has a penumbra where privacy is protected from governmental intrusion. The right of "association," like the right of belief (Board of Education v. Barnette, 319 U.S. 624), is more than the right to attend a meeting; it includes the right to express one's attitudes or philosophies by membership in a group or by affiliation with it or by other lawful means. Association in that context is a form of expression of opinion; and while it is not expressly included in the First Amendment its existence is necessary in making the express guarantees fully meaningful.

The foregoing cases suggest that specific guarantees in the Bill of Rights have penumbras, formed by emanations from those guarantees that help give them life and substance. Various guarantees create zones of privacy. The right of association contained in the penumbra of the First Amendment is one, as we have seen. The Third Amendment in its prohibition against the quartering of soldiers "in any house" in time of peace without the consent of the owner is another facet of that privacy. The Fourth Amendment explicitly affirms the "right of the people to be secure in their persons, houses, papers, and effects, against unreasonable searches and seizures." The Fifth Amendment in its Self-Incrimination Clause enables the citizen to create a zone of privacy which government may not force him to surrender to his detriment. The Ninth Amendment provides: "The enumeration in the Constitution, of certain rights, shall not be construed to deny or disparage others retained by the people."

The Fourth and Fifth Amendments were described…as protection against all governmental invasions "of the sanctity of a man's home and the privacies of life."

We have had many controversies over these penumbral rights of "privacy and repose." These cases bear witness that the right of privacy which presses for recognition here is a legitimate one.

The present case, then, concerns a relationship lying within the zone of privacy created by several fundamental constitutional guarantees. And it concerns a law which, in forbidding the use of contraceptives rather than regulating their manufacture or sale, seeks to achieve its goals by means having a maximum destructive impact upon that relationship. Such a law cannot stand in light of the familiar principle, so often applied by this Court, that a "governmental purpose to control or prevent activities constitutionally subject to state regulation may not be achieved by means which sweep unnecessarily broadly and thereby invade the area of protected freedoms." Would we allow the police to search the sacred precincts of marital bedrooms for telltale signs of the use of contraceptives? The very idea is repulsive to the notions of privacy surrounding the marriage relationship.

We deal with a right of privacy older than the Bill of Rights- older than our political parties, older than our school system. Marriage is a coming together for better or for worse, hopefully enduring, and intimate to the degree of being sacred. It is an association that promotes a way of life, not causes; a harmony in living, not political faiths; a bilateral loyalty, not commercial or social projects. Yet it is an association for as noble a purpose as any involved in our prior decisions. *Reversed.*"

Dissenting Opinions on Griswold

Not all Justices agreed with privacy being a Constitutional right. Justice Black, with whom Justice Stewart held dissenting opinions:

"(Sic) The Court talks about a constitutional "right of privacy" as though there is some constitutional provision or provisions forbidding any law ever to be passed which might abridge the "privacy" of individuals. But there is not. There are, of course, guarantees in certain specific constitutional provisions which are designed in part to protect privacy at certain times and places with respect to certain activities. Such, for example, is the Fourth Amendment's guarantee against "unreasonable searches and seizures." But I think it belittles that Amendment to talk about it as though it protects nothing but "privacy."

To treat it that way is to give it a niggardly interpretation, not the kind of liberal reading I think any Bill of Rights provision should be given. The average man would very likely not have his feelings soothed any more by having his property seized openly than by having it seized privately and by stealth. He simply wants his property left alone. And a person can be just as much, if not more, irritated, annoyed and injured by an unceremonious public arrest by a policeman as he is by a seizure in the privacy of his office or home.

One of the most effective ways of diluting or expanding a constitutionally guaranteed right is to substitute for the crucial word or words of a constitutional guarantee another word or words, more or less flexible and more or less restricted in meaning. This fact is well illustrated by the use of the term "right of privacy" as a comprehensive substitute for the Fourth Amendment's guarantee against "unreasonable searches and seizures." "Privacy" is a broad, abstract and ambiguous concept which can easily be shrunken in meaning but which can also, on the other hand, easily be interpreted as a constitutional ban against many things other than searches and seizures. I like my privacy as well as the next one, but I am nevertheless compelled to admit that government has a right to invade it unless prohibited by some specific constitutional provision. For these reasons I cannot agree with the Court's judgment and the reasons it gives for holding this Connecticut law unconstitutional.

The due process argument which my Brothers Harlan and White adopt here is based, as their opinions indicate, on the premise that this Court is vested with power to invalidate all state laws that it considers to be arbitrary, capricious, unreasonable, or oppressive, or on this Court's belief that a particular state law under scrutiny has no "rational or justifying" purpose, or is offensive to a "sense of fairness and justice." If these formulas based on "natural justice," or others which mean the same thing, are to prevail, they require judges to determine what is or is not constitutional on the basis of their own appraisal of what laws are unwise or unnecessary. The power to make such decisions is of course that of a legislative body. Surely it has to be admitted that no provision of the Constitution specifically gives such blanket power to courts to exercise such a supervisory veto over the wisdom and value of legislative policies and to hold unconstitutional those laws which they believe unwise or dangerous (Sic)."

Analysis of Griswold and the Conception of Privacy

Although there is no declarative textual mention of '*privacy*' within the Constitution, Justice Douglas who wrote the opinion of the majority argued that privacy was to be found the "*penumbras*" and "*emanations*" of other constitutional protections. Justice Goldberg, in a concurring opinion, went further. He argued that the Ninth Amendment (of the Bill of Rights) gave direct extension of privacy rights. Further, Justices Harlan and White went beyond this and centered on the due process clause of the Fourteenth Amendment as providing such a right.

Dissenting Justices Black and Stewart vehemently denied that privacy could be found within constitutional doctrine. If it could not be extracted textually, how then could it be a constitutional right. Justice Black criticized the interpretations of the Ninth and Fourteenth Amendments to which his fellow Justices adhered.

Thus, where no direct mention of '*privacy*' could be found, those who invalidated the Connecticut statute did so on the basis that such a right to privacy could be *inferred* from various areas of the Constitution and Amendments. This interpretive process by the Court set the stage for precedent, where future cases such as *Roe v. Wade* (1973) could be examined in similar light. The liberal shift of the Court in later rulings was substantiated with the due process rationale utilized by Justice Harlan. This marked the start of what many conservatives charged was judicial activism.

Although the Connecticut statute remained law since 1879, it was rarely enforced. There were some tests of the law's constitutionality. Two cases, *Tileston v. Ullman* (1943) and *Poe v. Ullman* (1961) were dismissed on technical grounds. Proponents of the due process model argued that the Court's apparent unwillingness to hear the cases was a sign that it could be ruled unconstitutional. Justice Harlan gave one of the strongest dissenting opinions ever in arguing that the Court should have heard the case (*Poe*) rather than dismissing it. Harlan favored a broader interpretation of the due process clause.

In that case, Harlan argued, "*the full scope of the liberty guaranteed by the Due Process Clause cannot be found in or limited by the precise terms of the specific guarantees elsewhere provided in the Constitution. This 'liberty' is not a series of isolated points pricked out in terms of the taking of property; the freedom of speech, press, and religion; the right to keep and bear arms; the freedom from unreasonable searches and seizures; and so on. It is a rational continuum which, broadly speaking, includes a freedom from all substantial arbitrary impositions and purposeless restraints.*"

Harlan's due process approach was utilized four years later in *Griswold*. This would serve as the precedent case that would set the course for the broader expansion of privacy rights. The three privacy victories that grew from Griswold's methodology were:

(1) ***Eisenstadt v. Baird (1972)***. Here, Harlan's interpretation of the Equal Protection Clause of the Fourteenth Amendment extended privacy rights for usage of contraceptives from married couples to unmarried couples.

(2) ***Roe v. Wade (1973)***. The Court ruled that this law was a violation of the Due Process Clause of the Fourteenth Amendment. The law was struck down, legalizing abortion for women up through the first trimester, and some restrictions for the second and third trimesters.

(3) ***Lawrence v. Texas (2003)***. The Court ruled that state law prohibiting sodomy between homosexuals was unconstitutional. This essentially overruled a decision 17 years earlier in *Bowers v. Hardwick* (1986) which upheld a Georgia statute prohibiting sodomy. The Fourteenth Amendment was used again in this case to grant privacy rights over intimate relations.

Eisenstadt v. Baird (1972) extended privacy rights of contraception for all couples. *Roe v. Wade* (1973) extended privacy rights for abortion for women. *Lawrence v. Texas* (2003) extended privacy rights to gay Americans over intimate relations. It can be argued then, that the Equal Protection Clause of the Fourteenth Amendment was essential in interpreting privacy rights where the Constitution fails to textually address it.

Uniqueness of the Decision

What is intriguing is that although majority Justices used the interpretive approach, not all used the same methodology. Indeed, some found an interpretation of privacy within the "*penumbras*" and "*emanations*" of other Amendments. Many liberal Justices have utilized the Equal Protection Clause of the Fourteenth Amendment in to incorporate various Amendments in the Bill of Rights to interpret privacy rights. Justice Douglas viewed the First, Fourth and Fifth Amendments as having them within their context. Justice Goldberg went on to focus exclusively on the Ninth Amendment. The latter is most intriguing, as most legal scholars argue that individual rights are limited to the first eight Amendments. Indeed, some have gone as far as to describe the Bill of Rights as only encompassing the first eight Amendments rather than ten.

Goldberg traces his logic to the arguments of the framers of the Constitution. The struggle to include the Bill of Rights was won by anti-federalists who were concerned that the new system threatened individual liberties. The original Constitution, as proposed in 1787 in Philadelphia and as ratified by the states, contained very few individual rights guarantees. The framers contended that the Constitution protected liberty primarily through its division of powers that made it difficult for oppressive majorities to form and capture power to be used against minorities. The anti-federalists were not convinced that this would be a sufficient safeguard and sought to include the Bill of Rights.

Justice Goldberg referenced statements of Madison and Story to argue that the Framers did not intend that the first eight amendments be construed to exhaust the basic and fundamental rights which the Constitution guaranteed to the people. He argues that the Ninth Amendment provides sufficient context to interpret privacy rights.

The dissenters maintained the traditional rigid constructionist approach: if privacy could not be specifically found within the text of the Constitution, then it could not be interpreted. Such an interpretation based on invalidating state laws, regardless of how "*arbitrary or capricious*" they could be would compromise the legitimacy of the Court. For conservatives, this amounts to judicial activism and perverts the role of the judiciary.

Are Justices legislating from the bench when they interpret the Constitution? Two considerations come into play here. First, by accepting to hear the case, the Court places itself in the line of judicial fire. It cannot escape charges of politicization because any decision it renders will have implications that extend beyond the legal system, and into the political and social realms. Second, by already having ruled on previous cases, precedence has been set. By clarifying *'privacy rights'* in prior cases, the Court, through its acceptance to hear the case, engaged in a struggle over how far the right of privacy should expand. Liberals won the struggle.

The victory for liberal agenda should be seen as the conservative rule (generally after the *Roe* decision in 1973) to refrain from challenging liberal landmark cases through other cases. Only in select cases, such as in *Lawrence v. Texas* (2003), has the Court essentially overturned earlier landmark decisions. There have been no challenges toward privacy cases that used selective incorporation approaches of the Fourth and Fifth Amendments in the 1960s (e.g., Miranda, exclusionary rule). Conservatives have restricted their ideological battles to two key areas: (1) maintain and expand conservative Justices on the Court, and (2) limit the expansion of incorporation of the Bill of Rights.

The *'total incorporation'* approach, whereby the Fourteenth Amendment can be utilized to have all ten of the Bill of Rights applicable and enforceable to the states, and be deemed fundamental rights, has been largely resisted by both conservatives and liberals. Instead, the *'selective incorporation'* approach has been utilized where judgments are made on a case-by-case basis.

Regardless of whether the *'total incorporation'* or the *'selective incorporation'* method is used, landmark cases provide the precedent by which future cases can be argued. Many legal scholars refer to this as a *'slippery slope'* which suggests that both conservatives and liberals fear what past cases can do to their ideological agendas in future cases. In the battle over ideological application, there is no monopoly on justice. Victories for either side occur in increments.

Bowers v. Hardwick **(Consensual Sex and Privacy)**

This case evolved out of the arrest of Michael Hardwick, an Atlanta bartender, for engaging in consensual oral sex with another male in his own bedroom. They were discovered by a police officer who had come to serve a warrant on Hardwick for not paying a fine for an unrelated offense. When the officer arrived at Hardwick's home, another individual in the premises allowed him entry. The officer proceeded to Hardwick's bedroom where he discovered the sexual dalliance.

Georgia Code Ann. § 16-6-2 (1984) accords the following:

> *"(a) A person commits the offense of sodomy when he performs or submits to any sexual act involving the sex organs of one person and the mouth or anus of another.*
> *(b) A person convicted of the offense of sodomy shall be punished by imprisonment for not less than one nor more than 20 years."*

Hardwick was charged under the Georgia statute. However, despite the charge, the District Attorney appeared to hold reservations about bringing the charge before a grand jury. Although the D. A. did not prosecute, he did not drop the charge. Hardwick then forwarded a civil suit challenging the state law's constitutionality in federal court. The defendant was Georgia's attorney general, Michael J. Bowers. The district court granted Bowers' motion to dismiss, but a divided panel of the Court of Appeals for the Eleventh Circuit reversed on the grounds that the Georgia statute violated Hardwick's fundamental rights.

The United States Supreme Court went on to allow Bowers' petition for certiorari. Of key not is that the only claim before the Court dealt with homosexual sodomy and not heterosexual sodomy. The Court did not offer an opinion about the constitutionality of the Georgia statute in its relation to heterosexual sodomy.

In a narrow 5-4 majority, the Supreme Court upheld, at least with regard to *homosexual sodomy*, a Georgia statute making *all* sodomy criminal. This decision was an ideological shift toward conservatism, and a direct rebuff of the arguments in *Roe v. Wade* (1973). It can be argued that the underlying impulse in Roe would have likely struck down the sodomy statute. It didn't.

The issue in *Bowers* involved the right of privacy. Since *Griswold v. Connecticut* (1965) the Court had held that a right to privacy was implicit in the due process clause of the Fourteenth Amendment to the United States Constitution. This is important in demarcating the ideological shift toward liberal views with regard to privacy. Where there was a judicial disconnect was in this case. Here, the Court held that this right *did not* extend to private, consensual sexual conduct, at least insofar as it involved homosexual sex.

Decision of the U.S. Supreme Court

Justice White delivered the 5-4 majority decision:

"(Sic) The only claim properly before the Court, therefore, is Hardwick's challenge to the Georgia statute as applied to consensual homosexual sodomy. We express no opinion on the constitutionality of the Georgia statute as applied to other acts of sodomy.

This case does not require a judgment on whether laws against sodomy between consenting adults in general, or between homosexuals in particular, are wise or desirable. It raises no question about the right or propriety of state legislative decisions to repeal their laws that criminalize homosexual sodomy, or of state-court decisions invalidating those laws on state constitutional grounds. The issue presented is whether the Federal Constitution confers a fundamental right upon homosexuals to engage in sodomy and hence invalidates the laws of the many States that still make such conduct illegal and have done so for a very long time. The case also calls for some judgment about the limits of the Court's role in carrying out its constitutional mandate.

We first register our disagreement with the Court of Appeals and with respondent that the Court's prior cases have construed the Constitution to confer a right of privacy that extends to homosexual sodomy and for all intents and purposes have decided this case. (Sic)

Accepting the decisions in these cases and the above description of them, we think it evident that none of the rights announced in those cases bears any resemblance to the claimed constitutional right of homosexuals to engage in acts of sodomy that is asserted in this case. No connection between family, marriage, or procreation on the one hand and homosexual activity on the other has been demonstrated, either by the

Court of Appeals or by respondent. Moreover, any claim that these cases nevertheless stand for the proposition that any kind of private sexual conduct between consenting adults is constitutionally insulated from state proscription is unsupportable.

(Sic) It is obvious to us that neither of these formulations would extend a fundamental right to homosexuals to engage in acts of consensual sodomy. Proscriptions against that conduct have ancient roots. Sodomy was a criminal offense at common law and was forbidden by the laws of the original 13 States when they ratified the Bill of Rights. In 1868, when the Fourteenth Amendment was ratified, all but 5 of the 37 States in the Union had criminal sodomy laws.

Nor are we inclined to take a more expansive view of our authority to discover new fundamental rights imbedded in the Due Process Clause. The Court is most vulnerable and comes nearest to illegitimacy when it deals with judge-made constitutional law having little or no cognizable roots in the language or design of the Constitution.

(Sic) Plainly enough, otherwise illegal conduct is not always immunized, whenever it occurs in the home.

Victimless crimes, such as the possession and use of illegal drugs, do not escape the law where they are committed at home. *Stanley* itself recognized that its holding offered no protection for the possession in the home of drugs, firearms, or stolen goods. And if respondent's submission is limited to the voluntary sexual conduct between consenting adults, it would be difficult, except by fiat, to limit the claimed right to homosexual conduct while leaving exposed to prosecution adultery, incest, and other sexual crimes even though they are committed in the home. We are unwilling to start down that road.

Even if the conduct at issue here is not a fundamental right, respondent asserts that there must be a rational basis for the law and that there is none in this case other than the presumed belief of a majority of the electorate in Georgia that homosexual sodomy is immoral and unacceptable. This is said to be an inadequate rationale to support the law. The law, however, is constantly based on notions of morality, and if all laws representing essentially moral choices are to be invalidated under the Due Process Clause, the courts will be very busy indeed. Even respondent makes no such claim, but insists that majority sentiments about the morality of homosexuality should be declared inadequate. We do not agree, and are unpersuaded that the sodomy laws of some 25 States should be invalidated on this basis.

Accordingly, the judgment of the Court of Appeals is *Reversed.*"

Analysis of Bowers

Justice White, in his opinion of the Court, set the parameters of discourse on the grounds that the case before them was that of homosexual sodomy. Although respondent Hardwick had challenged the constitutionality of the law with regard to homosexuality, and more specifically the case involving his homosexual acts therein, what was being challenged was the constitutionality of the Georgia statute. The statute did not demarcate heterosexual and homosexual conduct; rather, it defined sodomy as specific acts between parties. The Court's decision on the homosexual acts of sodomy would have to naturally extend to heterosexual conduct. Did it?

Justice White asserts,

> "*This case does not require a judgment on whether laws against sodomy between consenting adults in general, or between homosexuals in particular, are wise or desirable. It raises no question about the right or propriety of state legislative decisions to repeal their laws that criminalize homosexual sodomy, or of state-court decisions invalidating those laws on state constitutional grounds. The issue presented is whether the Federal Constitution confers a fundamental right upon homosexuals to engage in sodomy and hence invalidates the laws of the many States that still make such conduct illegal and have done so for a very long time.*"

What came before the courts (through both a charge that was not followed through and a subsequent constitutional challenge) was centered on homosexual sodomy. The U.S. Supreme Court could not divorce itself from a debate of all forms of sodomy. There was no mention of how many state statutes of prohibition of sodomy involved (1) heterosexual sodomy, (2) homosexual sodomy, (3) sodomy encompassing both, and/or (4) varied definitions of sodomy. It dealt specifically with the Georgia statute's definition of sodomy and the homosexual acts of sodomy before the Court. Yet, its ruling would have far reaching effects in upholding the Georgia statutes and legitimizing it as constitutional. Indeed, for 17 years it was given constitutional and legal credence.

Justice White rejected any assertion that consensual sodomy among homosexuals is a fundamental right. He argued:

> *"It is obvious to us that neither of these formulations would extend a fundamental right to homosexuals to engage in acts of consensual sodomy. Proscriptions against that conduct have ancient roots. Sodomy was a criminal offense at common law and was forbidden by the laws of the original 13 States when they ratified the Bill of Rights. In 1868, when the Fourteenth Amendment was ratified, all but 5 of the 37 States in the Union had criminal sodomy laws."*

White goes backward to fall upon laws against sodomy imposed by most states to resist a constitutional argument imposed by the Fourteenth Amendment. This is particularly intriguing. Law was being argued by the respondent to be unconstitutional. Both the Fourteenth Amendment (a part of the Constitution) and legal precedent in cases regarding privacy (e.g., *Griswold* with contraception, and *Roe* with abortion) were discounted in favor of historical prohibitions of sodomy by most states. Here, the Court utilizes discretion in applying greater weight to law rather than constitution.

Despite its 17 year tenure (from the 1986 ruling to the Supreme Court essentially striking down *Bowers v. Hardwick* in another decision in 2003) many states rejected the Court's constitutional recognition of prohibition of sodomy. Many state statutes were repealed as a symbolic denunciation of what could be considered a denial of application of the Fourteenth Amendment. How could this happen?

First, it would be expected that the Bowers decision would have long reaching effects on state laws. It did the opposite. In affirming the Georgia statute, many states repealed their laws. In doing so, it negated any power of prosecuting sodomy. Many states essentially did what the Supreme Court failed to do: grant the right of privacy to adults (despite their sexual orientation) to engage in sodomy, even though the Supreme Court stated that this was *not* a *fundamental right*.

This would explain why the decision remained unchallenged for 17 years. Many states repealed sodomy laws and those that retained them rarely pursued charges against individuals who violated such laws. There are laws in some states that have never been repealed (e.g., prohibition against interracial marriage, or marital aids) but continue to go unchallenged because the enforcement of them have been nonexistent. Unless legislatures repeal the laws, or someone charged challenges their constitutionality, they remain intact. So too did the Supreme Court's decision in Bowers remain as constitutional precedent, until it was challenged in 2003.

Lawrence v. Texas (2003)

The Court shifted from 1986's narrow 5-4 decision to uphold the constitutionality of a state statute prohibiting sodomy to a 2003's much greater majority decision to declare a state law unconstitutional. This shows a dramatic shift toward a liberal view toward privacy.

In a 6-3 decision, the Supreme Court declared unconstitutional a Texas law that prohibited sexual acts between same sex couples. Justice Kennedy, in his written opinion of the majority, argued the right to privacy extends to adults engaging in private, consensual homosexual activity. The decision essentially overruled the Court's decision in *Bowers v. Hardwick* (1986).

The Texas law was found to be unconstitutional by many on the Court based on equal protection grounds because it prohibits sexual acts between same sex couples that are allowed between opposite sex couples. Justice Scalia wrote a dissenting opinion, joined by Chief Justice William Rehnquist and Justice Clarence Thomas, in which he argued that states should be afforded the authority to prohibit homosexual conduct and have that enforced through law.

This case involved law enforcement receiving an anonymous tip of a disturbance at a residence. When officers arrived at the apartment they found two adult males embarking in homosexual conduct. The men were arrested and convicted under a Texas statute that prohibits '*deviate sexual intercourse.*' They received fines of $200. The decision was challenged in the state Court of Criminal Appeals on the grounds that the law was unconstitutional. The central arguments entailed constitutional rights privacy and equal protection. The Texas Court of Criminal Appeals rejected the challenges and upheld the original decision.

In the *Bowers* decision, the majority opinion argued *against* taking a more expansive view of their authority to discover new fundamental rights imbedded in the Due Process Clause. Majority Justices in that case argued that to make wide interpretations of the Constitution based on language that does not exist, compromises the legitimacy of the Court.

In that *Bowers* case, Justice White argued, *"There should be, therefore, great resistance to expand the substantive reach of those Clauses, particularly if it requires redefining the category of rights deemed to be fundamental. Otherwise, the Judiciary necessarily takes to itself further authority to govern the country without express constitutional authority."*

In the *Lawrence* case, Justice Kennedy used the polar approach. Indeed, the usage of the Due Process Clause of the Fourteenth Amendment extended the right for adults to engage in consensual sex as a fundamental right. What the Supreme Court did was essentially bring legitimacy to the decisions of many states to repeal their own statutes on sodomy after *Bowers*. The states, in their repudiation of the Bowers decision vis-à-vis state legislative repeal of their statutes essentially rendered the Supreme Court's decision constitutionally impotent.

If the Supreme Court ruled that homosexual acts of sodomy were *not* fundamental rights and hence immune from constitutional protection, why then did so many states repeal their laws? In the repeal of such legislation, state legislators redefined such fundamental rights within the scope of law, even despite its inconsistency with the 1986 Supreme Court's interpretation of the Constitution. The 2003 Court essentially followed suit, and overruled the Bowers decision.

Justice Kennedy wrote:

> *"The Court began its substantive discussion in Bowers as follows: 'The issue presented is whether the Federal Constitution confers a fundamental right upon homosexuals to engage in sodomy and hence invalidates the laws of the many States that still make such conduct illegal and have done so for a very long time.' hat statement, we now conclude, discloses the Court's own failure to appreciate the extent of the liberty at stake. To say that*

the issue in Bowers was simply the right to engage in certain sexual conduct demeans the claim the individual put forward, just as it would demean a married couple were it to be said marriage is simply about the right to have sexual intercourse."
He further stated: "When sexuality finds overt expression in intimate conduct with another person, the conduct can be but one element in a personal bond that is more enduring. The liberty protected by the Constitution allows homosexual persons the right to make this choice."

Lawrence v. Texas can be interpreted as a victory for civil liberties as it sought to impose limits on the State. However, the decision has not had far reaching effects. Indeed, 13 states still have not repealed legislation prohibiting private, consensual homosexual acts. Although there has been a relative reluctance to repeal such laws in these states, the prosecution of violators of such laws is nonexistent. It can be interpreted that states have done to this decision what other states have done in relation to the Bowers decision: directly oppose, or govern contrary, to Supreme Court rulings.

This, if anything, demonstrates the ongoing struggle between *legislators* and the *judiciary*. It also demonstrates that Supreme Court decisions can be revisited, and be overturned. This reinforces the argument that Justices use varied interpretations of the Constitution, and these interpretations in turn, affect how justice is defined.

Abortion

The constitutionality of privacy has been an ongoing ideological struggle for Supreme Court Justices. With regard to sodomy, conservative Courts have largely resisted the advancement of constitutional legitimacy on such issues. However, abortion was single-handedly won on the grounds of *privacy*. Of particular debate is (i) whether privacy can clearly be found within the text of the Constitution itself, and (ii) whether the courts implement judicial activism in interpreting the Constitution if privacy cannot be found within its text.

The Roe v. Wade (1973) Decision

Roe v. Wade was a Texas federal appeal involving a woman who argued that she was unmarried and could not legally obtain an abortion in Texas because her life did not appear to be in peril by the advancement of her pregnancy. At issue was whether the state of Texas statutes, or any state statutes relative to this, has the constitutional authority to be adhered to.

The Court had a difficult case before it. What should be acknowledged is that it agreed to hear the case, thus rendering it within its judicial jurisdiction. It could have denied hearing the case. Recall two more recent case examples where the Court acted differently based on varying rationale.

(1) A majority of the Court agreed in 2000 to hear *Bush v. Gore*, 121 S. Ct. 525, 550. This case involved the Florida supreme court, which ordered a manual recount of ballots cast in selected counties during the 2000 Florida presidential election. This order extended the December 12 deadline set by the Secretary of State of Florida. The Florida supreme court then ordered a manual recount of ballots (which earlier machines failed to record selections) in all counties. On December 9, the U.S. Supreme Court stayed the Florida state supreme court order. It argued that (i) the manual recount of ballots ordered by the state supreme court violated the equal protection clause of the Constitution, and (ii) given the December 12 deadline, remanding the case to the state supreme court for its ordering of a constitutionally proper contest would not be an acceptable solution.

(2) A majority of the U.S. Supreme Court did not agree to hear the case of Terri Schiavo. Schiavo was an American woman who suffered extensive brain damage and became dependent on a feeding tube. She received a diagnosis of persistent vegetative state (PVS) and received care for 15 years. 1998, her husband Michael Schiavo, petitioned the Pinellas County Circuit Court to remove her feeding tube. Her parents, Robert and Mary Schindler, opposed this, arguing she was conscious. The court sided with Michael Schiavo and ordered the removal of the tube.

By March 2005, the legal history around the Schiavo case included (i) 14 appeals and numerous motions, petitions, and hearings in the Florida courts, (ii) five suits in Federal District Court, (iii) Florida legislation struck down by the Supreme Court of Florida, (iv) a subpoena by a congressional committee that would have Schiavo's feeding tube temporarily reinserted to have Schiavo be present before them, and (v) four denials of *certiorari* from the Supreme Court of the United States (Tridico, 2009; Snead, 2005).

These two case examples illustrate the discretionary power the U.S. Supreme Court. It should be accounted that decisions are not always cast unanimously. With a nine member panel, most decisions are cast by majority. While majority decisions stand, dissenting opinions still show that there are varying views on the Court itself. However, by majority, the decisions made hold significant influences. These include, but are not limited to:

(1) *The Supreme Court determines if it even hears a case.* The vast majority of cases that are asked to be heard by the Court are not accepted. Thus, only a relative few cases come before the Court. Through its denial of bringing the case forward, the earlier decisions of the said cases are likely to stand.

(2) *The Supreme Court can accept a case to be heard but affirm earlier decisions by lower courts.* By rendering its decision (by majority consensus), the Court now affords constitutional legitimacy to earlier rulings. The risk or gain (depending on one's perspective) is that a Supreme Court ruling could render a decision a landmark precedent setting case. Here, future cases may be judged in accordance to this ruling.

(3) *The Supreme Court can accept a case to be heard but strike down earlier decisions by lower courts.* By rendering its decision (by majority consensus), the Court now *denies* constitutional legitimacy to earlier rulings. Once again, the risk or gain is that this ruling could be used as precedent. Future cases that come before it, as well as lower level courts, could be faced with arguments that these cases should be judged in accordance to the Supreme Court ruling.

In the first case (*Gore v. Bush*), the Supreme Court (by majority) agreed to impose itself in determining the outcome of the 2000 presidential election. What raises controversy is that although states are given jurisdiction over their own process vis-à-vis standards of an election, and although state supreme courts are given final legal jurisdiction to resolve issues, in this case, the U.S. Supreme Court (by majority) effectively circumvented the said protocol.

This move was substantiated by (i) the manual recount of ballots ordered by the state Supreme Court violated the equal protection clause of the Constitution, and (ii) given the December 12 deadline, remanding the case to the state supreme court for its ordering of a constitutionally proper contest would not be an acceptable solution. The first rationale utilized an argument for a constitutional violation. The second rationale, however, effectively judicially gelded the state supreme court's rulings and authority by taking it out of its jurisdiction altogether. Was this judicial overreaching?

In the second case (Terri Schiavo), the exact opposite occurred, perhaps with even greater fervor. Indeed, four denials of *certiorari* from the Supreme Court of the United States were issued. Could it have accepted this case and resolved a controversial issue that came before the lower courts and the Florida Supreme Court? The U.S. Supreme Court (by majority) chose to dismiss the repeated overtures for intervention. In doing so, it didn't allow for constitutional oversight into the matter, at least from the Supreme Court interpretation of the Constitution. This was left to the lower courts to decide, if at all, whether there were any constitutional violations.

The aforementioned are more recent examples of the discretionary moves by the highest court in the United States. They are not the only ones that can be critically assessed. The Court cannot be exempt from critique because any move it makes can be viewed as discretionary. It yields this power. What this does demonstrate however, is that consistency is the standard by which it should be judged. Moreover, the effects of its discretionary moves must be taken into account.

Decisions made by the U.S. Supreme Court carry greater weight than lower level courts, particularly since future cases are likely to be influenced by their rulings. Indeed, cases heard in lower courts will often hear arguments using past rulings from the Supreme Court level. Many attorneys often warn of this and refer to it as '*a slippery slope.*' The implications of past rulings come to bear in present and future cases.

Did the *Roe v. Wade* involve discretionary decisions on the part of those Justices? Discretion was used from the onset. The Court agreed by majority to hear the case. When the *Roe* Court relieved itself of the duty to define life by stating, *"We need not resolve the difficult question of when life begins,"* it can be argued that it essentially set the parameters of discourse for the case. It used discretion in not making the case about when life begins but rather when abortion should be allowed to begin. Whether or not this was correct or incorrect from a moral standard is not the focus. What can be asserted is that such discretion altered the course of judicial review.

Parameters of Discourse

Consider extracts taken from the briefs and arguments in the *Roe* case before the Supreme Court (Kurland & Casper, 1975):

[The Court]: Is it critical to your case that the fetus not be a person under the Due Process clause? Would you lose your case if the fetus was a person?

[Sarah Weddington (on behalf of appellant Roe)]: Then you would have a balancing of interests.

[The Court]: Well you say you have that anyway, don't you?

[The Court]: If it were established that an unborn fetus is a person protected by the Fourteenth Amendment, you would have almost an impossible case here, would you not?

[Sarah Weddington]: I would have a very difficult case.

[The Court]: Could Texas constitutionally, in your view, declare by statute that the fetus is a person, for all constitutional purposes, after the third month of gestation?

[Sarah Weddington]: I do not believe that the state legislature can determine the meaning of the Federal Constitution. It is up to this Court to make that determination.

[Robert Flowers (on behalf of the appellee)]: It is the position of the state of Texas that, upon conception, we have a human being; a person, within the concept of the Constitution of the United States, and that of Texas, also.

[The Court]: Now how should that question be decided? Is it a legal question? A constitutional question? A medical question? A philosophical question? Or, a religious question? Or what is it?

[Robert Flowers]: We feel that it could be best decided by a legislature, in view of the fact that they can bring before it the medical testimony.

[The Court]: So then it's basically a medical question?

[Robert Flowers]: From a constitutional standpoint, no, sir.

[The Court]: Of course, if you're right about the fetus being a person within the meaning of the Constitution, you can sit down, you've won your case.

[The Court]: Do you think you have lost your case, then, if the fetus or the embryo is not a person? Is that it?

[Robert Flowers]: Yes sir, I would say so.

[The Court]: Well, if you're right that an unborn fetus is a person, then you can't leave it to the legislature to play fast and loose dealing with that person. If you're correct, in your basic submission that an unborn fetus is a person, then abortion laws such as that which New York has are grossly unconstitutional, isn't it?

[Robert Flowers]: That's right, yes.

[The Court]: I gather your argument is that a state may not protect the life of the fetus or prevent an abortion at any time during pregnancy? Right up until the moment of birth?

[Sarah Weddington]: There is no indication that the Constitution would give any protection prior to birth. That is not before the Court.

[The Court]: Well, I don't know whether it is or isn't.

Critical Analysis of the Extracts

Readers should acknowledge that extracted dialogue in print fails to comprehensively demonstrate the precise complexity of this case. However, within its words, the conversational bantering between the counsel acting on behalf of the appellant and the appellee with the Court is evidence that the *Roe* ruling could have potentially been rendered the other way had the argument that the fetus is a person been able to be proven.

In his written opinion of the Court, Justice Blackmun affirms, "*Appellee argues that the fetus is a "person" within the language and meaning of the Fourteenth Amendment. [If so] appellant's case, of course, collapses, for the fetus' right to life is then guaranteed specifically by the Amendment.*" This of course raises particular controversy. On the one hand, the Court sought to relieve itself of whether the fetus constitutes a '*person*', on the rationale that the matter has yet to be resolved with any substantial consensus across other factions (religious, medical, philosophical, etc.)

On the other hand, it argued that had the fetus could be proven to be a person it would have Constitutional protection. Sarah Weddington (in the aforementioned excerpts) conceded that "*I would have a very difficult case*" if this were to be proven. Justice Blackburn went further than conceding it would be a '*difficult case*'; indeed, he specifically stated that the case would '*collapse*'. This indicates that from his view, the Court has already determined that in a case of balancing interests, it would be the life of the fetus (if defined as a person) that would be afforded greater Constitutional protection.

This raises particular concern. Justice Blackburn, though the written opinion of the Court, affirmed that the parameters of discourse essentially determined the outcome of the case. More specifically, the definition of the concept of '*person*' could have influenced the ruling. However, it can be argued that the Court played a central party in ensuring that this definition could not be effectively pursued.

The Court asked Weddington "*Could Texas constitutionally, in your view, declare by statute that the fetus is a person, for all constitutional purposes, after the third month of gestation?*"

Weddington replied, *"I do not believe that the state legislature can determine the meaning of the Federal Constitution. It is up to this Court to make that determination."*

The Court essentially asked if the state legislature can constitutionally use law to define a *'person'* after a said period of fetal development. Weddington used legal savvy in dismissing the jurisdictional authority of the state legislature by shifting the focus away from definition of person to another focus: the meaning of the Federal Constitution. She essentially argued that only the U.S. Supreme Court could make that determination.

Was this what the Court was asking Weddington? Did the Court need counsel to affirm that only it could determine the meaning of the Federal Constitution? State legislatures have the power to enact laws, but it is not within the jurisdiction of political officials to determine the Constitutionality of such laws. That is the role of the Courts. In this scope, Weddington is correct.

It then is ascertained that it is the Court's role to determine the meaning of the Federal Constitution. However, one can enter into debate how the *Roe* Court could dismiss the state's definition of *'person'* when it went on to argued that, *"We need not resolve the difficult question of when life begins."* Justice Douglas in his opinion of the Court essentially argued there is insufficient consensus on the definition of person, and if that is the case, how could the Court define it? Douglas stated, *"[The] protection of the fetus when it has acquired life is a legitimate concern of the State. Georgia's law makes no rational, discernible decision on that score. For under the Act the developmental stage of the fetus is irrelevant when pregnancy is the result of rape or when the fetus will very likely be born with a permanent defect or when a continuation of the pregnancy will endanger the life of the mother or permanently injure her health. When life is present is a question we do not try to resolve. While basically a question for medical experts, [it is] of course, caught up in the matters of religion and morality."*

Justice Douglas shifted the onus of responsibility of the question of whether the fetus is a *'person'* to medical experts and that it focuses largely on religion and morality. If this is the case, then medical experts are those that would be in the best position to define *'person'*. Why then should there be consensus across factions over this definition for the

Court to acknowledge it, if the medical community should be the proper authority?

Already we see that there are varying standards applied. One can further this argument by asking additional questions.

Do medical experts have the authority to determine the constitutionality that the *"fetus is a person, for all constitutional purposes, after the third month of gestation?"* Do religious or moral factions have this authority? By dismissing Texas' authority to define *'person'*, did the Court essentially argue that the legislative branch of government cannot define *'person'* through law?

In the rebuttal argument of Sarah Weddington, the Court asked *"I gather your argument is that a state may not protect the life of the fetus or prevent an abortion at any time during the pregnancy? Right up until the moment of birth?"*

Weddington replied, *"There is no indication that the Constitution would give any protection prior to birth. That is not before the Court."*

Weddington effectively set the parameters of the discourse by arguing that the Constitution does not give any protection of the life of the fetus, but that this issue was *not* before the Court. The Court responded with indifference, stating, *"Well, I don't know whether it is or isn't."* Was it?

Applying Critical Analysis

The purpose of critical thinking is not to argue the legitimacy of the *Roe v. Wade* decision but to assess the central dynamics of the process. The aforementioned excerpts between counsel for appellant and appellee with the Court show that the question of whether the fetus is, or should be defined as a *'person'* was of some concern. Moreover, it could have altered the outcome of the case.

Roe v. Wade is often assessed as a Constitutional right won on the basis of the First Amendment. The Court ruled that most laws against abortion in the United States violated a Constitutional right to privacy under the Due Process Clause of the Fourteenth Amendment. Pregnancy was essentially categorized into three trimesters, and added limitations to abortion procedures were placed with the ongoing development of the fetus. *Roe* was never a decision based on balancing the interests of mother with the fetus, as the definition of fetus was not accepted as one as a '*person*'.

Implications of *Roe v. Wade*

Prior to 1973, the abortion issue was left largely to state legislatures. *Roe* invalidated a century-old Texas law which prohibited abortion except where necessary to preserve the life of the mother. However, the judicial reach of *Roe* was so extensive that it overturned the abortion statutes of all 50 states.

The decision of the Court shows three very specific revelations.

(1) The U.S. Constitution does not define "*person*" in so many words. Justice Blackburn in the opinion of the Court stated that they "*listed each provision in which the word appears.] But in nearly all these instances, the use of the word is such that it has application only postnatally. None indicates, with any assurance, that it has any possible pre-natal application.*" Given this, the Court makes a discretionary judgment that if it is not specifically included in the Constitution that it must therefore not apply.

Blackburn uses observation that throughout most of the 19th century legal abortion practices were less rigid than at the time (circa 1973), thus applying credence to the judgment of the past. Who made such judgments? If they were legal, then legislators made that discretionary call. Could one not argue that these are the same branch of legislators that shifted from that paradigm and moved to criminalize abortion at a later stage? There is inconsistency in the application of whether the legislative body has the authority to enact laws on abortion. If there should be no credence placed on whether Texas imposed laws prohibiting abortion, why should there be credence placed on other legislators that did *not* prohibit abortion?

Further, Blackburn's contention in the written opinion of the Court was countered by dissenting Justice Rehnquist. He argued, "*[By] the time of the adoption of the Fourteenth Amendment in 1868 there were at least 36 laws enacted by state or territorial legislatures limiting abortion. [The] only conclusion possible from this history is that the drafters did not intend to have the Fourteenth Amendment withdraw from the States the power to legislate with respect to this matter.*" Rehnquist argues there was significant territorial legislation that placed legal rigidity to abortion, which is inconsistent with Blackburn's assertion that they were less rigid than in the time *Roe* was heard. This demonstrates a discretionary judgment on the part of the majority of Justices in this respect.

(2) The absence of the definition of '*person*' in the Constitution, particularly toward the unborn is relevant in the decision of the Court. They determined that since it could not be found, then it was subject to moving on to other considerations. This is dismissive and does not answer the relevant question of whether the fetus is a '*person*' or if it constitutes life. Justice Blackburn argued, "*We need not resolve the difficult question of when life begins. When those trained in medicine, philosophy, and theology are unable to arrive at any consensus, the judiciary, at this point in the development of man's knowledge, is not in a position to speculate as to the answer.*" Blackburn contends in his argument that the question of whether the fetus is a person does not fall within the jurisdiction of the Court.

Of relevance is whether the Court decided the question without admitting it. Did the Court imply that since it isn't defined as a '*person*' within the Constitution that it wasn't a '*person*'? Did the Court actually define '*person*' without having to hold itself accountable to its own premise that if the fetus is a person, then the appellant's case then collapses?

Justice Blackburn in his opinion of the Court argued, "We do not agree that, by adopting one theory of life, Texas may override the rights of the pregnant woman that are at stake. We repeat, however, that the State does have an important and legitimate interest in preserving and protecting the health of the pregnant woman and that it has still *another* important and legitimate interest in protecting the potentiality of human life. These interests are separate and distinct. Each grows in substantiality as the woman approaches term and, at a point during pregnancy, each becomes compelling."

The Court dismissed Texas' statutes prohibiting abortion because it was based on one theory of life. Yet it moved to set its own standard of theory of life based upon "the State having an important and legitimate interest in preserving and protecting the health of the pregnant woman and that it has still *another* important and legitimate interest in protecting the potentiality of human life." The Court set its own definition of '*potentiality of human life*' as growing substantiality as the woman approaches term. It stopped short of defining it as life, yet still afforded protection to that potentiality of human life. This, of course, furthers the central argument that the Court uses discretion in both the interpretation of the Constitution and to the cases that come before it.

(3) The Constitution does not explicitly mention any right of privacy. Justice Blackburn argued that "*in varying contexts the Court or individual Justices have recognized a right of personal privacy, or a guarantee of certain areas or zones of privacy, does exist under the Constitution.*" Blackburn referred to the roots of that right in the First, Fourth, Fifth and Ninth Amendment, in the penumbras of the Bill of Rights, and in the concept of liberty guaranteed by the first section of the Fourteenth Amendment. The Court sought to find Supreme Court decisions and/or parts of various Amendments that convey the spirit of the concept of right to privacy. However, there is a concession that the Constitution does not specifically mention such privacy directly.

This exemplifies a more aggressive approach by the Court to constitutionally legitimize the concept of privacy where it is not specifically defined. They did not use the same fervor where '*person*' was similarly not specifically defined. Here, we once again see power of discretion in judicial policy. It matters less of whether it was correct or incorrect, but that it follows that this is part of the judicial process.

Relevant Questions for Ongoing Discourse of Abortion

Question Number 1: Can *Roe v. Wade* be Overturned?

Dissenting Justice Rehnquist argued that the Fourteenth Amendment was adopted in 1868. Given that there were at least 36 laws enacted by state or territorial legislatures limiting abortion. Of relevance is whether the drafters did not intend to have the Fourteenth Amendment withdraw from the States the power to legislate with respect to the matter of abortion. Rehnquist believes they did not. The majority of the Court support the notion that the Fourteenth Amendment is relevant to the discourse in providing Constitutional legitimacy to a woman's right to choose.

Both sides use discretionary interpretation of what the founders of the Constitution would have wanted with reference to abortion. They can look carefully, but they won't find it. The absence of specific language will be a guarantor that on this issue, interpretation of the Constitution has been subjective and will continue to be subjective, even if it is overturned.

The *Roe* Court's relieved itself of defining the concept of *'person'* or specifically and clearly define when life begins. It also waged an aggressive move to substantiate/legitimize the right of privacy where the Constitution does not appear to specifically and clearly demarcate it.

Potential challenges to *Roe* will likely attempt to revisit the aforementioned controversy. However, the absence of such clear and specific language within the Federal Constitution will potentially only push different Courts in similar directions of discretionary interpretation.

If the issue is revisited, a future Court can decide the matter in three areas:

(1) *It can affirm the original ruling.* This can be done with greater specificity than the *Roe* Court provided in the matter, particularly if it can satisfy the Constitutional and procedural concerns of its dissenters.
(2) *It can strike down the original ruling based on new Constitutional challenges.* In this development, it would have significant implications legally, politically and socially. Given

that the *Roe* Court has given it Constitutional legitimacy, a reversal of status could be perceived to be an assault on the individual rights of women.

(3) ***It can shift jurisdictional authority to the states to decide the matter.*** In doing so, it would relieve itself of the burden of determining the constitutionality of abortion. To do this, the Court would have to take a strict constructionist view of the matter. It would have to take the position that if specific language is absent in the Constitution, then the matter should be left to the states to decide. The implications of this are profound. This would transform the current legality status of abortion into one where it would vary across state jurisdictions.

Question Number 2: Is the question of when human life something that cannot be defined by the judiciary?

In Justice Antonin Scalia Akron II (1990) (p.410) he argues, "*I continue to believe that the Constitution contains no right to abortion. It is not to be found in the longstanding traditions of our society, nor can it be logically deduced from the text of the Constitution - not, that is, without volunteering a judicial answer to the nonjusticiable question of when human life begins. Leaving this matter on the political process is not only legally correct, it is pragmatically so.*"

Scalia argues for a number of specific criteria here:

(1) He believes that there is no clear and fundamental right for abortion found within the Constitution.
(2) He believes that in order to be fully address the abortion issue, the question of when human life begins is crucial.
(3) He extends the authority to define human life to the political process.

Justice Scalia's logic is direct contrast to that of the *Roe* Court's view to deny the state legislature that very authority. The *Roe* Court (by majority) decided that the state legislature cannot impose one theory of life to deny abortion; Scalia argues it should. Scalia's logic would have the states decide on a definition and once that definition is established, the Supreme Court would have the ability, and authority, to comprehensively rule on the matter whether abortion is protected by the federal Constitution.

The *Roe* Court did three things. First, it relieved itself of the question of when human life begins, and appears to have ruled on the matter in its absence. Second, it denied the state legislature the legitimacy of defining life or 'person' by striking down its original legal stand. Third, the *Roe* Court, in the absence of a definition went on to decide the matter of abortion on other grounds, with *privacy* being central to its ruling.

Had the *Roe* Court applied Justice Scalia's views, it would have suspended legal oversight on the matter pending the state legislature legally forwarding a definition of when human life begins and what legally constitutes a '*person.*' However, Texas did just this. Scalia essentially argues that the Court's logic was flawed. He argues that by invalidating the Texas statute, and by failing to specifically define it from the judiciary's perspective, it could not have come to a constitutionally sound decision.

Jed Rubenfeld (1991) counters Scalia's arguments. He posits that given the contraception cases, a right to abortion cannot be denied without answering the question of when human life begins. Rubenfeld argues that '*personhood*' is not and cannot be a *political question*. Given that rights are constitutional, state legislatures should not be entitled to full jurisdiction over the matter. Rubenfeld argues that abortion cannot be completely prohibited unless the judiciary either (1) relinquishes its constitutional responsibility, or (2) decides that fetuses can be regarded as '*persons*' from the moment of conception.

Rubenfeld cautions that to extend authority of defining life to the legislature raises more concerns than it hopes to address. He argues that it is within the judiciary's authority to do this, because it is there where Constitutional application is determined. Rubenfeld believes that the political realm does not have the right to place prohibitions on abortion unless the Supreme Court extends that authority to them.

Here, we have two very different approaches. First, Scalia argues that the matter should be passed onto the states. On the other hand, Rubenfeld argues that the political realm does not, and should not, have this authority. The relevant concern at this point is to demarcate who may be, if at all, overreaching. Is the political realm overreaching in placing law before the Constitution, or is the judicial realm overreaching in denying the political realm the ability to enact laws that it may not concur with?

Certainly, it is within the power of the Federal Supreme Court to determine the constitutionality of law when the matters come before it. However, in the absence of specific language of abortion within the Constitution (either for or against), is it not logical that the Court arrive at consensus of a definition prior to it determining constitutionality on the issue? Scalia and Rubenfeld would take two very different paths to approach the matter. Scalia would extend greater powers to the state while Rubenfeld would enhance the authority of the judiciary. Given that the *Roe* Court ruled in favor of abortion, Scalia's approach would pose a direct threat to this ruling if it is to be revisited.

Question Number 3: Was *Roe v. Wade* a political or legal decision?

In *The Tempting of America* (1990), Robert Bork argues that in the 51 page explanation, the Court does not offer one sentence that can qualify as legal substance. He argues that the decision is undermined by the fact that abortion cannot be found within the text of the Constitution. As such, the Court is likely to be perceived as engaging in political activism.

Judge Bork is correct in that abortion or words relating to it are absent within the Federal Constitution. However, the Constitution does not specifically give reference to freedom of thought or liberty of association, yet these are areas where the Court has applied interpretation of the Constitution to cases that have come before it. Are those then, political rather than legal? Certainly, the Fourteenth Amendment states that no state may deny to any person '*without due process of law.*'

Judge Bork relies on a strict constructionist perspective which focuses exclusively on the reliance of specific language of the Constitution. To concur with his charges, one would have to consistently apply them across many other Supreme Court decisions. If the Court is to be charged with politicization, it should be judged across broader issues. In this vein, conservative Justices would have to show how decisions that favor conservative ideology are decided with the same precision as Judge Bork decrees on the *Roe* Court. This does not invalidate Bork's position. What it does do is expand the discourse to a more important context.

The matter is not so much whether the *Roe v. Wade* was a political decision? The matter should be whether the Court is political and if so, to what extent.

Conclusion

Liberal Justices have utilized the Equal Protection Clause of Fourteenth Amendment to interpret the context of various Amendments to include privacy. Most of the gains in the 1960s pertaining to the Fourth, Fifth and Sixth Amendments can be argued to be matters more to deal with personal liberty and limitations imposed on the State, than victories of privacy.

Liberal Justices have needed to adopt a *libertarian* premise to advance an ideological agenda. In *Griswold*, Justice Goldberg traces his logic to the arguments of the framers of the Constitution. The struggle to include the Bill of Rights was won by anti-federalists who were concerned that the new system threatened individual liberties. The original Constitution, as proposed in 1787 in Philadelphia and as ratified by the states, contained very few individual rights guarantees.

One could argue that the advancement of civil liberties pertaining to individual rights was made possible because they already exist within the context of the Bill of Rights. Privacy is a much more difficult concept to arrive at because it requires (i) landmark cases of various Amendments of the Bill of Rights to serve as precedent to advance further causes, (ii) interpretation of the Constitution in lieu of adhering to the rigid text of the document, and (iii) a shift in the ideological composition of the Court.

The first criterion has been well established. The second criterion has had some limited success. The third component has not been accomplished. The United States Supreme Court has been gaining more conservative composition since *Roe v. Wade* (1973). The conservative influence on the Court has demonstrated reluctance to selective incorporation of the Bill of Rights, and a resistance to total incorporation of the Bill of Rights, which has limited the expansion of civil liberty issues. The conservative influence on the Court has demonstrated some interpretation, but relied more heavily on the direct text of the document. Finally, conservative influence on the Court has slowly expanded the authority and power of the State, particularly in areas of law enforcement.

If *Roe v. Wade* is to be revisited, it will likely be challenged on the grounds that it was won: *privacy*. There is an ongoing political and ideological divide on the concept of privacy, and how the Constitution should be interpreted. This ultimately raises fundamental concerns over how justice is *defined* and *applied* in the United States.

References

Bork, R. (1990). *The Tempting of America: The Political Seduction of the Law*. New York, NY: Touchstone.

Kurland, P. & G. Casper (Eds.). (1975). 75 Landmark Briefs and Arguments of the Supreme Court of the United States. *Constitutional Law*, 64: 807-33.

Rubenfeld, J. (1991). On the Legal Status of the Proposition that "Life Beings at Conception." 43 *Stanford Law Review,* 599: 385-412.

Snead, O.C. (2005). Dynamic Complementarity: Terri's Law and Separation of Powers Principles in the End-of-Life Context. *Florida Law Review*, Vol. 57, Number 53.

Tridico, F. (2009). *Law and Social Order*. Sault Ste. Marie, ON: Landon Elsemere Press.

Supreme Court Cases

Bowers v. Hardwick, 478 U.S. 186 (1986)

Bush v. Gore, 531 U.S. 98 (2000)

Eisenstadt v. Baird, 405 U.S. 438 (1972)

Griswold v. Connecticut, 381 U.S. 479 (1965)

Lawrence v. Texas, 539 U.S. 558 (2003)

Poe v. Ullman (1961)

Roe v. Wade, 410 U. S. 113 (1973)

Tileston v. Ullman (1943)

About the Authors

Jacob Armstrong is currently a Doctoral Candidate and teaches in the Department of Sociology at Western Michigan University. Research and interests include the sociology of religion, comparative sociology, social psychology, and research methods. He has refereed co-authored articles recently published in *Humor: The International Journal of Humor Research* and *Personality and Social Psychology Bulletin*. He will also be presenting *"Religiosity and Tolerance Re-examined: The Case of Islamist Radicals"* at the 2009 Society for the Scientific Study of Religion conference in Denver, Colorado.

David Barry is a Doctoral Candidate in Sociology at Western Michigan University. He has taught courses in sociology at Western Michigan University and Lake Michigan College, and Non-Western Worlds course at Western Michigan University. His research interests include the sociology of religion and comparative sociology, with an emphasis on issues of religious tolerance, religion and national identity, and religion in post-communist Russia.

Darrick Brake is a part time faculty (and doctoral student) in the Department of Sociology at Western Michigan University. He has several major ongoing research interests ranging from the recognition of human trafficking as a modern social issue, to the development and history of sociological theory and metatheory, to the reconceptualization of the development of symbolic interactionist theory.

Carrie Buist is a Doctoral Candidate in Sociology at Western Michigan University with research concentrations in criminology, women in policing, policing organization, and gender and feminist studies. She has taught criminology and sociology courses at Eastern Michigan University and criminal justice and sociology courses at Western Michigan University.

Charles E. Crawford is Professor of Sociology at Western Michigan University and holds a PhD in Criminology from Florida State University. He has published numerous book chapters and refereed journal articles on criminal justice topics. Some of his articles have appeared in the journals *Criminology, Police Quarterly, Crime Law and Social Change, Crime Media and Culture,* and *Police and Society.* He serves as editor of *Spatial Policing* (Carolina Academic Press) and coeditor of *Policing and Violence* (Prentice Hall). He has served as a panelist for the National Science Foundation and a consultant for the Rand Corporation on police use of force policy, and the Kalamazoo Department of Public Safety.

Meghan Kenney received a M.Ed. in secondary education from Arizona State. In 2007, she joined Teach for America as an 8th grade science teacher in the Creighton Elementary School District. In 2009, she was named a Regional Semi-Finalist for the Sue Lehmann Excellence in Teaching Award. She continues to teach 8th grade in addition to graduate courses as an associate faculty member in Arizona State University's College of Teacher Education and Leadership.

Krim K. Lacey is currently a postdoctoral research fellow at the University of Michigan's Institute for Social Research, Program for Research on Black Americans (PRBA). He received his PhD in 2007 from Wayne State University. His research primarily focuses on violence against minority and immigrant women. Other research interests include substance use and abuse, and disparities in education. He has engaged in a federally funded (DOE/OSEP) research study that examined the contribution of demography in access, services, and outcomes of special education students.

Catherine Lysack is an Associate Professor in the Occupational Therapy, Department of Health Care Sciences, and Deputy Director for the Institute of Gerontology and Wayne State University. She teaches and conducts research on a range of topics related to disability, rehabilitation and aging. She has received funding to study the personal meanings of aging and well-being to older white and African-American women.

George P. Mason received a MA in Sociology from the University of Manitoba and is currently a Doctoral Candidate in Sociology at Wayne State University. He currently teaches Sociology and Labour Studies at the University of Windsor. His research has focused on autoworkers, educational workers, urban sociology, and in the field of social justice and inequality. He has published a number of items, held faculty positions in a number of different universities, is involved with a number of sociological associations, and has developed online materials for undergraduate and graduate students.

Joseph M. Pellerito, Jr. graduated and received a BS in Occupational Therapy, a MS degree in Technology Engineering in Rehabilitation and Special Education at Johns Hopkins University in 1995, and his PhD in Medical Sociology at Wayne State University. He served as Academic Program Director/Department Chair of the Occupational Therapy Program from 2000 until 2008, in the Eugene Applebaum College of Pharmacy and Health Sciences at WSU. Currently, he is an Associate Professor and Director of the Assistive Technology and Driving Simulation Research and Teaching Laboratories at WSU.

Charles Quist-Adade received his PhD in Sociology from Petersburg State University in Russia. He teaches racialization and ethnicity at Kwantlen Polytechnic University in British Columbia. He is the author of *In the Shadows of the Kremlin and the White House: Africa's Media Image from Communism to Post-Communism* (University Press of America, 2001).

Frank Tridico is Assistant Professor for the Criminal Justice Program and Department of Sociology at Western Michigan University in Kalamazoo, Michigan. He also serves as Undergraduate Director for the Department. He taught at Wayne State University in Detroit, Michigan from 1998 to 2007. He is co-author of *How Sociologists Do Research* (2003) with Richard Fancy, and author of *The Social Construction of Reality* (2003), *Contemporary Issues in Law and Society* (2004) and *Law and Social Order* (2009).

Andrew Verheek is a Sociology PhD student at Western Michigan University with research interests in offender reentry, social control, methods, and impression management/identity. He has also taught criminal justice and corrections courses at Grand Valley State University.